FOR RACHELI

Song of Songs 8:6–7

# CONTENTS

# PREFACE

THIS book had its origins over ten years ago, in a casual question from a colleague about the role of sexuality in I. B. Singer's story "Gimpel the Fool." Singer's stories revel in magic and the demonic, forces that he associates with sexuality. As I thought about Singer's idiosyncratic view of the role of Eros in Eastern European Jewish culture, I wondered whether he had created it himself or whether he was not perhaps embellishing upon some long-standing traditions. Little did I realize that I was embarking on a quest that was to lead me back from the modern period to the Middle Ages, talmudic culture, and finally the Bible itself.

Thinking about Singer led me first to investigate the literary culture of the Jews of nineteenth-century Eastern Europe. These writers, both highbrow and low-brow, created the Hebrew and Yiddish literary tradition to which Singer was heir. I became particularly interested in the autobiographies and other writings of the maskilim, the Jewish disciples of Enlightenment (Haskalah). As opposed to Singer, who drew upon popular culture, these writers held that traditional Jewish society suppressed erotic desire and created stunted and neurotic Jews, rather like Philip Roth's Alexander Portnoy. I suddenly realized that a novel like *Portnoy's Complaint*, with which this book begins, was not so much the bizarre creation of an obsessed American Jewish writer as it was another link in a long literary tradition.

Reading these nineteenth-century authors, I was skeptical that the Jewish culture they were describing reflected the real historical tradition. After all, did not Judaism, as opposed to Christianity, affirm sexuality as a healthy expression of this-worldliness? I noticed that the maskilim were particularly concerned with Hasidism, the eighteenth-century pietistic movement in Eastern Europe, and that their sweeping accusations against traditional sexual and marital practices seemed to be based primarily on their image of this movement. This led me to examine the attitude toward sexuality in Hasidism, and there I discovered expressions of extreme asceticism. But if, as I came to be convinced, Hasidism was radically ascetic on the question of sexuality, perhaps that was nevertheless an aberration, a sharp departure from the rabbinic traditions of the Talmud and the Middle Ages? And so I turned to these earlier sources, sometimes finding, again to my surprise, that things were quite different and often more complex than I had expected. Finally, I came to the Bible itself, the original Jewish source, and to ask whether the biblical discourse on sexuality had any connection with later developments.

In this circuitous, counterchronological fashion, the book gradually took shape over the course of more than a decade. My initial interest had been to describe the complicated, dialectical way in which Jewish culture negotiated the transition from the traditional world to modernity. But the further my research took me into the "traditional" world, the more skeptical I became that one could speak of a clean break between "traditional" and "modern." Instead, the modern period always seems to exist in dialectical relationship to its predecessors, and modern Jews define themselves in constant tension with their tradition, even if their knowledge of that tradition remains fragmentary. To do justice to the modern questions required extensive treatment of the tradition as a whole, going back to its very origins. Every attempt to discover the point of transition between tradition and modernity pushes the search further back in history, and ultimately these terms themselves dissolve and become increasingly unstable.

Yet another, even more personal quest prompted this "regressive" approach. As the son of a socialist Zionist father, I have always been curious about the personal dimensions of Zionism. From what I knew of my father's experience in the Zionist youth movement in the Poland of the 1920s, I was struck by the peculiar tension between eroticism and sublimation that characterized these idealistic young people, many of whom went on to found the State of Israel. After his death in July 1989, I chanced upon letters to and from my father, as well as a brief diary from the late 1920s and early 1930s that strikingly confirmed the ambivalence that I had found elsewhere.

But if indeed the relationship of Zionism to sexuality was one of ambivalence, how did this attitude derive from the Jewish culture of Eastern Europe out of which Zionism emerged? My attention turned to the renaissance of Hebrew literature at the end of the nineteenth century, and that, in turn, led me back to the Haskalah and then, in the fashion already described, farther and farther back into Jewish history. As I hope this study will show, there is a sense in which secular Zionism completed a grand circle with the very biblical, rabbinic, and medieval traditions against which it revolted.

Once I had completed the historical reconstruction of Jewish attitudes toward sexuality from the Bible to the early Zionist movement, Steven Fraser, my editor at Basic Books, pointed out that I had failed to close another circle: the connection between contemporary American Jewish culture and the earlier Jewish tradition. Chapter 9 is the product of that fruitful suggestion. Indeed, to close with the culture in which the author writes seems particularly appropriate to this subject and to the approach I have adopted. The very contention of historians that there *is* a history of sexuality is a product of contemporary culture, in which sexuality plays a central, if controversial, role. Since sexuality is a universal human experience, although one understood differently by every age and culture, it is virtually impossible to engage the past without the baggage of the present: like all modern men and women, the historian also struggles with his own sexuality. As I shall try to show in Chapter 9, to be a Jew in America today means, at least in part, to confront and attempt to understand oneself in terms of sexual relations both with other Jews and with non-Jews.

Instead of obscuring the contemporary questions that have compelled me to undertake this project, I have framed the book with them in the introduction and final chapter. Some will no doubt contend that these questions have led me tendentiously to choose certain sources and ignore others. To this charge, I plead guilty, but I believe that this is inevitable in all historical work. The story that I wish to tell *is* dictated to a large degree by contemporary concerns, but for author and readers alike, it cannot be otherwise. To write a history of Jewish sexuality means to place texts, many of them well known, into a radically new context, one that neither earlier historians nor the tradition itself might have anticipated. This history, like all histories, is not so much the *discovery* of facts or texts as it is the *construction* of a new way of looking at these "facts," a process that remakes them in its own image.

Although this book covers all periods of Jewish history, it will not—nor can it—be comprehensive; such a project would require the work of many scholars over many years. Since the contemporary issues I have raised are rooted in the modern history of the Ashkenazic, or European, Jews, I will make only occasional references to the culture of the Mediterranean Jews—the Jews of Spain, Italy, and the Muslim world (Chapter 4 is the main exception to this self-limitation). My purpose in this first overall history of Jewish sexuality is to give shape to what is an emerging new field and to encourage others to make their own contributions in their areas of specialization. I hope that the chapters of this book will be judged sufficiently provocative to encourage others to fill in the many gaps I will leave and to correct and add depth to those conclusions that require much more detail than either space or time would allow.

I began this project in the academic year 1980–81 with a research leave at the Hebrew University under the generous sponsorship of the Lady Davis Foundation, the American Council of Learned Societies, and my institution at that time, the State University of New York at Binghamton. Over the years since, I have accumulated many intellectual debts that are my pleasure to acknowledge. During that initial year of work, I received considerable assistance from Jacob Katz, Israel Bartal, Shaul Stampfer, and Michael Silber. The American Jewish Committee gave me the opportunity to develop some of my ideas, first in an essay on the Eastern European Jewish Enlightenment and later in a study on the Jewish family commissioned by the Committee's Steven Bayme.

Two editors have played key roles in this book. Several years ago Arthur Samuelson encouraged me to develop a book out of what seemed to me a rather uncohesive body of research and also acted as my *shadkhan* (marriage broker) with Basic Books. This book would simply not have come into the world without him. My editor at Basic Books, Steven Fraser, has also been unfailingly supportive and critical, pushing me to develop some of my ideas further than I was initially inclined and appropriately throwing cold water on others of my less promising inspirations.

In the last year of writing, I was blessed by the arrival in the Bay Area of two marvelous colleagues, Daniel Boyarin and Howard Eilberg-Schwartz, both of whom were already working on aspects of the history of Jewish sexuality. For the first time in my career, I have felt that I belonged to a true community of scholars engaged in the collective task of creating a new and distinctive approach to Jewish cultural studies. Their often very different perspectives forced me to look at things in new ways and to reconsider old conclusions. Both of them read and criticized more than one draft of this book, and it quite simply would not have taken the shape it did without them. Howard Eilberg-Schwartz wrote a trenchant response to my rabbinic chapter before we met, and we have been engaged in weekly and sometimes daily conversations ever since. The same chapter, written before I met Daniel Boyarin, is the subject of his forthcoming book; instead of competing with each other, we have succeeded in achieving that fruitful cooperation and respectful difference that can make intellectual life so satisfying.

Chana Kronfeld also played a central role in shaping the final revisions of this book. She read the manuscript with special care and made some important suggestions about my use of the Bible and Hebrew and Yiddish literature as well as about the methodological presuppositions of the book.

Since this is a work that spans so many periods and disciplines, I have imposed on many other colleagues and friends for their varied expertise. Steven Zipperstein read the whole manuscript with his usual keen historical and critical eye. Riv-Ellen Prell responded generously by sharing her work on gender stereotypes in American Jewish culture and by offering a feminist critique of my work. Others who read and criticized the whole manuscript from their different perspectives include Robert Alter, Jeremy Cohen, Sander Gilman, and Martin Jay. I was also assisted by specialists who read specific chapters: Steven Aschheim, Chana and Ariel Bloch, Arnold Eisen, Arthur Green, Hannan Hever, Deborah Kaufman, Thomas Laqueur, Daniel Matt, Jacob Milgrom, George Mosse, Adi Ophir, Regina Schwartz, and Eli Yassif. All of these readers made this a better book by saving me from errors and suggesting fruitful new approaches. I owe an incalculable debt to all of them for what is good in this book; what is less successful remains my own responsibility. I also thank Ehud Luz for helping me identify materials for the chapter on Zionism, and Bluma Goldstein for some insights on Freud.

The book has also profited from interaction with students at SUNY Binghamton, Haifa University, the Graduate Theological Union, the University of California at Berkeley, and the Lehrhaus Judaica. I am grateful especially for the unstinting and uninhibited criticism of the graduate students in my seminar on "Sexuality in Post-Talmudic Jewish History": Robert Daum, Laurie Davis, Charlotte Fonrobert, Yoel Kahn, Sophie Miron, Dan Prath, and Emily Silverman. I also benefited greatly at a critical period in writing from the conference on People of the Body—People of the Book that took place at Stanford University and the University of California, Berkeley, in April 1991.

I received much needed research assistance from Charlotte Fonrobert, my doctoral student at the Graduate Theological Union, and from Rochelle Rubinstein in Jerusalem. Lucinda Glenn Rand has been an unfailing source of secretarial help, often beyond the call of duty.

A number of people gave me much needed assistance beyond the academic. The Yuppie Bikers provided a great sounding board as we toiled breathlessly up and down the Berkeley Hills. I am also grateful to Robert Alter, Carol Cosman, Mollie Katzen, Deborah Kaufman, Fred Rosenbaum, Carl Shames, and Barry Stone for their support and friendship.

Finally, although it is customary to thank one's life partner at the end of a list of acknowledgments, my debt—marital and intellectual—to Rachel Biale, for helping me start and finish this book, is anything but perfunctory. Her book *Women and Jewish Law* provided me with a set of sources and questions from which to begin, and her unsparing readings and rereadings of my chapters were always my first source of criticism. The emotional support she has given me was no less unsparing, and the joy I have from our relationship and from our children, Noam and Tali, is proof that this book on Jewish sexuality takes its inspiration from real life.

# Dilemmas of Desire

IN February 1969 Philip Roth unleashed his most notorious novel, *Portnoy's Complaint*, the outrageous and hilarious confession of a sex-obsessed American Jew. Roth was certainly not the first Jewish writer or writer about the Jews to take up the theme of sexuality and the Jewish family, but his caricature of the American Jewish male and its attendant host of uncomfortable stereotypes brought him instant notoriety and also framed many of the questions that will preoccupy us in the chapters ahead. As a set of myths and countermyths, *Portnoy* is about the very discourse of Jewish sexuality and, beyond that, about what it means for Jews to live as a minority in the modern world.

Modern culture has a fascination with the sexuality of the Jews, a fascination marked by wildly conflicting beliefs. Perhaps because Judaism never embraced celibacy as a spiritual value, some hold that the Jews have a much more positive relationship to Eros than do Christians. Judaism, they claim, affirms the unity of the body and the spirit.[1] Some anti-Semites, by contrast, view the sexuality of the Jews as a threat to an ordered world, a barbaric affront to civility.[2] Yet others see Judaism as a chaste religion that elevates the spirit above the vulgar demands of the body; Jews, they say, know how to control their sexual impulses and are therefore the most ethical of peoples. For those less favorably disposed, however, there is a countermythology: this purported renunciation of sexuality is a sign of sexual repression, Judaism's deep hostility to eroticism and to the body.

In the wild monologue that is *Portnoy's Complaint*, Roth interwove these contradictory myths and touched a sensitive nerve. There were critics who saw in Roth nothing short of a Jewish self-hater who had resurrected the Nazi charge of *Rassenschande*, that the Jews lust after and defile pure Aryan girls.[3] The scandal of the novel is that it revealed the uncomfortable proximity of the erotic imaginations of Jews and anti-

Semites. Indeed, the furor that greeted *Portnoy* was perhaps greater than that aroused by any other Jewish novel published in this century. Reflecting back on his novel in 1974, Roth wrote:

> The man confessing to forbidden sexual acts and gross offenses against the family order and ordinary decency was a Jew.... Going wild in public is the last thing in the world that a Jew is expected to do.... He is not expected to make a spectacle of himself, either by shooting off his mouth or by shooting off his semen and certainly not by shooting off his mouth about shooting off his semen.[4]

This explanation for the book's notoriety is only half the story. After all, "going wild in public" in this fashion is also the last thing one might expect from, say, a New England Episcopalian.[5] *Portnoy* was believable, because on some level there existed an expectation that the Jew *was* capable of violating codes of civility.[6] Jews might present themselves as paragons of respectability, but below the surface, they think like Portnoy.

*Portnoy* appeared at that moment in American Jewish history when Jews had begun to believe that they had achieved full respectability and to relax about anti-Semitism. The end of anti-Jewish quotas and Israel's lightning victory in the 1967 War seemed to promise a utopian future. Roth's crime, in the eyes of his critics, was that he shattered this dream by flaunting Jewish sexual difference just as the sexual revolution was sweeping America and arousing profound anxieties in American culture. Perhaps, after all, the Jews were agents of cultural upheaval and degeneracy.

*Portnoy's Complaint* is the quintessential tale of the repression of sex and its displacement by words. Portnoy's "complaint" is precisely that the more he thinks—and speaks—about sex, the less he is able to achieve satisfaction. This is a book about how words substitute for sex and how the Jews, the quintessential People of the Book, live in eternal exile from their own bodies. The historical Judaism of Portnoy is a religion devoid of the erotic: sexual repression, rants the monologist, is the product of the heritage of Jewish suffering and compulsive legalism. The novel reduces this legalism primarily to food taboos, and those, in turn, are repeatedly linked to forbidden sexuality.[7] Food, like words, involves the mouth: yet again orality neutralizes Eros. Portnoy's Judaism is a religion of the mouth but decidedly not of the genitals.

The novel reduces the drama of Jewish history to a soap opera of family dynamics. Portnoy's mother has one implied purpose in life: to kill her son's sexuality by domination and intrusiveness; his passive father is the original victim of the crime now being perpetrated on the son. For Portnoy, the Jewish tradition boils down to this unholy trinity, making its way in a world of repression and secret cravings.

Since this repressive tradition has stifled Jewish sexuality, Gentiles are left with a monopoly on healthy eroticism. Indeed, the differences between Christianity and Judaism are no longer theological or historical but instead are utterly secular: "Religion ... is [the key not] to the mysteries of the divine and the beyond, but to the mystery of the sensual and the erotic, the wonder of laying a hand on the girl down the street."[8] The Jewish male has no choice but to seek out erotic fulfillment in the arms of the *shiksa*, the derogatory Yiddish term for the gentile woman, at once desired and despised. But since Jewish childhood and adolescence end in psychological castration, the *shiksa* can never fulfill her redemptive role. Repression breeds obsession but the object of obsession cannot liberate.

Curiously, it is the Monkey, Portnoy's gentile partner in sexual perversity and the culmination of his search for the perfect *shiksa*, who counters Portnoy's myth of the neurotic Jewish male. For the Monkey, the Jewish male is at once highly sexual *and* domestically responsible: "a regular domestic Messiah."[9] Here, Roth shrewdly suggests that it is not only Jews who have sexual myths about Gentiles, but Gentiles who have myths about Jews, myths that correspond to how Jews would like to see themselves. Both Jews and Gentiles, Roth seems to say, are trapped in imagined archetypes of themselves and the other.

It is therefore no surprise that the Jewish woman does not exist as a sexual possibility in the novel. Although the myth of the asexual Jewish American Princess is unarticulated in *Portnoy*, it clearly hovers in the background. Portnoy reflects such a thoroughgoing misogynist view of the world that Jewish women cannot be potential partners, and even gentile women are little more than anonymous cardboard stereotypes. But is not this very denial of an identity and an authentic voice to women also implicitly a product of the Jewish tradition itself, as Portnoy sees it?

For Portnoy, women and Gentiles are virtually synonymous.[10] Both are equally threatening. Only in the steam bath, surrounded by Jewish males, is there escape for Portnoy: "But here in a Turkish bath, why am I dancing around? There are no women here. No women—and no *goyim*. Can it be? There is nothing to worry about."[11] For all his ostensible success in American society (he heads the New York City Human Rights Commission, a symbol, as it were, of America's promise of social integration), Portnoy remains an alien in a gentile land, his sexual maladjustment a metaphor for the Jew in exile.

If the American Jewish woman has no sexual potential and the Gentile has too much, perhaps the solution is to be found in the allegedly healthy sexuality of the Jewish state, which Portnoy visits at the end of the novel. Here, Roth cannily alludes to a subterranean theme in Zionist ideology, a theme that is the cousin of anti-Semitic fantasy: the Jews of the Diaspora are sexually emasculated and perverted (and in the Zionist version, only a normal national life can restore erotic health). Zionism, then, is not just a political and cultural movement of liberation, it is also the sexual revolution of the Jewish people.

Yet Portnoy cannot escape his Diaspora fate: the Promised Land brings not Eros but impotence. The Israeli women, it turns out, are depressingly puritanical and Zionism offers no sexual liberation. Believing himself to have gonorrhea, Portnoy sets out to avenge himself on Zionism by infecting a healthy kibbutz woman and thereby poison "the future of the race" with a dose of Diaspora disease. And so with this bizarre twist on the anti-Semitic motif of Jewish race pollution, *Portnoy* comes to its crashing conclusion.

Between the covers of this novel lies more than an extended comic gig or an attempt to scandalize. With its hyperbole and nihilism, *Portnoy's Complaint* captures the dilemmas of modern Jewish life: Can the Jewish people perpetuate itself biologically in a culture that no longer links sex with procreation as had the old religious commandment that legitimated sexuality? Can Jews achieve sexual satisfaction with other Jews, or will they, like Portnoy, turn to the mythical Gentile? If the Diaspora proves to be a demographic dead end, is a Jewish state the solution not only to the political dilemmas of the Jews, but also to their sexual dilemmas?

Although these questions of procreation, sexual pleasure, and intermarriage are all modern, we will see that they also plagued the premodern Jewish tradition. Roth is not the first to meditate on the relationship between Jews and sexuality; on the contrary, he is heir to a long literary tradition, and, consciously or not, he reproduces many of the conflicts that thread through it. This novel of late-twentieth-century America is thus a lens through which we can view the major themes of Jewish discourse about sexuality since the Bible, as well as some of the major themes of this book itself.

Roth's *Portnoy* raises the fundamental question: does the Jewish tradition affirm or repress sexuality? To a certain extent, this very formulation of the question is modern, Freudian even—no surprise for a book written as a confession to a psychoanalyst and a Jewish one at that! The categories of "gratification" and "repression" can only be applied with great caution to cultures that thought of sexuality in very different ways.[12] As we take up different Jewish cultures, whether biblical, talmudic, or medieval, we shall identify the central concerns of each and try to refrain from imposing our own categories. At the same time, we cannot divorce ourselves entirely from our modern ways of looking at sexuality when we travel to the past; we would probably not even take the journey were it not for Freud and all those other modern thinkers who put sexuality at the center of our identities. Although I shall try to avoid applying psychoanalytic concepts anachronistically, it would be impossible to select and interpret texts dealing with sexuality without acknowledging some debt to modern psychology. The texts can speak for themselves only if we tell them first what we are interested in hearing!

Since psychoanalysis necessarily colors any study of sexuality, and is also explicitly Jewish in its origins, it is appropriate to reflect on what it has to say about our subject. The very lack of consensus on Freud's own Jewishness suggests that it would be a mistake to regard him primarily as a *Jewish* interpreter of sexuality.[13] This has not, however, prevented the claims that Freud's stand on sexuality was essentially Jewish.[14] In these discussions, Freud is enlisted to do battle for a "Jewish," as opposed to a "Christian," version of sexuality, the latter sometimes identified with Carl Jung.

In reality, Freud's own scattered remarks on the relationship between Judaism and sexuality are an excellent example of the very ambivalence that is one of the major themes of this book. On the side of sexual openness, he boasted of having liberated the erotic from "the condition of cultural hypocrisy" that prevents "the ventilation of the question," hinting that he was able to do so because, as a Jew, he remained outside conventional morality.[15] While Freud himself never explicitly said that Jews were less sexually repressed than others, his disciple, Otto Rank, did. In an essay written shortly after his conversion to psychoanalysis, Rank defined the "essence of Judaism" as its "stress on primitive sexuality."[16] Jews were forced to repress their essential sexuality as a result of exile, said Rank, but the original "essence of Judaism" might still offer a radical cure for the sexual neurosis of civilization.

Whether or not these views even partially reflected Freud's when Rank composed his essay in 1905, Freud often took quite the opposite position, especially in his later writings. He argued in numerous famous essays that civilization requires sublimation of the sexual drive. As his own life attests, Freud remained a sexual puritan, even as he gave sexuality its most systematic discourse; and after the birth of his fifth child, he seems to have become largely celibate, if not impotent.[17] He argued in *Moses and Monotheism* that the Jews were spiritually superior because monotheism led them to renounce instinctual gratification.[18] The Jews, it would seem, were the original masters of sublimation. Freud's science of sexuality therefore combined liberation and sublimation in an uneasy dialectic, with Judaism somehow straddling both antinomies.

The contradictions in Freud's view of Jewish sexuality capture the central argument of this book: the Jewish tradition cannot be characterized as either simply affirming or simply repressing the erotic. Our story is about the *dilemmas* of desire, the struggle between contradictory attractions, rather than the history of a monolithic dogma. As such, it is the story of a profoundly ambivalent culture.

We will follow our theme from biblical times to the modern period, that is, this tension between procreation and sexual desire in a culture that required everyone to marry. Is sexual fulfillment an end in itself or is it to be subordinated to other goals, whether a theology of fertility in the Bible, a divine commandment in rabbinic law, a mystical theosophy in the Middle Ages, or the building of a modern Zionist nation-state?

From the period of the Talmud onward, Jewish culture always wrestled with sexual asceticism, trying to find ways to incorporate the virtues of renunciation, as it absorbed them from Greco-Roman and Christian culture, into its theology of procreation. Influenced first by philosophy and then by mysticism in the Middle Ages, this struggle took on new forms, leading to much more ascetic expressions, especially in the Hasidic movement of the eighteenth century. In the nineteenth and twentieth centuries, secularized forms of sexual renunciation appeared in both the Jewish Enlightenment and the pioneering collectives of the Zionist movement. Asceticism then, as an attraction and a challenge to Jewish culture, is a persistent, if ambiguous, subtext to our story.

By attributing the Jews' ostensible renunciation of the instincts to monotheism, Freud suggested another issue that must be addressed. A God lacking any sexual biography was unique in the ancient world— what were the consequences of such a theology for the way Jews viewed their own sexuality?[19] The answers to this question varied as much as did the Jewish cultures of different ages. Sexuality occupied a no-man's-land between theology and secularism, sometimes serving as a symbolic displacement of erotic energies onto the divine realm, as in the case of eighteenth-century Hasidism, and sometimes as an instrument of revolt against the strictures of divine commandments, as in secular Zionism. In the biblical cult of fertility or in medieval Jewish mysticism, sexuality was an integral part of theology; by contrast, one strand of rabbinic literature and also medieval philosophy relegated it to the secular world, with all the attendant ambivalence that world aroused. No study of Jewish sexuality can ignore the changing role of theology, which continues to resonate even in the secular culture of contemporary America.

Roth's method in *Portnoy's Complaint* points to the approach I propose to take in this book. Following the initial storm over *Portnoy*, the *New York Times* published interviews with Jewish mothers (including Roth's own mother) who unanimously rejected Roth's portrayal of the Jewish mother and the Jewish family in general.[20] This approach to the novel missed the point. *Portnoy* is decidedly not a sociological description or a mimetic representation of reality; it is expressly a study in erotic fantasy, a Jew imagining how Jews imagine themselves.[21] Like Roth, my goal is not to discover what Jewish sexual behavior actually was in the past so much as to investigate how Jews have constructed notions of sexuality, how they have thought about it and struggled with it in the texts they produced.

The question is not primarily what actually happened, but rather how

Jews *wrote* about sexuality. If sex is the physical act that takes place between people, sexuality or eroticism is the way a culture imagines sex, the framework in which it places it, and the meanings it assigns it.[22] Thus, I understand Eros to encompass the cultural and social constructs, such as love and marriage, that define and control sex to be part of our subject. Similarly, desire may mean specifically sexual desire, but it may also signify what we would call, in modern language, romantic desire, those aspects of erotic relationships that include but also go beyond the physical. Throughout this book, *Eros* and *desire* will sometimes be understood in these broader contexts and sometimes more narrowly to refer specifically to the meaning of the physical aspect of sex itself; we will allow each period to define these concepts in its own terms.

Literary constructs of the erotic are not necessarily disconnected from the world of experience. Wherever possible we want to understand the relationship between the lives of those who created a culture and the ideas they expressed. The erotic theology of the thirteenth-century Jewish mystics must be located in the particular concerns of the culture of southern France and Spain; similarly, the texts produced by the eighteenth-century Hasidim and the nineteenth-century maskilim cannot be divorced from their life experiences. Like the modern historian of sexuality, those who wrote about sexuality in the past were themselves people with bodies possessed by erotic desire.

Texts, furthermore, do more than merely reflect experience; they also *shape* experience or, rather, the way people view their experience: discourse defines desire. Roth's *Portnoy* may have represented what some readers believed to be reality, but, much more importantly, it created a perception of reality. Texts can also have contradictory effects. The puritanical preacher who denounces sexual excess may actually arouse himself or his congregation by his very words.[23] Of course, we cannot know how texts from the past were read and understood without some explicit evidence, and we must be careful not to impose our reactions upon readers from other centuries. Nevertheless, we must be attuned to the fact that the written word can be, and often is, the main vehicle by which a culture creates the erotic.

The chapters ahead present texts produced by a cultural elite: priests, rabbis, philosophers, mystics, Hasidic masters, Enlightenment literati, and Zionist ideologists, among others. The elite produced a canonical literature, some of which was read widely but large portions of which, such as medieval philosophy and mysticism, were accessible only to the elite itself. In the Jewish context, there is also a close connection between those who write and those who wield authority: knowledge and power are frequently linked. The rabbis of the talmudic period, for example, developed their singular culture in order not only to make sense of themselves but also to exert control over those outside the elite, including the poorer, ignorant classes and, perhaps most significantly for a study of sexuality, women.

Rarely can we hear the distant voices of those not included in this elite, and only in the modern period do they emerge as equals. Yet throughout Jewish history, dissident cultures, including popular culture, challenged the canon. No cultural elite arises in a vacuum. On the contrary, the so-called normative tradition is always embedded in a social matrix, in part defining it and in part struggling against it. I see this tension not as a conflict between a normative system and its deviants but rather as a conflict between competing cultures that often differed far more than the authoritative norms themselves might suggest. Throughout this book, we shall try to capture traces of these alternative cultures through other kinds of texts, such as literature, folklore, and court documents, which often convey visions of sexuality quite different from those of the canonical texts.

As the elite that produced the vast majority of the texts we will be considering was male, we will be concerned primarily with the way these male writers viewed their own sexuality, as well as the sexuality of others, whether women, Gentiles, or the unlearned. With very few exceptions, what we know of women's sexuality was filtered through male eyes; even the *tekhines*, women's prayers written in Yiddish, were often composed by men, sometimes masquerading as women.[24] Producing a history of the experience of Jewish women remains one of the great tasks of the new Jewish historiography, and I do not propose to offer more than fragments for such a history, primarily by suggesting some possible feminist readings of certain texts.

What does it mean for the history of sexuality to have only a one-sided, male perspective? If feminist theory is correct that men's and women's experiences of sexuality are fundamentally different, the way in which an all-male cultural elite imagines the erotic will differ from the imaginings of an elite that included women. Might it be that the struggle with asceticism which so dominated Jewish culture from Hellenistic times onward reflected a particularly male set of concerns? Would women have defined the problem in quite this way? We might compare the Jewish tradition with the Christian, which carved out an official place for female religiosity and therefore preserved women's voices, too. But Christianity placed such a high value on celibacy that women often had to renounce their sexuality in order to find a place in the religious order; in fact, since Christian asceticism sometimes defined the celibate state as "becoming male," women had to renounce their gender as well.[25] Female experience in the church was therefore frequently shaped by male concerns, although male domination did not entirely erase the distinctive perspective of women from the history of Christian spirituality.

The Jewish case is more difficult because women's voices were much less commonly preserved. Since this was a culture in which knowledge was one of the main forms of power, the exclusion of women from the creation of texts—our main historical source—signaled their exclusion from power. The situation is not as hopeless as it might appear at first glance, however. Although folklore and court records, to take two examples, were written and transmitted primarily by men, they contain unmistakable traces of women's voices. Furthermore, the male authors of canonical texts often projected onto women points of view, sometimes subversive and radical, that they were not prepared to express as their own. At times, patriarchal and antipatriarchal voices compete in the texts and, as part of our effort to describe both the canon *and* alternative discourses, we will try to disentangle these voices. Although we will still be left with a predominantly male culture of sexuality, it will at least be one in which male writers, who were by no means always misogynistic, at times tried to construct sympathetic versions of female sexuality. Only in the modern period will we discover attempts by women to recover their own erotic voices.

Finally, we wish to know how specifically Jewish images of sexuality relate to the larger, non-Jewish cultures in which the Jews lived. In *Portnoy's Complaint*, Roth showed how entangled Jewish self-perceptions are with the attitudes of the majority culture: Portnoy's pathology reflects the anti-Semitic trope of Jewish hypersexuality. Although Jewish culture generally did not adopt anti-Jewish images, neither did the tradition evolve in some splendid isolation from the rest of the world. Too many histories of the Jews unconsciously fall back on the theology of Jewish uniqueness and assume that the development of the culture is determined by an autochthonous textual tradition. Jewish attitudes towards sexuality were certainly the product of such a tradition, but that tradition was always open to external influences from the larger societies in which Jews lived. An old Arabic proverb has it that "men resemble their own times more than those of their fathers." Whether the larger culture was Canaanite, Roman, medieval European, or modern nationalist, the Jews' construction of their sexuality reflected the issues of their times, even as their vocabulary was often inherited from their ancestors. The history of Jewish sexuality must therefore be the history of a cultural system in all its conflicts, varieties, and interactions with other cultures; it is not merely the history of norms developed by an ivory-tower elite.

That Jewish culture throughout the ages consists of actual people with bodies and not only rarified ideas may seem almost a commonplace in the waning years of this century.[26] Yet the reaction that greeted Philip Roth's work suggests that the relationship between sexuality and the Jews continues to arouse enormous discomfort, as if the very subject might undermine the vexed struggle of the Jews to survive in the modern world. Some years before Roth published *Portnoy*, a rabbi named Seligson attacked him for ignorance of "the tremendous saga of Jewish history" in his portrayal of a middle-aged Jewish adulterer in the story "Epstein." Roth responded that his story was not about Judaism or Jewish history as a whole but about a Jew named Epstein:

> Where the history of the Jewish people comes down in time and place to become the man whom I called Epstein, that is where my knowledge must be sound. But I get the feeling that Rabbi Seligson wants to rule Lou Epstein *out* of Jewish history.[27]

In response to the Seligsons of the Jewish world, Portnoy answers in his characteristically outrageous fashion: "LET'S PUT THE ID BACK IN YID."

This book has been written in the conviction that sexuality in all its manifestations is indeed part of Jewish history: Eros, for all its Hellenistic overtones, also belongs to the Jews. Epstein the adulterer and Seligson the moralizing rabbi, Alexander Portnoy and his critics—all are part of that history. And the ongoing dialogue between them, from biblical to contemporary culture, is the story we shall tell in the chapters ahead.

# Sexual Subversions in the Bible

THE contemporary debate over whether Judaism liberates or represses sexuality must begin with the Hebrew Bible. This foundational document of Jewish culture, like any other such document, is subject to contradictory readings. Those who wish to portray Judaism as a this-worldly affirmation of sexuality look to the Bible, best represented on this subject by the Song of Songs, as setting the tone for all subsequent Jewish tradition. Indeed anti-Semites who hold that the Jews are hypersexual contrast the "lustful" nature of Judaism, which, they say, has its roots in the same biblical texts, with the more ascetic spirituality of Christianity. Taking the opposite position are those who believe that Judaism is sexually repressive. In their eyes, the basis for sexual repression in Western culture lies in the biblical laws of sexual purity. Feminists who hold this view argue further that the Bible is the origin of patriarchy: the male God of the Old Testament—the paragon of stern monotheism—jealously stamped out the erotic matriarchy of the pagan gods. Biblical culture, they charge, treated women as dangerous temptresses whose sexuality had to be controlled and domesticated.[1]

Each of these contradictory accounts assumes that the biblical text and biblical culture were stable and monolithic. But the Bible is less a factual history of ancient Israel than the record of a culture in conflict over its own identity, a conflict frequently represented by tensions between law and narrative and, just as often, by contradictions between different laws and different narratives. The conflicting genres and ideas within the Bible are not unlike the cultural conflicts that appear in texts from later periods of Jewish history. Thus, the Bible, itself the canonical text, includes material that foreshadows the later struggles between canon and alternative voices.

Since biblical culture was not monolithic, all of the contemporary interpretations of the Bible can find some support for their contradictory positions in the text. But as partial interpretations, they are often more misleading than helpful. The biblical legacy cannot be reduced to the harsh and repressive strictures of patriarchal custom. In addition to divinely ordained laws and patriarchal custom, the Bible also contains narratives in which these norms are suspended or undermined. Biblical culture takes on issues of sexuality with a remarkable theology of sexual subversion in which erotic brashness, often on the part of women, becomes a metaphor for the political brashness of a young, upstart nation. God is both the author of the laws and the hidden force behind their mythic subversion. Within what was undoubtedly a patriarchal legal culture, one finds surprisingly subversive alternatives that survive, not necessarily because there was external resistance to patriarchy, but because the dominant culture itself was neither monolithic nor utterly self-confident.

Sexuality was a central issue in Israel's self-conception,[2] with adultery and fidelity the dominant metaphors both for Israel's relationship to God and for national identity. The prophet Ezekiel combines the two explicitly in his accusation that Israel is whoring with her neighbors, the "well-endowed Egyptians" (16:26); Israel's depravity, he explains, derives from her origins: "You are daughters of a Hittite mother and an Amorite father" (16:45). Sexual anxiety is thus at the very heart of the struggle with this ambiguous identity. Would intermarriage with the competing nations in the land dilute a discrete Israelite identity, or was there no choice for a small, poorly defined people but to strengthen its position through such marital alliances? Intermarriage, as we shall see, was as defining and controversial an issue in biblical times as it is for Jews today.

Closely linked to problems of sexuality were deep concerns about fertility. The religion of ancient Israel is frequently seen as a refutation of the fertility cults of the Canaanites and the other peoples who lived in the area that became the land of Israel. Fertility rites are thought to be particularly characteristic of polytheists, who are said to engage in wild sexual orgies that will incite the gods and goddesses to copulate, which, in turn, is meant to bring fertility to the worshipers and their land. If it is highly doubtful that this is an accurate picture of Canaanite religion, it is equally false that Israelite religion lacked interest in fertility. On the contrary, ancient Israelite religion is not reducible to the abstract monotheism of later Jewish theology. Rather, it flourished in complex interaction with its milieu, at once adopting, transforming, and resisting Canaanite ideas and practices.

Fertility was a central component of biblical religion, a result, no doubt, of the Israelites' sense of their origins as a small, weak people.[3] As Psalms 105:12 puts it: "They were then few in number, a mere handful, sojourning there [in the land of Canaan]." Psalms 127:3–7 beautifully captures the connection between fertility and national power, represented respectively by female and male metaphors:

*Sons are the provision of the Lord;*
  *the fruit of the womb, His reward,*
*Like arrows in the hand of a warrior*
  *are sons born to a man in his youth.*
*Happy is the man who fills his quiver with them;*
  *they shall not be put to shame*
  *when they contend with the enemy at the gate.*

This sense that fertility was a precarious matter accompanied the ancient Israelites from the recurring stories of female infertility in Genesis to the thundering threats of the later prophetic texts:

*From birth, from the womb, from conception*
*Ephraim's glory shall be like birds that fly away.*
*Even if they rear their infants, I will bereave them of men.*
*Give them, O Lord—give them what?*
*Give them a womb that miscarries*
*And shriveled breasts! (Hosea 9:11–12, 14)*

Like intermarriage, the fear of the demographic demise of the Jewish people is an ancient theme in Jewish history, with its roots in biblical culture.

Preoccupied as it was with defining its national myth, biblical culture repeatedly situated sexuality in national and political contexts that pertained to fertility. With the exception of the Song of Songs, the Bible displays little interest in erotic desire as such. Desire was instead subordinated to communal concerns, and as long as it was expressed in its proper place, it did not pose a problem, as it would for later Jewish cultures. In this respect, the Hebrew Bible—although it is the sacred text on which all of subsequent Judaism is based—is in some ways disconnected from the later tradition. Let us therefore consider biblical culture on its own terms, as the first chapter in our history of Jewish sexuality.

## Ruth: Sexual Subversion and the Origins of King David

We begin with the Book of Ruth. This ancient folktale artfully reveals many of the central themes of sexuality in ancient Judaism.[4] As the story of the journey of an Israelite family out of the land of Israel and then back again, it defines many of the boundaries—both geographic and metaphoric—that would preoccupy the Jewish people in the ancient period and, indeed, throughout the subsequent ages. Ruth addresses questions of fertility and lineage, and its iconoclastic solutions to these problems are emblematic of similarly surprising solutions found elsewhere in the biblical record.

Ruth is the story of the family of Elimelech of Bethlehem. In time of famine the family emigrates to Moab, where Elimelech's two sons marry Moabite women but fail to have children. After all the men in the family die in the foreign land, Elimelech's wife, Naomi, and her two daughters-in-law begin the journey back to Bethlehem. One of the two, Orpah, returns to Moab on the advice of Naomi, but the other, Ruth, pledges eternal loyalty to Naomi and stays with her. In Bethlehem, Naomi instructs Ruth to glean in the fields of Elimelech's distant kinsman Boaz and then to approach him at night on the threshing floor, where he has fallen asleep from drink. Boaz awakes and pledges to marry Ruth and thus redeem the inheritance of her deceased husband and father-in-law. After persuading an anonymous closer relative of Elimelech to forgo his duty as redeemer, Boaz marries Ruth, who then conceives and bears the child who will be the grandfather of the future King David. Thus, a story that begins with death and infertility ends with the birth of David's ancestor.

Eroticism, procreation, and agricultural fertility are intertwined throughout the book, as befits a tale from a predominantly agrarian society.[5] The "house of bread" (Bethlehem) has become infertile and the man, Elimelech, seeks fertility in the "fields" of Moab. Yet he and his sons die there, childless: the fields that had appeared so fertile from afar become the graveyard of Elimelech's lineage, the burial ground of his own fertility. Indeed, the Hebrew word for a barren woman, *akarah*, literally means "uprooted."[6] To leave one's land is to become infertile, and, in this story it is the foreigner, Ruth, who restores fertility.

Naomi and Ruth return to Bethlehem at the beginning of the barley harvest. The ensuing action, from Ruth's gleaning in the fields to her probable seduction of Boaz on the threshing floor, connects the harvest of grain with sexuality and reproduction. These interlocked themes may well have been taken directly from older Canaanite myths.[7] If so, however, the author of Ruth, like other biblical authors, covered up the cultic origins of the story.

The lineage of Elimelech is restored by an act of implied sexual transgression. In the charged scene of Ruth accosting the drunken, sleeping Boaz on the threshing floor, the text repeatedly uses words like "to lie down" and "to know," both of which have clear sexual connotations.[8] Ruth uncovers Boaz's legs, an occasional biblical euphemism for the genitals.[9] The text alludes to a Genesis legend here, for Noah, too, had his nakedness revealed, in his case when he lay drunk in his tent after leaving the ark (Genesis 9:21). To "uncover the genitals" is the technical term in biblical law for a sexual violation,[10] and Ruth's act alludes suggestively to the sin of Noah's son Ham.

The ancient audience would have recognized these terms as implying that Ruth actually seduced Boaz. After this delicately suggested seduction, Ruth invites Boaz to spread his "wing" (the corner of his cloak) over her, a phrase that evidently means marriage.[11] To "uncover" the genitals is a transgression, but to "cover" them by marriage makes sexual activity permissible. Thus, Ruth subverts sexual custom in order to secure her marriage to Boaz; only by bending the social norms can she win her destined mate and give fertility to the line of David.

The erotic initiative in this tale falls, significantly, to women.[12] When Ruth chooses to remain with Naomi and return to Bethlehem, the text says that she "clung to her" (*davkah bah*), just as Genesis 2:24 states that when a man leaves his father and mother, he "clings" (*davak*) to his wife. It is this "clinging" of Ruth to Naomi, the bond between these women, that guarantees the continuity of Elimelech's line. So predominant is the role of Naomi that the women of the town, who form a kind of Greek chorus, name Ruth's son after her, rather than after her deceased husband, saying "a son has been born to Naomi" (4:17). Ruth is a surrogate for the postmenopausal Naomi, much like the famous concubines of Genesis: Hagar for Sarah, Zilpah for Leah, and Bilhah for Rachel. Thus, although the story concludes with the male lineage that leads from Boaz to King David, Ruth's great-grandson, it is really Naomi whose name is perpetuated.[13]

The Book of Ruth therefore at once reinforces *and* subverts patriarchy. Women play the critical role of ensuring fertility—a role perhaps dictated by patriarchy—but they do so by subversion of sexual custom. This ostensibly antipatriarchal role is implicitly based on a view of women as erotic creatures whose sexuality could just as well be destructive.[14] We shall presently see how this projection of ambivalent sexual power onto women is repeated in other stories, some of which are explicitly connected to Ruth, as if for the biblical authors women represented the subversion of norms necessary for fertility.

The ultimate purpose of Ruth's sexual initiative is to bear the child who will be the grandfather of King David. Here too, however, the story challenges biblical norms by emphasizing Ruth's Moabite origins; no fewer than five times in this short book she is referred to as "Ruth the Moabite" or the "Moabite girl." Readers over the centuries, including the rabbis of the talmudic period, could not fail to notice the glaring contradiction between Ruth's origins and the law of Deuteronomy 23:4: "No Ammonite or Moabite shall be admitted into the congregation of the Lord."[15] The Moabites were not only periodic enemies of the Israelites, but the Bible's own account of their origins casts doubt on their legiti-

macy. According to Genesis 19:30–38, the Moabites were the product of
an incestuous union between Lot, Abraham's nephew, and one of his
daughters. Following the destruction of Sodom and Gomorrah, from
which they were saved, Lot and his daughters found refuge in a cave. Believing that they were the only people left in the world, the two women
got their father drunk and had sexual relations with him. Out of this incest came two sons, Moab, the eponymous father of the Moabites, and
Ben-ammi, the first of the Ammonites, precisely the two nations forbidden by Deuteronomy to enter the congregation of the Lord. As in Ruth, it
is women who ensure fertility by bending or breaking with convention;
and as in Ruth, the sexual ruse involves the seduction of an inebriated
older relative.[16]

The story of Ruth, then, reunites the two branches of Abraham's family. Boaz represents the line of Judah, Jacob's son and Abraham's great-
grandson, whereas Ruth represents Moab, the son of Lot, Abraham's
nephew. King David is the eventual product of this genetic recombina-
tion, and to complete the story, the son Solomon chooses to succeed him,
Rehoboam, is born of an Ammonite mother (1 Kings 14:21). According
to these genealogies, the Davidic dynasty had Moabite and Ammonite, as
well as Israelite, origins. These stories may have been primarily ideological in intent; since David had conquered the Moabites and Ammonites,
the legend that the Judean kings shared the blood of their vassal peoples
would have served the political end of helping to solidify the Davidic empire.

But there may have been a broader motive at work, as well. The biblical concept of fertility demanded the suspension of norms when it came
to the birth of heroes. The crossing of boundaries, both sexual and ethnic, became a central component in the ideology of the monarchy as well
as in the national ideology of the Israelite people. Ruth is doubly antinor-
mative: a woman who takes the sexual initiative in a patriarchal culture
and a Moabite who becomes the ancestor of King David, despite legal
bans on intermarriage.[17]

## The Politics of Sexual Subversion

The sexual deceits practiced by Ruth and by Lot's daughters are but two
of many more instances in the biblical record in which subversion of sexual norms is central to the lives of heroes like David or to the survival of
whole nations, including Israel itself. Both Abraham and Isaac become
dangerously entangled with foreign kings by passing off their wives as
their sisters (Genesis 12, 20, and 26), in clear violation of biblical law.

Sarah may actually have been Abraham's half sister, for so he claims to Abimelech in Genesis 20:12. If so, their marriage would violate the incest law of Leviticus 18:11: "The nakedness of your father's wife's daughter [that is, a half sister born of a common father but different mothers]... she is your sister; do not uncover her nakedness." Furthermore, Genesis 12 says that when Sarah poses as Abraham's sister in Egypt, she is taken into Pharaoh's household, implying that they have sexual relations. If so, she has committed adultery with Abraham's complicity. This is precisely the argument made by Abimelech in the case of Isaac's wife Rebecca (Genesis 26:10–11). Finally, Jacob, the eponymous father of the Israelite nation, marries two sisters, Leah and Rachel, in seeming violation of the law of Leviticus 18:18, which prohibits marrying two sisters while both are alive.

All of these stories no doubt preceded the Levitical incest laws by many centuries; what is therefore noteworthy is that they were included in the biblical text. The authors or editors who produced the text were surely aware of the flagrant contradictions between the laws and the narratives, but they must have seen those contradictions as serving an important cultural function. The creation of the Israelite nation was seen by these later authors as a result of the suspension of conventions, a sign, perhaps, of divine favor for a ragtag, ethnically mixed people. Far from a disgrace to be hidden, sexual subversion, like the repeated preference for younger over older sons, hints at the unexpected character of God's covenant with Israel.[18]

All of these themes found their most vivid expression in the stories of David's origins, his rise to power, and his reign as king of Israel and Judah. This is perhaps not surprising since the Davidic dynasty, which was to rule the Kingdom of Judah until its demise in 586 B.C.E, was the dominant political force in whose shadow and later memory most of the biblical text was composed. The royal theology became a synecdoche for Israel's national identity.

The sexual transgressions that underlie David's lineage are particularly manifest in the last chapter of Ruth. The people at the gate conclude their fertility blessing to Boaz: "And may your house be like the house of Perez whom Tamar bore to Judah—through the offspring which the Lord will give you by this young woman" (4:12). According to the genealogy appended to the end of the book, Boaz's ancestor was Perez, the son of Jacob's son Judah. The author of Ruth alludes specifically to Perez because of the striking similarities between the story of the birth of Perez, recorded in Genesis 38, and the Book of Ruth.[19]

Genesis 38 interrupts the Joseph stories to relate the following account of Jacob's son Judah.[20] Judah has three sons by his marriage with a Canaanite woman. He marries his eldest son, Er, to a woman named Tamar; when Er dies, he gives her to his second son, Onan, in order to perpetuate Er's name. Onan resists this levirate duty by spilling his seed on the ground instead of engaging in procreative intercourse. He, too, dies. Judah promises Tamar to give her his third son, Shelah, when the young boy reaches maturity, but he breaks his promise. Tamar then disguises herself as a prostitute, seduces her father-in-law, and becomes pregnant. Instead of paying the "prostitute," Judah leaves his staff and seal with her as pledges, and Tamar subsequently uses them to prove his paternity. Out of this transgressive affair come the twins Perez and Zerah.

If the author of Ruth only hints at Ruth's sexual deviousness to achieve her end, Genesis 38 is much more explicit: relations between daughter-in-law and father-in-law are forbidden as incest (Leviticus 18:15). Yet the story treats Tamar's subterfuge as thoroughly justifiable to right the failure of Judah and his sons to provide her with children. The story allows her to take matters into her own hands and violate sexual norms.

The associations between the Ruth and Tamar stories are too remarkable to be coincidental. Both stories begin with the death of two brothers (and, in the case of Ruth, their father as well). Both involve levirate (Deuteronomy 25:5–10), the custom by which the brother (or, in the case of Ruth, a more distant relative) of a man who dies childless must marry the widow in order to perpetuate the dead man's name and provide for the continuity of his inheritance.[21] In both stories, the levir, or redeemer, fails to fulfill his obligation, and the widow must take bold action, including sexual transgression, to ensure a child.

The levirate law itself is, in fact, the consummate violation of sexual boundaries for the sake of fertility. The incest laws of Leviticus 18:16 and 20:21 explicitly forbid a man from having sexual relations with his brother's wife; in the second law, the punishment for violation is childlessness. The case of the levirate is a complete reversal: the very point of allowing a man to marry his deceased brother's wife is to produce a child. The levirate and incest laws therefore appear to be conscious mirror images of one another: just as the levirate custom takes effect only if the deceased brother is childless, so relations with the wife of that brother when he is alive will result in infertility for the offender. In the first case, levirate practice suspends the normal incest laws in order to guarantee the continuity of a lineage; in the second, violation of the incest law results in the disruption of the offender's lineage. Even though the levirate served to guarantee a family's fertility, it still aroused enormous ambivalence: because there were circumstances, albeit unusual, when a brother-in-law was permitted sexually, he might have been a more tempting object of incest than other relations.[22]

It is this problem implied in the levirate law that gives the erotic charge and overtones of subversive sexuality to the threshing-floor scene in Ruth and to Tamar's seduction of Judah. The two stories cast long shadows on the legitimacy of David's lineage, from both a strictly legal and a broader cultural point of view. Neither story is presented as polemic or apology, though, which suggests that the subversion was meant to be emphasized rather than obscured.

In terms of comparative mythology, these stories reverse the pattern of many ancient myths in which the king-hero has legitimate origins that are then lost by circumstance: his parents abandon him, he is raised by peasants or animals, and through a series of adventures, he eventually returns to his parents' household and to his predestined status.[23] Thus, Oedipus murders his father and has sexual relations with the mother out of ignorance of his true, royal identity. This typology is absent in the David stories, as well as in other myths of the origins of biblical heroes. The biblical stories correspond instead to a different kind of folkloric motif: the powerless youngest son (often, as in the case of David, the seventh son) who outwits his older brothers and surprises everyone by attaining fame and fortune through cleverness and sheer good luck.[24] The hero, like Israel as a whole, is the least expected: legitimacy is not preordained, but is instead achieved by subverting the established order.

David's rise to power and his reign are no less bound up with violation of sexual boundaries than are his origins, just as his whole political career is marked by an unconventional, even scandalous path. He appropriates two mens' wives, Abigail, the wife of Nabal (1 Samuel 25), and Bathsheba, the wife of Uriah the Hittite (2 Samuel 11). In the first case, Nabal (the name itself is derogatory, meaning "boor" or "scoundrel") is said to wrong David by refusing to pay him protection money. As a reward to David for not attacking Nabal himself and as punishment for Nabal's "crime," God strikes Nabal dead, thus clearing the way for David to marry Abigail. Abigail is portrayed as God's agent in the death of her husband: he becomes like a stone and subsequently dies when she tells of David's intention to murder him. Her words, it is implied, are what actually kill him. Here is truly a lethal woman, but one whose behavior appears to be fully legitimated by God.

David's adultery with Bathsheba is the dark version of the Abigail story: the author roundly condemns David's theft of another man's wife.[25] David sleeps with Bathsheba while her husband, Uriah, is at the battlefront: the king is having fun in bed while the general is in the trenches. When Bathsheba becomes pregnant, David tries to cover up his own paternity by ordering her husband back, in hopes that he will sleep with his wife. Uriah refuses, even when David gets him drunk. Unable to hide his crime, David has Uriah killed at the front. Bathsheba then marries David, but the child born of their adulterous union dies at the hand of God.

The reference to alcohol here suggests that the story of Uriah and Bathsheba should be read against that of Nabal and Abigail. Nabal, too, becomes drunk while he is having a feast "fit for a king" (1 Samuel 25:36), ominously foreshadowing David's drunken feast with Uriah. When the effects of the wine wear off the next morning, Abigail utters her deadly words. Uriah, however, does not succumb to the effects of drink: as opposed to Nabal and David, who is now subtly equated with his late enemy, Uriah is a righteous man. Indeed, Uriah's behavior under the influence of alcohol contradicts the standard type scene in which figures like Noah, Lot, and Boaz succumb to sexual temptation while drunk.[26]

David has therefore murdered a man who was not only innocent but, we are led to understand, righteous as well. The prophet Nathan then prophesies that God will "make a calamity rise against you from within your house; I will take your wives and give them to another man before your very eyes and he will sleep with your wives under this very sun" (2 Samuel 12:11). The prophecy is fulfilled: David's adultery with Bathsheba unleashes a chain of sexual violations by his sons that sunder his house and bring civil war to Israel. Amnon rapes his half sister Tamar and Absalom, Tamar's full brother, avenges the incest by killing Amnon. Absalom flees David's wrath, and a full-fledged revolt breaks out. At a critical stage in the revolt (2 Samuel 16:20–22), Absalom fulfills Nathan's prophecy by sleeping with David's concubines, a sexual violation that, like Reuben's intercourse with Jacob's concubine (Genesis 35:22 and 49:4), signifies political and familial usurpation.[27] Absalom performs this politico-sexual ritual in public, on the rooftop "with the full knowledge of all Israel." Moreover it symbolically mirrors David's first view of Bathsheba bathing on her rooftop. Sexual betrayal thus comes full circle.

When read against each other, however, the stories of David's marriages to Abigail and Bathsheba reveal a startling reversal of moral judgment. Despite the apparent divine sanction for David's marriage to Abigail, it is not Abigail but Bathsheba, the wife acquired by adultery and murder, who gives birth to Solomon, arguably Israel's greatest king. The civil war wrought as a result of David's sexual crime has a hidden teleology: it clears the way for Solomon to become king by eliminating his competitors. Once again, erotic transgressions are covertly positive in the political fate of ancient Israel: God, it would seem, straddles both sides of the legal fence in order to advance the fortunes of his chosen people.

## The Political Theology of Intermarriage

A related conflict between law and narrative, with similar theological surprises, surrounds intermarriage. We have already observed the role that intermarriage played in Ruth: the emphasis on her Moabite origins may have functioned as imperialistic propaganda for the early Davidic monarchy. Nevertheless, the sexual relations between Israelites and their neighbors had far greater ramifications than just this. Intermarriage was highly controversial in biblical culture, and it reflected deep conflicts over the nation's ethnic identity.[28]

Biblical law forbids intermarriage between Israelites and the so-called Canaanite nations:

> When the Lord your God brings you to the land that you are about to enter and possess, and He dislodges many nations before you—the Hittites, Girgashites, Amorites, Canaanites, Perizzites, Hivites and Jebusites, seven nations much larger than you— ... you shall not intermarry with them: do not give your daughters to their sons or take their daughters for your sons. (Deuteronomy 7:1, 3)[29]

This ban is explicitly theological: intermarriage leads to idolatry. An even more vivid denunciation of sexual relations with foreigners as idolatrous is the sin of Baal-Peor (Numbers 25). During their wanderings in the desert, the Israelites "fornicate" (from the root *znh*, meaning literally "to commit prostitution") with Moabite women and then sacrifice to the Moabite god Baal-Peor. The contrast with Ruth could not be more striking, since Ruth abandons Moabite religion for Israelite religion.

To take foreign wives led to idolatry because the covenant with God was understood as a metaphorical marriage. This is especially so in the prophetic literature, with Israel feminized as the wife.[30] Thus, the prophet Ezekiel:

> You were still naked and bare when I passed by you and saw that your time for love had arrived. So I spread My robe over you and covered your nakedness, and I entered into a covenant with you by oath—declares the Lord God; thus you became Mine. (Ezekiel 16:8)

The legal language of marriage—covering nakedness—is explicit here, but the sexual component of the biblical marriage ritual—intercourse—has been transformed into the making of a covenant. The prophet Malachi, who lived about the time of Ezra's assault on intermarriage in the fifth century B.C.E., specifically connected this marriage metaphor to foreign wives:

> For Judah has profaned what is holy to the Lord—what he desires—and espoused daughters of alien gods.... The Lord is a witness between you and the wife of your youth with whom you have broken faith, though she is your partner and covenanted spouse. (Malachi 2:11, 14)

Just as the covenant between God and Israel is a metaphorical marriage, so actual marriage between Israelites is a social expression of the covenant. To marry the daughter of another religion was a violation of the covenant. But since marriage between Israelites was covenantal, Malachi also forbade divorce, a stance so radical that it only struck roots later on in the sectarian movement of early Christianity.

Despite this legal and theological exclusivism, however, the biblical narratives are filled with intermarriages: Mahlon and Boaz to Ruth, Judah to the daughter of the Canaanite Shua, Joseph to the Egyptian Asnat, and Solomon to women from virtually every imaginable nation. Bathsheba herself was married to Uriah, a Hittite, although Uriah's name suggests that he was a worshiper of the Israelite God. Some historians try to explain this contradiction between law and narrative by arguing that the legal bans on intermarriage were late developments in biblical history. They point out that Ezra the scribe waged a campaign against intermarriages in the period after the return from the Babylonian exile (ca. 440 B.C.E.).[31] But there is also a good deal of seemingly early material that suggests disapproval, such as Rebecca's disgust with Esau's choice of Hittite women and the opposition of Samson's parents to his Philistine wife.[32] In fact, despite Ezra's ban, disputations over intermarriage persisted throughout the later Second Temple times.[33] Only with rabbinic law did the ban on intermarriage become a more or less accepted social norm.[34] It would appear that for ancient Jewish culture as a whole, the issue aroused great ambivalence and controversy.

Two stories capture this ambivalence. The first is the Samson cycle in Judges 13–16. Samson marries one Philistine woman, has relations with a Philistine prostitute, and, finally, falls in love with Delilah, who, although not ethnically identified, is certainly an ally of the Philistines, if not a Philistine herself. As opposed to Ruth, foreign women, and especially Delilah, are the instruments, not of fertility, but of death.[35] The narrator's position on the sexual deceit practiced by these women is nonetheless far from negative. He or she interjects a comment when Samson's parents oppose his choice of a Philistine wife: "His father and mother did not realize that this was the Lord's doing: He was seeking a pretext against the Philistines, for the Philistines were ruling over Israel at that time" (Judges 14:4). In each case, Samson's submission to feminine wiles leads to a violent confrontation with the Philistines in which he ends up killing hordes of the oppressors of Israel. What appears to be his downfall, in fact, is revealed as the vehicle for national salvation. In this way, the narrator depicts sexual relations with the foreigner as covertly orchestrated by God to serve Israel's political ends.

Equally ambivalent is the story of Jacob's daughter, Dinah, in Genesis 34.[36] Shechem, a Hivite (and therefore prohibited according to Deuteronomy), rapes her and then proposes marriage. Jacob accepts the offer as a way of settling his family in the land, but his sons object. Portrayed as better protectors of their sister than their father, they demand that the Shechemites circumcise themselves as the price for obtaining Dinah, a ruse that renders the Shechemites temporarily unable to defend themselves: while recovering from the circumcision, they are slaughtered by Simeon and Levi, and the other brothers pillage the town. The punishment fits the crime: the organ that committed the rape is the device by which Jacob's sons avenge their sister.

This is more than a simple account of vengeance for a sexual crime, however; it is a contestation over intermarriage, a competition among contradictory voices. The Shechemites themselves are presented in certain verses as far from hostile to the Israelites. They propose that the two peoples intermarry, and Jacob acquiesces. To make Jacob's position more plausible, the rape is turned into romantic seduction. Thus, immediately after the rape, we read: "Being strongly drawn to Dinah, daughter of Jacob, and in love with the maiden, he spoke to the maiden tenderly" (Genesis 34:3). Is this rape or seduction? Both possibilities are presented, although Dinah herself remains silent: the battle over intermarriage is fought by men over her passive body.

It seems that the narrator of Genesis 34 favors Simeon and Levi, but the claims of Jacob, the eponymous father of all the Israelites, cannot easily be dismissed. He curses his two sons in his deathbed testament: "For when angry they slay men, and when they please they maim oxen" (Genesis 49:5–7). Thus is Jacob himself associated with the affirmation of intermarriage, whereas his two violent sons are on the other side. The contradictions in this story attest to a real split in Israelite opinion over whether intermarriage is a legitimate way of settling in the land. As today, intermarriage in biblical times was a kind of code for the general problem of Jewish self-definition: would the Jews separate themselves religiously, politically, and ethnically, or would they find their identity by assimilating with those around them? Where the legal and prophetic texts are clear in their theological denunciation of intermarriage, the narrative traditions reveal the conflicting attitudes on the subject that ran through biblical culture. And where did the two sides believe that God came down on the issue? The very contradictions between law and narrative suggest that no monolithic theology was possible: all sides invoked the deity for their own purposes.

## Fertility and the God of the Bible

Fertility, then, was a central preoccupation of biblical culture, and subversion of sexual codes cropped up again and again in the struggle to ensure fertility. I have suggested that God played an equivocal role in these

conflicts between law and narrative, serving at once as author of the law
and author of the covert force that undermined it. And in examining the
role of the divine in the struggle for fertility, we will find some surprising
reversals of convention.

Many interpreters of the Bible through the ages have argued that poly-
theism is a corporeal religion associated with sexuality, whereas abstract
monotheism posits that God has no body and is consequently not involved in human sexuality. But this reading of the Bible is anachronistic,
based on medieval theology rather than the text itself. Whether monotheistic or not, Israelite religion was profoundly concerned with fertility,
and the biblical God was by no means devoid of sexual characteristics.

Israelite religion was deeply intertwined with Canaanite religion. It
has been generally assumed that the Canaanites, following a pagan, polytheistic religion, practiced fertility rites in which male and female ritual
prostitutes (*kedashim* and *kedashot*) engaged in sexual intercourse as a
way of promoting intercourse between the gods. Thus, the prophet
Hosea thundered against Israelites who followed Canaanite religion:

> *They sacrifice on the mountaintops*
> *And offer on the hills,*
> *Under oaks, poplars and terebinths*
> *Whose shade is so pleasant.*
> *That is why their daughters fornicate*
> *And their daughters-in-law commit adultery ...*
> *For they themselves turn aside with whores*
> *And sacrifice with kedashot. (Hosea 4:13–14)*

Yet the Canaanite texts themselves contain almost no corroboration of
such practices, so these graphic images were more likely propaganda.[37]
Just as the covenant with the Israelite God was understood as a
metaphorical marriage, so worship of a foreign God came to be seen as
metaphorical adultery. The prophets regarded Canaanite religion with
such hostility that they may have projected a whole range of sexual fantasies onto their enemies, much as later anti-Semites were to accuse the
Jews of a variety of deviant sexual practices.

If Canaanite religion probably contained no such erotic rituals, its theology *was* nevertheless deeply concerned with fertility. Far from rejecting
this belief in fertility, the ancient Israelites transferred it to their own
theology. One of the jobs of the Israelite God is to make barren women
fertile: "He sets the childless woman among her household as a happy
mother of children" (Psalms 113:9). Barrenness is normally considered a
sign of divine disfavor, and the Bible repeatedly suggests that God will
make all of Israel infertile as punishment for rebelliousness. Yet all the
matriarchs in Genesis, with the exception of Leah, are barren and re-

quire divine intervention in order to conceive. Similar stories are told of the mother of Samson (Judges 13) and of Hannah, the mother of Samuel (1 Samuel 1). Barren women, such as Sarah, Leah (after she stops conceiving), and Rachel, might give concubines to their husbands as ways of achieving fertility, but surrogate children such as Ishmael were quickly replaced by those natural sons whose birth is made possible by divine action.[38]

Against the belief that barrenness was a punishment, certain narratives even suggest that infertility might be a sign of a special status. Rachel, Jacob's preferred wife, is barren, while Leah, whom he married under coercion, conceives with ease. Elkanah, the father of Samuel, also has two wives: the one he loves, Hannah, is barren; the other, Peninah, is fertile.[39] This repeated pattern of infertility, especially of the preferred wife, suggests that we are not dealing with real gynecological histories but with a theological archetype. As opposed to the norm, barrenness in these stories opens the way for an act of divine favor. By rendering the Israelite matriarchs barren and then having them miraculously conceive, the biblical authors reinforced the theology of divine election: just as God chooses the younger son and allows other violations of legal norms to establish the Israelite nation, so there is divine intervention in procreation to provide the nation's heroes.

In other ancient myths the parents of heroes also frequently suffer from infertility, and the solution is sometimes divine impregnation.[40] Israelite theology explicitly rejected this possibility. In the strange story of Genesis 6:1–4, the "sons of God" have sexual relations with the "daughters of men," but God intervenes to prevent a recurrence of this divine miscegenation: the divine and human realms must remain distinct. Something of this mythology remained, however, in the form of divine intervention to open the wombs of barren women. Thus, God might still be involved in the births of the heroes of ancient Israel without actually impregnating their mothers. The divine plays the role, quite literally, of the godfather, facilitating conception but not physically intervening in acts of human sexuality. Only with Christianity did this fertility theology revert to a literal myth of divine impregnation.[41]

It is striking that infertility is attributed solely to women, just as in other texts, it is women who take the initiative to ensure fertility. The virility of men is never explicitly called into question. When Rachel reproaches Jacob for her lack of children, he replies angrily: "Can I take the place of God, who has denied you fruit of the womb?" (Genesis 30:2). But because biblical culture specifically excluded literal divine impregnation, God's role remained ambiguous. Is this a male God, as the marriage metaphor suggests, who brings fertility, or is it perhaps, as another distinct tradition hints, a God with female characteristics, a divine midwife rather than a godfather?

This latter fertility tradition is to be found in the so-called priestly texts that have been identified by modern biblical criticism.[42] Perhaps because of their particularly intense interest in lineage, as represented by many of the genealogical lists thought to come from this school,[43] the priests developed a systematic theology of fertility. The repeated blessings of fertility in the Book of Genesis ("be fruitful and multiply") also stem from this priestly school.[44] A precise parallel to these blessings appears in Leviticus 26, one of the key examples of a priestly text. God tells the Israelites that if they follow his laws, "I will look with favor upon you and make you fertile and multiply you" (verse 9). Adherence to the laws governing sexuality in the priestly books of Leviticus and Numbers therefore guaranteed progeny.

El Shaddai is the name of God that is connected with all of the Genesis fertility blessings from Abraham on.[45] One verse (49:25) that uses the name may explain why. Genesis 49 contains the series of deathbed blessings ostensibly delivered by Jacob to his twelve sons. The blessing for Joseph bears great similarities to the priestly fertility blessings: "And El Shaddai will bless you with the blessings of the heavens above, blessings of the deep lying below, blessings of breasts and womb." Here we have an explicit wordplay associating Shaddai with breasts (*shadayim*). Thus, for the author of Genesis 49 and quite possibly also for the author of the priestly blessings, the name El Shaddai meant something like the "God (El) with breasts" or the "God who suckles."[46]

Those who believe that the biblical God was either perceived as masculine or without gender altogether may find this startling. Many of the images of God in the Bible are masculine, and biblical thought also lays the basis for the much later Jewish denial of any human attributes to God. Nevertheless, none of the biblical images of a masculine God reveals any anatomical signs of gender (penis, beard); the "sexuality" of God as male required concealment, it seems, just as human beings are required to conceal their genitals.[47]

When anatomical signs are mentioned they are invariably female. This notion that the biblical God might have female characteristics is quite consistent with a variety of biblical texts.[48] The priestly account of creation in which the first fertility blessing appears speaks of God creating man and woman in his (*sic!*) image. If both men and women are created in God's image, then, God's image must logically contain both genders. Other biblical texts, such as Deuteronomy 32:18, speak of God as giving birth to the Israelite nation. Just as it is women who bear primary responsibility for fertility, then, God's fertility functions are most clearly associated with female markers.

Much of this use of language may have been metaphorical; the authors of these texts did not necessarily believe that their God literally had breasts and womb. Yet, the Canaanites among whom the Israelites lived worshiped goddesses such as Asherah and Anat, whose iconography featured prominent breasts and whose sexual activities with their male consorts El and Baal were intimately connected to earthly fertility. These goddesses are referred to in one Canaanite text as "the wet nurses of the gods."[49] Another speaks of "the divine breasts, the breasts of Asherah and Raham,"[50] which looks suspiciously like the "blessings of breasts and womb [rehem]" in Genesis 49.

Were the Israelites influenced by the Canaanite fertility cult? Since the Bible was ultimately edited by those who waged holy war against Canaanite religion, it might appear initially that Israel's monotheism had nothing to do with Canaanite pagan religion. The historical reality was otherwise, however. The worship of the goddess Asherah seems to have been particularly prevalent, until very late in the biblical period.[51] When Elijah destroyed the prophets of Baal, he did not take similar action against the prophets of Asherah mentioned in the text (1 Kings 18:19). At the end of the First Temple period, the goddess Asherah was worshiped in the Temple itself. In 622 B.C.E., only a few decades before the Babylonian exile, the Judean king Josiah carried out a sweeping reform in which he destroyed the house in the Temple where "the women wove clothes for Asherah" (2 Kings 23:7). Archaeological evidence corroborates the Bible. Asherah figurines from the Israelite period were found at Tel Beit Mirsim (the biblical Devir).[52] Most striking, inscriptions found at Kuntillet 'Ajrud in the Sinai record blessings to "YHWH ... and to his Asherah."[53] Later monotheism notwithstanding, this ninth- or eighth-century text seems to imply that the Hebrew God had a Canaanite consort. The worship of Asherah seems therefore to have been a well-established part of Israelite religion until a very late date.

We do not know what the attitude of the priests was to the Canaanite fertility cults before the great monotheistic reforms of the late seventh century. But the priestly school was concerned to amalgamate all of the gods of the patriarchal period, including the Canaanite El, into the worship of the one God Yahweh (YHWH).[54] It makes sense that the priests would want to give Yahweh the fertility functions of El's consort, Asherah, whom the Israelites so venerated. Hence, it is possible that just as El was assimilated to Yahweh, so Asherah was adopted into priestly Yahwism by a surreptitious sex change: the Canaanite "wet nurse of the gods" was reincarnated as El Shaddai, the God with breasts, in a kind of androgynous monotheism. Instead of rejecting the Canaanites' cults outright, the priests "monotheized" the powerful fertility imagery of their neighbors.

At the same time, the prophets (a number of whom, such as Jeremiah and Ezekiel, were themselves priests) came increasingly to view any involvement with Canaanite religion as both a sexual and a theological violation. This orthodox Yahwism did not reject a divine role in fertility.

Rather, it saw itself in competition with the Canaanite gods: to whom would the Israelites turn for fertility, Yahweh or the gods of Canaan? The stories of God's intervention to make barren women fertile are therefore one Israelite answer to the Canaanite fertility religion.

## Sexuality and the Purity Code

God's intimate role in fertility was directly linked in priestly theology to the power of the procreative fluids: semen and menstrual blood. We encounter in this realm a great puzzle that raises new questions about biblical attitudes toward sexuality. According to the priestly purity code, sexual intercourse causes ritual impurity for one day (Leviticus 15:16). Why did the priests, who were so concerned with fertility, regard intercourse as ritually defiling? Was this indicative of a negative attitude toward sexuality, an association of semen with demonic forces? How can God's intimate role in fertility be reconciled with the polluting character of procreative fluids? The answer here, too, lies in a dialectical process: just as sexual norms were tied to narrative subversions, in this instance purity and impurity were linked.

The Israelites believed, along with many other ancient peoples, that the sacred, cultic site was a dangerous place since the face-to-face encounter with God could lead to death.[55] Many commentators have pointed out that there is a strong association between impurity and death in the Levitical laws.[56] Indeed the most extreme source of impurity is a human corpse (Numbers 19:11–22). All lesser impurities can be understood as lesser forms of death. A person who enters a sacred site in an impure state is not protected against the extraordinary divine powers that reside there and will die: "You shall put the Israelites on guard against their uncleanness, lest they die through their uncleanness by defiling My Tabernacle which is among them" (Leviticus 15:31).[57]

Many religions contain paradoxical notions of the defiling character of sacred or creative powers.[58] The power to contaminate need not be a negative force, as in the case of a corpse. Instead, it may be a vital life force that symbolizes death when it is not in its proper place. Nevertheless, that these forces were at times out of their proper place was not in and of itself a crime or a transgression. On the contrary, impurity in biblical religion is frequently a result of normal life processes and is therefore unavoidable: purity and impurity, that is, are inevitably linked.

In the priestly cult the only fluids that create impurity are those that come from the procreative organs: semen, menstrual blood, and also discharges from genital diseases. These fluids are more than the forces of life; unlike blood, they are also the forces of *new* life. Although the priests regarded blood as the force of life,[59] bleeding from an ordinary flesh wound does not defile, and neither does urine, feces, saliva, or mucus. Semen and menstrual blood undoubtedly aroused a much greater sense of mystery and awe than did other bodily fluids. They were obviously not waste products, nor were they a passive life force like blood. Precisely because they are the sources of new life, they must have been seen as having enormous power. The priests seem to have believed that a man who has ejaculated temporarily loses his vital power; the impurity he acquires symbolizes a brief loss of fertility, which was the symbolic equivalent of death.[60]

The connection between loss of procreative fluids and death is equally clear with respect to menstruation. The priests evidently regarded menstrual blood as female seed, the equivalent of semen. The Levitical laws on menstruation resemble those of many other Near Eastern cultures, as well as of other traditions, except that the menstruating woman was not isolated from the community during her period. The law did not regard a menstruating woman as any more repugnant than a man who had ejaculated: both had incurred cultic impurity by loss of their respective seed, but the woman's period of impurity was longer because the flow continued for seven days.[61]

Just as male ejaculation represented temporary infertility, biblical culture seems to have associated menstruation with a period when a woman could not conceive.[62] This explains why the priests included the prohibition on intercourse during menstruation among the other sexual prohibitions (Leviticus 18:19 and 20:18). The priests saw a close connection between proper sexual behavior and fertility; in their view violations of the law led to childlessness. Most of the laws of Leviticus 18 and 20 concern sexual deviance such as incest, adultery, bestiality, and homosexuality, but they also include sacrificing one's children to Molech and insulting one's father and mother. What unifies all these acts is that they are considered affronts to procreation, either because they are sterile (homosexuality and bestiality), produce illegitimate progeny (adultery, incest), destroy progeny (sacrifice to Molech), or represent rebellion against the source of one's own legitimacy (insulting one's parents).[63] To have sex during menstruation is therefore, by implication, to engage in a nonprocreative act.

Those who have intercourse during menstruation will be "cut off from among their people," which means that they will have no progeny.[64] The strange phrasing of the law in Leviticus 20:18 also suggests this reading:

> If a man lies with a woman in her infirmity and uncovers her nakedness, he has laid bare her source and she has uncovered the source of her blood; both of them shall be cut off from among their people.[65]

The term "to uncover nakedness" (*giluy arayot*) is the technical term for incest. The woman whose "nakedness" is otherwise permitted to her husband is suddenly in a condition where she becomes like a prohibited relation. To "uncover the source" (*mekor*)[66] of her blood is to reveal her reproductive power, which must be hidden in order to function properly. When she is menstruating, her "inside" becomes her "outside," and she cannot conceive.

This priestly belief system explains the association of menstruation with idolatry and intermarriage. Ezra, the priest who led the community of returned exiles, launched his campaign against intermarriage with these words:

> The land that you are about to possess is a menstruous land [*eretz niddah*] through the menstruation of the peoples of the land, through their abhorrent practices with which they, in their impurity, have filled it from one end to the other. Now then, do not give your daughters in marriage to their sons or let their daughters marry your sons.[67]

Menstruation here has exceedingly negative associations, as a symbol of the threat to Israel's fertility represented by intermarriage. This threat is both literal and metaphoric. It is literal in that marriage with foreigners will dilute the Jewish population; to marry foreigners is, like menstruation, to turn one's "inside" into one's "outside." And it is metaphoric in that it stands for idolatry, much as the prophets associated idolatry with sexual violations. The polytheistic practices of the "peoples of the land" defile what is cultically pure because, like menstruation, they violate the boundaries between the sacred and impure.

The Israelites must preserve these boundaries, represented here by menstrual blood, if they wish to receive the divine blessing of fertility. Indeed, God's intimate role in fertility is directly linked to the power of procreative fluids. In Genesis 1:27, the priestly author states that God created man in his image and, in the next verse, that God blesses men and women with fertility. For people, as opposed to animals, to reproduce is to become a partner with the divine, to act in God's "image." Since fertility represents divine power, to reveal one's reproductive source means to reveal something that is sacred. In the Garden story in Genesis, it is said that to feel shame at one's sexual nakedness is to be like God (Genesis 3:5 and 3:22). Since God's sexuality is thoroughly hidden,[68] "imitation" of the divine means that the procreative organs and fluids are scrupulously covered and controlled by the sexual prohibitions.

Yet just as the sexual laws must be bent in order to ensure fertility, so human beings must periodically become impure by uncovering their genitals and releasing their procreative fluids. Procreation would otherwise be impossible. No one can live solely within the sacred precinct, the one realm where constant purity is necessary; all must live in the secular world, the world in which impurity is a necessary part of life itself. Sex defiles, but it is also divine. It is this dialectic between the pure and impure, the sacred and the secular, norms and subversions that lies at the heart of the biblical construction of sexuality.

## Sacred and Secular Fertility

Although biblical culture clearly regarded God as the hidden puppet master of Israelite history, the role played by God varies remarkably from text to text. God, so much in the foreground in the infertility stories of Genesis, is virtually absent in Ruth.[69] This is true for other transgressive stories as well, such as the story of Tamar and Judah. It is as if God must step backstage in order to make space for human actors, and particularly women, to bend social custom and law, just as the world itself contains both impurity and purity. God's absence implicitly sanctions these inversions and subversions.

Perhaps the most secular of all books of the Bible is the Song of Songs, the most erotic text in the Jewish tradition. There have been those who have argued that the Song has a Canaanite or perhaps even Indian cultic background and that many of the strange images can be explained in light of religious rites.[70] Yet, the author of the collection of poems that has come down to us suppressed any such religious overtones, if ever they existed. The Song appears to be a deliberate attempt to write a secular poem in which the Shulamit and her lover are human. Unlike Canaanite religion and unlike many other biblical texts dealing with sexuality, the Song is not directly concerned with fertility. Instead, it explores the tension between desire and fulfillment.[71] As a poetic treatment of the problem of pure desire, the Song of Songs anticipated later talmudic and medieval Jewish culture more than it resembled other books of the Bible.

What the Song does share with other biblical literature is the theme of transgressive female behavior.[72] The woman plays a sexually aggressive role; she violates boundaries by searching in the streets for her beloved; she also uses a bold, incestuous metaphor as she addresses her lover: "If only it could be as with a brother, as if you had nursed at my mother's breast: then I could kiss you when I met you in the street, and no one would despise me" (8:1). But the watchmen who find her in the street beat her, as if to control her unconventional behavior (5:7), much as her brothers force her to guard their vineyards (1:6). Perhaps the Song of

Songs represents, then, a poetic rendition of the tensions between narrative subversions and legal constraints that are so essential to the Bible's
treatment of sexuality elsewhere.

In its affirmation of eroticism, the Song of Songs tells us something
critical about the biblical view of sexuality. For biblical culture, sexuality
within its proper boundaries was not a problem, although the boundaries
themselves were repeatedly contested. The sexual act itself was cultically
defiling, but this was because of the divine power associated with it. The
celebration of erotic desire in Song of Songs must surely be related to
this dialectical theology. Because the divine was only indirectly involved
in procreation, however, eroticism was properly the realm of the secular,
as it is in the Song. God might intervene to guarantee fertility, but actual
sexual relations take place between human beings, and the Israelite cult
itself involved no ritual sexual acts, either literal or metaphoric.[73]

Later rabbinic and patristic interpretations of the Song of Songs
would infuse a theological dimension into this most secular of poems:
the poem, they would say, is really about the love between God and Israel
or God and the Christian church. In advancing this argument, the rabbis
and church fathers unwittingly resurrected the possible Canaanite cultic
background of the Song. Such theological allegories also contained a
radical new possibility: human love may be the model for the love of
God, but love of God might come to compete with human love. The marriage metaphor of the biblical covenant demanded exclusive love between Israel and God: monotheism is the theological version of monogamy. Taken to an extreme unimaginable in biblical culture, the exclusive
love of God demanded by monotheism might lead to the renunciation of
physical sexuality altogether.

The following chapters look at how this possibility played itself out in
subsequent Jewish history. Influenced by Hellenistic and Roman notions
of sexuality, Jewish culture of late antiquity was forced to struggle with
negative attitudes toward Eros, even within marriage. Although the rabbis of the talmudic period continued to affirm sexuality, especially within
the context of procreation, they came to regard the sexual act itself with
great ambivalence. Sexual renunciation and asceticism, which had
played no significant role in the Bible, now posed a major challenge to
Jews and Judaism. Some adopted it in part, and others resisted. Where
fertility had been the main concern of the Bible, the problem of desire
would now become predominant.

# CHAPTER 2

# Law and Desire in the Talmud

I N a famous incident in the Book of Numbers, Miriam and Aaron criticize their brother Moses "because of the Cushite woman he had married" (Numbers 12:1). This opaque criticism is immediately followed by their attempt to usurp Moses' leadership: "Has the Lord spoken only through Moses? Has He not spoken through us as well?" A number of early rabbinic midrashim (commentaries on the Bible) addressed the puzzling relationship between these two verses and concluded that the reason for this sibling rivalry was that Moses had taken a vow of celibacy at the time of the revelation of the Torah.[1] If the male Israelites were required to refrain from sexual intercourse for three days at Mount Sinai, then the one who was to be in constant communication with God must surely do so permanently. Here is how one version of the story goes:

> How did Miriam know that Moses had abstained from sexual relations [*peresh mi-priyyah u-riviyyah*]? She saw that Zipporah no longer ornamented herself in female jewelry. [Zipporah] said to her: your brother does not perform in this matter [*eino makpid ba-davar*]. Miriam therefore knew and she spoke to her brother [Aaron] and the two of them spoke against [Moses].... [They said]: "Did God only speak to Moses? Didn't He speak to our ancestors and they didn't refrain from sexual relations? And didn't he speak to us and neither did we abstain?"[2]

In suggesting that the controversy was over Moses' vow of celibacy, the midrash introduces a set of concerns that had been absent from the biblical text. Instead of criticizing the Cushite woman, as the Bible suggests, Miriam and Aaron take her side against her husband. Indeed, Miriam takes the lead in speaking on behalf of her sister-in-law, which explains why God singles her out for punishment, and not Aaron. Most important, the conflict is not over who is a legitimate prophet, as it is in the Bible, but over the status of sexuality in relation to prophecy. For Miriam and Aaron, there is no theological justification for abstention from sexual relations, even for so holy a man as Moses.

The midrashic rereading of the biblical text conveys a new struggle over sexuality that was characteristic of rabbinic and other late antique Jewish cultures.[3] Was Moses' celibacy a mark of the holy man to be emulated by other rabbis? Moses was regarded, after all, as the archetypical rabbi (rabbinic literature calls him "Moses *our* rabbi"). Or, as the text itself seems to confirm by stating that Moses was unique among prophets, perhaps celibacy may have been necessary only for Moses and not for the other rabbis. If the latter, then Miriam, a woman, surprisingly represents the mainstream of rabbinic culture in this struggle over the relationship between holiness and marital sexuality.

A midrash on Noah after he left the ark contains a similar controversy.[4] According to Rabbi Judah, Noah was commanded by God to procreate upon leaving the ark, but he planted a vineyard instead and was humiliated sexually as a result of his subsequent drunkenness. But according to Rabbi Nehemiah, Noah had been commanded to refrain from sexual intercourse while in the ark (a story that appears elsewhere), and because he continued of his own volition to be abstinent after the Flood, he was rewarded with a divine revelation. In this latter version, as in the case of Moses, sexual abstinence is connected to communication with God. Rabbi Judah's point of view certainly reflects the norm: yes, people must procreate, but they must also take care to observe the sexual prohibitions. Noah's unhappy fate suggests that perhaps the two are even causally linked. Nevertheless, Rabbi Nehemiah appears to teach that there is a higher level of holiness, such as that practiced by Moses, that requires abstinence.

Our investigation of rabbinic attitudes toward sexuality begins with the celibacy of Moses and Noah. The rabbis clearly did not see Moses or Noah as models for subsequent holy behavior, especially since they believed that prophecy no longer existed in their time. They never advocated an unmarried life and, Ben Azzai, the one rabbi known to have renounced marriage on principle, was clearly the exception who proved the rule. Rabbinic law commanded procreation for all Jewish males. Paradoxically, the most extreme statement of this obligation is attributed to the celibate Ben Azzai: those who fail to procreate are the equivalent of murderers.[5]

But the imagined abstinence of Moses and Noah reveals a culture in conflict. It is often just such cases at the margins, which are not meant to be emulated, that betray the contradictory values of those who live within the limits. These two midrashim suggest that the norm of procreation did not go unchallenged and that an ideal of sexual abstinence had penetrated rabbinic culture to the point that it became a bone of contention. Projected by the midrash onto the biblical text, traces of this struggle can be discerned in these fanciful stories.

Rabbinic culture, like its biblical predecessor, was anything but monolithic. Like the Bible, the legal and literary texts produced by the rabbis consist of many disparate strata, composed over many centuries and in two culturally and geographically distant centers, Palestine and Babylonia.[6] The many contradictory points of view found in this literature make it difficult to speak of *the* rabbinic position. It may instead be more useful to consider this a culture struggling with certain tensions and ambivalences.

In biblical culture, sexual relations within marriage did not attract attention, as long as they were carried on within legal bounds. For the rabbis, however, sex had become a problem to be discussed, investigated, and possibly controlled. If for the Bible, sex was always an issue of bodily practices and their cultic implications, for the rabbis, the problem was not the body as such, but desire, the psychic state of the passions, that might overpower the body. Where biblical culture had taken desire for granted, rabbinic culture made desire itself the subject of much discussion, both as something necessary for the existence of the world and as a potentially destructive, evil force. The challenge confronting the rabbis was to channel this desire so that it might equally serve the ends of Torah study and procreation, the twin values that animated rabbinic culture. At the heart of this discourse was a profoundly ambivalent attitude toward sexuality as such, an ambivalence not found in the biblical sources.

In the Bible, procreation was a blessing to be sought; there was no hint that it must be required. The Bible recounts the trials of people who wish to have children, but cannot; rabbinic law turned this concern into a divine commandment. Several explanations have been proposed for this surprising piece of legislation. For one, it paralleled the Roman law requiring men to marry and have children; as in Rome, the Jews of Palestine, especially after the devastating Bar Kokhba rebellion of the second century C.E., had a desperate need to increase their population. According to this understanding, the rabbinic commandment to procreate was a piece of population policy modeled on Roman law.[7] Others have argued that the rabbis were attempting to give divine status to an activity that was otherwise considered "natural"; by applying this commandment only to Jewish men, they distinguished themselves from women, Gentiles, and animals.[8]

Both of these explanations are plausible and no doubt contain part of the truth. I would like to suggest several additional possibilities. While it is always tricky to argue from a law to a social reality, it is possible that the very insistence on a divine commandment to procreate and the drastic punishment threatened for those who fail to obey attest to a significant cultural conflict. Perhaps Ben Azzai, the one avowedly celibate rabbi, represented the tip of an ascetic iceberg. Where no one in the Bible entertained the possibility of celibacy, perhaps the fact that the rabbis turned the biblical fertility blessing into a commandment suggests that some of their contemporaries were attracted by sexual renunciation.

There may be a social explanation as well. Like the church fathers, the rabbis were members of a wider community and they could ill afford to offend the heads of households who sought legitimacy and sanctity in their domestic lives. One talmudic text speaks of marital alliances between the rabbis and the wealthy householders.[9] Deeply and personally entangled in this upper class as the rabbis were, celibacy would have meant forfeiting the considerable benefits that marriage conferred upon them. They could, of course, have adopted the patristic solution: that marriage was the lesser of evils or, at best, a good way of life, with celibacy the most virtuous way of all. To have embraced celibacy would, however, have required a radical restructuring of the social matrix of the rabbinic elite. Instead, they imposed the requirement of marriage on themselves as well as on all other Jews and they did so in unashamedly positive terms.

The rabbis saw themselves as an elite, distinct caste, preserving a higher state of holiness than other Jews. The study of Torah, which they held to be a divine commandment, was only incumbent on men and, in practice, was only truly fulfilled by those men who were rabbis. Though couched in general terms, the sexual ethic that we shall presently describe was only really prescriptive for this narrow elite. In the same talmudic passage that treats marriage with the wealthy elite, the rabbis warn against marrying their daughters to the *ammei ha-aretz*, the poor and uneducated. Rabbi Meir, a second-century Palestinian authority, is reported to have said that "whoever marries his daughter to an *am ha-aretz* is as though he bound and laid her before a lion: just as a lion tears [his prey] and devours it and has no shame, so an *am ha-aretz* … engages in intercourse and has no shame."[10] The sexual self-restraint preached by the rabbis was obviously irrelevant to such lower-class animals, just as this class has no business studying Torah: "Rav Hiyya taught: Whoever engages in the study of Torah in the presence of an *am ha-aretz* is like one who has intercourse with his fiancée in his presence."[11] For the rabbis, the association between proper sexuality and study of Torah was more than just an arbitrary analogy. In similar fashion, a dominant rabbinical faction banned women from the study of Torah on the grounds that it would teach them "lasciviousness."[12] In this culture, as in every other, the way sexuality is constructed is a map for the hierarchies of the society as a whole. For the rabbis, the dominant male role in sexuality and study of Torah were intimately, indeed inseparably, linked.

## The Greco-Roman Setting

It is frequently argued that rabbinic Judaism represents a moderate, this-worldly affirmation of sexuality. This position is contrasted with the asceticism of the Stoics and Cynics, as well as with that of Second Temple Jewish sectarians and the early church fathers.[13] For these varied groups, procreation was not necessarily the highest good, and total celibacy was often celebrated. Rabbinic moderation is equally contrasted with the alleged hedonism of Greek and Roman society in which homosexuality, orgies, and sexual debauchery are presumed to have run rampant.

There is, of course, much truth to these characterizations of both the rabbis and their milieu. All too often, however, the very project of contrasting the culture of the rabbis with that of their Greco-Roman surroundings subtly implies that they developed their ideas in a vacuum, building and revising the biblical tradition and, at most, pausing to reject their surroundings. This model of cultural interaction seems questionable.[14] Rabbinic Judaism had its origins in Greco-Roman Palestine in the first three or four centuries of the Common Era and it both participated in and resisted the wider culture of Hellenism.[15] The Bible played a central role in the evolution of rabbinic Judaism, but it often furnished no more than proof texts for the rabbis' own original constructions; rabbinic speculations on sexuality were a complex hybrid of reinterpreted biblical concepts and Hellenistic ideas.

There is also a tendency to speak of Hellenism, or Greco-Roman culture, as if it were monolithic. In reality, there were many Hellenisms, just as there were many Judaisms in late antiquity. By taking the most extreme expressions from the ancient world as yardsticks against which to measure rabbinic culture, one risks misunderstanding the rabbis' position.

The Roman world of the second century, the formative period of early rabbinic culture, was not a "Garden of Eden from which repression was banished." Instead, it was a time of increasing domestic sobriety in which the nuclear family became the symbol of the well-ordered state.[16] This was a culture that emphasized procreation. To be sure, there were those like the Cynics, who saw the bearing of children as a bothersome distraction from the calling of philosophy.[17] But the times favored marriage and reproduction on both political and philosophical grounds. To increase the population required not hedonistic sexual liberation but, on the contrary, restraint in the conjugal bed.

The Stoics provided philosophical support to this *raison d'état*, arguing that the purpose of intercourse was procreation. At the same time all sexual activity intended solely for pleasure was condemned as "gratuitous acts."[18] The Stoics denounced any nonprocreative sexual posi-

tions as against "nature," the great plumb line for all of Stoic philosophy. They therefore largely divorced pleasure from procreation: too
much of the first was deemed inappropriate to proper cultivation of the
second.

Nevertheless, the Stoics were not thoroughly hostile to the pleasures
of the body. Agreeable physical feelings are permitted even to the wise
man; but when these pleasures arouse excessive passion and lead to loss
of control, they must be curbed, a position shared by many rabbis.[19] The
Stoics were concerned with "cultivation of the self" as a whole, which included the health of both body and soul.[20] Following the medical opinion
of the day, they emphasized the importance of controlling the passionate
"heat" of intercourse[21]—excessive sexual activity could diminish fertility
and harm the body. As the medical writer Soranus put it: "Men who remain chaste are stronger and better than others and pass their lives in
better health."[22]

Just as Roman attitudes toward sexuality were frequently moderate,
so early Christian views cannot be reduced to the fierce renunciations of
the wild-eyed Egyptian monks. Many of the church fathers sought to do-
mesticate the more extreme antifamily positions taken by Jesus and Paul.
For the author of the Epistle of Barnabas, good Christians should act like
pious Jews and only forbid those sexual practices that do not lead to procreation or that violate marriage. Clement of Alexandria saw sexuality
not as a sin but, in the service of procreation, as a holy partnership between man, woman, and God. Like the Stoics, Clement called for a "self-
controlled marriage" in which sexual desire is conquered by the will.[23]
Most church fathers did, of course, consider celibacy a higher virtue than
marriage, but they also struggled to legitimate the marital lives of the
wealthy householders who supported the church.

Stoic teachings found their way into Hellenistic Jewish culture. Perhaps the best-known representative of that culture was Philo of Alexandria, who lived in the first century C.E. Philo denounced any sexual activity that was not for the purpose of producing children: "For they are
pleasure-lovers when they mate with their wives, not to procreate children and perpetuate the race, but like pigs and goats in quest of the enjoyment which such intercourse gives."[24] And further: "Even natural pleasure is often greatly to blame when the craving for it is immoderate and
insatiable, as for instance, the passionate desire for women shown by
those who in their craze for sexual intercourse behave unchastely, not
with the wives of others, but with their own."[25] But whereas Philo
blamed an "incurably diseased soul" for the sin of adultery, he regarded
sexual excess within marriage as a peculiarly physical ailment:

> But the blame in most of these cases rests less with the soul than with the
> body, which contains a great amount both of fire and of moisture ...; the

moisture is sluiced in a stream through the genital organs, and creates in them irritations, itching and titillations without ceasing.[26]

The cure for sexual excess was ascetic moderation and control of the body (*enkrateia*).[27] Philo held that the commandment of circumcision was designed for this purpose. This Hellenized Jew, and his audience as well, must have been perplexed by the seeming barbarity of the ritual. He therefore constructed an antisexual rationale for circumcision, one that would recur in medieval Jewish philosophy. The function of circumcision, he writes, is to excise pleasure: "The legislators thought good to dock the organ which ministers to such intercourse, thus making circumcision the symbol of the excision of excessive and superfluous pleasure."[28] Circumcision is a physical reminder to the Jew to engage in intercourse not for pleasure but for procreation.

Writing later in the first century, Josephus Flavius betrayed a similiar Stoic influence. In his polemic against Apion, he says of the Jewish law of marriage: "That law owns no other mixture of sexes but that which nature has appointed, of a man with his wife and that this be used only for the procreation of children."[29] Although Josephus was trained as a Pharisee, his description of one of the Essene sects seems to correlate well with his own views on the proper role of sexuality in marriage: "When conception has taken place, intercourse ceases—proof that the object of the marriage was not pleasure but the begetting of children."[30]

Although Josephus may have deliberately dressed his Essenes in Stoic garb to make them familiar to his Roman audience, we know from other sources that there were sects of Jews who practiced complete or partial celibacy in response to the potential pollution of sexual desire. Philo reports on some of these, whom he calls Therapeutae, in the region of the Upper Nile, in Egypt.[31] One of the documents from Qumran, the so-called Messianic Rule, forbids intercourse before the age of twenty when a man presumably "knows [good] and evil."[32] Since the sect believed that it would fight an apocalyptic war against the "children of darkness," it constituted itself as a holy army and envisioned, along biblical lines, that the soldiers would refrain from relations with women.[33] The sect also forbade all sexual intercourse in the city of Jerusalem, a geographical extension of the biblical prohibition on entering the Temple less than a day after a seminal emission.[34] In all of these types of abstinence, the biblical concept of purity bulks large but is typically extended and elaborated far beyond the Levitical laws.

A striking Greek Jewish text that deals with sexual ethics is the *Sentences of Pseudo-Phocylides*, a pseudepigraphical work probably written in Alexandria between 50 B.C.E. and 150 C.E. The author celebrates marriage but, in the fashion of the wisdom literature, warns against excesses:

*Remain not unmarried, lest you die nameless.*
*Give nature her due, beget in turn as you were begotten ...*
*Outrage not your wife for shameful ways of intercourse.*
*Transgress not for unlawful sex the natural limits of sexuality ...*
*And let not women imitate the sexual role of men.*
*Do not deliver yourself wholly unto unbridled sensuality towards your*
*wife.*
*For "Eros" is not a god, but a passion destructive of all.*[35]

Like the Stoics and Philo, who may well have been his contemporary, the author of *Pseudo-Phocylides* unequivocally viewed procreation as a law of nature. Nonprocreative sex was unnatural in his view, and control of one's sexual impulses was clearly linked to proper procreative intention.[36]

For other writers of the time, sexuality was dangerous because even if it began licitly, it could, once aroused, slide all too easily into sin. The author of the *Wisdom of Solomon*, who probably also wrote in the first century C.E. in Alexandria, praised barren women and eunuchs, two categories of people regarded by the Bible either as unfortunates or as outcasts.[37] Following a messianic prophecy in Isaiah 56:3–5, but against biblical law (Deuteronomy 23:2), the author not only permits eunuchs in the Temple but even grants them special favor.

In both its clear contradiction of the Deuteronomic ban on castrati and its advocacy of childlessness, the *Wisdom of Solomon* took a radical position, but there is evidence from the first and second centuries C.E. that there actually were Jewish eunuchs. The Mishnah contains a legal category of "man-made eunuchs" (*seris adam*) and a *baraita* (a nonmishnaic text from the period of the Mishnah) reports that Joshua ben Bathyra knew a eunuch named Ben Megosath who lived in Jerusalem.[38] Thus, when the Gospel writer Matthew spoke of "eunuchs for the sake of Heaven," he may have been referring to a particular group of Jews who eschewed procreation and embraced celibacy.[39]

These, then, are some of the diverse aspects of the wider Greco-Roman and Jewish culture in which the rabbis lived and that influenced them, as when they turned procreation into a duty. At the same time, they resisted and opposed part of it, particularly in their affirmation of marriage against both Jewish and non-Jewish advocates of celibacy.[40] Their views of sexual pleasure were far less negative than those of writers like Philo, even though they shared with him, and with Greco-Roman culture in general, a concern for the overall problem of how to reconcile the sober duty of procreation with sexual passion. They, too, troubled over "all the disturbances of the body and the mind, which must be prevented by means of an austere regimen."[41] Their struggles and ambivalences were those of their age, and their solutions, although often distinctive, sought to relieve the same set of anxieties.

## Sex in the Garden of Eden and the World to Come

Like their stories of the celibacy of Moses and Noah, the rabbis' portrayal
of sexuality in the Garden of Eden and in messianic times defines their
discourse. Differing with many church fathers, virtually all of the rabbis
adopted an older Jewish belief that Adam and Eve had sex in the
Garden.[42] The dominant position seems to have been that the "fall" was
punishment for disobedience rather than for the discovery of sexuality itself. Those blessings chanted in the marriage ceremony that stem from
rabbinic times state "make happy the loving friends, as you made your
creature happy in the Garden of Eden in the beginning."[43] The context of
the blessings indicate that this happiness is clearly sexual.

A number of midrashim pick up the Greek idea of a primordial androgyne, a first human who preceded the division into male and female.
But while Hellenistic thinkers, including Philo, saw this androgyne as devoid of gender and thus devoid of sexuality, certain rabbis regarded the
primordial Adam as both embodied and engendered.[44] The rabbinic androgyne had both sexes at once rather none at all; human beings were
created with full sexual potential. Another rabbinic tradition, however,
adopted the Hellenistic notion of an "astral body" and argued that the
primordial Adam possessed a nonmaterial body of light.[45] This probably
minority point of view held that the "image" of God in which Adam was
created was without a body. Sexuality, then, was not an essential part of
human nature, but rather was acquired by human beings after their creation.

If most of the traditions about the Garden of Eden affirmed sexuality
as an essential aspect of humanity, views of the *Endzeit*, the "world to
come," were more ambivalent. In no case, though, do the rabbis describe
paradise in the manner of the Koran, as a place with "gardens and vineyards and maidens with swelling breasts, like of age, and a cup overflow-
ing."[46] On the contrary, according to a "favorite saying" of the third-
century Babylonian Rav: "The world to come is not like this world, for in
the world to come there is neither eating, nor drinking, nor procreation."[47] The Palestinian Talmud attributes to Rav a contradictory saying:
"In the world to come each person will have to give an accounting for
everything which his eyes saw but he did not eat."[48] But against such an
antiascetic statement, Judah the Prince, the presumed editor of the Mishnah, is reported to have said: "Whoever accepts the pleasures of this
world is denied the pleasures of the world to come. And whoever does
not accept the pleasures of this world is granted the pleasures of the
world to come."[49] On balance, these eclectic sayings about the world to
come suggest a world without bodily pleasures.

One midrash on the verse "He sets free the bound" (Psalms 146:4) supports the ascetic position:

In the time to come, sexual intercourse itself will be forbidden, and you should know that this is true, for on the day that the Holy One, blessed be He, appeared on Mount Sinai to give the Torah, He forbade sexual intercourse for three days ... [Exodus 19:15]. Now, since God forbade intercourse for three days when He revealed Himself to them for one day, in the time to come, when the Shekhinah [the divine presence] dwells among them [permanently], will not intercourse be entirely forbidden?[50]

The text may mean that the constant presence of God, as in the case of Moses, requires sexual abstinence. Or perhaps intercourse will no longer be necessary, since there will no longer be any distance between God and man; that is, with the messianic resurrection of the dead, man will become immortal like God and will therefore neither need to procreate nor suffer from sexual desire. In either case, the midrash strikingly understands the "freedom" of messianic times ("He sets free the bound") to be freedom from sexuality.

The same midrash, however, reports an alternative interpretation of the verse "He sets free the bound": that sex with a menstruant woman (*niddah*) will be permitted in messianic times:

Though nothing is more strongly forbidden than intercourse with a menstruant ... in the time-to-come, God will permit such intercourse. As Scripture says, "It shall come to pass in that day, says the Lord of hosts, that ... I will cause the prophets and the unclean spirit to pass out of the land" [Zechariah 13:2], the "unclean" clearly denoting a menstruant, and of such it is said, "And you shall not approach a woman to uncover her nakedness, as long as she is impure by her uncleanness" [Leviticus 18:19].

In this interpretation, the boundaries between pure and impure, permitted and forbidden, will be erased. This antinomian interpretation may have been a voice of protest raised against the legal strictures on sexuality and perhaps also against the rabbinic obsession with procreation. The way the passage is immediately refuted by the statement that sexual intercourse will be forbidden makes it clear that this is a minority point of view, but one that the editor of the midrash felt he could not censor.

A similar kind of conflict, this time possibly between the rabbinic establishment and contrary popular belief appears in another text: "Three things are a taste of the world to come: the Sabbath, sunshine, and *tashmish*" (a term literally meaning "to serve" but generally used in rabbinic language as a euphemism for sexual intercourse).[51] This passage comes in a longer text containing a variety of medical sayings, quite likely of a folk nature. The rabbinic commentator on this saying immediately refutes the notion that sexual intercourse gives one a taste of the world to come since it "weakens" the body, a view derived from ancient medicine. Rather, the saying must refer to *tashmish* of the other bodily orifices—whatever that might mean. For this rabbi, too, sexuality cannot possibly have any place in messianic times, although popular opinion may have held the opposite.

What can we conclude from these statements? For the rabbis, procreation is essential to the definition of humanity in this world. As one aggadic saying has it "the world was created only for procreation."[52] The commandment to procreate defines man as a bridge between God, who is immortal and does not procreate, and the animals, who procreate but are not commanded to do so.[53] One must, in fact, prepare for messianic times by giving birth to all those souls who are destined to be born; anyone who fails to procreate delays the coming of the Messiah.[54] For some, however, a perfect world requires neither sexuality nor procreation. The radical midrash on the abolition of the prohibitions of *niddah* further suggests that the biblical impurity associated with sexuality is itself a function of the imperfection of this world. These views do not negate the rabbis' strong affirmations of procreation in this world, but they cast them in a much different light: for those who believe that the ideal world will be asexual, one's behavior in this world might serve as a *preparatio messianica,* a paradoxical nonascetic asceticism. By engaging in the sexual act of procreation in the properly chaste manner, one prepares the way for the asexual world to come.

## The Dialectic of Desire

This dialectical way of thinking characterized much rabbinic speculation on sexuality: "Resh Lakish said: Come and let us give thanks to our ancestors, for had they not sinned, we would not have come into the world."[55] This recalls the biblical idea of sexual subversions, also to be found in certain midrashim. For example, the midrash confirms our reading of the story of Lot and his daughters, who, although they had incestuous relations, produced the nation of Moab, the ancestor of Ruth, great-grandmother of King David.[56] Similarly, Cain is said to have married his twin sister and this incestuous relationship is called an act of divine grace (*hesed*).[57]

Certain texts regard perfectly licit sexuality as driven by forces of sin: "If it were not for evil desire [*yetzer ha-ra*], man would not build a house, marry a wife, or have children."[58] Procreation requires man to harness

the dialectical energies of sin and evil. Another midrash in the name of
Rav Aha states of King David:

> Even the most pious person cannot possibly be without an element of iniq-
> uity [avon], for David said before God, "Master of the universe, did my fa-
> ther Jesse really intend to bring me into existence, or did he rather intend it
> only for his own pleasure? You can tell that this is so because after each
> one performs the sexual act, he turns his face one way and she turns hers
> the other and you introduce every drop that a man has."[59]

The sexual act, then is inherently iniquitous, its iniquity apparently stem-
ming from the physical pleasure that drives it. Only God's intervention
can turn the hedonistic act to the holy purpose of reproduction.

To understand the peculiar status of sexuality as at once evil and an
instrument for good, one must first understand what the rabbis meant by
the yetzer ha-ra.[60] Although they considered the yetzer to be the force that
drives man toward all types of sin, they associated it primarily with sexuality.[61] The yetzer may best be understood as natural desire or, to use the
Stoic term, the passions. The Bible, by contrast, had used the term to
mean a person's mind or thought. In giving it a new meaning, the rabbis
may well have been attempting to translate Stoic concepts into a Hebrew
idiom.

One point of view sees the yetzer ha-ra as implanted at birth;[62] another
considers it to be present from conception: "Rabbi Reuben ben Astroboli
says: How can a man escape from the yetzer ha-ra within him? For the
first seminal drop that a man puts in a woman is the yetzer ha-ra."[63] The
yetzer is part of what makes man distinct from both animals and angels;
although man shares procreation with the animals, they are not impelled
by the yetzer as he is.[64] Moreover, as opposed to the later Christian doctrine of original sin with which it is sometimes confused, the yetzer is the
force that gives man his very capacity to choose between sin and correct
behavior—that uniquely human quality that is at once potentially creative and destructive.

The yetzer is said to be "king over [man's] two hundred and forty-eight
limbs":

> When a man excites himself [mehamem et atzmo] and goes off to commit
> some licentious act [le-devar zimah], all of his limbs obey him.... When he
> goes to fulfill a commandment, they begin to become lazy ... for his good
> inclination [yetzer ha-tov] is like a captive in prison.[65]

Man's natural will is to act with sexual abandon, whereas the aspect of
the will that inclines toward good is a prisoner in the body, acquired only
at thirteen, the age of maturity. The good inclination is learned; the evil

one is instinctual, rather like Freud's superego and id. Seen in this light, the commandments are the opposite of natural law: a supernatural legislation imposed on the natural inclination toward sexual license.

The body itself is neutral in this midrash, as it is in much of rabbinic thought; that is, it is not the materiality of the body as such that constitutes the threat but rather the contaminating effects of the passions that all human beings possess from birth. The struggle for control of sexuality is therefore not primarily a war between body and soul, but a struggle within the realm of the will, a position similar to those of both Hellenistic writers and some of the early church fathers.[66]

Although the rabbis generally regarded the body as a neutral vessel, their sexual rhetoric sometimes suggests physical repugnance: "Know from whence you come—from a smelly drop" (tippah seruha, that is semen).[67] A related verb is used to describe why the ten tribes were exiled: they committed adultery by "befouling" (heserihu) their beds with "semen that was not theirs."[68] This revulsion toward semen has its roots in the biblical notion that seminal emissions cause ritual impurity, but in rabbinic writings it is extended far beyond the cultic sphere.[69] According to another midrash, the serpent was the first to have intercourse with Eve and he injected her with "filth" (zohama).[70] This last text blames the snake rather than Eve for contaminating sexuality, but yet another text evinces an almost violent misogyny toward the female body: "Although a woman is a vessel filled with excrement and her mouth is filled with blood [probably a euphemism for menstrual blood], everyone runs after her."[71] The "mouth" is probably a displacement here for the vagina; the female genitalia in particular aroused the revulsion of the author of this text.[72]

The female body in general seems to have aroused anxiety: "Anyone who looks at the little finger of a woman is as if he looked at [her genitals] ... the handbreadth of a woman is [like] her genitals, and even that of his wife."[73] One should therefore avoid looking at women or even speaking to them, except when there is absolutely no alternative. Although this prohibition is intended primarily to prevent illicit liaisons, it might even be extended to one's own wife, as the formulation suggests. At the same time, however, other texts treat women as legitimate sexual companions and affirm the importance of wives making themselves sexually attractive to their husbands.[74] It would therefore be a gross distortion to say that rabbinic literature universally regarded women's bodies as repugnant or demonized women themselves.

Indeed, despite expressions of distaste and even revulsion at the sexual act and at the female body, rabbinic literature also contains a good deal of materia¹ on sexuality that is in keeping with the thinking of ancient medicine.[75] Sexual intercourse is said to be one of eight things that are beneficial in small quantities but harmful in large quantities.[76] Intercourse weakens the body and, in excess, causes premature old age.[77] The literature also proposes a kind of sexual eugenics, according to which different sexual positions will affect the physical and moral character of the child born of the union.[78] These medical speculations tended to reinforce the idea that moderation and control are physically as well as spiritually beneficial. Thus, although the physical aspects of sexuality sometimes aroused disgust, the rabbis' primary concern was for the ambiguous, dialectical nature of desire. The passions, rather than the body, were the danger that needed to be controlled.

## Law and Desire

Like the Stoics' belief that study of philosophy can control the passions, the rabbis held that study of Torah is a way to channel libidinal energy. For example:

> The Holy One, blessed be He, said to Israel: "My children, I have created for you the *yetzer ha-ra*, [but I have at the same time] created for you the Torah as an antidote. As long as you occupy yourselves with the Torah, he shall not have dominion over you."[79]

In more graphic terms: "if this vile creature [*menuval*] encounters you, drag him to the house of study; if he is of stone, he will dissolve and if of iron, he will be shattered."[80] The study of Torah thus acts as a form of sublimation, to use the modern psychoanalytical term. But the rabbis may also have imagined the Torah to have magical properties, to judge from a collection of stories listing rabbis (sixty in one account!) who became impotent as a result of the lessons given by Rav Huna.[81] While the language of these stories makes them appear hyperbolic and humorous, the belief that holy study might redirect sexual desire—even to the point of causing impotence!—was evidently taken quite seriously.

Study of Torah could serve as an antidote to excessive sexual desire because the *yetzer* is itself the passion necessary for study: "Every [scholar] who is greater than his fellow, his *yetzer* is greater also."[82] Because one's *yetzer* is necessary for both procreation and Torah study, competition between them was inherent and inevitable. At times, the Torah is described as an object of desire in terms that are frankly erotic.[83] Although the rabbis were not prepared to opt for celibacy as a way of resolving this tension, both the Palestinian and Babylonian schools struggled mightily with the problem. According to the Palestinian rabbis, one should first study and then marry, for like the Cynics, they feared that household concerns would distract one from scholarly concentration: "With a millstone around the neck, can he study Torah?" The Babylonian authorities prescribed that one should marry first and study later, presumably so that sexual desire would not distract from study.[84] They were evidently skeptical about the belief that study by itself can control the *yetzer ha-ra!* But in Babylonia scholars also tended to absent themselves from home for long periods, despite the laws requiring men to provide their wives with regular sexual satisfaction.

The idea that Torah and sexuality tap the same desire may shed new light on the most famous bachelor of the Talmud, Ben Azzai. When confronted by his colleagues for preaching the necessity of procreation while himself remaining unmarried, he retorted: "But what shall I do, since my soul lusts [*hashkah*] for the Torah?"[85] His response suggests that his inability to marry was not his choice: the Torah had utterly consumed his desire, sublimating it to the point where none was left for a sexual partner. Here was scholarship turned explicitly sexual!

If study of Torah channeled the *yetzer* of the rabbis, obedience to rabbinic law was to serve the same function for the Jewish people as a whole. The Torah is an anaphrodisiac, a kind of divine immunization against excessive sexuality. Because the Jews have the Torah, says one text, they do not suffer from the same uncontrolled sexuality as the Gentiles:

> Israel's lust ceased when it stood at Mount Sinai [and received the Torah], while the lust of the idolatrous nations, which did not stand at Mount Sinai, has not ceased. The idolators are always to be found with their neighbors' wives and when they can't find their neighbors' wives, they find their animals.... They love the animals of the Jews even more than their own wives.[86]

Here was a Jewish myth of the hypersexuality of the Gentiles!

The very details of the law provide a method for channeling sexual energy, a series of substitutions for natural desires:

> Observe, for everything that the divine law has forbidden us it has permitted us an equivalent: it has forbidden us intercourse during menstruation but permitted us the blood of purification;[87] ... it has forbidden us the married woman, but it has permitted us the divorcée during the lifetime of her former husband; it has forbidden us the brother's wife but it has permitted us the levirate marriage; it has forbidden us the non-Jewess but it has permitted us the beautiful [non-Jewish] woman [taken captive in war].[88]

In each case, as well as in others, the law offers a substitute for the thing forbidden. Indeed, the rabbis regarded the forbidden as precisely that which man desires the most and which he forgoes only because of a divine command that runs against his nature.[89] The natural desire for the forbidden is so great in this text that the law permits something that yields the same "taste," a kind of flirtation with antinomianism.

This text is placed in the mouth of a woman, Yalta, the wife of Rav Nahman. As in the biblical stories of sexual subversion, here, too, it is a woman who tests the boundaries of the law. In fact, there are several other talmudic stories in which Yalta challenges male legal authority and wins significant victories over patriarchal interpretations of halakhot pertaining to women.[90]

One law, circumcision, was viewed as particularly related to the problem of sexual desire. In biblical times, circumcision was most probably connected to fertility, and since it was practiced by most other Near Eastern Semitic peoples (as well as Egyptians), it only gradually came to be a physical sign distinguishing Jews from other ethnic groups.[91] By the rabbinic period, it had become a definitively "Jewish" mark, although some of the old fertility associations were retained. Like Philo, some rabbis held that circumcision curbed excessive sexual desire. The Gentiles, says one rabbinic text, are hypersexual not only because they lack the Torah but also because they retain their foreskin: "It is hard for a woman to separate herself from an uncircumcised man with whom she has had intercourse."[92] Jewish males are presumably less sexually attractive and active because they all undergo surgical prophylaxis at the age of eight days.

This same point is made more obliquely in stories about biblical heroes born circumcised,[93] a long list that stretches from Adam to Job. Verses are brought to underscore the perfection and virtuousness of these figures; the sexual significance of this congenital miracle is explicitly attested by Job, who, we are told, would never even look at an unmarried girl because "if I should look upon her today and on the morrow another man comes and weds her, it will turn out that I have been looking upon another man's wife." The much later Midrash Tadshe, possibly reflecting as much an early medieval as a rabbinic view, argued that the effect of circumcision was more psychological than physiological: "The covenant of circumcision was therefore placed on the genitals so that the fear of God would restrain them from sin."[94]

## Marriage as a Framework for Control

Within the legal system, the most important framework for channeling sexuality was undoubtedly marriage itself. Though necessary to fulfill the commandment to procreate, marriage has an additional value quite apart from reproduction: "Even though a man has children, he must not remain without a wife."[95] The Babylonian and Palestinian Jewish communities evidently differed on these additional reasons for marriage: "He who has no wife lives without joy, without blessing, without goodness. In the West [that is, Palestine] they say: without Torah, without a [protecting] wall."[96] While the Babylonian tradition tended to emphasize the emotional blessings of marriage, the Palestinian focused more on marriage as a utilitarian defense against sexual temptation.[97] We will see additional evidence later on that the Palestinian Jewish community may have been more sexually ascetic than its Babylonian counterpart.

So deeply entrenched and universal was marriage in Jewish culture that it became a polemical issue between Jews and Christians as early as the fourth century. In Babylonia at that time a defender of Christianity named Aphrahat attacked Jews who mocked the Christian practice of celibacy. These Jews evidently claimed that Christians who failed to marry and procreate were thereby rendered impure[98]—a startling reversal of the biblical belief that sexual intercourse creates impurity. This view also has no basis in rabbinic law, which commands all men to marry and procreate but says nothing about the ritual status of those who fail to do so. It is possible that the Jews quoted by Aphrahat represented a kind of popular opinion, rather than the legal view of the rabbis. Nonetheless, for these Jewish polemicists as well as for the rabbis, sexual relations within marriage were not only permitted but required.

From the records available to us, it would appear that celibacy among the rabbis was exceedingly rare.[99] Still, the extensive praise for marriage in the rabbinic literature may well have been a response to the considerable attraction that celibacy exercised in the surrounding culture, possibly on Jews as well. A midrash on the biblical figures of Nadab and Abihu may hint at the social reality of the times. It attributes the violent death of these two sons of Aaron at the hand of God (Numbers 3:2–4) to the fact that they never married: they thought that no woman was worthy of them because they were members of the aristocracy (their father Aaron was high priest and their uncle was Moses). As a result, says the midrash, many women remained unmarried since they desired only these two.[100] Perhaps this story represents no more than literary imagination, but it might also be a veiled polemic against members of the elite who considered spurning marriage. If the latter was the case, then perhaps the way of Ben Azzai may have represented a real threat, a temptation that few followed but that had to be actively resisted.

Since marriage was intended to control sexual energy, the age of marriage was an important consideration. One passage that would echo long and loud for Ashkenazic Jews throughout the Middle Ages held that a man who marries off his sons and daughters near the period of puberty (*samukh le-firkan*) will receive the scriptural blessing: "you shall know that your tent is in peace" (Job 5:24),[101] evidently understood to mean that if one's children were married, they would not succumb to sexual temptation.

Most rabbis at that time married considerably later. Rav Huna, the Babylonian authority whose lectures were thought to have caused impotence, held that "he who is twenty years of age and is not married spends all his days in sin" (the editor, baffled at this extreme position, hastens to add, "in sinful thoughts").[102] Another, similar tradition embellishes this teaching with a theological warning: "Until the age of twenty, the Holy One, blessed be He, sits and waits. When will he take a wife? As soon as one attains twenty and has not married, He exclaims: 'Blasted be his bones!'" Rav Hisda is quoted as saying: "The reason I am superior to my colleagues is that I married at sixteen. And had I married at fourteen, I would have said to Satan, an arrow in your eye."[103] This last saying is perhaps the clearest expression that marriage and, especially early marriage, serves as prophylaxis against the evil potential of the sexual passions, personified as Satan.

## Sexual Practices

Unlike the Bible, rabbinic literature devoted considerable attention to actual sexual practices between husband and wife. Most of this wealth of material is designed to hide sexual behavior in a cloak of modesty and moderation, yet the law itself allows any sexual practice, as long as it is procreative.[104] As the following text on the menstrual prohibitions suggests, the legal authorities seem to have recognized the limitations on their enforcement powers in the face of patriarchal prerogatives:

> When one's wife menstruates, she is alone with him at home. If he wishes to, he has intercourse with her; if he does not wish, he does not have intercourse with her. Does anyone see him or does anyone know so that they might say anything to him? He fears only [God] who has commanded [the laws] concerning menstruation.[105]

Although the law allows any procreative sexual activity, rabbinic texts nevertheless take up the question of practices under the guise of medical advice. The Babylonian Talmud recounts a debate between Rabbi Johanan ben Dahabai and the legislative majority:

> R. Johanan b. Dahabai said: ... people are born lame because they [that is, their parents] overturned their table [that is, had intercourse in a nonmis-

sionary position]; dumb, because they kiss "that place"; deaf, because they converse during intercourse; blind, because they look at "that place."[106]

Johanan's eugenic warnings, though not intended as law, are part of rabbinic medical lore, similar to the statement: "If a man has sexual intercourse standing, he will be liable to convulsions; if sitting, to spasms; if she is above and he below, he will be subject to diarrhea."[107] The majority rejects Johanan ben Dahabai's position as binding law and invokes against him (a thoroughly minor rabbinical figure) a series of such major mishnaic figures as Judah the Prince and Rabbi Eliezer to demonstrate that "a man may do whatever he pleases with his wife."[108]

The question of sexual practices thus aroused a good deal of controversy. Johanan ben Dahabai claims to have his genetic information straight from the "ministering angels" (*malakhei ha-sharet*), a claim that a later rabbi tries to neutralize by identifying these angels with the rabbis themselves. But in the process of rejecting the legal status of this medical knowledge, the text makes it available to its readers. Did these readers consider it as a warning to be heeded, even though the practices were legally permitted, or as a covert rabbinic *Kama Sutra?* The text brings two cases of women who complain to Judah the Prince that they "set a table" for their husbands, who then "overturned them." Evidently such practices were not theoretical! The response of Judah is instructive: "My daughter, the Torah has permitted you to him and I, what can I do for you?" In his reluctance to intervene, Judah confirms that the law does not restrict the sexual privileges of men, but by symbolically throwing up his hands, he also implicitly criticizes such practices.

These tensions are repeated in another text brought in the Talmud together with this one. The story concerns Imma Shalom, wife of the first-century rabbi Eliezer, and sister of the patriarch Rabban Gamliel; she is said to have had beautiful children because her husband had intercourse with her as fast as possible and by removing only a minimum of clothing.[109] The Talmud brings the story to refute Johanan ben Dahabai: it suggests that even though Eliezer conversed with his wife during intercourse, they still had beautiful children.[110] Nevertheless, Eliezer's other ascetic practices actually support Johanan ben Dahabai. Thus, once again, even as it attempts to establish that the law allows any sexual practice, the Talmud betrays its deep ambivalence about sexual pleasure.

To promote modesty, most rabbinical opinion held that intercourse should take place only at night or in the dark: "Israel is chaste because they do not have intercourse during the day. Rava said: if the house is dark it is permitted, and Rava said and some say Rav Papa, a scholar can darken the house with his cloak [tallit] and then it is permitted."[111] No living creature is supposed to witness the act, and especially holy men such as Abaye are said to have chased away even flies.[112] But another opinion held that one might have intercourse during the day, since otherwise the husband, overcome by sleep, might perform perfunctorily and end up despising his wife.[113]

Opinion was also divided on the question of whether sexual relations should take place clothed or naked. The second-century Rabbi Simon bar Yohai denounced those who engage in sexual intercourse naked.[114] The story of Imma Shalom suggests that she remained clothed during intercourse. Both of these accounts refer to first- or second-century Palestinian rabbis. By contrast, two later Babylonian rabbis, Joseph and Huna, reject such practices as "the manner of the Persians": sexual relations must take place without clothes and a man who requires his wife to wear clothes must divorce her and pay her (marriage contract) [ketubah].[115] Although medieval Jewish law adopted this lenient position, it would appear that those who lived in Palestine inclined toward remaining clothed while in the conjugal bed.

Roman culture provides the explanation for the greater modesty of the Palestinian rabbis. Not only did the new moral code that became accepted by the early second century dictate chastity until marriage, but the sexual taboos between man and wife clearly resemble rabbinic prescriptions: lovemaking was to take place at night or in a darkened room, and women were to keep their clothes on. Thus, wall paintings in Pompeii reveal that even servants and prostitutes wore brassieres while making love.[116]

Despite the influence of Roman practices on early rabbinic Judaism, the Palestinian rabbis were so hostile to Rome that they rarely had anything positive to say about Roman sexual customs. Some sources from Palestine do, however, speak admiringly of the Persians (or Medes) as paragons of sexual virtue. The first-century patriarch, Rabban Gamliel, is said to have remarked: "There are three things for which I love the Persians: they are modest in their eating, modest in the toilet, and modest in another matter [davar aher],"[117] the latter a clear reference to sexual behavior. In a number of other midrashim, the chastity of the "sons of the East" is contrasted with the immoral life of the Canaanites, probably a veiled reference to the Romans.[118] Indeed, some of the sexual practices of the Sassanian Persians bore similarities to those of the rabbis, especially in such prohibitions as sex with a menstruant.[119]

The sexual act therefore required both moderation and modesty. Restraint breeds restraint: "Man has a small member—if he starves it, it is satisfied, but if he satisfies it, it remains starved."[120] It was this saying, which the Talmud refers to as a "law" (halakhah), that King David is said to have forgotten in his lust for Bathsheba.[121] In addition, rigorous, even excessive application of the biblical purity laws might promote moderation. According to a Palestinian tradition, such extra purifications ensured, in a much-quoted phrase during the Middle Ages, that "scholars would not hang around their wives like roosters.... Whoever is strict with himself in this regard will have his days and years prolonged."[122] For those who believed that sexual moderation and self-control were signs of holiness, biblical rituals of purification became autodidactic devices.

Naturally enough, the actual behavior of members of the rabbinic elite did not always measure up to the strict norms suggested by their teachings, as in the following amusing story:

> Rav Kahana lay under the bed of Rav who was carousing and speaking frivolously with his wife of sexual matters; afterward, [Rav] had intercourse with her. Rav Kahana said to Rav: "You appear to me to be like a hungry man who has never had sex before, for you act with frivolity in your lust." He [Rav] said to Kahana: "Are you here? Get out! It is improper for you to lie under my bed!" [Kahana] said to him: "This is a matter of Torah and I must study."[123]

Whose side does this text take, the teacher's or his pupils'? Does Kahana's shock at Rav's behavior suggest that Rav behaved wrongly? Or if this is, indeed, a "matter of Torah," perhaps the prudish Kahana has learned something new about proper behavior.

The story is embedded in a larger text that relates accounts of disciples who conceal themselves in toilets in order to learn from their teachers how one performs this similarly private function.[124] These other stories follow the same structure: the disciple is caught but protests that "this is a matter of Torah and I must study." Unless this line is intended as a parody of overzealous discipleship, it would seem to support the notion that even the most private acts are part of Torah learning and that privacy, which is otherwise sacrosanct, may be violated in order to observe them. At the same time, by placing sexual behavior in the same category as defecation, the text covertly undermines any affirmation of Rav's unbridled sexuality. These contradictions cannot be resolved; indeed, I would argue, they reveal the ambivalences in rabbinic culture toward both sexual practices and the degree to which they might be controlled.

## Procreation and Pleasure

Although the central purpose of sexual relations for the rabbis was to fulfill the commandment of procreation, they recognized a separate, legitimate realm of sexual pleasure. These laws, called *onah*, guarantee every married woman the right to regular sexual relations, though the frequency depends in part on the husband's occupation.[125] As opposed to at least one Jewish sectarian text, sex on the Sabbath was not only permitted but, in fact, required of scholars.[126] The laws of *onah*, moreover, pertain regardless of procreation: the woman has the right to sexual satisfaction even if she is pregnant or menopausal, that is, incapable of conceiving. Not only is there a *commandment* to engage in sexual relations independent of procreation, but the purpose of such relations is explicitly to give pleasure.[127]

Pleasure and procreation may not have been totally separated from each other in rabbinic thought, however. Ancient medicine held that both male and female sexual pleasure is essential to conception.[128] The very physical mechanics of the sexual act seemed to physicians like Galen necessary to produce the mixtures of fluids necessary for reproduction. While the rabbis do not appear to have discussed male orgasm, they seem to have believed, based on Galen's two-seed theory, that women released some kind of seed during orgasm.[129] Since female pleasure was evidently necessary for conception, the commandment of *onah* was implicitly linked to procreation, even though the two were formally distinct.

*Onah* applies only to women; men do not have similar rights, as they do in the Paul's marital debt.[130] This assymmetry is connected to the sharp distinction the rabbis drew between the sexuality of men and women: "A man's sexual impulse is out in the open: his erection stands out and he embarrasses himself in front of his fellows. A woman's sexual impulse is within and no one can recognize her [arousal]."[131] Nevertheless, "a woman's passion is greater than that of a man."[132] Women were thus considered to be highly sexual but incapable of asking for sexual satisfaction. Men must attend to these needs to ensure a peaceful household: "It is a man's duty to pay his wife a 'visit' before a journey, for it is said 'and you shall know that your tent is in peace'" (Job 5:24).[133] Women who take the sexual initiative are so rare that if they do solicit their husbands to perform the marital obligation, they will "have children the like of whom did not exist even in the generation of Moses!"[134] This text seems to suggest that women who act against female nature are praiseworthy: rabbinic culture, like its biblical predecessor, cannot be labeled unequivocally patriarchal.[135]

The laws of *onah* clearly had the effect of protecting and advancing women's sexual rights, although the motivation behind the law may have had more to do with the temptation of total abstinence that existed in rabbinic culture than with a protofeminist agenda. It is noteworthy that the law of *onah* first appears in the Mishnah right after a dispute between Hillel and Shammai about the permissible length of time a man may take a vow of celibacy without his wife's permission.[136] While it is always difficult to infer social reality from law, it may be that by mandating regular sexual relations the Palestinian mishnaic schools were trying to control a problem of scholars absenting themselves to study for excessive periods.

This suspicion is strengthened in the Babylonian *Gemara,* the commentary by the Bablyonian rabbis on the Mishnah.[137] A series of stories suggest that the Babylonian rabbis absented themselves from home in order to study for much longer periods of time than did their Palestinian colleagues. These stories show that the Babylonians not only attempted to modify the strict mishnaic limitations on vows of abstinence but that there was enormous conflict in their culture over the question. According to one account, Rav Rehumi failed to return home because he was so engrossed in his studies; his wife cried bitter tears and he then died. The famous story of how Rabbi Akiva's wife, Rachel, gives him permission to go to study for decades was evidently intended to refute the criticism of Rav Rehumi's practice and to legitimate long periods of marital abstinence. If these stories had their roots in an actual social problem, then there must have been an enormous sense that marital duties conflicted with study of Torah. The laws of *onah* were designed to resolve the conflict, but they clearly did not provide a definitive solution.

Rabbinic law imposed both positive and negative temporal controls on sex. If *onah* dictated when men must have sexual relations with their wives, *niddah,* the prohibition on sex with a menstruating woman, prescribed the period of abstinence. Instead of the biblical period of five to seven days of impurity that ended with the end of the woman's flow, the rabbis imposed a twelve-to-fourteen-day separation, in effect, abstinence for half of every month.[138] The rabbis derived their law of menstruation from the biblical law pertaining to *nonmenstrual* bleeding: it is only the latter, which is the result of illness, that requires a week of cleanness after the bleeding has ceased.[139] The result of this legal innovation was to enforce extensive periods of sexual abstinence on married couples.[140]

Modern observers have repeatedly noted that the extension of the menstrual taboo to nearly two weeks means that resumption of sexual activity coincides with the greatest moment of fertility: the laws of *niddah* seem almost tailor-made to promote procreation.[141] Some rabbis may have been aware of the fertility consequences of *niddah.* Rabbi Johanan is quoted to the effect that a woman becomes pregnant "close to [her] immersion," that is, immediately after the end of the full rabbinic period of menstrual abstention.[142] Following certain strands of ancient medicine, the rabbis held that menstrual blood is necessary for conception:

> A woman's womb is full of standing blood and from there it flows out in
> menstruation. And at God's will, a drop of whiteness goes and drops into

her and instantly, the fetus is created. This is likened to a bowl of milk: if you put rennet in it, it curdles and stands; if not, it remains liquid.[143]

Menstruation was considered a time when this blood is not in its proper place and is therefore not available for conception, a view reflected in the Bible, but without the physiological explanation. Like *onah*, which also seemed on the face of it unrelated to procreation, the laws of *niddah* turn out to have a hidden connection to this cardinal rabbinic precept.

Given these implicit connections between pleasure and procreation, the rabbis' attitude toward nonprocreative sex was ambiguous. On the one hand, they permitted a wide variety of sexual practices designed purely for pleasure and they mandated marital sex even when a woman was unable to conceive. On the other hand, they were opposed to sexual acts such as coitus interruptus that could never be procreative, even with a fertile woman; coitus interruptus was considered the crime of Er and Onan in Genesis 38.[144] Other types of nonprocreative intercourse, such as anal and oral intercourse, were more problematic. The law frowned upon, but did not technically forbid, nonvaginal intercourse, which it labeled "unnatural" (*she-lo ke-darkha*), possibly because it assumed that Jews did not engage in such practices.[145]

One nonprocreative practice that the rabbis condemned without reservation was masturbation, typically designated *hashhatat zera* (destruction of seed) or *shikhvat zera le-vatalah* (emission of wasted seed).[146] According to biblical law, masturbation, like any other seminal emission, would presumably have created ritual impurity, but no more so than normal sexual intercourse.[147] The rabbis turned masturbation into a heinous crime. The Mishnah states the earliest form of the law by contrasting women who examine themselves to determine if they are menstruating with men who masturbate: "Every hand that makes frequent examination is praiseworthy in the case of women, but in the case of men, it should be cut off."[148] This statement is followed by a series of equally extreme pronouncements in the *Gemara*.[149] Rabbi Johanan is quoted as saying: "Whoever emits semen nonprocreatively deserves capital punishment."[150] Similarly, the biblical verse "your hands are filled with blood" is taken to refer to those who "fornicate [that is, masturbate] with their hands." Rabbi Eliezer adds: "Whoever holds his penis while he urinates is as though he brought a flood to the world." Although urination does not seem a particularly erotic activity, Eliezer was concerned about the consequences of a man becoming accustomed to touching his penis. He may also have associated urine with semen based on a midrash that one of the primary causes of the Flood in Genesis was "wasting of seed."[151]

It is perhaps no coincidence that the laws against masturbation appear in the tractate Niddah of the Talmud. This association between masturbation and menstruation may explain the statement "he who deliberately causes himself an erection shall be in *niddui*" (usually translated "excommunicated" or "ostracized"). Figuratively speaking, he will be like one who has sex with a *niddah*. He, like a *niddah*, is beyond the sexual pale because his sexual fluids are neither retained in his body nor deposited in the body of his procreative partner. But the difference between a menstruating woman and a masturbating man is crucial: the woman cannot control her menstruation, for it is a function of her biology, but a man *can* avoid masturbation.

In this distinction lies the fundamental rabbinic ethic that accepted the sexuality of women as a biological fact but required that men "conquer their desire" (*yetzer*).[152] As women are condemned to be prisoners of their own biology, incapable of willed sexual restraint, there is no point in teaching them the law. In a circular way, this assumption naturally reinforced the male orientation of the whole legal discussion of sexuality: since only men can learn to control their sexuality, the texts are also directed exclusively toward men.

Also at stake in the condemnation of masturbation, in addition to its being deliberately nonprocreative, is that it is the ultimate solipsistic act, the "solitary vice."[153] The rabbis did not reject male sexual pleasure, but they did not believe that it was a legitimate end in itself. According to one midrash, the generation of the Flood took two wives, one for sexual pleasure and one for procreation.[154] This division was a sign of the utter depravity of antediluvian man, who could not subordinate his sexuality to larger social goals, whether procreation, marital harmony, or national survival.[155] The rabbis thus shared with Hellenistic culture the attention to the needs and passions of the individual,[156] but they also agreed with prevailing opinion in late antiquity that sexuality could not remain a private matter.

## The Body as a Temple

The rabbis believed that prophecy had ceased with the destruction of the Temple, so that God was no longer as directly accessible as he had been through the Temple cult. The rabbis therefore "secularized" the purity laws by applying them to all areas of life, as opposed to just the sacred site of the cult. The laws of menstruation are a particularly striking instance of this perpetuation and extension of biblical purity laws when the Temple no longer stood.[157] Purity now became necessary for the sake of the body, rather than for the sake of the cult. The sexual laws were to turn the body into a sacred site, a substitute for the Temple, reminiscent in a way of Paul's exhortation that "your body ... is the temple of the Holy Spirit."[158] When sexual relations are properly conducted the divine presence stands between man and wife, much as it did in the Temple when the cherubim were "intertwined with one another."[159] Once the Temple no longer stood, the eroticism implicit in its cult was transferred to the marital bed. As one Palestinian text stated long after the destruction of the Temple: "The Holy One has greater affection for fruitfulness and increase than for the Temple."[160]

Yet, alongside this affirmation of sexuality, another rabbinic voice sounded a far more pessimistic note, though probably not meant to be taken literally. Rav Judah quotes Rav:

A man once conceived a passion for a certain woman and his heart was consumed by his burning desire [this is, his life was endangered]. When the doctors were consulted, they said: "His only cure is that she shall submit [and have intercourse with him]." The rabbis replied: "Let him die rather than she should submit." Then [the doctors said]: "let her stand nude before him"; [the rabbis answered]: "Sooner let him die." Then, said the doctors, "let her converse with him from behind a fence." "Let him die," the rabbis replied, "rather than she should converse with him from behind a fence."[161]

Later rabbis speculated that this text made perfect sense if the woman in question were married, since any contact with her might lead to adultery. But what if she were unmarried? Why not marry her? No, says Rabbi Isaac, "marriage would not assuage his passion, for *since the destruction of the Temple, sexual pleasure [taam biah] has been taken [from those who practice it lawfully] and given to sinners*" (emphasis added). With the Temple destroyed, the cultic constraints on erotic passion could no longer operate. The intimate role of the divine in human sexuality, which was so central to biblical theology, was now shattered with God himself now in exile with the Jewish people. In this view, the body cannot serve as a substitute Temple, since, even within marriage sexuality remains an ambivalent and dangerous desire.

Here, then, are the two poles of rabbinic ambivalence about sexuality. Properly channeled and controlled, the erotic body becomes the site where the divine can still be found in this world, a world from which biblical prophecy has vanished. Yet the rabbinic emphasis on reproduction was not merely a continuation of the biblical theology of fertility. A new contrary view, current in Greco-Roman culture, held that sexuality was a thoroughly secular, material activity that conflicted with the life of the spirit. In the culture of late antiquity, the competition between holy abstinence and the duty to produce children created a deep anxiety to which the rabbis were not immune. Like the Stoics, the rabbis embraced the virtue of study as equal to and, in some cases, greater than procreation. The same ambiguous and dialectical passion was thought to drive both. The rabbis were not prepared to embrace celibacy as did certain pagans and Christians, but as the midrashim about Moses and Noah attest, neither could they easily resolve the tensions between these conflicting values.

And so it was that Rabbi Akiva, like the church father Origen, argued for transforming the Song of Songs from an erotic poem into a theological allegory, the love affair between God and Israel.[162] Although early Christianity took a much more radical course than did rabbinic Judaism, sexuality was deeply troubling for both and had to be subordinated to loftier goals. If the Song, allegorically read, was, indeed, the Holy of Holies in relation to the rest of Scripture, this was because human sexual relations in and of themselves could not be the unambiguous site of the new Temple. The midrashic reading of the Song certainly did not efface the eroticism of the text, but neither could it embrace it fully on the human plane.

In the centuries after the talmudic period, different medieval Jewish cultures would take up these opposing strands of rabbinic ambivalence. Where the northern European elite was to emphasize the more affirmative view of sexuality, the Jewish philosophers of the Mediterranean, under the impact of Greek philosophy, would opt for a more radical asceticism than had ever existed in rabbinic thought. Finally, Jewish mysticism would create a hybrid between philosophical hostility to the material world and an erotic theology, which would come to dominate the culture of the Ashkenazic Jews by the end of the Middle Ages.

# CHAPTER 3

## Rabbinic Authority and Popular Culture in Medieval Europe

WHEN he came to comment on the talmudic passage with which we ended the last chapter, the great medieval French commentator Rashi (Rabbi Shlomo Yitzhaki, 1040–1105) noted dolefully that "because of the power of great worries [since the Temple was destroyed], the spirit does not arise in men to desire their wives, and therefore, the pleasure of intercourse has been taken away."[1] Where the passage in the Talmud had signified some ontological change in the status of sex, Rashi offers a much more mundane explanation for the phrase "since the destruction of the Temple, sexual pleasure has been taken away and given to sinners." The political and economic burden of living in exile prevented Jews from enjoying sexuality as they had in their own land. Was Rashi in this commentary reflecting something of the belief structure of either the French rabbis or the Jewish population of his day? Did these Jews share the talmudic ambivalence toward sexuality, or was their position more positive?

In this chapter we will describe the distinctive erotic culture of the Ashkenazim, those Jews who lived in France, Germany, and Eastern Europe in the period from roughly the eleventh to the eighteenth centuries. This is a long span of time and it covers a wide geographical area, so that, as with the talmudic literature, it is difficult to make sweeping generalizations. Just as differences arose between Babylonia and Palestine, so the Jews of twelfth-century France did not necessarily follow the same customs as did the Jews of sixteenth-century Poland. Our task here is not, however, to chart the chronological changes in this diverse culture comprehensively; rather, it is to examine selected examples of the sexual norms and practices of these Ashkenazic Jews in order to identify the dilemmas and conflicts that gave this society its character.

The central problem for this culture was to define the appropriate object of desire. Would parents, rabbis, or communal authorities decide whom their children would marry or would the children themselves make that decision? Would men be allowed to divorce their wives with ease if they found more desirable mates? Control of the institution of marriage became the central issue in the control of desire. Marriage and divorce were critical issues in this culture because, as we shall see, the normative authorities were preoccupied with the threat of sexual temptations outside of marriage, and they regarded sexual satisfaction within marriage as the appropriate defense against temptation. All of these themes can be found in the talmudic literature, but with one major difference: the talmudic rabbis were concerned primarily with their own social class and therefore focused less on the threat of alternative values and external desires than did the Ashkenazic authorities. Where the problem in the Talmud was largely the conflict for scholars between law and desire, the rabbis and communal leaders of medieval Ashkenazic culture were preoccupied with the threats to legitimate marriage in Jewish society at large.

The norms of this elite must therefore be seen against the backdrop of the wider culture—both Jewish and non-Jewish—in which these authorities lived. The laws they enacted and the sermons they preached should not be mistaken for the norms of society as a whole but should instead be viewed as elements that both shaped and sometimes opposed these alternative values. The alternative voices of popular culture were not mere deviations from the universally accepted norms;[2] rather, they represented a wider range of possibilities than the official literature of the legal codes was prepared to admit. Such an alternative culture certainly existed in talmudic times, and rabbinic literature contains traces of the conflicts between the rabbis and the other classes of society, the *amei ha-aratzot*. But in the Middle Ages new genres of literature flourished alongside the writings of the rabbis, making the claims of popular culture more accessible to us today. We can therefore listen to both the sexual norms propounded by the Ashkenazic rabbis and the alternative voices of popular culture.

Popular culture generally does not come to us directly but is instead typically filtered through literary sources written by members of a cultural elite. Folktales, for example, may reflect popular attitudes, but they come down to us in forms that tell little about what their original transmitters intended or what their audiences thought of them. Similarly, although court cases transmit the voices of the plaintiffs, the transcriptions of these voices were made by rabbis, who, perhaps unconsciously, shaped the cases according to their own lights. Thus, tensions between popular culture and the legal tradition may reflect struggles between competing literary elites.

Indeed, the rabbinic elite itself was not always of one mind. The pietistic movement of the early thirteenth century that produced the *Sefer Hasidim* (Book of the Pious) had its own position, which departed at times
from the legal tradition. The jurists and commentators of northern
France and Germany also held views on sexual questions that differed
dramatically from those held by the philosophers and mystics of southern France and Spain.

## Communal Control of Marriage

The Jewish communities of northern Europe enjoyed a large degree of political autonomy, and their courts largely controlled matters of marriage
and divorce. This control was by no means absolute, however, and certain
features of the social structure tended to resist the hegemony of the rabbinic and communal authorities. In some areas, such as the enforcement
of the commandment to marry and to procreate, the authorities often
chose to relax or even ignore the law. As Moses Isserles, the sixteenth-century legal commentator, wrote about the talmudic prescription to marry by
age twenty: "For several generations, courts have not enforced this [law]."[3]

The relatively high level of mobility within this society, a function of
the large numbers involved in commerce, tended to weaken social controls. The Jewish communities of France and the Rhineland during the
High Middle Ages were often very small, sometimes numbering no more
than a hundred souls each. It was often necessary for men to travel to
other towns, often at some distance, to find appropriate mates. Thus, a
man might contract a marriage to a woman in a distant town with the
understanding that he would live in her community. But some men exploited this circumstance for unscrupulous gain: after the betrothal, they
would refuse to move and would extort large sums of money from the
bride's family before giving a writ of divorce.[4]

As this kind of case indicates, maintaining control over marriage and
sexuality in a society without centralized political institutions was difficult. The problem was exacerbated by a legal issue rooted in both the
Bible and the Talmud. According to Jewish law, individuals can contract
marriages without the prior consent of either parents or religious authorities. There is already evidence in the Talmud of attempts to constrain
this individual freedom and to require prior engagement, presumably
under parental control, as well as rabbinic certification of betrothal formulas. Nonetheless, religious and parental control of sexual relationships remained problematic throughout the Jewish Middle Ages, as it

was for the medieval Christian church. There were many parallels between the struggle of the church to assert clerical authority over marriages and the legislation of the medieval rabbis, possibly reflecting some mutual influence.

Jewish law also holds that "all families are presumed fit,"[5] which means that a Jew could marry any other Jew. Social criteria for marriage contradicted this theoretical principle of equality, however, since medieval Jewish society was rigidly stratified along class lines. The specific criteria that governed marriages were lineage, wealth, and learning, three factors that guaranteed an alliance between the wealthy and the scholarly class within the Jewish community and that created a singular Jewish aristocracy. Although this marital system tended to preserve the Jewish elite class, the possibility of upward mobility existed for a poor but intellectually gifted boy, through marriage with a wealthy girl.[6]

A text that repeatedly struggled with the conflict between parents and children over marital choices and sexual initiative was the *Sefer Hasidim* of Judah the Hasid (Judah the Pious). This early-thirteenth-century work is a unique collection of ethical advice, literary exempla, and mystical theology.[7] Although it is unclear whether the *Sefer Hasidim* reflects the views of a discrete sect or only those of its author, its pietistic teachings came to have a major influence on the values of Ashkenazic Jews throughout the subsequent centuries. Contrary to the idea that the will of parents must reign supreme and that love played no role in marital norms, Judah the Hasid taught:

> If a father commands his son to take a close relative as a wife and the son does not desire her and he fears that if he marries her, he will come to hate her, or he fears that he will not be able to resist the temptation to sin with other women, he should not marry her. But if he can resist the temptation to sin with other women, even though he despises her, he does a great thing for the sake of his father and mother [in marrying her]. But his father and mother sin in forcing him to take the woman whom he does not love.[8]

We shall see how important marital sex was for the German pietists in preventing extramarital temptation. The attempt to reconcile the conflicting demands of love and desire with the duty to honor one's parents in *Sefer Hasidim* reflects the struggle between individual desire and convention that appears to have been characteristic of Ashkenazic Jewish culture starting with the High Middle Ages. The ongoing concern of *Sefer Hasidim* with problems of love may reflect the influence of the new European tradition of courtly love,[9] although the particular problem that this text deals with has little to do with the strict etiquette of unrequited romance between a married woman and her knightly suitor.

Given the enormous stake that both Jewish parents and social authorities in general had in preserving a stable marital order, the possibility that individuals might exercise their nominal legal right to marry as they wished could only produce enormous anxiety. For both Jews and Christians, the problem was what canon law called *matrimonia clandestina* (secret marriages). In response to this problem, Jewish communal councils throughout the Middle Ages enacted harsh legislation, such as the following from sixteenth-century Lithuania:

> Anyone who deliberately and brazenly violates the customs of Israel by marrying ... without a quorum of ten and a marriage canopy [*huppa*] shall, together with the witnesses who assisted him in this foul deed, be excommunicated and ostracized in this world and in the world to come. Their sin shall not be forgiven, and the court shall punish them severely by hanging them from a post and administering forty lashes without any possibility of substituting a fine. They shall be punished and tortured with all manner of suffering and excommunications as a means of preventing the promiscuity of this generation.[10]

The last sentence of this piece of legislation makes it clear that the community regarded such uncontrolled marriages as sexual license. This kind of legislation was similar to the requirement of the church that marriages be performed in the presence of a priest and two or three witnesses. The Jewish legal authorities, however, never went quite as far as the Council of Trent, which, in 1563, annulled all marriages that did not conform to officially prescribed sacraments.[11]

The communities might also specify the age until which a boy required parental consent to marry. The Council of the Four Lands, the governing body of the Polish Jews from the sixteenth to the eighteenth centuries, stipulated that "youths [*bahurim*] who have not reached the age of twenty and who contract to marry a woman without the knowledge or consent of their relatives and parents shall have their engagement contracts declared void."[12] These Polish Jews evidently had a concept of adolescence as that problematic period between the ages of thirteen and twenty for a boy, when he has the legal capacity to act as an adult but should not be allowed to do so.[13] Throughout the Middle Ages the pattern among the Ashkenazic Jews who could afford to do so was to marry their sons off shortly after their thirteenth birthdays (if not, as in some cases, earlier) in order to prevent them from exercising their own wills. This early marriage age was distinctive of the Ashkenazic Jews, and it distinguished them from the Jews of the talmudic period and from the Jews of the contemporary Muslim world; in both of those cultures men tended to marry in late adolescence or their early twenties.

These legislative actions were responses to real-life stories that are found throughout the centuries in the responsa literature. Time and again rabbinic courts were presented with cases of "clandestine marriages" such as that of the son of a wealthy family in Germany who secretly married the family maidservant.[14] Once it was found out by the father, the boy was evidently coerced into renouncing the marriage, but the girl refused to accept a divorce. The outraged rabbi annulled the marriage on an obscure legal technicality. Not all such cases involved servants, but many authorities saw that group as a serious threat to the class structure of the Jewish community.[15] Writing in the 1630s, Joseph Hahn prescribed in great detail what a householder must do to avoid the possibility of relations with his servants.[16] Similar concerns were expressed about itinerant beggars and bachelor teachers.[17]

Despite the attempts by the communal and rabbinic authorities to discourage these clandestine marriages, the norm of publicly approved engagements following the standard criteria did not always go uncontested. Yair Hayyim Bachrach (b. 1638) relates in his responsa a case that occurred in 1636 during a plague in the German town of Worms.[18] Since the case occurred before his birth, Bachrach was asked to rule on it as a theoretical matter. In fact, the style of the narrative suggests a folktale as much as a historical event. The case concerns the daughter of a wealthy man who falls ill during the plague and "there was neither a male nor female servant prepared to nurse her except for a tall and handsome butcher's assistant." The young man tells the girl's father that he is in love with her and extracts a promise of her hand in marriage if she should recover. He nurses her faithfully but when she recovers, he becomes ill and she then nurses him "because her soul had become connected to his and she fell greatly in love with him." When the young man comes to redeem the pledge, the father reneges, embarrassed that his only daughter, who was "educated, learned, and beautiful," was to marry a servant. He claims that he had given his promise under coercion, out of fear for his daughter's life. The girl is not to be swayed and she threatens to have sexual intercourse with the boy, even without the father's permission, which would effect a marriage. The question that is posed to Bachrach is whether the father was justified in refusing to give the girl any dowry. Bachrach rules that the father does not have a case and must give the girl her dowry.

Several conclusions can be drawn from this case. Bachrach's ruling was based on the legal status of a pledge, but by presenting the case in the form of a classic romantic tale, he implicitly validates the young couple's emotions. The father's pledge, of course, means that this was not a true clandestine marriage; nevertheless, it still represented a power struggle between parents and children, in which the daughter uses the threat of sexual relations with the boy. Perhaps young women were less passive in this culture than is often assumed! As we go on to consider other cases and other tales, we will see that love and sexual desire played a role as alternative norms.[19]

Popular Yiddish literature also offered an alternative to the official norms. Let us consider two stories. The first is a sixteenth-century manuscript of what must have been a much older folktale. Entitled *Maase Beriah ve-Zimrah* (The Story of Beriah and Zimrah), it is the story of a daughter of the high priest of Jerusalem and her love for a lower-class boy named Zimrah.[20] The high priest will not allow them to marry, despite the intercession of the king. They nevertheless meet while others go to pray in synagogue and "they kiss each other a thousand times." Then, the pope [*sic!*] decrees that Jewish women may not go to the ritual bath and also forbids circumcision, two commandments connected to Jewish sexual purity. Zimrah is promised Beriah if he can gain access to the pope and persuade him to annul the decrees. As a result of his great cleverness, he succeeds, but the high priest reneges on his promise. The couple meets and kisses many times, and she dies. Zimrah is then taken to the "other world" where Beriah is being punished for kissing him. "Dear Zimrah," she says, "I committed no sin on earth other than permitting you to kiss me." He kisses her again, and she ascends to paradise. Elijah appears and assures Zimrah that he has committed no sin. Three days after returning to earth, Zimrah dies and comes to paradise, where he marries Beriah. Moses and Aaron lead them to the canopy, where God himself pronounces the marriage formula and King Solomon recites the seven blessings.

Although derived from European romances, this tale was rewoven into a Jewish fabric, as the many details about the pope and the wedding attest. The author concludes with a pious admonition: "Therefore, let no one kiss anyone." But the narrative itself subverts this homily by taking the side of the couple against the machinations of Beriah's father, the high priest, whom the audience may well have taken as a synecdoche for religious and parental authority. Against the blinkered vision of the hypocritical father, the story invokes biblical figures and, finally, God himself on the side of love. Yet, if this was a match made in heaven, it can only be consummated in heaven, after the protagonists' deaths. In good romantic fashion, the quotidian norms of this world will not permit the fulfillment of such desire. The story therefore affirms the power of the normative marital system but at the same time undermines it by offering a fictional alternative. Whether actual romantic rebellions against parental dictates were common or rare, the existence of such stories demonstrates that official norms were not accepted without countervailing fantasies.[21]

Another story takes on the problem of "frivolous marriages" (*kiddushei hitul*).[22] In these cases, a boy would give a girl some object worth a small amount of money, such as a loaf of bread, and jokingly pronounce the marriage formula. If done in front of witnesses, this act legally effects a marriage that can then be dissolved only by a formal writ of divorce. Many such cases were probably no more than jokes that went awry. But some may actually have been attempts to circumvent parental and communal authorities; in order to obtain annulments, the parents later characterized them to the courts as frivolous.

The story concerns a rabbi's son who places a ring on a hand that reaches out of a hollow tree; he then recites the marriage blessing. The hand belongs to a female demon who proceeds to kill the boy's first two wives. The third wife pleads for her life and the demon agrees, on condition that she can spend an hour each day with the rabbi's son. The wife finds her husband deep asleep with the demon and lays the demon's long hair on a bench. The demon awakes and is so moved by the wife's courtesy that she surrenders the ring and disappears. In this story, it is the wife who succeeds in banishing the demon; in others, the intervention of a rabbinical exorcist is required.

This tale and its parallels reflect the same deep anxiety about frivolous marriages that one finds in the legal literature.[23] The story not only recounts the legal difficulty of extricating oneself from such a marriage but also voices the fear that improper behavior between the sexes might evoke malevolent erotic forces. Only by allowing her husband to pay the demon a sexual debt can the third wife save herself. Although saved in the end, the hapless husband has been warned, as have all men, about the sexual dangers that lurk in the outside world. Indeed, a common motif in these stories is that the joke marriage takes place out in nature (by a hollowed tree, in the countryside, or near a river). To wander beyond the confines of the community into nature is to risk exposure to demonic eroticism. Nevertheless, warning though this story may be, it also evokes a male fantasy of sexual relations with a long-haired erotic demon, and justifies such relations by claiming that they save the life of the man's wife.[24]

## Popular Erotic Culture

Jewish law does not forbid relations between two unmarried Jews. Here, too, as with supervision of marriage, the Ashkenazic rabbis attempted, with less than total success, to impose controls beyond the letter of the law.[25] The problem was complicated by the existence of public spaces where men and women might meet outside strict communal controls. Examples of such liminal territories were the great commerical fairs, where Jews gathered from a wide geographical area. Since women were active in commerce, the Council of the Four Lands, the supracommunal council of the Polish Jews, negotiated with the city of Breslau in 1617 to allow women to attend that city's fair. Breslau at first resisted this request but finally agreed to let women attend for only one fair, evidently a compromise to decrease the possibility of ongoing romantic liaisons.[26]

Equally problematic places in this highly mobile society were inns that put up itinerant merchants. Such a place was an especially likely site for sexual violations, since both guests and residents might sleep in the same room. In an eighteenth-century case from Brody, in Galicia, for instance, the married daughter of an innkeeper was raped in her bedroom during the night.[27] Despite the curtain that she pulled around her bed, a guest staying in the same room assaulted her in the dark. She initially relented on the assumption that it was her husband, who had been sleeping on a bench nearby. The accused was dragged to the local rabbi's house, where he was beaten until he confessed.

Weddings were a popular place for men and women to meet, and as early as the eleventh century, an anonymous authority ruled, as did his successors for centuries thereafter, that "it is forbidden for men and women to intermingle [at a wedding] whether at the meal, at the dancing, or at any other part [of the celebration]. The women must be by themselves and the men by themselves ... for at a happy occasion, especially, the sensual passions are aroused."[28] But these strictures were not always heeded; one folk song that appears in a sixteenth-century German collection appears deliberately to contradict the rabbis:

> *Singing and jumping,*
> *Cheerfulness at all times,*
> *Is certainly permitted.*
> *Promenading, courting*
> *Embracing and playing.*
> *Turn all my suffering to joy.*
> *As long as it takes place honorably*
> *No one can forbid it.*[29]

Erotic relations between unmarried people not only took place with some hard-to-determine frequency, but, more important, they were enshrined in a popular erotic culture, attested by these love songs and poems.[30] Some of the songs were intended as dances and may have actually been sung when men and women, against rabbinic strictures, danced together:

> *Young maiden, will you not*
> *Do a little dance with me? ...*

*Your delicate young body*
*Has wounded me with love;*
*So also your clear little eye*
*As well as your red mouth.*
*Link your arm, dear love, with mine*
*Then will my heart be healed.*[31]

The authorities themselves were fully aware of the subversive nature of these songs. The author of *Shevet Musar*, an ethical advice book that was translated into Yiddish in 1726, warns women not to sing love songs (*shirei agavim*) to their children, as was evidently the custom, since not only do they corrupt the children but the women themselves are led to promiscuity by emulating them.[32]

These folk songs suggest that the Jewish population as a whole was attracted to a very different erotic code from the one that the rabbinic authorities wished to enforce. Court cases also reveal the conflict between the popular and rabbinic codes. Here is a particularly rich example from the responsa of the Polish authority Joel Sirkis (1561–1640):

> An accusation circulated about a woman after her second marriage and the birth of a daughter seven months later that the pregnancy had been caused by another man. When she saw that she was pregnant, she quickly arranged her marriage to her second husband in order to cover up her fornication, claiming that the accusation was a calumny. The truth, however, is that the time of wedding was [as stated] since she gave birth seven months later and the child was large as one gestated for nine months. The accusation came from the mouth of a woman who was a servant in the house. When the accusation had been broadcast widely and without ceasing, the woman's relatives came and brought charges against the woman who had slandered her.... There is also a rumor that the man [who was alleged to have had relations with her] boasted that he had had intercourse with her several times. Now, her husband had lived with her seven years and more after the birth of the daughter and he loved the daughter greatly.[33]

The story then becomes more complicated: the husband dies and leaves a substantial inheritance to the daughter. Involved legal questions, which need not detain us, arise about both the inheritance and whether the woman is subject to the levirate law. The man accused of having fathered the child cannot be easily questioned, since he is now located a considerable distance away.

This case offers a fascinating window onto social relations among these medieval Polish Jews. Second or third marriages were quite common for many people in premodern times due to high rates of mortality and, in the case of Jews, divorce as well. A widow or divorcée might act with considerably greater autonomy than a young girl before her first marriage, especially since the Ashkenazic Jews tried to marry their daughters, like their sons, in early adolescence.[34] In this case, the woman seems to have had a number of relationships after the end of her first marriage, and if the accusation was true, she arranged her second marriage in order to make her pregnancy appear legitimate. Although the actors' motivations are not stated, the servant woman evidently guarded her knowledge of her mistress's premarital activities for a long time and made her accusation when she did in order to settle some old, unspecified score. At the same time, if the rumors were accurate, the earlier lover, far from feeling repentant about the relationship, had no qualms about broadcasting his own involvement with her. In the relatively small community in question, the affair quickly became a public matter and the accused woman's relatives entered into the fray in order to protect her honor. If this reconstruction is correct, then sexual ethics and behavior within this Jewish community were grounded less in rabbinic law than in codes of family honor and social resentments, much as in European village life in general.[35]

Although older women, such as the one in the case reported by Joel Sirkis, were more likely to assert their sexual freedom than younger ones who had never been married, a great many cases in the court literature suggest that sexual activity might well start before the first marriage. In seventeenth-century Germany a man had intercourse with his fiancée but discovered that she was not a virgin.[36] He refused to marry her, and she ultimately confessed that she had, indeed, had relations with another man. Then, she turned the tables on her fiancé, pointing out that he himself obviously did not care whether he married a virgin since he had willingly had intercourse with her. As she tellingly put it: "Since I am not pregnant, what do you care, for if you hadn't done this [that is, had sex with me], you wouldn't have found out about this until after the wedding?" He answered with a round of name-calling, saying that he had no desire to marry a "wanton fornicator and lover of strangers [foreigners?] willing to take up with anyone who would make her a vessel." He proclaimed his desire to marry a virgin and piously insisted that if he had sinned ("the sin of sleeping with a menstruant!"), he is willing to repent. The woman's logic may have been unassailable, but the court ruled in the man's favor and allowed the engagement to be broken off without penalty.

Sexual relations between an engaged couple were a perennial issue in the Jewish courts, and—like these two people, at least before the man's ostensible change of heart—many evidently assumed it to be quite acceptable.[37] As early as the thirteenth century, Meir of Rothenburg tried to counter common practice by ruling that a bride and bridegroom are forbidden to live in the same house after their betrothal, since they are not permitted sexual relations until after the marriage.[38] The custom persisted, however, so that in the early seventeeth century, the ascetic moralist, Isaiah Horowitz, felt compelled to denounce those authorities who continued to permit it:

> One should scrupulously prevent the bride and groom from living together before the wedding as is the custom in this wicked generation. For not only do they live together, but he even hugs and kisses her ... and I am appalled at the authorities of this generation who tolerate this great iniquity.... For, even if she is still a minor, the groom's lust will overcome him as a result of his love and he might have an ejaculation, ... and even if he does not ejaculate, it would in any case be impossible for him to avoid having an erection.[39]

Horowitz assumes that even two very young people might engage in sexual activity, especially "as a result of his love," which may mean both sexual desire and what we would call romantic affection. An almost identical phrase can be found in Ezekiel Landau's responsum in the eighteenth century about a traveling merchant who would stay over periodically in the house of his fiancée's family: "She had intercourse with him several times and became pregnant by him. [The groom told the rabbi] that the bride had had no intimate contact with any other man, but only with him [as a result] of the love which was between them."[40] The circumstances here suggest a reasonably well-off family, which would refute the presumption of some historians that such practices were limited to the poorer classes. Either the parents exercised little control in their household, or they followed a very different set of norms from that preached by Isaiah Horowitz.

This evidence suggests the possibility that many Jews may have engaged in a practice similar to the widespread peasant custom of "bundling," a part of courtship in which some sexual contact, usually short of intercourse, was permitted between an engaged couple.[41] In the eighteenth century Jonah Landsofer joined his predecessor Horowitz in criticizing the Jewish practice, which he describes in terms quite similar to those found elsewhere in Europe: "From the day they conclude the engagement between the boy and the girl, they allow them to live together and give the girl over to fornication in the house of her father with hugging, kissing, and sexual foreplay [*maase hidudim*] with the sanction of all those gathered there."[42] Landsofer's contemporary Jonathan Eibeschutz notes that this practice was considered so socially acceptable that if the bridegroom "should fail to do this, he would be counted a fool and the girl's parents would speak to him in anger that he does not know proper manners or he has ceased loving his bride."[43]

In a later chapter, we will see how eighteenth- and nineteenth-century

Enlightenment memoirists would complain that they met their brides only on the day of the wedding, which was probably the accepted custom for the rabbinic elite during most of the Middle Ages as well. The very different practices described here reflect more than just a failure to follow rabbinic norms; rather, they are evidence of another set of norms operating among other classes of society, and not necessarily the poorest. It is even possible, although harder to establish, that before the impact of ascetic values on marriage in the eighteenth century, this looser norm regarding the period of engagement may have obtained for most of Jewish society. In this case, the complaint of the Enlightenment memoirists would have reflected a relatively recent practice rather than a long-standing medieval tradition.

## The Problem of Sexual Temptation

The popular erotic culture that appears to have existed among the Ashkenazic Jews aroused deep anxiety on the part of the thirteenth-century pietists. The dangers of adultery and other sexual sins are recurring themes in works like *Sefer Hasidim*. Seeing sexual temptation everywhere, the author of *Sefer Hasidim* considers and then rejects the possibility that there might be some reward for successfully resisting temptation. In one passage, the text tells of three who confess to deliberately inciting their desire for forbidden things and then come to ask the rabbi for a reward for resisting temptation. The third describes a complicated sexual scenario:

> I love a woman who is married, and my love for her is as strong as death. I walked with her when her husband was on a journey, and she loves me greatly, too. I hugged and kissed her and fondled her whole body, but I did not have intercourse with her. I regarded all my kisses and caresses as if they were between two men or two women, for I intended to conquer my desire. I burned with desire to have intercourse with her, but my desire did not overcome me....
>
> I behaved in this way for days and for years and I could have done with her whatever I wished, since her husband journeyed to a distant land and could not prevent me from doing what I wished, including to have intercourse with her. Yet, I refrained from doing so for the sake of God, but I permitted myself fondling and kisses. But I did not enjoy them, for my heart was set on having intercourse with her. And I did this for years in order to receive a reward.... And now I ask you whether I need to perform acts of penance or if I will receive a reward, for I am pure from any transgression.[44]

The rabbi responds that any reward is up to God but that the petitioner must perform penitential acts, since he is virtually guilty of a deliberate transgression.

This is probably not a true story. The petitioner not only claims that he has acted in this fashion but that his father did likewise. Moreover, the story is related to a folkloric tradition, going back at least to an Arabic source, and has been fit into a didactic framework that serves Judah the Hasid's purposes.[45] The story also bears similarities to the courtly love tradition, in which desire for a married woman remains unconsummated.

We have no way of knowing whether there were those who actually believed in so deliberately seeking out temptation in order to receive a reward or whether Judah the Hasid adapted and elaborated the story to reject a hypothetical position.[46] In either case the story is a very graphic account that could only excite its author or its readers: the text subverts its stated intent by telling a highly erotic story. In the process of resisting the erotic temptations of his culture, Judah the Hasid ended up unwittingly reinforcing it.

Like their Christian contemporaries, the pietists prescribed detailed penances for transgressions ranging from looking at or talking to women to full-fledged adultery. Sefer Hasidim suggests that one who has committed adultery and is prepared to repent should, in place of being flogged, sit in an icy river for as long as it took from the moment he began speaking to the woman to the consummation of the affair.[47] And what if it is summer? Instead of the cold-water treatment, the adulterer is instructed to sit on an anthill. One senses from these penances that even the pietists had great difficulty resisting temptation or, at least, suffered from great anxiety that they would be tempted.

How realistic were these anxieties? The struggles over control of marriage demonstrate that popular culture did not necessarily operate according to the same values and codes as those prescribed by the rabbinic authorities. As one finds in every society, not everyone lived within the letter of the law, and virtually every volume of responsa contains cases of sexual relations outside of marriage. We cannot draw any statistical conclusions from this material, and it would be as mistaken to assume that promiscuity was rampant as to claim that all Jews were chaste during marriage. Nevertheless the record of responsa from the time of the Ashkenazic pietists leaves no doubt that adultery, real or alleged, was a repeated issue for the German Jews.

Meir of Rothenburg, writing in the thirteenth century, time and again handled cases of men accusing their wives of sexual misconduct.[48] To prevent easy divorce, he tried to impose the strictest rules of evidence. In one case, for example, a man claimed to have seen his wife in the company of a young man on several occasions; once he heard them breathing heavily from the other side of a wall and came to the court claiming that they had had intercourse. The court compelled a divorce, but Meir, who heard the case on appeal, pointed out that hearing heavy breathing is not sufficient evidence that intercourse has taken place.[49] Writing a generation before Meir, Judah the Hasid describes a similar situation, in which a man divorces his wife on the basis of no more than his servant's evident attraction to her.[50] Such problems were not limited to the Jews, for Christian jurists at the same time were also confronted by husbands accusing wives of infidelity without sufficient witnesses.[51]

Fear of sexual promiscuity was one motivation behind the efforts of medieval Ashkenazic authorities to impose strict communal controls on divorce, much like the controls on marriage. Biblical and talmudic law make it quite easy for a man to divorce his wife, while women have no right to initiate a divorce and only a few grounds to ask a court to compel the husband to grant one.[52] The *ketubah*, or marriage contract, offered some protection against easy divorce, since it required that the husband pay a sum of money to the wife if he had no grounds, such as adultery, for divorcing her. But the sums specified in the Talmud for the *ketubah* were quite modest in medieval terms, and there was little to prevent a man from divorcing his wife if he developed a desire for another woman.

As early as the tenth and eleventh centuries, however, the Jews of France and the Rhineland dramatically increased the size of the *ketubah*, eventually adopting a standard amount regardless of the wealth of the partners at the time of marriage.[53] This high *ketubah* standard made it financially much more difficult to divorce than it had been previously. By the mid-twelfth century, if not earlier, legislation attributed to the tenth-century authority, Rabbenu Gershom, forbade divorce without a woman's consent.[54] This radical revision of talmudic law was probably influenced by the Germanic tradition of consensual divorce. In the thirteenth century, an additional law, this time quite possibly influenced by earlier developments in Christian canon law, forbade divorce without the explicit consent of the communal authorities.[55] Like the others, this last reform was clearly intended, as one contemporary put it, "to make it more difficult and expensive for the couple to divorce, so that they might come to regret the intention and abandon it."[56]

These legislative moves all had the effect of protecting and enhancing the position of women, and they may even have been a response to demands made by women themselves. In fact, women in the French and German Jewish communities of the High Middle Ages appear to have enjoyed rather astonishing freedom, probably a result of their active role in business and other public professions.[57] Women may have also demanded a greater liturgical role, for lively debates were carried on in legal circles about the place of women in the synagogue and in talmudic study.[58] We have already seen that divorcées and widows often exercised a great deal of autonomy in their sexual lives. Perhaps the anxiety over sexual promiscuity evinced by the male authorities came in response to this relative freedom enjoyed by women.

Despite moralistic appeals and the reforms of the eleventh to the thirteenth centuries, divorce still remained a legal avenue for realizing sexual desires. In the fifteenth century, divorces in Germany not only became extremely common, but people evidently contracted to marry others before even completing their divorce proceedings. Concerned that existing laws were not sufficient to control such rampant promiscuity, a rabbi named Seligmann of Bing attempted unsuccessfully to convene a rabbinic synod to impose a three-month waiting period before one could enter into a new engagement contract and to forbid any marital negotiations whatsoever before completion of a divorce. Seligmann's opponents implicitly confirmed his alarmist views by arguing that the public would not follow his proposed regulations.[59]

## The Temptation of the Other

Adultery with a Jewish woman was only one of the sexual temptations that vexed the Ashkenazic pietists. No less of an issue was the possibility of relations between Jews and Christians. The *Sefer ha-Rokeah* written by Eliezer of Worms, a disciple of Judah the Hasid, prescribes penances for such relations as part of a long list of sexual trangressions with Jewish women; the author evidently considered the problem in roughly the same category as adultery and the like.[60] One who commits this infraction should not eat meat, drink wine, or bathe for at least forty days, which is less taxing than the icy rivers and anthills prescribed for adultery. The penalty for having sex with a gentile servant is somewhat less than for having sex with other Christian women, possibly reflecting the political reality that a Christian servant represented less of a threat than a person of a higher class: one must only refrain from bathing for forty days and fast every Monday and Thursday.

*Sefer Hasidim* also warns its readers against relations with Christian women.[61] It invokes the figures of Samson, David, and Solomon, individuals whose excessive love of foreign women got them into trouble; if such holy and righteous heroes were brought down by this temptation, how much more dangerous must it be for others. While it is true, says Judah the Hasid elsewhere, that Samson had relations with non-Jewish women and God worked miracles for him, he had permission because he was trying to convert them![62] This is a remarkable revision of the biblical story, which insists that Samson's marriages were part of God's plan for

Samson to *kill* the Philistines. But what might have been legitimate for Samson is not acceptable for thirteenth-century German Jews; on the contrary, Judah's main concern is that any offspring of such relations would become idolators, which was evidently his view of Christians.

This concern with the attractions of the non-Jew was not limited to the Ashkenazic pietists. The responsa literature also reveals such anxieties in the thirteenth century. Meir of Rothenburg writes:

> I have known of a woman who was reported to have received permission to enter upon marital relations with a Gentile. I have also heard in France that some women were permitted to have marital relations with Gentiles.... I, for my part, can find no justification for granting permission to a woman who wants to live with a Gentile merely in order to gratify her carnal desires.[63]

We thus learn from Meir's opposition that some authorities acquiesced in such relations.

That such relations existed is corroborated by repeated church and secular bans on intercourse, sexual and otherwise, between Jews and Christians of the opposite sex.[64] The Fourth Lateran Council of 1215 imposed the wearing of a special badge on the Jews to help prevent fornication between Jews and Christians. A particular concern was the vulnerability of Christian servant girls in Jewish houses. Non-Jewish opinion seemed to be more threatened by the possibility of Jewish men having relations with Christian women than of Jewish women having relations with Christian men. A number of stories about relations between Christian men and Jewish women, such as the Oxford deacon and the Jewess and the Polish king Casimir I and the beautiful Esterka, circulated during the later Middle Ages.[65] This motif of the *belle juive* (the beautiful Jewess) became more prominent in the literature of the Renaissance, with plays by Racine and Corneille about the love affair between Berenice, the great-granddaughter of Herod the Great and the last Judean princess, and Titus, the Roman general who destroyed Jerusalem.[66]

It is possible that actual relations between Jewish women and Christian men formed the social basis for this literary trope, even though such relations were legally forbidden. But quite beyond social reality, the *belle juive* fulfilled an important symbolic function as a projection of the desire for the exotic in a culture that, in practice, required strict observance of social barriers. Whether or not this literature was based on real-life experiences, both the fear of the sexuality of Jewish men and the attractiveness of Jewish women must have motivated both clerical and secular lawmakers to prescribe strict penalties for infractions. In practice, however, such penalties varied widely and were sometimes limited to minor monetary fines.

There is no Jewish literary genre that corresponds to that of the *belle juive*, although there were Yiddish versions of the Polish legend that King Casimir I married a Jewess named Esterka.[67] Yet despite—or perhaps because of—the fascination with Christian women hinted at in the ethical literature, the tone of these works was unequivocally condemnatory. There is a sense of real threat. Even in Eastern Europe, where one usually thinks of the Jews as quite segregated from their surroundings, a sixteenth-century Yiddish work thundered:

> For the sin of lying with a gentile woman is more grievous than adultery with a Jewess, and anyone who finds a man lying with a gentile woman may freely kill him. Indeed, it is a great *mitzvah* to slay him immediately.... Also, there is no need to obtain permission from any rabbi or from any judge or from any leader of the community.[68]

We may be justifiably skeptical as to whether this hyperbolic prescription was ever put into practice, but no doubt the passion with which it is written demonstrates the existence of a real social problem or at least a real anxiety.

We should, of course, not be surprised that relations between Jews and Christians could become intimate. Despite the Crusader massacres, expulsions, and other persecutions, relations between members of the majority and minority cultures were not uniformly hostile. Beyond mere business relationships, there could develop friendships based on trust and affection.[69] In the final analysis, as much as they were outsiders, Jews were also a part of the medieval Christian world. *Sefer Hasidim* strikingly recognized this reality in its instructions to a Jew looking for a town in which to live:

> Check the various settlements of the land to determine whether the Gentiles [living there] have loose sexual morals. You should know that if Jews live in a certain city, their sons and daughters will follow the ways of the Gentiles, since in every city the customs of Jews are those of the Gentiles....[70]

This statement should not be taken at face value. One searches in vain to find a Jewish version of the romantic tragedy of Abelard and Heloise.[71] The sexual code of the Ashkenazic authorities was certainly not the same as that of the contemporary church. But there are a great many parallels between the way the church interacted with popular culture and the interactions between the rabbinic elite and the wider culture of the Ashkenazic Jews, from the problem of clandestine marriage to rituals of sexual courtship.

## Sexual Pleasure as Prophylactic against Temptation

The Ashkenazic authorities proposed to deal with the temptation of extramarital relations by affirming sexual pleasure within marriage, a significant modification of the ascetic pole of talmudic culture. This development is particularly remarkable in the case of the Ashkenazic pietists,
who renounced all other worldy pleasures but affirmed eroticism,[72] as
opposed to the authors of the otherwise similar Christian penitentials of
the time. *Sefer ha-Rokeah* describes sex after the conclusion of the menstrual period in the following language:

> He should give her pleasure and embrace her and kiss her and sanctify him-
> self with sexual intercourse. He should not use foul language and should
> not see in her anything contemptible, but should rather arouse her with ca-
> resses and with all manner of embracing in order to fulfill his desire and
> hers so that he doesn't think of another, but rather only of her, since she is
> his intimate partner, he should display affection and love toward her.[73]

It is rare to find such an explicit affirmation of *male* sexual desire in the
legal literature.[74] In another passage, Eliezer of Worms states: "One
should avoid looking at other women and have sex with one's wife with
the greatest passion because she guards him from sin."[75] The visual
temptations of forbidden women are everywhere, and only sexual satisfaction within marriage can overcome them.

The texts themselves may have functioned unconsciously to arouse
erotic excitement, as we have already observed about the story in *Sefer
Hasidim* of the man who lives for years with a married woman. Similarly, when Eliezer of Worms describes those parts of the forbidden female body one should *not* look at, he lingers over the details: "her
clothes, her face, the jutting out of her breasts, and her genitals." The
very description of what is forbidden serves at once as incitement and
displacement: reading the text would surely arouse those very desires
that are presumably forbidden, but if the reader then follows the text's
prescription, he would turn this desire toward his wife.

In extolling sexual pleasure within marriage, the author of *Sefer Hasidim* provided detailed prescriptions for sexual practices. Commenting
on the biblical verse "your wife should be like a fruitful vine" (Psalms
128:3), he writes:

> Your wife should dress and adorn herself like a "fruitful vine" so that your
> lust [*yetzer*] will become inflamed like a fire and you will shoot semen like
> an arrow.... You should delay your orgasm until [your] wife has her orgasm
> first and then [she will conceive] sons.[76]

Although Judah the Hasid justifies his prescriptions for male and female orgasms by linking them to the conception of male children, the consequence of his argument, which was based on both the Talmud and contemporary science, was to affirm sexual pleasure.

Elsewhere, he takes up the question of sexual positions.[77] A man should engage in sex in the missionary position after the end of his wife's menstrual period, since "she has no pleasure when he is below, and then she will become pregnant." Whether drawing on a talmudic source or contemporary medical lore, Judah is persuaded that a woman is most fertile at the end of the period of *niddah*, which in fact corresponds to the modern discovery of ovulation. Moreover, he holds that conception is most likely in the missionary position and, in line with the previous passage, if a woman experiences pleasure and has an orgasm first, she will conceive sons. But at other times: "He should follow his own pleasure so that he doesn't think about other women." He is permitted any position, since the purpose is not only procreation.

This permissiveness even extended, surprisingly, to male masturbation. *Sefer Hasidim* poses the question of whether one whose sexual drive is strong and is afraid of committing a sin is allowed to masturbate in order to cool his desire. Judah the Hasid answer that, indeed, he may masturbate in order to avoid a sexual sin, but he must then perform the penances of sitting in ice water during the winter or fasting for forty days in the summer.[78] These penances are not particularly severe as compared with others prescribed by the Ashkenazic pietists; and the length of the fast falls at the low end of the range imposed by the Christian penitentials.[79] The pietists evidently regarded the problem of temptation as much greater than that of "wasting of seed," which was to become a virtual obsession with the later Jewish mystics.

In one fascinating passage, Judah the Hasid declares that even if one could lessen sexual desire by taking some kind of medicine, it would not be permitted:

> The relatives of an adulterer once came to the wise man to request that he do something to prevent the adulterer from committing adultery. The wise man said, "I could give him something to eat so that he would not have any desire, but I am not allowed to do so, since he would then not have sexual relations with his wife, even if he already has sons; and if he does not have a wife, he might still take one."[80]

Thus, there is no legal recourse in this case. Excessive sexual desire is regarded as a physical disease, the result of a legitimate drive gone wild, a kind of erotic cancer. Yet so committed is Judah to marital sex that he prefers adultery to some form of chemical castration.

It is interesting that the Ashkenazic pietists prescribe physical solutions to problems of sexual temptation or transgression. If one has transgressed, the penance is to afflict the body in some manner, such as sitting in an icy river. Presumably, the penance will cause the body quite literally to cool off and will serve both as punishment *and* prophylactic. Similarly, the solution to temptation is sex with one's wife. The pietists therefore appear to eschew any psychological theory of penance or resistance to temptation. Not only is there no mind-body dualism at work here, but the way to deal with problems of the passions is by the instrument of the body. This approach contrasts dramatically with that of the Spanish philosophers and mystics and that of the eighteenth-century Hasidim, all of whom placed great importance on spiritual intention.

The pietists were not the only Ashkenazic authorities to advocate sexual pleasure in marriage. Following talmudic law, all the law codes of the Middle Ages clearly specify that a man may engage in sexual relations in any way he pleases with his wife, but he should not force her against her will.[81] Marital harmony presupposes sexual compatibility. Building upon the talmudic commandment of *onah*, the sexual rights of married women, the medieval legal authorities argued for the legitimacy of pleasure in marital relations.[82] *Onah* remained a commandment separate from the commandment to procreate. Thus, sexual relations are required even with a woman incapable of conceiving, whether pregnant, nursing, or postmenopausal, no less than they are with one fully fertile, as long as it is done in the same manner as procreative sex. Some authorities even understood the talmudic permission to engage in "unnatural intercourse" as permitting occasional acts of anal or oral intercourse, even though these were clearly not procreative.[83]

The medieval legal literature contains very explicit instructions for sexual foreplay. In his commentary on an obscure talmudic passage concerning advice that Rav Hisda had given to his daughters, Rashi expounds:

> When your husband caresses you to arouse the desire for intercourse and holds the breasts with one hand and "that place" [that is, the vagina] with the other, give the breasts [at first] to increase his passion and do not give him the place of intercourse too soon, until his passion increases and he is in pain with desire.[84]

Although the nature of the talmudic passage required Rashi to write as if to women, he probably intended this advice for his male disciples.

There were, however, texts directed explicitly to women that were often informed by the same principles. The *Shevet Musar*, for example, exhorts women always to think of their husbands, and especially during intercourse, in order to avoid thoughts of promiscuity.[85] Women are told to please their husbands and to undertake intercourse with joy, since their mood will affect the character of their offspring. The text also instructs women to assume the blame for sexual transgressions by their husbands. For instance, if a woman fails to keep a clean house, her husband will come to covet the house of their neighbors—from there but a short step to coveting the neighbor's wife.

These kind of strictures on women's behavior can also be found in the *tekhines*, prayers written for and, in some cases, by women.[86] The rhetoric of the prayers that deal with women's reproductive lives, and especially menstruation, emphasizes the importance of sexual purity. As one prayer on the laws of menstruation puts it: "God takes pride in the daughters, that means the wives, of the children of Israel, because their garden is locked in the face of debauchery."[87] It is hard to say how these prayers affected the women who chanted them. Did they create additional anxiety about menstruation, sexual intercourse, pregnancy, and childbirth? Or did they give these female experiences a spiritual dimension often lacking in the male-authored law? The answer is probably something of both, but it is interesting to note that the profound fear of masturbation and nocturnal emissions that would characterize the kabbalistic devotional literature directed toward men is totally missing from the *tekhines* on women's reproductive lives. Little direct attention is given to women's sexual experience as such, and menstruation is treated as normal and nonrepugnant, as long as the laws of separation are properly obeyed. Women's sexuality is treated in both the male- and female-oriented texts as something dangerous outside of marriage but as necessary within marriage to prevent external temptation.

The ascetic pole of talmudic thought was not, however, entirely absent from medieval Ashkenazic culture. A text called *Hukkei Torah* (Laws of the Torah), from the thirteenth-century French school of the Tosafot, advocates setting up houses where men would study all week and only return to their homes on Friday evening, perhaps inspired by similar talmudic traditions.[88] The anonymous author equates these *perushim* (abstinents) with the biblical *nezirim*, even though the biblical nazirite vows had nothing to do with abstention from sex. Such abstinence is necessary, the text insists, so that these young students "will not be destroyed by sexual trangressions and will not have nocturnal emissions; their intention will be directed toward speaking words of Torah in purity." The *Hukkei Torah* evidently had an influence in Germany and as far east as Bohemia and Moravia, but it is unclear how widespread this practice actually was among the medieval Ashkenazic Jews. However, more than a century before the *Hukkei Torah* was written, Rashi, the great biblical and talmudic exegete of late-eleventh-century France, referred to Friday evening as the appropriate time not only for scholars (*talmidei hakhamim*) to have sex with their wives, which is the talmudic position, but also for *perushim*.[89] It is therefore possible that small groups of students pursued their studies in semimonastic fashion, returning to their wives only on the Sabbath to fulfill their sexual obligations. We will see in a later chapter how this ideal was realized in a much more extreme way in the great Lithuanian yeshivot of the nineteenth century.

Within the Ashkenazic elite itself, therefore, there coexisted different attitudes toward sexuality within marriage. The predominant tendency, though positive, had its roots, especially for the thirteenth-century pietists, in a profound anxiety about the dangers of sexual temptation, whether from premarital sex, adultery, or the attractions of Christian women.

## Challenges to the Norms

As permissive as the rabbinic elite was toward sexuality within marriage, popular culture sometimes pushed the boundaries even farther, just as it contested the prohibitions on premarital relations. In the twelfth century, the French biblical commentator Joseph Bekhor Shor observed that "there are those whose only concern is their own pleasure" and they therefore practice coitus interruptus in order to avoid the burden of raising children.[90] How common this practice may have been is hard to tell, but what is significant is the discomfort Bekhor Shor felt with such a pure pleasure principle divorced from any procreative intent.

A more extreme form of resistance to normative marital law was the failure to observe the prohibitions on sex during a woman's menstrual period and especially during the seven so-called "white days," the additional, talmudically legislated period of abstinence after the end of the menstrual flow. It is of course very difficult to say how many people might have violated these laws, which essentially required sexual abstinence for half of every month. The polemical literature of the Middle Ages insists that all Jews scrupulously observed the laws of menstrual purity, but the detailed penances for having sex during menstruation imposed by the *Sefer ha-Rokeah* in the thirteenth century suggests that violations of the law were not uncommon.[91] In Eastern Europe in the eighteenth century a man was accused of beating his wife and forcing her to have sex with him during the "white days."[92] According to the testimony of neighbors, he was overheard "attacking the rabbis for instituting the restriction of the white days," and he tried to convince his wife that one need not follow this aspect of rabbinic law. From the sources available to us, it is impossible to say whether there were others like this man—an evidently simple Jew who explicitly rejected rabbinic sexual norms.

It is, however, in folklore rather than in records of actual sexual practices that we find the most striking subversions of rabbinic authority,
just as we found alternative values around questions of love and marriage in this kind of literature. One of the most sexually outrageous
pieces of Jewish writing from the Middle Ages, if not from all of Jewish
history, is the *Alphabet of Ben Sira,* a compilation of stories about and
sayings attributed to the Second Temple author of the Book of Ecclesias-
ticus, Jesus Ben Sira.[93] Although originating in a Muslim country sometime about the late ninth or early tenth century, the *Alphabet of Ben Sira*
was known and utilized by the German Jewish pietists in the early thirteenth century; and from 1610 on the work was translated and published
in a number of shortened Yiddish versions.[94]

The *Alphabet of Ben Sira* opens with the miraculous birth of Ben Sira,
which, like that of two other saintly figures, Rav Zera and Rav Papa, is
said to have occurred without intercourse:

> Once, Jeremiah went to the bathhouse where he found wicked men from
> the tribe of Ephraim and he saw them masturbating.... When he saw this,
> he began to rebuke them. They surrounded him and struck him, saying,
> "Why do you rebuke us? You won't get out of here until you do the same as
> us." Said he to them: "Please let me be and I swear that I will never reveal
> this." But they said: "... If you act like us, well and good, but if you don't, we
> will sodomize you." Immediately, he did as they demanded and began to
> curse the day [he was born]....
>
> That semen remained and did not decompose [literally "did not smell"]
> until his daughter came to the bathhouse. The semen entered her intestines
> and she became pregnant. After seven months, she gave birth to a son. This
> son was born with the power of speech, and his mother was ashamed that
> people would say that the daughter of Jeremiah gave birth to him out of
> fornication.[95]

Ben Sira then reassures his mother that she has nothing to be embarrassed about since just as Lot of the Book of Genesis impregnated his
daughters by coercion and without his knowledge, so did she become
pregnant.

One is immediately struck by a sense of subversive ambiguity, such as
we found in the Bible, that permeates this story.[96] The text condemns
masturbation, and Jeremiah rebukes the wicked men of Ephraim, but it
is as a result of masturbation that Ben Sira is born. "Wasted seed," it
turns out, may have a miraculously procreative fate. The story of Lot and
his daughters is rendered—perhaps close to its original biblical intention—as a dialectical narrative in which a violation of sexual ethics pro-

duces a positive result. The narrator at once professes to be shocked by the story he (or, less likely, she) tells, but also turns the scandal into a virtue.

This opening story is followed by others that also revel in sexual scandal. One such story has received much attention in recent feminist circles: the creation of Lilith, Adam's first wife. Fashioned from the earth like her husband, she demands equality in terms of sexual positions and flees when Adam refuses to acquiesce. She then becomes a demon who destroys male children before their circumcision and female children up to the age of twelve days. The text gives instructions for making an amulet to protect against her powers.[97]

Against talmudic law allowing all sexual positions, this Lilith story demonizes women who demand sexual equality. Lilith's desire for sexual pleasure is implicitly contrasted with the later Eve's maternal role: the former kills children, whereas the latter gives birth to them. Pleasure and procreation are binary opposites, personified by two different women. But the very presentation of Lilith's story allows a voice to women's demand for sexual pleasure. Thus, in one and the same breath, the story is sexually less permissive than the law but also more daring: a woman expresses sexual desires, in contrast to the talmudic materials, which presume an exclusively male prerogative to initiate different sexual practices. The *Alphabet of Ben Sira* must have resonated in some very complex way for Ashkenazic Jews: it raised anxieties about women's desires in a culture that affirmed female sexual pleasure but also feared female temptation.

Yet another story asks why the raven inseminates its mate "through the mouth." Several reasons are given, the most interesting being that the raven was punished on his mouth for accusing Noah in the ark of wanting to have sex with the raven's mate. This story is immediately followed by another that asks why the nonkosher animals have sex with their parents and with the "wives" of their fellow animals.[98] These fables conceal fantasies of oral sex and forbidden unions by displacing them onto unclean animals. The raven is punished by being forced to perform cunnilingus. The audience is permitted an outlet for its erotic imagination, but the outlet is safe since the stories contain the appropriate normative criticisms of deviant practices.

The *Alphabet of Ben Sira*, like many of the other folktales and songs we have investigated, challenged the boundaries of official norms, but the norms themselves allowed wide latitude for sexual expression within marriage. The authorities frequently struggled against the alternative voices of popular culture, but their own values were not always antithetical to them. In response to their anxieties over temptation, rabbinic lawyers and pietists came to celebrate sexuality within marriage, even as they resisted it from without. Thus, when Rashi claimed that only because of the great anxieties prompted by exile did "the spirit not arise in men to desire their wives," he was affirming the value of sexuality within marriage and lamenting those conditions that prevented its full enjoyment.

If the Ashkenazic elite took such a positive position on Eros, the Jewish philosophers and Mediterranean mystics—our subjects for the next two chapters—would re-create the talmudic struggle with asceticism, but in a much more radical key. When these new ideas were imported back into the Ashkenazic world in the seventeenth and eighteenth centuries, they would reshape the sexual norms of the Eastern European Jews in a way that was quite different from that of their medieval predecessors.

# Sensuality, Asceticism, and Medieval Jewish Philosophy

THE Jews of southern France and Spain and, indeed, the Mediterranean basin as a whole shared the same legal system as their Ashkenazic cousins to the north and east. They, too, had to find ways of reconciling the law with often divergent social practice. But the culture of these Jews was dramatically different from that of the Ashkenazim. During the High Middle Ages, the so-called golden age of the eleventh to the fourteenth centuries, they shared a cultural idiom with their Muslim and Christian neighbors to a degree unknown in the Ashkenazic world. The result of this remarkable participation in their wider society was a diverse and creative Jewish culture in which secular literature flourished alongside religious literature. If tensions between elite and popular values characterized the Ashkenazic Jews, the polarities were even more sharply drawn among the Sephardim, the Jews of Spain.

Indeed, two souls often beat within the breast of the elite itself and sometimes within the breast of the same individual. On the one hand, Jewish culture shared with its surroundings an extraordinary openness to the erotic and a willingness to cast it in purely secular terms. Poets experimented with a range of hitherto unheard-of subjects, including unbridled sensuality and homosexuality; many of them found inspiration for secular love poetry in a return to a literal reading of the Song of Songs.[1] On the other hand, Jewish philosophers, under the influence of Greek philosophy mediated through Arab sources, took the ascetic leanings of talmudic culture even further. The result was a much more negative stance on sexuality and the body than anything to be found in northern Europe. A more ambiguous movement was the Kabbalah, as medieval Jewish mysticism was known. Like the philosophers, the mystics

were deeply suspicious of the sensual, but they also constructed a remarkably erotic theology. As we shall see in this chapter and the next,
this was a culture (or cultures) that, like its talmudic predecessor, struggled mightily with sexuality, determined to affirm marriage but also attracted to a spirituality that often seemed to eschew bodily pleasure.

## An Intelligentsia at War with Itself

The intellectual and cultural movements of southern France and Spain
emerged out of a particular social context. Both the Jewish and secular
court records from the period suggest that, as in northern Europe, social
behavior among Jews was frequently at odds with legal norms.[2] These
cases include premarital and extramarital sex, prostitution, and rape.
Jewish men not only frequented Muslim and Christian prostitutes, but
there were Jewish prostitutes as well. Of particular interest are the many
instances of amorous relations between Jews and non-Jews in both
southern France and Spain, probably a much more widespread phenomenon there than among the Ashkenazim.[3] Most of the cases in Spain
seem to have involved Jewish men and Muslim or Christian women, usually as concubines. In 1281 the Jewish community of Toledo issued a formal ban against sexual immorality with a particular clause against non-
Jewish concubines. The ban evidently had little effect.[4] Moses of Coucy,
who visited Spain from France in 1236, denounced what he believed to
be this widespread practice, equating it with idolatry.[5] That Moses found
the situation in Spain more scandalous than at home may be an indica-
tion that relations between Jews and Christians were, in fact, more common in the south than in the north.

How widespread were these practices, and were the Spanish Jews
more permissive than their Ashkenazic relatives? On the basis of court
records, it is almost impossible to give more than an impressionistic answer to such a question. Folklore would seem to support the contention
that, as in northern Europe, a popular erotic culture coexisted with more
restrictive rabbinic norms. For instance, wedding poems from the fourteenth century advise couples in very explicit detail how to remain sexually attractive to each other and how to make love.[6]

Of interest to us is less the social history of the Sephardic Jews than
how the intellectual elite perceived and responded to these practices. The
Jewish leadership of Spain was deeply concerned about both the abstract
question of sexuality and about the actual sexual practices of the Jewish
community. Solomon ben Adret (1235–1310), perhaps the most important Spanish legal authority in the second half of the thirteenth century,

tried to defend the virtue of Jewish women but was forced to admit that sexual laxity was rampant: "Today, unruly persons are on the increase and there is no one to reproach his fellow man.... The daughters of Israel are chaste, but the generation corrupts them."[7] In 1281 Todros Abulafia (1247–1298?) corroborated Ben Adret in a sermon condemning the sexual lasciviousness and promiscuity of his congregants.[8]

Moses Nachmanides (1194–1270), the mystic, philosopher, and exegete, warned his son about the dangers of engaging in sexual relations with non-Jewish women,[9] while Moses de Leon, the author of the great late-thirteenth-century kabbalistic work, the *Zohar*, hinted darkly that the leaders of the nation are themselves guilty of such behavior.[10] Two addenda to the *Zohar*, the *Raaya Meheimna* and the *Tikkunei ha-Zohar*, written by an anonymous Kabbalist at the end of the thirteenth century, are filled with attacks on the materialism and sensuality of the Jewish elite. Like the teachings of the Christian Spirituals of the same time, to which these texts have been compared, we find an ascetic style of life deliberately counterposed to the conventional practices of both the community and its leaders.[11]

The intellectuals of Spain were deeply troubled that their own class, and not just the poor and uneducated, lived a sexually dissolute life. This was an elite very much in conflict over its own sexuality, torn between the competing norms and practices of the Jewish and non-Jewish cultures in which they lived. They struggled not only against other classes of society but also against their social equals and, even more poignantly, against themselves. Todros Abulafia, the same thirteenth-century poet and preacher who chastized his congregation, reveals in his poetry how he himself pursued both Jewish and Christian women in his youth but became more restrained as he grew older. His poems suggest a continual oscillation between indulgence and repentance.[12]

In the twelfth century, Moses Ibn Ezra reflected the controversy around sexual license in one of his poems:

> *Caress a lovely woman's breast by night*
> *And kiss some beauty's lips by day*
> *Silence those who criticize you,*
> *Those who give you their own counsel.*
> *Take advice rather from me:*
> *With beauty's children only can we live*
> *For they were kidnapped from Eden to subjugate*
> *The living—and there is no living man who does not desire them....*[13]

Possibly drawing on the Muslim fantasy of heaven,[14] the poet pictures beautiful women as erotic foreigners imported into our world to seduce men.

Did Moses Ibn Ezra, like Todros, really indulge in the sensual behavior he describes in his poem? Or, more radically, did the many Jewish poets who celebrated erotic attraction to other men engage in homosexuality?[15] These questions are particularly sensitive, because these poets were not just frivolous literati but often were statesmen and communal leaders—the political elite of the community expressing daring, even antinomian, views. Whether poems such as these reflect actual practices by the poets or mere literary conventions remains a highly vexed question that we will not try to answer. Even if they were only imitating conventions, they were powerful vehicles for their authors' fantasies.

Also hotly debated by the elite in the twelfth and thirteenth centuries was the nature of women. Some authors blamed women for the ruination of men, while others glorified women and the virtues of marital love.[16] The very institution of marriage was troubling for elements of the Spanish Jewish intelligentsia, who projected their ambivalences onto women as either the source of the problem or its cure.

Ambivalence over erotic behavior therefore plagued the Jewish elite. If the philosophers rejected sexual pleasure, they did so in the context of a culture that affirmed it. The Jewish mystics similarly sought to distance themselves from the frank sensuality of Moses Ibn Ezra's poem, while seeking to indulge their desires in another realm. This may be the reason that the male and female emanations of God are described in the symbolic system of the Jewish mystics as engaged in acts of explicit sexual intercourse. Moreover, these aspects of God are permitted, and perhaps even required, to engage in sexual transgressions, such as incest, which are prohibited by Jewish law.[17] In this way, the mystics may have guarded against sexual license in this world by projecting it into a higher realm.

The mystics also revived the old allegorical reading of the Song of Songs, infusing it with their own unique symbols.[18] Might this intense spiritual interpretation of the Song of Songs not be a reaction against the repeated secular use of the book's metaphors by the Spanish Jewish poets? Both the rich erotic metaphors of the thirteenth-century Kabbalists (mystics) and the extraordinary theological weight they placed on the sexual act are inconceivable divorced from the culture they both accepted and resisted.

## The Philosophical Tradition

The intellectual culture of the Spanish Jews was heavily influenced by medieval Muslim philosophy. Drawing first upon Neoplatonic and then Aristotelian ideas as translated and transmitted by Arabic authors, Jewish philosophers sought to reconcile these Greek systems of thought with their own religious tradition.[19] The sharp duality between spirit and matter drawn by these philosophies posed a problem for the Jewish thinkers, since neither the authors of the Bible nor the rabbis of the Talmud recognized such rigid distinctions. The law they had inherited clearly pertained to all functions of the body, but they understood it in the spirit of one strand of rabbinic thought, as a way of channeling and controlling physical desire so that it might serve spiritual ends.[20] With the advent of medieval philosophy, the competition between study of Torah and the obligations of marriage intensified, turning now into a struggle between love of the spiritual and love of the material.[21]

Abraham Ibn Ezra (1092–1167), possibly a relative of Moses Ibn Ezra and one of the foremost Neoplatonic philosophers and biblical exegetes of twelfth-century Spain, exemplified the attitude toward sexuality of many medieval philosophers. His views, at least in his exegesis, were strikingly different from those of Moses. In his commentary on Leviticus 18:20 ("Do not have carnal relations with your neighbor's wife and defile yourself with her"), Ibn Ezra notes that sexual intercourse has three purposes. The first is procreation, which is to be divorced from desire. The second is to improve the health of the body, following ancient medical prescriptions still current in the Middle Ages. And the third is to satisfy desire, which, for Ibn Ezra was akin to the carnal nature of the animals. This tripartite division corresponds roughly to Ibn Ezra's division of the soul into three parts, in which the highest, or rational, soul is divorced from the demands of the body. This last soul is only truly developed by the philosophers.[22]

Ibn Ezra therefore saw procreation and desire as polar opposites, with only the philosopher able to understand what it means to have sex for purely procreative purpose, without the physical desire of the animals. This radical division between procreation and desire, something new in the Middle Ages, reflected the influence of Neoplatonic philosophy.[23] But since Ibn Ezra, like all other Jewish philosophers, followed halakhah, the philosophical soul could not renounce procreation. Sexual renunciation, if it was to be entertained as an option, had to be within the framework of the commandment to marry and produce children.

The philosophical position was inseparable from the name of Moses Maimonides (1135–1204), the greatest legal and philosophical mind of the Jewish Middle Ages. Although both his great legal code, the *Mishne Torah,* and his philosophical masterpiece, *The Guide of the Perplexed,* provoked hurricanes of controversy after his death, Maimonides' ideas continued to resonate even among those who rejected their author. Maimonides spent most of his career in North Africa, but he was born in Spain and his work had a major impact on the culture of the Sephardic Jews.

Maimonides vehemently denounced matter as the cause of "every defi-
ciency affecting [man] and every disobedience."[24] Following Aristotle,
Maimonides recoiled from the sense of touch in particular, even though
he was prepared to allow some pleasure from the other, less material
senses.[25] This particular emphasis on the sense of touch departed from
talmudic thinking, which seems to have regarded the senses of sight and
hearing as more problematic: the rabbis held that the sight of a woman's
hair, foot, or even little finger, and the sound of a woman's voice were all
as dangerous as actually touching a woman.

The general purpose of Jewish law, according to Maimonides, is "to
quell all the impulses of matter."[26] Thus, in explaining the meaning of the
sexual prohibitions, Maimonides argues that the laws against both har-
lotry and illicit sexual unions were designed to prevent "an intense lust
for sexual intercourse and for constant preoccupation with it."[27] By creating categories of prohibited women, the law effectively lessens desire, a
notion that would seem to contradict the talmudic idea that forbidden
fruit are always sweeter! For Maimonides, the dulling of desire that
comes from being confined to a sexual relationship with one woman is
precisely what the law seeks to achieve. Even the language of the Torah
promotes this end, since, Maimonides says, the Bible does not have a
word for sexual intercourse or for the sexual organs and therefore requires the use of euphemisms.[28] What should not be seen also should not
be spoken directly, so that desire is curbed both physically and mentally.

Such, too, is the purpose of circumcision, which was commanded in
order

> to bring about a decrease in sexual intercourse and a weakening of the
> organ in question, so that this activity be diminished and the organ be in as
> quiet a state as possible.... The bodily pain caused to that member is the
> real purpose of circumcision. None of the activities necessary for the
> preservation of the individual is harmed thereby, nor is procreation ren-
> dered impossible, but violent concupiscence and lust that goes beyond what
> is needed are diminished.... For if at birth this member has been made to
> bleed and has had its covering taken away from it, it must indubitably be
> weakened.[29]

The foreskin, Maimonides seemed to believe, is highly innervated and
therefore generates intense sexual pleasure (much like the clitoris in the
female, which was yet to be discovered).[30] Excising it serves two purposes: it removes this seat of pleasure and imprints the memory of physical pain on the unruly organ. Circumcision comes suspiciously close to
effecting something like castration, but with the ability to procreate left
intact. If Origen's solution to the problem of sexual desire—self-
castration—was outside the pale of halakhah, circumcision might serve

as a Jewish alternative: the cut that separates pleasure from procreation.[31]

One might expect Maimonides to entertain the possibility of celibacy, as had others. Saadia Gaon, for example, devoted a whole chapter of his *Book of Beliefs and Opinions* two centuries earlier to criticizing those who regard the begetting of children as a primary good and to enumerating all the perils of raising children.[32] Maimonides' own son Abraham, who was influenced by Sufi mysticism, espoused an ascetic argument against the burdens of family life.[33] Both of these writers accepted the duty to procreate and married and had children, but they voiced their ambivalence, nevertheless. One searches in vain, however, for such antiprocreative statements in Maimonides' work. Certainly, it would have been difficult for such a preeminent legal authority to take such a stance, but I would suggest that his position flowed logically from his philosophical and political thinking.

Philosophically, Maimonides held that since form cannot exist without matter and since that which is material must necessarily perish, human beings have no choice but to reproduce themselves continually, thus passing their forms into new matter. Like it or not, humans are embodied creatures, and it is no accident that Maimonides considers the soul a "corporeal faculty" and not a rarefied spirit.[34] When one succeeds in controlling his bodily desires, "that matter [becomes] a divine gift."[35] Since "moral qualities of the soul are consequent upon the temperament of the body,"[36] the body itself must be controlled, just as the physical organ itself needs to be cut in circumcision. Given this kind of argument, it would be a mistake to call Maimonides a dualist: mind and body *are* linked, even though the relationship between the two must be hierarchical.

This is precisely the spirit of moderation and restraint with which Maimonides presents the law of sexual intercourse for the scholar in his *Mishne Torah* and in his medical writings. Although the law permits a man to act in any way he chooses with his wife, both ethics and health require modesty and temperance.[37] Following Abraham Ibn Ezra, he holds that one engages in sexual intercourse to promote health and to procreate. As his critics were to note, Maimonides fails to mention the commandment of *onah* in these passages; physical pleasure is an animal drive that has no place in a philosophical life.

Yet, for Maimonides, it was not possible to attain true spirituality by denying the claims of the body. Asceticism, if it was to be entertained as an option, had to be practiced within the framework of the commandment to marry and bear children. Maimonides might well have subscribed to the Muslim saying attributed to Ibn Abbas, a companion of the prophet Muhammad, that "the asceticism of the ascetics cannot be complete without marriage."[38]

Further, following Aristotle, Maimonides held that human beings are political animals; he saw the family as the basis of the state. The Jewish laws governing sexual relations were designed to guarantee the legitimate genealogies necessary for a well-ordered polity.[39] Although Maimonides does not say so explicitly, he considers procreation a necessary component in the creation and maintenance of a political community. The philosopher must live within a community and, according to the Arab Platonist al-Farabi, his ideal role is to serve also as lawgiver, a role that Maimonides himself fulfilled as a leader of the Egyptian Jewish community and as a codifier of Jewish law.[40] In this last role, the philosopher is surely not exempt from the laws governing the community and, indeed, is called upon to exemplify them. Thus, the philosopher, too, must marry, have children, and take a personal part in the orderly functioning of the state.

This portrait of Maimonides is therefore complicated; it reveals how ultimately problematic sexuality was for medieval Jewish philosophers. Because the problem as they saw it was materiality, their position was intrinsically much more extreme than that of the talmudic rabbis. The material body is a necessary dimension of existence, but it is also the source of destructive desires. The disciplines of medicine, ethics, and political theory all require that the body receive its due, but it must be kept under the firm control of the intellect. Since most human beings are not philosophers, the divine law of the Torah provides the appropriate methods for restraining the passions and for establishing a sober and ordered community. As much as possible, procreation must be kept separate from desire.

## Maimonides' Influence

The work of Maimonides would influence, negatively and positively, a wide circle of intellectuals who lived in the century after his death. There were those mystics in southern France and Spain who struck out in a different direction, based in part on a rejection of Maimonides. But there were others, in the same time and place, who followed closely in Maimonides' footsteps. Levi ben Gerson (Gersonides, 1288–1344) lived in southern France and was perhaps the most important philosopher after Maimonides. He gave an explicit account of how the law divorced procreation from desire, noting in his commentary on the biblical verse "be fertile and increase" that only human beings need to be *commanded* to procreate since, as opposed to the animals, man can choose to engage in sex for reasons of pleasure alone.[41]

A much more radical follower of Maimonides was Isaac ben Yedaiah, who wrote several philosophical commentaries on talmudic *aggadot* in southern France sometime after the middle of the thirteenth century.[42] Quoting Maimonides, Isaac labels the sense of touch a "disgrace" and proclaims that "a man should not be drawn after this shameful thing even with his wife, for it confuses his intellect."[43] Nowhere does Isaac mention the commandment of *onah*, nor does he appear to be particularly interested in procreation. The purpose of marriage is to prevent a man from pursuing other women, including non-Jewish women, a theme he may have taken from northern European sources. Jews are not only protected against sexual desire by their wives but also, again following Maimonides, by circumcision. As his explicit language strongly suggests, however, Isaac himself seems to have been obsessed with sexual fantasies. His lengthy passage on circumcision is filled with vivid sexual imagery as well as highly eroticized views of the sexual difference between Jews and Christians:

> [A beautiful woman] will court a man who is uncircumcised in the flesh and lie against his breast with great passion, for he thrusts inside her a long time because of the foreskin, which is a barrier against ejaculation in intercourse. Thus she feels pleasure and reaches an orgasm first. When an uncircumcised man sleeps with her and then resolves to return to his home, she brazenly grasps him, holding on to his genitals and says to him, "Come back, make love to me." This is because of the pleasure that she finds in intercourse with him, from the sinews of his testicles—sinew of iron—and from his ejaculation—that of a horse—which he shoots like an arrow into her womb. They are united without separating and he makes love twice and three times in one night, yet the appetite is not filled. And so he acts with her night after night. The sexual activity emaciates him of his bodily fat and afflicts his flesh and he devotes his brain entirely to women, an evil thing....
>
> But when a circumcised man desires the beauty of a woman, and cleaves to his wife, or to another woman comely in appearance, he will find himself performing his task quickly, emitting his seed as soon as he inserts the crown.... He has an orgasm first; he does not hold back his strength. As soon as he begins intercourse with her, he immediately comes to a climax. She has no pleasure from him when she lies down or when she arises and it would be better for her if he had not known her ..., for he arouses her passion to no avail and she remains in a state of desire for her husband, ashamed and confounded, while the seed is still in her "reservoir." She does not have an orgasm once a year, except on rare occasions, because of the great heat and the fire burning within her. Thus he who says "I am the Lord's" will not empty his brain because of his wife or the wife of his friend. He will find grace and good favor; his heart will be strong to seek out God.[44]

This complex man was preoccupied with images of beautiful women, and although he strives bravely to defend the chaste behavior of the Jewish philosopher, he can scarcely conceal his admiration for the virility of the uncircumcised lover. Similarly, although failure to satisfy one's wife turns out to be a virtual prerequisite for engaging in philosophical contemplation, there seems to be some unintended sympathy evinced for the woman's sexual frustration.

Isaac's understanding of the physiology of circumcision differs significantly from Maimonides'. The result is the same, however. Instead of serving as a highly erogenous zone that must be removed, the foreskin is rather a barrier that retards quick ejaculation. Though the Jew may feel more intense sensation than the Christian, he expends his sexual desire faster and thus is able to return to his philosophy without exhausting his body. In perhaps no other text that I have come across is the economy of erotic energy so linked to theology: the Christians spend their sexual reserves and remain slaves to their bodies, while the parsimonious Jews expend just enough to neutralize desire so that they can "seek out God."

Although we know little about Isaac's biography, it is hard not to see these ideas as products of the particular social and cultural context of southern France. The Jews did not have easy relations with their Christian neighbors, as Isaac's sexual polemic suggests, but neither were they entirely isolated from them. The possibilities for erotic relations between Jews and Christians were not merely theoretical, as we have already seen. Isaac's sexual fantasies demonstrate that the problem of Jewish sexuality in a Christian world has a long history.

## In Defense of Desire

Maimonides' philosophy and legal writings were received with approbation by some in southern France and Spain; but for others they sparked fierce controversy, which led, in some cases, to outright bans on the teachings of the great philosopher.[45] Abraham ben David of Posquières (ca. 1120–1198), usually referred to by the acronym Rabad, was one of Maimonides' earliest and most vociferous opponents.[46] Rabad composed a searing gloss on Maimonides' code of Jewish law. Commenting on one of the passages in which Maimonides had prescribed intercourse for medical or procreative purposes, Rabad restored the commandment of onah as equally legitimate.[47] The sexual rights of the woman now found a defender against the misogynist philosophers!

About 1180 Rabad wrote a treatise on marriage entitled *Baalei ha-Nefesh* (roughly translated as "The Masters of the Animal Soul") in which he goes into much greater detail about how sexual satisfaction of one's wife fits into the law.[48] This text was the first in a series of "marriage manuals" produced by medieval Jewish writers. Rabad itemizes the legitimate reasons for engaging in intercourse, many of which are already familiar to us: the commandment to procreate, improving the health of the fetus, the commandment of *onah* (that is, when the wife desires sex), and avoidance of sin. With regard to *onah*, Rabad advances two views at once: the man owes his wife not only the *minimum* that is required by the law but as much as she desires. Here is a view of women's sexual rights diametrically opposed to that of Isaac ben Yedaiah.

But if women are allowed as much sexual activity as they wish, the opposite is the case for men. A man who engages in sex in order to avoid sexual temptation receives a reward, to be sure, but it is a lesser reward than for engaging in sex for other reasons. Moreover, if a man does it to satisfy his own desire for pleasure, not only is there no reward but he is close to sin. Rabad compares such a man to one who eats and drinks too much and then vomits. This analogy between sex and gluttony was a favorite in medieval Jewish ethical texts, and it points to an anxiety about food that does not seem to have its source in earlier texts.[49]

Despite Rabad's permissive understanding of the sexual rights of women, his text is addressed chiefly to men; viewed in this context, his views on *onah* take on a rather less positive air.[50] The very title suggests, as he spells out in his introduction, that his intention is to teach men how to control their animal soul, which, in good Maimonidean language, "drags them after this world and its pleasures to the point where they forget God."[51] Rabad then gives an account of the creation of woman: whereas all other animals were created equally male and female, only woman was created from man's ribs; she therefore exists to serve him, just like the other limbs of his body or like a field that he owns.[52] The word for intercourse, *tashmish* (service), indicates that woman serves man and desires him the way in which the other limbs desire the pleasures of the body.[53] Thus, a man must satisfy his wife's sexual desires just as he must satisfy the demands of his own body, but he must also rule his wife as he is commanded to rule his body. This introductory passage, which is rarely quoted by those who highlight the positive sexual prescriptions of the last chapter of the book, shows that Rabad did not consider women to have an emotional status equal to that of their husbands. A real tension exists in the *Baalei ha-Nefesh* between this patriarchal view of women as servants to be controlled, like the limbs of one's own body, and Rabad's expansive position on *onah*.

Rabad's whole discussion of sexuality within marriage revolves around the problem of intentionality, or motivations (*kavvanot*). The hierarchy of reasons for intercourse—from the virtuous to the merely permissible to the virtually sinful—relies upon the inner purpose of the male agent and not on the act itself. Although the talmudic rabbis occasionally considered motivation as relevant to acts, Rabad made it central, a development that would be crucial for all subsequent medieval treatments of sexuality. It is not the physical pleasure itself that is at stake, but one's inner psychological state. Does the man intend procreation or is the motivation to satisfy his wife? Only when his intention is dominated by his own physical desire does the act become problematic. The attention, one need hardly point out, is only on the *man's* intention; women, viewed as limbs of the male body, are assumed to be creatures whose intentions are not so easily controllable.

This overwhelmingly psychological emphasis on sex, to use a modern formulation, may explain why Rabad and his successors devoted less attention to physical penances than did the Ashkenazic pietists.[54] Since it is not so much the body that is to blame for sexual excess as it is the mind's inability to control the body, rectification of the body's errors should be made through the mind, by concentrating one's intention in the right direction.

## The Christian Context

Rabad's introduction of intentionality into the sexual act was an innovation in Jewish tradition, but he did not develop it in a vacuum. Instead, his teaching reflected the intense debate that was going on simultaneously among Christian theologians.[55] While the Jews of the Ashkenazic world did not lack contacts with their Christian neighbors, the interpenetration of Jewish and Christian culture was much greater in southern France and Spain, and Jewish intellectuals there were undoubtedly aware of developments in canon law and scholastic theology. Although their relations with Christians were not always peaceable, it would have been only natural for them to formulate their own thinking in response to the tumultuous debates of the times. There is good evidence, for example, that eleventh-century changes in Jewish marital customs, which reinforced the sacramental nature of marriage, may have owed much to contemporary developments in the Christian theology of marriage.[56]

Christian theologians of the High Middle Ages were deeply concerned with problems of sexuality and marriage. In precisely this period, southern France, Spain, and Italy were gripped by the Catharist (or Albigensian) dualistic heresy, which preached renunciation of the material world. As medieval heirs of Gnosticism and Manichaeanism, the Cathars vehemently rejected marriage and procreation.[57] It is not unlikely that the challenge of these heretics prompted a renewed Catholic affirmation of marriage: at the same time that the newly established Inquisition turned its sights on the Cathars, church lawyers developed the medieval doctrine of marriage as a sacrament and of procreation as divinely decreed.[58] During the twelfth century, though, the church also experienced a movement of reform that dissolved clerical marriages and unequivocally established clerical celibacy.[59] As opposed to the Catharist desire to equalize clergy and laity under a common doctrine of celibacy, the church drew a sharp distinction between a celibate clergy and a married laity.

The rabbinical class, which no doubt saw itself as the counterpart of the Christian clergy, must have felt the need to defend its own continuing marriages against the ideal of a celibate clergy. For example, the *Sefer Nizzahon Yashan*, a late-thirteenth-century compendium of Jewish polemical arguments, repeatedly attacks Christianity for its celibate priesthood. Christian celibacy was a fake; the priests, says the text, "wallow in licentiousness in secret."[60] The implication is that celibacy can never work; on the contrary, it forces the practitioner into secret sex.

Perhaps in response to the asceticism of the heretics, the Christian theologians devoted considerable attention to the question of the legitimacy of sexual pleasure. The discussion revolved around issues raised by Augustine in the fifth century over whether sex within marriage was a sin.[61] Against more radical church fathers, Augustine defended the notion that God had instituted sex in the Garden of Eden and that it was the Fall that caused human beings to experience concupiscence, that excess of desire that polluted the act. Augustine asserted that sex for the purpose of satisfying physical desire was a pardonable sin within marriage.

Augustine's various formulations of this last principle left ambiguities that his medieval successors exploited to advance their own positions. A wide range of views characterized this medieval debate.[62] At one extreme, Peter Abelard, who had a personal stake in the matter because of his notorious affair with Heloise,[63] contended that neither the sex act nor the desire that accompanies it is sinful and that only the intention of the actor is relevant—a position not unlike that held by Rabad.[64] At the other extreme, Huguccio, one of the twelfth-century commentators on Gratian's code, the *Decretum*, listed four reasons for intercourse that were also almost identical to those in the *Baalei ha-Nefesh*.[65] Huguccio declared that no matter what the reason, all sexual relations within marriage were sinful to some degree, because they were contaminated by lust.[66] Huguccio suggested that the only way to avoid sin was to suppress one's pleasure during intercourse and avoid orgasm. This highly ascetic practice, which surely seems more difficult than outright celibacy, came to be called *amplexus reservatus* (restrained embrace) in subsequent Christian literature; it also surfaced in later Jewish sources, especially in eighteenth-century Hasidism.

Most of the Christian theologians took a moderate position between these extremes. Thomas Aquinas (1224–1274) is a good representative of this golden mean. Although he was an Aristotelian philosopher who respected Maimonides, Aquinas took a more positive stance on sexuality than did his Jewish predecessor. Aquinas rejected those who held that the sex act is always sinful, and he argued, with Augustine, that if sex had taken place in the Garden of Eden, it would have been without sin, an interpretation of the Garden story that can also be found in the earlier midrash and that is found in medieval Jewish mysticism. Sex in the Garden would have involved the same intense pleasure, but it would not have "squandered itself in so disorderly a fashion on this sort of pleasure when it was ruled by reason."[67] Since intercourse serves the goal of procreation, a purpose created by God, it is consonant with "right reason" when it follows that purpose, and the "abundance of pleasure in a well-ordered sex act" is not the cause of sin.[68] When undertaken for pleasure alone, sex creates a pardonable (venial) sin, which the marriage blessing itself pardons. Rendering the marital debt, as Paul called it, entails no sin, while receiving the debt from one's spouse—that is, requesting sex in order to satisfy one's physical desire—is venial.[69]

This last distinction corresponds almost exactly to the Rabad's distinction between fulfilling the commandment of *onah*—satisfying one's wife—and engaging in sex for one's own pleasure. The most significant difference between Aquinas and Rabad on the question of sex within marriage is the difference between the Christian and Jewish traditions: for Christians, the marital debt is shared equally by husband and wife, while for Jews, only the man is obligated to have sex with his wife.

Rabad's discussion of intentionality and the distinctions he draws between one's own pleasure and other reasons for sex all point to a common language with contemporary Christian intellectuals. It is not necessary to show that he or other Jewish writers on sexuality were influenced by this or that Christian theologian. We do not know whether they even read these Latin scholastics; it is possible that their sources were oral rather than written. In any event, the way they cast their arguments shows that they were part of a specifically medieval intellectual culture. Although the Christian clergy was now celibate, the arguments developed for the married life of the laity show that Christians and Jews did not differ all that much in their thinking. Both Jews and Christians affirmed sexuality within marriage, especially for the purposes of procreation and fulfilling the marital debt, but both were ambivalent about sexual pleasure for its own sake.

Rabad was not only a legal scholar; he was also one of the first adherents of the new movement of Jewish mysticism that arose in Provence in the late twelfth century—precisely when the Catharist heresy was at its peak in that region. We know of no Jewish "Cathars," although the sect's gnostic doctrines may well have been familiar to the early Jewish mystics as well as to other Jews.[70] This radical, antimaterialist heresy must have had an impact on the way Jews thought about sexuality, even if no one in the Jewish community actually followed it. The mystical marital theology developed by the Kabbalists, starting with Rabad, can best be understood in this context. Although the Kabbalah was not a polemic, its erotic theology may have resulted from the desire to demonstrate the sacramental nature of Jewish marriage while at the same time renouncing any vulgar desire for physical pleasure. Where the orthodox Christians could resolve the contradictory claims of celibacy and procreation only by creating two rigidly distinct classes of people and where the Cathars rejected sexuality altogether, the Kabbalists proposed a dialectical doctrine in which the married mystic might transmute the physical into the spiritual.

The philosophers and mystics must also not be divorced from the Jewish setting in which they lived. We have observed how the intellectuals of the Sephardic world were caught between ideals of sensuality and asceticism. They believed that the Jews of their community and especially the members of their own class were infected by a culture of erotic license, a culture they themselves could not ignore. Whether they advocated renunciation of the pleasures of the body, as did the philosophers, or a more complex doctrine that linked the physical to the spiritual, in the manner of the mystics, they did so in response to their surroundings. Whether *amor dei* was the product of a philosophical or mystical system, it remained Eros displaced from the material world in which it seemed so rampant.

# CHAPTER 5

# Sexuality and Spirituality in the Kabbalah

Sometime in the early part of the thirteenth century, an anonymous Spanish Kabbalist wrote a treatise on marital relations that was to become a standard work for the Jewish Middle Ages.[1] It remains for many today evidence of an astonishingly positive attitude toward sexuality in traditional Judaism. Reacting against Maimonides' philosophy, the author of this *Iggeret ha-Kodesh* (Letter of Holiness) writes:

> The matter is not as Rabbi Moses [Maimonides] thought and supposed in his *Guide of the Perplexed*, where he praises Aristotle for saying that the sense of touch is despicable to us. God forbid! That impure Greek is wrong inasmuch as his statement contains an imperceptible trace of heresy. For if he believe that the world was created intentionally [by God], he would not have said this. But we who have the Torah and believe that God created all in his wisdom [do not believe that he] created anything inherently ugly or unseemly. If we were to say that intercourse is repulsive, then we blaspheme God who made the genitals.... Marital intercourse, under proper circumstances, is an exalted matter.... Now you can understand what our rabbis meant when they declared that when a husband unites with his wife in holiness, the divine presence abides with them.[2]

According to many modern commentators,[3] the Jewish mystics, or Kabbalists, of which our author was an early representative, rejected the philosophers' hostility to the material world and sought to restore the integrated relationship of body and soul that had prevailed in biblical and rabbinic culture. By these accounts, the mystics celebrated human sexuality as a requirement for divine harmony, itself portrayed in sexual terms. As opposed to many medieval Christian writers who believed that the Holy Spirit could not be present while human beings were engaged in carnal intercourse, the Kabbalists—and medieval Judaism in general— held the very opposite: intercourse between man and wife brings the Shekhinah, the divine presence, into the conjugal bed.

There is much truth to this characterization of medieval Jewish mysticism, but the story is more complex. We have already seen that the stark contrast often drawn between medieval Jewish and Christian thought does not stand up to scrutiny: as Rabad's *Baalei ha-Nefesh* shows, Jews and Christians often spoke a similar language about marital sex, even though the Christians put a more negative value judgment on it and also valorized clerical celibacy. The radical distinctions between philosophy and mysticism also cannot be sustained. The early Kabbalists often saw mysticism as taking up where philosophy left off.[4] Many began their intellectual careers as Maimonideans, and even though they may eventually have rejected the great master, much of the philosophical way of thinking persisted in their doctrines. We have seen that even Maimonides did not argue for a totally dualistic split between body and spirit, although he certainly denigrated the former in favor of the latter. The mystics would agree with the *Iggeret ha-Kodesh* in rejecting Maimonides' attack on sexuality, but they perpetuated much more of the philosophical ambivalence toward the material world than the above quotation might suggest.

## The *Iggeret ha-Kodesh*

The *Iggeret ha-Kodesh*, although framed in a specifically Jewish idiom, was part of a larger genre of coital guidance literature that had Christian and Muslim versions as well. When placed in this literary context, the *Iggeret* appears to be less uniquely Jewish and more typical of its wider culture. Some decades before the *Iggeret* was written, there came into circulation a treatise entitled *De secretis mulierum* (On the Secrets of Women), which was falsely attributed to Albertus Magnus.[5] The text gives detailed instructions on sexual technique, including how long to wait after eating, what kind of foreplay to engage in, and at what point to commence intercourse, all themes that appear in the *Iggeret*. The author advocated that women assume a certain position during intercourse and think certain thoughts in order to ensure a healthy child, a kind of sexual eugenics that we have already observed in rabbinic sources.

Muslim writers were no less interested in the subject of sexual technique. In the early twelfth century the Sufi mystic al-Ghazali composed his *Book on the Etiquette of Marriage,* a Muslim version of the same kind of text. A strong advocate of procreation as the main purpose for sexuality, al-Ghazali nevertheless affirmed, along with his Christian and Jewish counterparts, the husband's duty to satisfy his wife:

> Let him proceed with gentle words and kisses. The Prophet said: "Let none of you come upon his wife like an animal and let there be an emissary between them." He was asked, "What is this emissary, O Messenger of God?" He said, "The kiss and [sweet] words." ... Once the husband has attained his fulfillment, let him tarry until his wife also attains hers. Her orgasm may be delayed, thus exciting her desire.... Difference in the nature of [their] reaching a climax causes discord whenever the husband ejaculates first.[6]

The *Iggeret*'s advice to husbands runs along virtually the same lines as al-Ghazali's:

> Therefore engage her first in conversation that puts her heart and mind at ease and gladden her.... Speak words that arouse her to passion, union, love, desire, and Eros [agavim].... Never may you force her.... Rather win her over with words of graciousness and seduction.... Do not hasten to arouse passion until her mood is ready; enter [her] with love and willingness so that she "seminates" [that is, has an orgasm] first.[7]

The author of the *Iggeret,* like his Muslim and Christian counterparts, recognized the existence of female orgasm, which he labeled "semination" on the basis of Leviticus 12:2.[8] Although his advocacy of noncoercive sex was very much in line with halakhah, the context in which he composed these lines was broader than just the Jewish tradition.

The *Iggeret* clearly validates the physical pleasure of sexual intercourse, but its position is not unambiguous. The epigraphic poem at the beginning makes it clear that the purpose of text is eugenic: to teach the sexual behavior necessary for producing learned sons. Following both the Talmud and ancient medical lore based on Galen's two-seed theory, the author held that female orgasm is necessary for conception.[9] This physiological construct at once legitimates female sexual pleasure *and* subordinates pleasure to procreation.

In line with a long medical tradition reaching back to antiquity, the author holds that the physical and moral character of one's offspring is determined by the nature of the male seed, which is a kind of homunculus. The character of the seed is in turn determined by the behavior of the sexual partners. Moreover, the author's genetic counseling is not merely personal; it also contains a national component. The Jews are separated from the rest of the nations and are said to be holy "just as God is holy."[10] This ethnic holiness is not a genetic given to be automatically inherited; rather, it must be imprinted in each generation by proper sexual behavior.

But the stakes in every act of intercourse are higher than national eugenics. Our author writes as a Kabbalist, and his text must be interpreted not only on the manifest level, as a form of medieval genetic engineering, but also esoterically, as a mystical theurgy. The demand that Israel imitate God's holiness hints at the kabbalistic belief that the male and female emanations of God are engaged in a perpetual state of sexual intercourse with each other. Men and women not only become holy by engaging in sex, as do these aspects of God, but they actually cause the divine powers (known as *sefirot*) to come together in holy intercourse. This sexual theurgy would become even more explicit in the *Zohar*, the great mythological text of the end of the thirteenth century.

What is the function of the sense of touch, the physical aspect of sexuality, in this erotic theology? The answer begins to take shape in the second chapter of the text directly following the author's denunciation of Maimonides and Aristotle. If these philosophers had believed in God's creation of the world, rather than its eternality, they would have had to admit that everything created had its legitimate utility and that nothing created could be contemptible or ugly. Adam and Eve were therefore not ashamed of their nakedness before they sinned, since their genitals were "like eyes or hands or the other limbs of the body." The original couple was "engaged in [contemplating] the intelligences [*ha-muskalot*], and their whole intention was toward heaven." The philosophical term our author uses and the activity he describes are remarkably similar to Maimonides' description of Adam and Eve in the Garden.[11]

For the *Iggeret*, if there was sex in the Garden, it occurred without any particular physical desire, a theme that is also found in various other medieval Jewish exegetes.[12] After eating from the tree of knowledge, however, sexuality changed: "When they strayed after bodily pleasures and did not direct their intention toward heaven, [they became aware] that they were naked."[13] Sexual shame is the *consequence* of the desire for sexual pleasure, which was evidently first produced by the fruit of the tree. In other words, the knowledge acquired by eating the fruit was physical desire, the desire that distracts from proper focus of the will upon God during the act of intercourse. Proper sex, as it was carried on before the first sin, was sex without any special physical pleasure.

In its view of sex in the Garden, the *Iggeret* was very much at home in the medieval Christian milieu. The Christian arguments were based on Augustine, who held that sex between the first couple was under the complete control of the will and without lust.[14] Although Augustine believed that the purity of this original intercourse could never be recovered, the more liberal of his medieval heirs thought that the intention to procreate might nullify the sin of sexuality. Thomas Aquinas took an even more expansive view than did the author of the *Iggeret:* he believed that sex in the Garden involved the same sensation as after, with the difference that pleasure in the first instance remained under the control of reason.

The author of the *Iggeret* solved the problem of how to get back to the Garden: one could recover that state through kabbalistic knowledge. Even after the Fall it is possible to redirect one's intention back to God during sex, to recapture, as it were, the experience of having sex as if the genitals were no different from the hands. In kabbalistic terms intercourse is the uniting of the male and female aspects of God, rather than a merely physical act. In fact, from an esoteric point of view, the secret (*sod*) meaning of carnal knowledge (*daat*) is kabbalistic knowledge. When a man understands the mystical meaning of intercourse, he transforms the act into communion with the divine: the physical becomes epistemological. In the act of reproducing, the Kabbalist also produces mystical knowledge.

Proper intercourse must therefore be divorced from the merely physical. This explains why Jewish law prescribes that the scholars (understood here as Kabbalists) have sex on the Sabbath, rather than the other days of the week, which our author calls "the days of corporeality." The Sabbath represents, kabbalistically, the tenth *sefirah*, which mediates between the supernal realm and the lower worlds. It is the day when the mystic can commune with God, since only on this day does sex transcend its base materiality and become a theurgic instrument.

But if kabbalistic knowledge allows the mystic to transcend the physical act, does this mean that the *Iggeret* should be interpreted not as an affirmation of sexuality but rather as a gnostic *rejection* of the material?[15] Such a rereading would be far too extreme; our author's much more subtle understanding of the relationship between the physical and the spiritual becomes clear from chapter 4 of the text, which treats the digestion of food and its effect on the formation of the semen. This chapter, which is generally ignored in most commentaries on the *Iggeret*,[16] contains the key to understanding the status of the physical in this kabbalistic theory of sexuality. The author raises the question of why human beings are allowed, even commanded, to slaughter animals for food when fruits and vegetables would have done as well. His answer, based on a detailed physiology of digestion taken almost entirely from Galen,[17] is that eating animals is a way of raising them to a higher level, since they are incorporated into the limbs of their eaters: what we eat becomes us.

The incorporation of food into the body of the eater reaches its end state with the formation of the semen, which is why one must digest one's food fully before engaging in intercourse.[18] Semen is the most rar-

efied element of the body, the "most clarified form of blood." Following
the homunculus theory, semen contains miniature versions of each limb
of the body. Although a material substance, it is nevertheless purified of
all physical dross. The *Iggeret* never makes this point explicitly, but it
seems that for the author semen is the mediator between the material
and the spiritual, a *res divina*.[19] All lower forms of materiality, including
both food and the actual limbs of the body, are transmuted in the seed
into a pure substance that has the capacity not only to create new life but
also to influence the very potencies of the divine.

The quasi-material, quasi-spiritual character of semen explains why it
Digestion is therefore the proper model and analogy for sexuality. Just
as the digestive system raises the meat of an animal to a higher level, cul-
minating in the formation of semen as the most clarified form of blood,
physical desire has to be transformed into spiritual intention. But digestion is not just a metaphor, since food is precisely that material substance out of which semen is made. Proper sex, one might say, is the
spiritual extension of digestion, as that which started as food becomes
semen and finally effects the union of the male and female *sefirot*.

The quasi-material, quasi-spiritual character of semen explains why it
is so susceptible to the effects of thought during intercourse. The author
of *Iggeret ha-Kodesh* is preoccupied with the power of the imagination.
Although he bases his argument on a number of talmudic passages,[20]
there can be no doubt that he was following the earlier *Baalei ha-Nefesh*
in making the psychological state of the sexual partners paramount. In
the *Iggeret*, intention (*kavvanah*) is the code word for a mystical and magical theory of thought.[21] Since the brain is linked to the upper spheres,
thoughts are more likely than physical deeds to disturb the harmony of
God's emanations. But the power of thought works in the other direction
as well: whatever one imagines during intercourse will form an impression in the semen and will reproduce the same form in the child born
from that seed. Although he does not say so, our author may have taken
this theory from the widespread medical belief, inherited from the an-
cients and repeated in later kabbalistic texts, that the semen first forms
in the blood, then passes to the brain, and finally moves through the
spinal column to the genitals.[22] Thus, if one's thoughts are directed toward heaven, the semen will be pure, but if one's thoughts are about
pleasure or the physical beauty of one's wife, then the seed will become
"smelly" and polluted.[23] The language used here is identical to that of the
mishnaic tractate Avot, but the difference is startling: for the Mishnah,
*all* semen is smelly, while for our author, the semen changes its valence
according to the thoughts of the man who produces it.

So powerful is this force that if one's thoughts are not focused on
heaven and away from materiality, one's intercourse becomes nothing
short of "destruction of seed," which in turn is equivalent to idolatry![24]
This is an extraordinary set of equivalences that effectively subverts the

traditional meanings of the terms. "Destruction of seed" was understood from the Talmud on to refer specifically to masturbation. The sexual act here *is* procreative, but what is produced is a Jew with the soul of a non-Jew (*ben nokhri*). This is because such intercourse fails to engage the divine in the procreative process, as it would do if one's theurgic thoughts were directed toward heaven. By turning an act of intercourse motivated by desire for pleasure into nothing short of idolatry, our author surely did not allay the anxieties that his readers might have felt after reading Maimonides. On the contrary, one might say that sexuality became even more problematic than it had been for the philosophers.

The centrality of thought in the *Iggeret* explains why arousing one's wife is so important for the male mystic. Since each partner is connected symbolically with the male and female *sefirot*, the thought or intention of each is equally powerful. Their thoughts must be in conjunction even more than their bodies; indeed, only if their thoughts are in conjunction and are directed toward heaven will their intercourse produce the appropriate theurgic effect. Women are, however, at once equal players in this duet and also subordinate: nowhere does our author direct his advice to women; rather, he instructs his male audience to educate their wives in proper conduct. To judge from the language he prescribes for husband and wife, the husband is not expected to turn his wife into a Kabbalist; her intention is sufficiently pure if she possesses the appropriate "fear of heaven." The Gnosis (*sod*) of intercourse remains the monopoly of the male mystic.

The commandment to give sexual satisfaction to one's wife is clearly linked to this kabbalistic theory of marital sexuality, but our author offers what seems to be a radical theory of the function of *onah*. This theory is contained in an interpretation of the story of Rabbi Eliezer and Imma Shalom to which we alluded previously.[25] Eliezer, says the *Iggeret*'s author, performed sexually with as much modesty and speed as possible such that

> he did not intend sexual pleasure alone, but rather, for him, it was like someone who engages in a craft that is not his own, an obligation that he was required to fulfill as a result of the commandment of *onah* that is spoken of in the Torah.[26]

In other words, because satisfaction of the wife is *commanded*, a man can and should have sexual relations as if alienated from himself ("a craft not his own"). The purpose of *onah* is not just to satisfy one's wife but also to constrain one's own physical desire and force one's thought to be pure. The fact that it is a commandment makes it possible to transform the physical pleasure into a desire for heaven by divorcing desire from the physical act of intercourse.

The underlying problem that preoccupied the author of our text, as it did virtually every other medieval Jewish philosopher and mystic who addressed the subject, was how to perform one's sexual obligations without experiencing distracting pleasure. At no point in this text do we find a demand to eliminate physical arousal altogether, as the canon lawyer Huguccio advocated and as we will discover in eighteenth-century Hasidism. The goal was to recover sex as it had been practiced before the first sin, when the genitals experienced no greater desire than did the hands or the eyes. Lust had to be removed from the driver's seat and, if possible, banished from the vehicle of mystical ascent. The sense of touch, or the carnal encounter between man and woman, could not be spiritualized, but it could be divested of what Augustine called "concupiscence."

In light of the elaborate instructions to regulate intercourse found in the *Iggeret* (a reflection of the enormous theological stakes involved in human sexuality), one cannot conclude that this text represents a "permissive" or "sensual" approach to the conjugal act. On the contrary, the act itself must take place within rigid boundaries; even the seemingly spontaneous way in which one arouses one's wife is highly formalized. The *Iggeret ha-Kodesh* is a sex manual, to be sure, but one aimed at a very restricted audience of male mystics who were instructed to channel their physical practices very narrowly in the service of an elite spirituality. If anything, the text may have implicitly functioned as a response to more popular erotic prescriptions such as those found in the wedding songs referred to in the last chapter. Here was advice that a mystic, bewildered by the frank eroticism of his culture, might safely follow.

The *Iggeret ha-Kodesh* has been misunderstood by modern readers looking to find something akin to a "modern" affirmation of sexuality in medieval Judaism. The interpretation presented here suggests a much more ambivalent and dialectical position and one that was very much in tune with the Christian and medical discourse of the Western High Middle Ages. In its emphasis on thought and intention, the *Iggeret* was not far from certain medieval Christian writings that drew upon the legacy of Augustine. It was also closer to the philosophical ambivalence toward sexuality than its denunciation of Maimonides and Aristotle might imply. Indeed, the text says that the words of the "wicked Greek" against the sense of touch are invalid *"in one sense [only]."*[27] They are invalid, that is, when proper intention presses the sexual act into the service of the divine, but when it does not—when physical desire becomes the driving force—our author could not agree more with both Maimonides and Aristotle.

Maimonides and our Kabbalist part ways on sexuality on the basis of an underlying theological disagreement only hinted at in the text. The author points out that Maimonides would never have denounced the sense of touch if he really believed that God had created the world, for he could not have judged any of God's creations contemptible. But behind the issue of creation lay the even more vexing question of the very nature of God. For the author of the *Iggeret ha-Kodesh*, as for all Kabbalists, God's emanations, the *sefirot*, can be known mystically, and man can interact with them by proper channeling of his physical activities, including prayers, sacrifices, and sexual intercourse. For Maimonides, however, God cannot be known at all and human physical existence is utterly incommensurate with his existence.[28] The symbolic interaction in the Kabbalah between human intercourse and divine intercourse would have been anathema to Maimonides. Thus, the issue is not two different views of the material world as such, but differing views of the relationship between the material and the divine.

## Ascetic and Erotic Kabbalism

In defending the sense of touch, albeit with many severe qualifications, our author may have been addressing other contemporary Kabbalists as well as philosophers. Two schools of Kabbalah coexisted in the thirteenth century, as later. The theosophical school, to which the author of *Iggeret ha-Kodesh* belonged, was concerned with knowledge of the *sefirot* and with how human actions might influence the divine. The other school, usually called "practical" or "ecstatic" Kabbalah, stressed the experience of the divine through a kind of mystical, prophetic communion. Adherents of this latter school did not imagine that human actions, such as sexual intercourse, might have a theurgic effect upon the *sefirot*, and their attitude toward the body was similar to that of the philosophers. Abraham Abulafia, a major representative of this approach, wrote: "Intercourse is called the Tree of Knowledge of good and evil and it is a matter of disgust and one ought to be ashamed at the time of the act."[29] Although this school used erotic symbolism as extensively as did the theosophical Kabbalists, it considered human sexuality nothing more than a metaphor for relations between God and the mystic, who was often, as in philosophical allegory, "feminized" as he was "impregnated" by the divine intellect.

But if ecstatic Kabbalah was as hostile to sensuality as were the philosophers, the theosophical Kabbalists were by no means entirely on the other side of the fence.[30] Let us turn briefly to the *Zohar* (Book of Splendor), written at the end of the thirteenth century, the *summa mystica* of theosophical Kabbalah. The *Zohar*'s ideas about sexuality do not differ significantly from those of the *Iggeret*, and, indeed, one theory holds that the *Iggeret* was written by Joseph Gikatilla, who was close to Moses de Leon, the author of the *Zohar*. The *Zohar* treats the sexual relations between the male and female aspects of God with great mythological imagination.[31] As with the *Iggeret*, it considers that proper sexual relations between the mystics and their wives produce harmonious intercourse between the *sefirot*, whereas sexual infractions arouse male and female demons to destructive deeds.

Like the philosopher Isaac ben Yedaiah, the author of the *Zohar* was particularly perturbed by sexual relations with Christian women, which may have been a social reality of his time. He condemns the practice by construing the consequences in kabbalistic terms. By "inserting the sign of the covenant [that is, one's circumcised penis] into a foreign domain," one damages the *sefirah yesod*, God's symbolic penis.[32] The divine itself is disrupted by miscegenation.

The *Zohar* carries the talmudic strictures against male masturbation to an even greater extreme—as equivalent to sex with a forbidden woman, both being forms of "destruction of seed."[33] While all other sins, including even murder, are susceptible to repentance, masturbation is beyond atonement: "What is the reason? They kill other people, but this one literally kills his own sons."[34] This unrelenting position was to have ominous consequences for later Kabbalists, who struggled with the uncomfortable notion of a sin (that, one assumes, must have been much more commonplace than murder) for which there was no repentance.

In addition to masturbation, the author of the *Zohar* had a particular obsession with nocturnal emissions. In the talmudic literature, *keri*, as it is called in Hebrew, was merely a source of transient impurity, but for our author it was evidence of intercourse with female demons: "When a man dreams in his sleep, female spirits often come and have relations with him and so conceive from him and subsequently give birth. The creatures thus produced are called 'plagues of mankind.'"[35] With these strictures against masturbation and nocturnal ejaculations, the *Zohar*, like other works of Kabbalah, vastly expanded on the sexual anxiety already present in the Talmud. Given the laws of *niddah* and the other constraints on sex incumbent on the scholar, it is likely that *keri* was a frequent occurrence, so that the *Zohar*'s condemnations must have been particularly terrifying.

Like the *Iggeret ha-Kodesh*, the *Zohar* is much more ambivalent about marital sexuality than is initially apparent. Relations between the mystic and his wife bring the female aspect of the *sefirot*, the Shekhinah, down to him, and she accompanies him when he is away from his wife.[36] Moses de Leon gives the most detailed account of why the *onah* for scholars (read mystics) must be on the Sabbath eve: as this is the night associated with the Shekhinah, it is the proper moment for aligning human intercourse with the intercourse between the Shekhinah and the male *sefirah*, *Tiferet*.

But this is only half of the story. Commenting on the verse "These are the words of the Lord concerning the eunuchs that keep my Sabbaths" (Isaiah 56:4), the *Zohar* notes that the "eunuchs" refer to those scholars who abstain from sex during the week.[37] Thus, to become a voluntary eunuch during the week is necessary preparation for sexual activity on the Sabbath. As in the *Iggeret ha-Kodesh*, the days of the week are material, while the Sabbath is spiritual, and one should therefore observe abstinence in order to avoid contamination by the forces of evil. Sexuality is, once again, to be divested of its purely physical aspect and endowed with transcendent spirituality. Abstinence for six days was as necessary to the life of the mystic as was sex on the Sabbath.[38] Taken together, the two sides of this doctrine attest to a powerful ambivalence about sexuality and a desire to reconcile the attraction of celibacy with marital obligations by subsuming the physical act of sex into a mystical theology.

Though the Kabbalists evidently found the commandment of *onah* quite troubling, they certainly could not ignore it. When the author of the *Zohar* specifically states that sex with a wife incapable of conceiving should not be understood as destruction of seed, one may infer that the idea had occurred to him, as it had to others.[39] But elsewhere he expresses his distress at the fact that Abraham and Sarah had sex when she was barren.[40] He explains that these acts of seemingly nonprocreative intercourse produced the souls of the converts, as does the intercourse of the "righteous in the Garden of Eden," a theory that explains how those born of non-Jewish parents might still receive Jewish souls and why they subsequently convert to Judaism. It is unclear whether the "righteous in the Garden of Eden" refers to Adam and Eve before the first sin or to some kind of spiritual intercourse that takes place between the righteous after they die, as one commentary has it.

In either case, the author of the *Zohar* was perturbed enough by the commandment of *onah* to contruct an ideal form of sexuality in which every act of intercourse produces some kind of progeny. In the seventeenth century, the kabbalistic moralist Isaiah Horowitz (1565?–1630) extended the *Zohar*'s comment to include all acts of nonprocreative intercourse by the righteous in *this* world.[41] One may wonder that there are not millions of converts to Judaism as a result of this mystical process! But the consequence of this bold interpretation was to transform the law requiring a man to have sex with his wife even when she is unable to conceive into a justification for procreation after all. For these mystics, sex for pleasure, even female pleasure—the commandment of *onah*—was too troubling to stand as an independent value.

An even more extreme position was taken by Moses Nachmanides, one of the most important biblical exegetes among the thirteenth-century Kabbalists. Ignoring *onah* altogether, he wrote: "Know that sexual intercourse is a matter alien and detestable to the Torah with the exception of that which propagates the species, and anything connected to it that does not lead to procreation is forbidden."[42] Nachmanides also explicitly states in his commentary on the Levitical menstrual laws that the Bible forbade sex during menstruation since it wished to permit intercourse only for purposes of procreation.[43]

This ambivalence also found expression in the theology of the thirteenth-century Kabbalah toward women. As opposed to the Aristotelian view of Maimonides, women in kabbalistic thought are no less created in the image of God than are men, since God's emanations are both male and female.[44] Although men—and male seed—are the active elements in the mystical doctrine of intercourse, women are not merely passive recipients of male seed. The feminine is given pride of place in the system of the *sefirot*, as the element that mediates between God and the world.[45] A man cannot fulfill his mystical duties without a woman, for, as noted above, she is required to bring the female element of God down upon him.

For all this, though, the Kabbalah is not a protofeminist theology.[46] As we have already seen in Abraham ben David's *Baale ha-Nefesh*, texts that appear to defend the sexual rights of women can also be quite hierarchical. The Kabbalah's own theology contains this tension in the feminine tenth *sefirah (malkhut)*. As one text in the *Zohar* points out, the nature of *malkhut* is that it has no stable identity but instead reflects the configuration of powers above it, sometimes loving and sometimes angry.[47] According to the alignment of the other *sefirot* and the consequent power of the evil "other side," *malkhut* can be transformed instantly from the "tree of life" to the "tree of death." In mythological terms, *malkhut*, or Shekhinah, is at once the Great Mother and the Devouring Goddess, the nurturing power of fertility and the violent demoness of destruction. Oscillating between positive and negative poles, she is the very definition of ambivalence.

This mixed attitude toward women should not come as a surprise. The Kabbalists' interest in incorporating a female dimension into its image of God resembles in many ways the contemporaneous new cult of the Virgin Mary as a part of the Christian pantheon.[48] But as opposed to medieval Christian mysticism, which involved both men and women, the Kabbalah was exclusively a movement of men. Although its theology was far from that of a purely male, patriarchal God, anxieties about women and sexuality were nevertheless woven in brilliant colors into its mystical tapestries. There is no better symbol for the ambivalence of these Kabbalists than their mercurial image of the feminine element of divinity.

What can we learn about the actual lives of the mystics from their teachings? One recent scholar, noting that, as far as we know, all the Kabbalists were married or at least regarded marital sex as legitimate, has argued that they "can hardly be regarded as persons who employed sexual metaphors as a compensation for the frustration of 'real' erotic experiences."[49] This seems to me highly debatable. It is very difficult to determine exactly how to understand Kabbalists (or for that matter others who employed erotic symbolism in their theology). When a writer refers to the relation between God and a mystic as like that of the "desire of a bridegroom for his bride,"[50] or when the Song of Songs is turned into a set of mystical symbols,[51] what is the status of the human experience upon which the analogy is based? If a mystic is married, does he translate his own sexual experience into a mystical theology or does he substitute the latter for the former? Is human sexuality an analogy for a process within the divine, or is it an allegory emptied of physical content?

As our analysis of the *Iggeret ha-Kodesh* and other mystical texts of the thirteenth century suggests, the Jewish mystics did not renounce human sexuality in favor of a spiritualized erotic relationship with God, but neither did they embrace it unambiguously. Although we know little of Moses de Leon's personal life, the image of the mystic as a "eunuch" for the six weekdays who then has sex on the Sabbath hints at a real personal struggle with the sexual obligations—and pleasures—of marriage. Isaac of Acre, de Leon's contemporary, reveals something of these tensions in a passage on the biblical Jacob:

> I saw it said in the matter of our father Jacob, that when he was still with the physical Rachel outside of the Land [of Israel], his soul was not united with the supernal Rachel, whose domicile is in the Land of holiness, but as soon as he came to the Holy Land, the lower Rachel died and his soul communed with the upper Rachel.[52]

This kabbalistic text immediately brings to mind the midrashim on the celibacy of Moses and Noah. It would seem to contradict the *Zohar's* idea of the mystical ménage à trois between the Kabbalist, his wife, and the Shekhinah. Instead, for those who wish to emulate Jacob, the physical and the spiritual remain very separate realms, divided like the borders between the Holy Land and the rest of the world. The physical experience of sexuality thus remained very present for these mystics as they searched for an erotic relationship with God, but it had become a source of deep anxiety and ambivalence.

## The Later Career of Mystical Asceticism

The kabbalistic doctrines we have pursued remained the property of small, sectarian groups who circulated their manuscripts from hand to hand. Following the expulsion of the Jews from Spain in 1492, the mystics carried these texts in their baggage, as they, like the other Spanish Jews, flooded the countries bordering the Mediterranean, as well as Holland, Germany, and even Poland. In the century following the expulsion, a small, but highly dynamic community of such mystics formed in the little town of Safed in the north of Palestine.[53] Here, they were to develop a set of new speculations, building upon the work of the earlier Kabbalists. These ideas, in turn, began to circulate throughout the Jewish world and became by the seventeenth century perhaps the most widely accepted theology of Judaism.[54] Thus, the ideas we have charted were to become central to the consciousness of a large proportion of the Jewish people, even if their mystical subtleties remained the province of an intellectual elite.

Perhaps as a result of the intense messianic expectations and the unique communal character of mystical practice in Safed, asceticism in general and sexual renunciation in particular held great attraction, indeed, were taken to an extreme. The earlier theoretical doctrines were turned into communal and household rituals, which created a need for teachings that would instruct disciples in how to apply kabbalistic doctrine to their everyday lives.[55] Elaborate penances were prescribed for all manner of infractions, rivaling those of the medieval Ashkenazic pietists. These penances were accompanied by kabbalistic explanations of how particular transgressions affected the *sefirot*.[56]

In addition, the *musar* (ethical) literature and other writings produced by these Kabbalists detail much more explicit accounts of personal experiences and practices than had previously been described. Where earlier mystics generally effaced their own lives from their writings, the Safed Kabbalists were much more open to discussing the relationship between the personal and the cosmic. In this feverish mystical atmosphere, the personal struggles of the leaders of the community seem to have become part of the public discourse.[57]

The *Maggid Mesharim* of Joseph Karo (1488–1575) is an extraordinary example of this type of autobiographical expression. Karo, one of the greatest figures of medieval rabbinic Judaism, authored the *Shulhan Arukh*, which was to become the definitive code of Jewish law. But he was also a mystic who received communications over a good many years from a *maggid*, or revelatory voice, which claimed to be the personification of the Mishnah (the first collection of Jewish law).[58] The *maggid* typically admonishes Karo for failing to live up to the severe ascetic ideals then current among the Safed brotherhoods. Karo's relationship to his *maggid* has definite erotic overtones; his biographer has speculated that the *maggid* represented a demanding mother figure for whom Karo had unresolved Oedipal feelings.[59]

Karo's autobiography also includes revelations about his own sexual life. Following earlier kabbalistic teachings, he believed that his wives (he had three over his lifetime) protected him from demonic powers. He relates that one night he had a nocturnal emission, which the *maggid* blames on his having passed by a monastery. But he is able to rescue himself an hour later by having intercourse with his wife.[60] Such emissions must have been common enough for those who practiced sexual renunciation even beyond the requirements of the menstrual laws. Isaac Luria, perhaps the preeminent Safed Kabbalist, shared Karo's concern and was reported to have had intercourse with his wife every night just after midnight in order to avoid nocturnal emissions.[61] What an extraordinary inversion in which a doctrine of sexual asceticism requires frequent sex!

Even though the *maggid* compliments Karo on restoring his purity by having intercourse with his wife, the text nevertheless voices considerable unease over marital sex. The *maggid,* for instance, reveals to Karo that his third wife was really a male scholar reincarnated as a woman—she cannot therefore be his real mate. Given her former identity, Karo is warned that he should treat her with great respect and "be ashamed of having intercourse with her for pleasure."[62] The *maggid* then stammers and fails to reveal the wife's true former identity. Perhaps the gender switch was a way of neutralizing female sexual attraction, or, alternatively, perhaps it reveals latent homosexuality. Whatever was the case, the *maggid*'s sudden stammer suggests that Karo's relations with his wife were a source of great conflict for him.

In a fascinating extension of the sexual taboos, Karo refers to *all* physical pleasures as sexual infractions (*gilui arayot*).[63] Small wonder that when he came to compose his monumental code of Jewish law, Karo should have taken one of the most extreme positions on male sexuality, forbidding any male pleasure as sinful.[64] Despite the preachings of the *maggid,* he eliminates the husband's desire to avoid sin as a reason for intercourse, as well as the benefits to one's health. He defines the frequency listed in the Talmud as the *maximum* allowable, rather than, as Rabad had argued, a minimum that the woman could exceed.

Karo's dour view was very much in agreement with a prevalent opinion in Safed. Hayyim Vital (1542–1620), the main compiler of Isaac Luria's teachings, took the prescription of weekly sex for scholars to an extreme by decreeing that "it is *forbidden* for scholars to have sexual intercourse on any of the days of the week and it is only permitted to them on the eve of the Sabbath."[65] The *Zohar*'s celebration of the "eunuchs" who voluntarily refrain from sex during the week is here turned into a commandment.

Vital also struggled with the problem of nonprocreative intercourse (as when a woman was pregnant or lactating) that could only serve the woman's sexual needs. Although the law of *onah* required affirmation of such intercourse as both permitted and required, Vital argues that a man might refrain from it with the consent of his wife, since "the sexual union of the supernal world takes place by itself, without any action from below,"[66] a position that would seem to contradict the *Zohar*. Vital brings reports from others who "observed signs" that Isaac Luria himself refrained from the commandment of *onah* when his wife was unable to conceive, although Vital's own observation of his teacher did not bear this out.

The problem of sexual pleasure also worried Elijah da Vidas, who composed a massive work of kabbalistic *musar* entitled *Reshit Hokhmah* (The Beginning of Wisdom). Quoting extensively from *Baale ha-Nefesh* and the *Iggeret ha-Kodesh*, he declares: "If, God forbid, he should think of vain pleasure during this act, the garment of his spiritual soul will be found in the realm of the evil inclination."[67] Yet the sin of Adam has clothed man in a material body that necessarily experiences pleasure, making it impossible to anesthetize one's sensations totally. Da Vidas therefore explains that sexual heat is appropriate if it comes from the supernal world: male sexuality comes from above and it is the mystical function of one's wife to send it back to its source in the *sefirot*. In a similar way, Isaiah Horowitz warned that one should be careful not to arouse evil desire for one's own pleasure.[68] But like da Vidas, he also developed a complicated dialectical doctrine in which one "should seize the evil impulse in order to fulfill the good."[69] These often contradictory doctrines testify to the struggle of these Safed mystics to strike a balance between severe asceticism and the requirements of marriage.

The Safed Kabbalists exhibited great concern with actual sexual practices. In 1548 a woman came to the court and testified that her husband had had anal intercourse with her. The court, which included Joseph Karo, expelled him from the land of Israel, despite the much more permissive talmudic law. One Kabbalist who reported the case devoted a lengthy passage of an ethical treatise to explaining why the correct interpretation of the Talmud should be much stricter than either its literal meaning or the earlier Ashkenazic understanding of it.[70]

An even greater concern was masturbation. Hayyim Vital decreed that masturbation is the only sin for which minors are liable, since, by his accounting, the biblical Er and Onan were only seven.[71] Vital also listed a variety of elaborate penances for different masturbatory techniques and fantasies.[72] Isaiah Horowitz also tried to show that, despite the contrary stance of the *Zohar*, repentance is possible for this most grievous of sins.[73] Building on the belief that the sperm is born in the brain and travels through the spinal cord to the genitals, he argues that this sin involves the *whole* body (as opposed to other infractions involving only a single limb), and thus the whole body must do penance. Perhaps influenced by views such as these, the Kabbalists produced a profusion of books about the perils of masturbation and nocturnal emissions with titles such as

*Penitential Remedies for the Impairment of the Sign of the Covenant.*[74]

If the body and its desires posed a knotty challenge for the sixteenth-century Kabbalists, at least the realm of the spirit promised solutions. Karo's often erotic relationship with his *maggid* suggests that the competition between one's earthly wife and personified female spirits became even sharper in the sixteenth century than it had been earlier. The Sabbath rituals in Safed included processions and hymns to welcome the Sabbath Bride, with the mystics playing the role of the bridegroom. Solomon Alkabez's popular Sabbath hymn "Lekha Dodi" is a classic example of this practice.

Like Karo's Mishnah, the spiritualized women in these mystical romances were often the very texts that the mystics studied. Following earlier kabbalistic exegesis, Alkabez composed a commentary on the Song of Songs, which he interpreted as an erotic dialogue between the Torah and its mystical lover.[75] One of the popular *musar* manuals of the period, Eliezer Azkari's *Sefer Haredim* (literally Book of the Anxious), states: "Behold the Torah, she is the wife God has given thee ... and the other wife is of flesh and blood.... The King, blessed be he, commanded us to love her [too], but the real love should be for the former."[76] Human sexuality may be the model for the secrets of supernal intercourse, but it is decidedly inferior. Thus, Horowitz contrasts sexual desire, which ends after intercourse, with desire for God, which results in a permanent union.[77]

Philosophers and mystics in the High Middle Ages had struggled with the conflict between body and soul, but they had rarely envisioned a totally disembodied existence. Their descriptions of the Garden of Eden typically refer to Adam and Eve as possessing bodies, even though their bodies might not have experienced lustful desire. But there was a competing tradition that went as far back as the talmudic period and that also appeared in the thirteenth-century Kabbalah. In this view, the body of the primordial Adam was a luminous ether;[78] and after death, the material body would be replaced once again by this ethereal "astral" body.

These notions took on an urgency in the apocalyptic atmosphere of Palestine after the Spanish expulsion. Abraham Azulai, who lived in Hebron in the seventeenth century, spoke of the eschatological future when "men will divest themselves of their material bodies and ascend to the mystery of the [spiritual] body which Adam possessed before the fall."[79] Isaiah Horowitz popularized an old theme in Jewish literature, one that also had Christian associations: he referred to death as the liberation of the soul from the pollution of the body; this, he suggests, was the state of the first human beings before they sinned.[80] Solomon Alkabez maintained that Moses' body was already spiritual while he was alive,[81] which correlates nicely with the midrashim about his state of permanent celibacy.

What we have found in the small, but extremely influential town of

Safed is the radical working out in mystical brotherhoods of the ascetic tendencies that had come from medieval Spain and Provence. These practices were to have an enormous impact on the mass pietistic movements of Poland in the eighteenth century and, beyond, to the images of traditional Judaism in the modern period. And, in the early Zionist communes of twentieth-century Palestine, which may have taken the name "kibbutz" from the Safed Kabbalists,[82] a secular version of this mystical asceticism was to compete with an ideology of erotic liberation.

## The Sabbatian Heresy

Safed Kabbalism was to produce another, perhaps even more bizarre by-product before it reached the modern period. In the 1660s a messianic movement gathered around a Kabbalist from Jerusalem named Sabbatai Zevi.[83] Based on various motifs in the earlier Kabbalah, the Sabbatians believed that the advent of the Messiah meant that a higher, "spiritual" Torah would now be revealed. After the putative Messiah was forced to convert to Islam in 1667, the Sabbatians developed an antinomian doctrine of "redemption through sin," which sought to justify the Messiah's entry into the domain of evil. Some of the more radical followers of Sabbatai Zevi, including a group in eighteenth-century Poland, decided to emulate him by violating the law themselves.[84]

This antinomian doctrine naturally enough had erotic reverberations, some of them real and others in the imaginations of the opponents of the Sabbatians. In fact, many of the reports about Sabbatai Zevi place him initially squarely within the traditions of sexual asceticism. According to one extraordinary story, "when he was six years old, a flame appeared in a dream and caused a burn on his penis; and dreams would frighten him."[85] Like other Kabbalists, he was tormented by sexual temptations and engaged in severe ascetic practices, which, like the dream, were designed to eradicate desire. Legends claimed that he did not consummate his three marriages. In addition, he apparently married the Torah in a wedding ceremony in Salonika, thus making concrete one of the various spiritualized erotic fantasies.[86]

As the eschatological expectations of the movement escalated, however, these ascetic practices gave way to the beginnings of sexual libertinism. Rumors circulated that Sabbatai's third wife, Sarah, had been a prostitute, and after their marriage, there were other rumors that she had committed sacred adultery.[87] At one point, Sabbatai called women to the reading of the Torah and allegedly organized a banquet at which men and women sat together. He himself met privately with his two divorced wives, also a violation of sexual etiquette. His biographer, Gershom Scholem, believes that he may have intended to institute a real change in the traditional status of women, although how many of these reports are fact and how many fiction remains unclear.[88]

One anonymous Sabbatian text, the *Gali Razaya*, was fascinated by the marriages between biblical heroes and foreign women such as Judah and Tamar, Moses and Zipporah, Samson and Delilah, Boaz and Ruth, and Joshua and Rahab (the latter is midrashic): "The souls of these women are descended from the pious Gentiles and the pious Gentiles thereby acquire a share in the world to come because they mingle with Israel."[89] Because women are under control of the *sitra ahra*, the realm of evil, these women provide points of contact between the great souls of Israel and the demonic world. This radical Sabbatian author thus resurrected the sexual subversions of the biblical text and at the same time undermined the strict legal segregation of Jews and Gentiles.

There can be no doubt that Nathan of Gaza, Sabbatai's first disciple and the theoretician of the movement, entertained ideas of sexual liberation. He thought that with the coming of the Messiah, the Tree of Life replaced the Tree of Knowledge. In the mystical world of this higher tree, the prohibitions on incest no longer exist.[90] Equally startling is his bold declaration, which brings us back full circle to the *Iggeret ha-Kodesh*:

> The patriarchs came into the world to repair the senses and this they did to four of them. Then came Sabbatai Zevi and repaired the fifth, the sense of touch, which according to Aristotle and Maimonides is a source of shame to us, but which now has been raised by him to a place of honor and glory.[91]

Although he must have been aware of the *Iggeret* and its claim to have saved the sense of touch from the onslaught of the philosophers, Nathan attributes this innovation to Sabbatai Zevi. In accordance with the Lurianic kabbalistic meaning of "repair" (*tikkun*), what Sabbatai and the patriarchs before him did was to rescue the sparks of holiness from the material senses and restore them to their divine source. Only in messianic times might the sense of touch—that most material of senses—be rescued from the realm of evil.

Nathan is very perceptive in his understanding of the relationship of the Kabbalah to eroticism and to the material world. Far from celebrating a "positive and natural attitude toward sexuality,"[92] the earlier Kabbalists could only be ascetic, just as Sabbatai Zevi himself was until he revealed his messianic vocation. In its frank eroticism, Sabbatianism was, then, not so much the direct product of the Kabbalah as its dialectical negation, in which the urge toward sexual renunciation was turned into its opposite. Only with the coming of the messianic age might the sensual, now liberated from evil materiality, be indulged in all its antino-mian possibilities.

This revolutionary outburst, with its inversion of asceticism into sex-ual license could not, however, be long maintained. With the pietistic movements of eighteenth-century Poland, the asceticism of the Kabbalah was once again given pride of place, but now, for the first time, in the context of a mass religious movement in the Ashkenazic world.

# The Displacement of Desire in Eighteenth-Century Hasidism

N the waning years of the eigh-
teenth century, David of Makov, a follower of the great Lithuanian rabbi
Elijah, the Gaon of Vilna, wrote a devastating critique of Hasidism, the
pietistic movement that was sweeping the Jewish communities of Eastern Europe. Among his many accusations, he counted the sexual excesses of the ecstatic Hasidim:

> The Hasidim commit the sin of involuntary ejaculation at all times during
> their prayer, for they deliberately give themselves erections during prayer
> according to the commandment of Rabbi Israel Baal Shem [the founder of
> Hasidism], who said to them that just as one who engages in intercourse
> with an impotent organ cannot give birth, so one should be potent at the
> time of prayer and, in prayer, it is necessary to unite [sexually] with the
> Shekhinah [the female emanation of God]. It is therefore necessary to move
> back and forth as in the act of intercourse.[1]

In the view of this enemy of Hasidism, prayer for the new populist mystics was not merely analogous to an act of intercourse, as it had been for
many earlier Kabbalists; it had become scandalously equivalent. The
characteristic swaying of the Hasid at prayer was imagined to be intercourse with the female emanation of the divine itself, and so great was
the arousal that it might culminate in ejaculation. What had been
metaphorical and symbolic in the past had become literal.

The bitter hostility between the adherents of this new movement of religious revival and their opponents (known as *mitnagdim*) was no doubt
responsible for the unrestrained style of this polemic. With its courts of

miracle-working holy men (zaddikim—literally righteous) and their far-flung adherents (Hasidim), Hasidism was considered a threat to local rabbinic power. It is not unusual for new religious movements that challenge existing power structures to arouse sexual anxieties, as if sexual license must necessarily accompany a revolt against authority. Sexuality came to embody the critique of Hasidism as a whole, as a coarse, lower-class movement of illiterates. But did our author, and others like him, make up their accusations? Was Hasidism a movement of sexual rebellion against the strict standards of medieval kabbalistic *musar*? Or, conversely, were such accusations baseless calumnies, with Hasidism of the eighteenth century representing, instead, the extreme sexual abstinence with which it has come to be associated among the ultra-Orthodox Jews of today?[2] Or, finally, did the truth lie somewhere in between?

Hasidism did have a major impact on the sexual and marital attitudes of Eastern European Jews, but the story is complicated: the stance of Hasidism on sexuality captured in an extreme way the dualism of the rabbinic tradition as a whole and the ambivalence of the mystical tradition in particular. There is an affirmation of sexuality, but it is transferred to the relationship between man and the divine realm. Hasidism made God the object of erotic desire and constructed an affective community of male companions around a charismatic leader. This eroticized community in turn had a direct impact on Hasidism's construction of human sexuality. In its attitude toward relations between men and women, Hasidism radicalized some of the ascetic tendencies in earlier traditions and introduced the most extreme antierotic values ever to appear in any Jewish texts, values that in some respects resemble Christian monastic renunciations of sexuality. On the threshold of modernity, then, one finds one of the most widespread movements of sexual asceticism in Jewish history.

Nonetheless, like all of the movements and cultures we have dealt with from the Bible on, Hasidism cannot easily be reduced to a monolithic doctrine. Since Hasidism was less a unified movement than it was a loose association of autonomous sects, each following its own zaddik, a comprehensive theory such as the one just proposed can always be refuted by counterexamples. I shall present some of these other positions alongside those that support my thesis. Hasidism was a dynamic movement, and by the second half of the nineteenth century, it was much more conservative than it had been in its first hundred years. As a result, it drifted closer to the mainstream medieval rabbinic attitudes that it could not entirely replace. More recently, some of the better-known sects, especially the Habad or Lubavitch Hasidim, have been sufficiently influenced by modern ideas to present themselves in ways even more remote from their origins. Our interest here, however, is in the major theological tendency in the Hasidic movement in its first fifty or seventy-five years, when it revolutionized attitudes toward sexuality within broad sectors of the Ashkenazic culture of Eastern Europe.

## Sexual Radicalism and the Background to Hasidism

Hasidism must be understood as a response to the crisis that engulfed Polish Jews in the eighteenth century. The flourishing world of the Eastern European Jews was shaken to its core by the great massacres perpetrated by the Ukrainians in their revolt against Polish rule in 1648–49. Although precise statistics are hard to come by, many tens of thousands of Jews were killed by the Ukrainians then and during the wars of the following two decades. By the eighteenth century the community had begun to rebuild itself, but the Polish state continued to weaken, finally succumbing to its powerful neighbors in the three partitions of the last quarter of the century. The proud institutions of Jewish autonomy were eroded during this process and, in 1764, the Council of the Four Lands, the supracommunal governing body of the Polish Jews, was disbanded. As the Jewish population increased in this period, many moved out of the old towns owned by the nobility to the countryside and thus escaped from the authority of the established communities.[3]

This disintegrating society was ripe for religious renewal. Throughout the eighteenth century and into the nineteenth, a variety of new movements and sects emerged to fill a vacuum that must have seemed both spiritual and political. These included followers of the seventeenth-century Messiah, Sabbatai Zevi; an ascetic movement of preachers and miracle workers; the Lithuanian yeshiva movement; the *musar* teachings of Israel Salant; the Eastern European Jewish Enlightenment (Haskalah); and Hasidism itself. These movements typically featured new authority figures who directly challenged or replaced traditional figures. The zaddikim who led the Hasidic sects were perceived by both their followers and opponents as replacing rabbinical authorities. But even the heads of the Lithuanian yeshivot, a movement that ostensibly constituted a conservative response to Hasidism, took on many of the charismatic features of the Hasidic zaddikim. The forces of tradition felt compelled to adopt the tactics of their enemies, precisely because authority had become so problematic in the fractured Polish Jewish community.

Sexual experimentation is often a feature of religious upheaval, a way of shattering the oppression of the everyday world in the quest for spirituality. This experimentation can often take contradictory forms that nonetheless serve the same purpose. On the one hand, it may manifest itself as antinomian permissiveness, in which all repressed desires are allowed expression. On the other hand, it may take on the form of sexual asceticism. This "coincidence of opposites" may actually exist in social practice, or it may be the product of the imaginations of observers who believe asceticism to conceal its opposite, as in the case of the polemics against Hasidism. Whether or not sexual excesses actually took place in eighteenth-century Poland, the anxieties of the age led observers to believe that it was widespread, a sign, evidently, of the breakdown of authority.

The vestiges of Sabbatianism, which had already gained a reputation for sexual license in the seventeenth century, attracted similar notoriety in the mid-eighteenth century. Some areas of Poland had already succumbed in the 1660s to the worldwide messianic movement of Sabbatai Zevi, and in the 1750s a Polish adherent of Sabbatianism, Jacob Frank (1726–1795), led a radical, heretical cult that ended up converting to Catholicism.[4] The Frankists were accused of sexual excesses not unlike those attributed to the Hasidim. According to testimony brought before a rabbinic court in Satanow, the group danced around naked women, kissing their breasts. Some confessed to adultery and promiscuity. As with the accusations against Hasidism, so those leveled against the Frankists accused them of sexual depravity committed in the name of ritual, as expressions of an antinomian theology. Since the sources for these rumors and confessions were anti-Frankist, the truth about Frankist practices may never be fully known. Again, whether fabrication or fact, the accusations stand as compelling evidence of the sexual obsessions of the period.

Although the vestiges of Sabbatianism had resonance for some, a much more widespread movement, which emphasized asceticism, emerged in the early part of the century. Based on the kabbalistic *musar* tradition, this movement was less a product of messianic ideas than of the particular social and religious needs of the lower middle class. Moving into a spiritual vacuum, a variety of itinerant preachers and mystical magicians, all peddling alternatives to the classical regimen of talmudic study, swarmed about the countryside.[5] This movement, which preceded Hasidism, may also have been influenced by Ukrainian pietistic sects, particularly in the Carpathian mountains, in which holy men gathered disciples and engaged in ascetic practices, often by secluding themselves on mountaintops. The stories of the Baal Shem Tov, the founder of Hasidism, resemble the legends about these Ukrainian preachers, but the Baal Shem Tov was not the only Jewish counterpart to these Christian ascetics.[6] It is likely, indeed, that Hasidism, both in its social structure and in its teachings, was part of this larger pietistic groundswell in the remote regions of eighteenth-century Eastern Europe. In the parlous conditions of life in eighteenth-century Poland, many Jews were attracted to severe asceticism as the route to religious perfection. Yet they were also taken with the bold call to transform evil into good by confronting the evil instinct on its own terms. Baruch of Kosov (d. 1795), a contemporary of early Hasidism, typifies this ambivalence in his discussion of how the spiritually elevated soul experiences sexual pleasure:

> I was once listening to a humble man bemoan the fact that sexual union naturally entails physical pleasure. He preferred that there be no physical pleasure at all, so that he could engage in union solely to fulfill the command of his creator.... In accord with his words, I composed a simple explanation of the saying of the rabbis, may their memory be a blessing, "Everyone should sanctify himself during sexual union." ... I concluded that the meaning of this sanctification is that one should sanctify his thought, excluding from thought any intention of feeling one's own physical pleasure; one should bemoan the fact that feeling such pleasure is inherent to this act....
>
> Sometime later, however, God favored me with a gift of grace, granting me understanding of the true meaning of sanctification during sexual intercourse: the sanctification derives precisely from feeling physical pleasure. This secret is wondrous, deep and awesome.[7]

We note that Baruch articulated this position in response to a question from a "humble man," suggesting that we are dealing here with a popular urge for asceticism that sought legitimation from a spiritual authority. In his response, Baruch takes the ascetic tendency in the *musar* tradition to an extreme: the spiritual goal is to eliminate sexual pleasure. But his later position also draws upon another kabbalistic notion: the use of pleasure for a spiritual purpose.[8] Baruch, then, reflects the struggle between these two competing conceptions of sexual pleasure, one severely ascetic and the other dialectical, but both rooted in the earlier kabbalistic literature. Hasidism in turn fell prey to the same struggle.

The religious turmoil in the middle of the eighteenth century produced some very radical figures, whom the opponents of Hasidism sometimes confused with the Hasidim themselves. One such figure was Leib Melamed.[9] Expanding on earlier traditions of "transgressing for the sake of repentance,"[10] Leib Melamed advocated radical use of sexual temptation:

> I say that it is proper to stand at the time of ritual immersion. Believe me that once I stood while a woman immersed herself and I saw "that place" [that is, her genitalia] and it was like seeing nothing and afterward, when I left the place, a spirit of great holiness came down on me.[11]

It is unclear just what kind of *mikveh* (ritual bath) may have occasioned this particular practice. Perhaps men and women bathed in the same *mikveh*, separated by some kind of divider. Thus, "standing" would make it possible to see naked women in the bathhouse.

Another passage recounts the following tale of temptation:

Once I was alone with a woman and she was lying naked on a bed and she asked me to "be with her." But I did not heed her words and I only contemplated her flesh and her great beauty until a spirit of holiness came upon me and told me to desist. Therefore, it is proper for a man when he sees a woman to have great desire for her, but nevertheless not to have intercourse with her, but rather to contemplate her and look at her intensely and he will pass the test and rise to great [spiritual] heights.[12]

In both texts Leib first recounts a personal experience and then draws a didactic conclusion from it. Even if all these accounts were the inventions of an anti-Hasidic author, they testify to a powerful urge to imagine scenes of temptation rather than just denounce a radical teaching: the anti-Hasidic polemicists were as concerned with sexuality as they alleged the Hasidim were. Whether or not such events ever took place, the text becomes its own provocation: the author of the polemic transforms the visual into a powerful verbal form of temptation.

Leib applies this doctrine of visual temptation to prayer. His statement bears a striking resemblance to the quotation at the beginning of this chapter:

One should imagine during prayer that a woman stands in front of him and then he will rise to a great height.... One is even permitted to have an ejaculation as a result of the great arousal of prayer.[13]

Here the spiritual purpose of the sexual arousal—unification with the feminine principle of the divine—has been subsumed by the doctrine of overcoming temptation: it is a woman of flesh and blood who constitutes the vehicle for achieving spiritual heights.

To what extent were Leib Melamed's teachings unique? It is clear from other eighteenth-century sources that a rather wide group of preachers not associated directly with Hasidism flirted with religious radicalism.[14] One anti-Hasidic text reports a case that allegedly came to a rabbinic court; it concerned several men who secluded themselves with a married woman and afterward came to a rabbi to perform penitence (a case that resembles narratives from *Sefer Hasidim*). The rabbi, following the talmudic precept on returning to the scene of temptation (b. Yoma 86b), instructed them to return to the same place and to the same woman, but this time to resist the temptation. But instead, they had intercourse with the woman and, according to the text, died as a result of their sin.[15]

Perhaps this case was also a fictional construction. But the belief that such practices were widespread in eighteenth-century Eastern Europe led Ezekiel Landau, the great legal authority from Prague, to comment that most of the world is mistaken in thinking that the prohibition on secluding oneself with a woman applies only to an actual deed [that is, intercourse] ... but this is not correct, for even if no thought of transgression crossed his mind, if he was with a woman forbidden to him, this is already a transgression against the laws of the Torah.[16]

This was, then, a culture caught between severe ascetic practices on the one hand and dialectical dances with temptation on the other—with both approaches preoccupied with the dangers of sexuality. Was this preoccupation greater in the eighteenth century than it had been earlier in the Jewish Middle Ages? It is difficult to judge. But it would seem that the predilection for radical solutions became more widespread as the esoteric teachings of earlier authors found greater popular resonance. With Hasidism, this concern with sexuality found a social framework in a movement of teachers and disciples.

## The Problem of Jewish Adolescence in Eighteenth-Century Poland

The eighteenth century saw the spread of sexual ideologies and theologies to large groups of people, indeed, to whole social movements. No longer were such ideas confined to narrow groups of intellectual elites. The new religious movements, in search of adherents, framed their teachings and practices around the issues of personal concern to their audience. This process may or may not have been conscious, and it may have emerged out of a complex interaction between the movements' theorists and the largely unarticulated desires of their followers. I believe that many of these movements of reform attracted their followers as adolescents, often newly married, and that much of their ideologies and theologies were shaped to address the problems of this particular group of young male Jews.[17] This is not to suggest that the sexual dilemmas of Jewish adolescence were new to the eighteenth century; rather, the breakdown of authority at that time made sexual behavior much more problematic than it had been before.

Since the early Middle Ages, the Jews of northern Europe who could afford to married their sons off very young, frequently at age thirteen or fourteen and sometimes even younger—this possibly in imitation of the nobility. The responsa literature over the course of centuries contains case after case of children married as minors, under thirteen for boys and under twelve for girls. A distinct split developed between the Sephardic and Ashkenazic legal traditions about how to handle these "child marriages." In general, the Sephardic authorities, following Maimonides, tended to invalidate such marriages when the boy was under age, while the Ashkenazic tradition tried to find legal devices for affirming them.[18] Early marriage was clearly a practice that had become intrinsic to the culture of the northern European Jews, so that there was great pressure to accept even marriages between minors. The Jews of the Mediterranean, by contrast, tended to contract marriages when the men were a good deal older, so their legal tradition was largely spared the problem of accommodating a prevalent but problematic social practice.

By at least the eighteenth century, early marriage had become a thing of the past for the Jews of Germany and the areas immediately to the east such as Bohemia and Silesia.[19] One reason for this change was the rise of absolutist states, which sought to regulate Jewish marriages, something medieval rulers had left in the hands of the Jewish communities. During the eighteenth century laws were passed in places like Bohemia to force the Jews to marry in late adolescence. In response to such legislation or rumors of such legislation, a number of waves of "panic marriages" swept Jewish communities, as parents sometimes married off their children as virtual infants.[20]

In Eastern Europe, the age of marriage, especially among the elite, remained very young throughout the eighteenth century, and it became one of the marks that distinguished the *Ostjuden* (Eastern Jews) in the eyes of the German Jews. A number of Central European rabbis from the period noted that their cousins to the East married at uncommonly young ages, writing as if these Jews were from some exotic tribe.[21] The early age of Jewish marriage also attracted much unfavorable comment from non-Jewish Enlighteners, occasioning a medical theory that such marriages made the Jews hypersexual.[22] The Haskalah, or Eastern European Jewish Enlightenment, treated the traumas of early marriage as a touchstone for the oppressiveness of traditional Jewish society. Even within traditional Jewish society itself, the practice of early marriage came increasingly under challenge. In 1793 the communal council of the Lithuanian Jews banned child marriages altogether.[23] An admittedly nonstatistical survey of the responsa literature from Eastern Europe suggests that many more cases reached the courts in the eighteenth century than in earlier periods.[24]

A celebrated case from eastern Galicia in the 1760s suggests the extreme sexual tensions that might be generated by such marriages.[25] A twelve-year-old boy was married to a girl of the same age and forced by family pressure to have sexual relations with her in order to consummate the marriage. During the act, a member of the household, presumably waiting with bated breath outside the room, knocked on the door, thus causing the young boy to have a premature ejaculation. Their attempt at sex thus aborted, the two subsequently refused to approach each other, and shortly before his fourteenth birthday, the boy disappeared. Although the rabbi, Ezekiel Landau, found it impossible to nullify the marriage and thus allow the girl to remarry, his framing of the narrative and the comments he appended at the end of the responsum on the practice of such child marriages convey his sympathy for both the boy and the girl.

This case suggests that at least some couples experienced sexual trauma as a result of early marriages. This is not meant to imply that such was true of all marriages; on the contrary, there is evidence that some were very successful. For instance, a case from about the same time and place tells of a minor boy who has sexual relations with his young wife on a number of occasions even though the two continued to live with their respective parents.[26] There is no evidence of coercion and one has the sense that relations between the two followed an entirely accepted pattern. Similarly, Glückel of Hameln reports in her famous memoir of her very successful relationship with her husband, even though they were married in early adolescence.[27] Cultural expectations certainly shaped the way many individuals adapted to their early marriages.

Nevertheless, we see from Landau's case that early marriage could exert sexual pressures and cause severe anxiety. We cannot say how the girl responded, but it would seem that the boy had more options. The eighteenth century offered men organized alternatives to the pressures of family life, whether in the court of the Hasidic zaddik or in the study hall of the yeshiva; it had less to offer women.

For young newly married men, the new movements seemed to address the anxieties of early marriage: not only did they offer a legitimate place to which to escape but they also provided ideologies that justified such escape. Eliezer Zweifel, a moderate nineteenth-century Enlightener who wrote one of the first relatively unbiased accounts of Hasidism, observed that most of those who came to the zaddik were newly married young men.[28] Obsessed with the "sins of youth" (that is, masturbation and nocturnal ejaculations), these teenagers found in the zaddik a model of sexual purity and abstinence: in eighteenth-century Poland the connection was close indeed between sexual anxiety and the search for new forms of authority.

Hasidic sources themselves confirm this connection between an ideology of sexual abstinence and an audience of teenagers. Menachem Nachum of Chernobyl, for instance, advocated intensive study immediately following marriage, but "study" as it came to be understood in Hasidic practice also meant regular and prolonged attendance at the court of the zaddik:

This was in order to break down desire by means of circumcising the heart, setting their moral lives aright and especially uplifting any fallen love through the study of Torah.... After these qualities were in their proper place, they returned home to produce offspring, fulfilling this commandment of their Creator just like any other, filled with love of God and with nothing extraneous.[29]

The audience for such a text would clearly have been newly married teenagers in turmoil over the sexual demands of marriage. The term "circumcision of the heart," taken from Jeremiah, is especially pointed, for it appears to be a metaphorical play on the philosophical belief that circumcision lessens sexual desire. Following talmudic dicta, study of Torah serves as an anaphrodisiac. But while the rabbis of the talmudic period may have been ambivalent about sexual desire within marriage, Menachem Nachum is utterly negative. Marriage may be necessary for procreation, but it appears almost as threatening as bachelorhood, since the newlywed experiences sexual desire for his wife! Only an immediate cold shower in the house of study—or the court of the zaddik—could inoculate him against such temptation. The later Hasidic master Mendel of Kotzk (1787–1859), perhaps the most extreme ascetic in the whole history of Hasidism,[30] agreed with this prescription. He, too, urged that young men come to his court immediately after marriage, so that when sexual desire was at its peak, he could crush it once and for all.[31] In these statements, we have evidence of a powerful ideology of sexual renunciation, shaped in response to the perceived problems of Jewish adolescence.

## The Teachings of the Baal Shem Tov

Hasidism developed in the middle of the eighteenth century in the context of the wider pietistic movement of its milieu. Despite its proper image as a revolutionary movement, Hasidism actually took a conservative position with respect to these radical preachers. The circle of Israel Baal Shem Tov (the founder of Hasidism, who died in 1760) rejected the radical doctrine of actively seeking out temptation in order to achieve spiritual elevation. Jacob Joseph of Polonnye, one of the Baal Shem Tov's closest associates and the author of the first published Hasidic text, explicitly labeled these practices "heretical."[32] Some from this circle seem to have evolved their own teachings on prayer in almost explicit opposition to the visual temptations sought out by those like Leib Melamed. Instead of imagining a woman during prayer, one must strive for the opposite: "I heard from Nahman [of Kosov] that in order to avoid developing an erection, he would imagine God standing in front of him [as if] visually portrayed."[33]

The Baal Shem Tov himself took a moderate position on asceticism. His teachings, as reported by some of his disciples, would seem to affirm the physical against the severe practices of renunciation followed by many of the itinerant preachers: "It is better to serve the Lord in joy, without self-mortification."[34] The Baal Shem Tov's doctrines of joy in prayer and of "uplifting sparks" belong to the dialectical school of Kabbalah in which the material is transmuted into the spiritual and evil into good: "Every *mitzvah* or act of holiness starts with thoughts of physical pleasure,"[35] and "it is proper for a man to have physical desires and out of them he will come to desire the Torah and the worship of God."[36] Rather than merely suppressing such desires, the Baal Shem Tov taught, one should elevate or transform them, for they are in fact useful or even necessary tools for achieving spiritual transcendence.

The second doctrine of Baruch of Kosov, according to which sexual pleasure is the source of sanctification, thus made its way into the circle of the Baal Shem Tov in the doctrine of using the physical as a stepping-stone to the spiritual. An example of this doctrine applied to sexuality is in the commentary of Benjamin of Zalozce, a member of the Baal Shem Tov's circle, on the Song of Songs: "If you wish to adhere to God with some form of worship, allow yourself some kind of material desire and lust."[37] Here is an interpretation that reconnects the allegorical theology of the Song of Songs with actual sexuality. According to this aspect of the Baal Shem Tov's teaching, neither the body nor women are to be regarded negatively. Thus, the Baal Shem Tov is said to have treated the second wife of his companion Nahman of Kosov (no relation to Baruch) with great honor, "since she merited to lie next to so holy a body for some years, she herself is worthy of respect."[38] Here the woman gains in status because of her physical relations with her husband: the body conveys spirituality.

The earliest concern of Hasidism was with "wayward thoughts" (*mahshavot zarot*), primarily sexual, especially during prayer.[39] The Baal Shem Tov was less concerned with actual physical temptations than with thoughts and fantasies. This emphasis on thoughts rather than deeds appears in a striking teaching about involuntary seminal emissions (*keri*):

> One should not worry over an impure accident, an involuntary emission not occasioned by any wayward thought or fantasy, for if he had not had the emission, he would have died, but he was saved from death because the evil departed from him.... For if the emission comes to him without any fantasy, it is good.... Therefore, one should only worry if one has not purified one's thought.[40]

In light of the increasing anxiety since the thirteenth century over such involuntary emissions, the Baal Shem Tov's teaching was nothing short of revolutionary, and his disciples soon reverted to the more traditional thinking on the subject.[41] For the Baal Shem Tov, though, the emission by itself is a form of purification of evil that otherwise would have caused death. The danger lies in one's thoughts. Thus, an emission before one's thoughts are purified is ominous, but it is salutary afterward.

This teaching expands on the kabbalistic doctrine of intentionality. The degree to which these inner states are dissociated from the physical world becomes especially clear in another text, also attributed to the Baal Shem Tov: "When a woman begins to fantasize about a man, a fantasy about the woman arises in the man, and when the woman is modest and does not fantasize about the man, he does not fantasize [either]."[42] Aside from holding women responsible for male fantasies about women, what is new here is the lack of any visual contact between the two: the fantasies are conveyed "telepathically."

Sexually illicit thoughts must be elevated to their divine source. Here is a particularly striking passage from Menachem Nachum of Chernobyl, based on a teaching of the Baal Shem Tov:

> We have to raise up our love to the Love above.... This the Baal Shem Tov ... said on the verse "If a man takes his sister, that is *hesed*" [literally "grace" but in context "disgrace"; Leviticus 20:17]. This refers to fallen love and it has to be uplifted. The wicked and the foolish say that they can do nothing about ... bad love.... They say that this evil love has come into the body from God Himself, like a fetus into a full belly.... But what did God answer...? In the moment when that bad love comes to you, you should be taken aback and tremble greatly before the Lord.... Then you begin to make this love resemble the Love above, saying "is this not fallen from that higher Love, the quality of Abraham [that is, the *sefirah hesed*, also known as "love"]?"[43]

The Hasidim agree with the "wicked and foolish" that thoughts of incest are a degenerate form of supernal love, a "fetus into a full belly," in the colorful phrase of the text. This image may well be drawn from the talmudic belief that a woman can become pregnant during pregnancy and, if she does, the second fetus will crush the first "like a sandal."[44] Thoughts of incest are therefore dangerous to the gestation of legitimate spiritual love. But as opposed to their foolish opponents, the Hasidim believe that this superfluous fetus can be purified from its evil form and returned to its proper place in the divine world of the *sefirot*. By doing so, the Hasid "gives birth" to a purified thought.

## Ascetic Reaction

The Baal Shem Tov's doctrine of using material desire as the basis for achieving spiritual desire for God would seem to affirm the erotic, and some of his followers understood him in this way. But there were those among his most influential disciples who rejected this understanding of his teaching in the half century after his death. They returned to the more ascetic tendencies in sixteenth-century Kabbalah and in the contemporary Polish *musar* movement.[45] Even Menachem Nachum of Chernobyl, who might generally be grouped with the less ascetic disciples, laid the groundwork for the new asceticism in passages such as this:

> It sometimes happens that a person feels himself to be in a fallen state, overtaken by the negative side of his own inner qualities, especially by improper love in the form of sexual desire. *This may even happen when the desired sexual act is a permitted one.* Such a person should know that heaven desires to uplift him, using his own natural emotions in order to open his heart to the love of God.... He must use that arousal of love itself for the love of God. This may be done even if a person in fact has to fulfill his conjugal duty.... Even then he may perform only for the sake of his Creator, fulfilling this commandment as he would those of *tzitzit* [the ritual fringes on garments] or *tefillin* [phylacteries], making no distinction at all between them, and not seeking to satisfy his lust.[46]

Any sexual desire, including that toward one's wife, exists only as an instrument for uniting with God. Even permitted sexual acts must be divorced from desire; or, put differently, the fantasies and emotions connected with sexual arousal must be transformed into a spiritual love of God. By doing so, the act itself becomes like the performance of any other commandment, rather as the earlier Kabbalists had described sex in the Garden of Eden: the genitals experienced no greater sensation than did the hands.

In this teaching, the doctrine of using the material world to attain spirituality begins to reflect very negatively on the material. In fact, the question of just what Hasidism thought of the material world has been one of the most controversial issues in twentieth-century scholarship of Hasidism. Martin Buber understood the Hasidic phrase *avodah be-gashmiyut* (worship through the material) to indicate a positive relation to the everyday world.[47] Gershom Scholem argued against Buber that Hasidism sought to "annihilate the material" (*bittul ha-yesh*) by raising the divine sparks back to their source.[48]

Scholem based his interpretation primarily on the teachings of Dov Baer, the Great Maggid (Preacher) of Mezeritch (d. 1772), whose followers created the institution of the Hasidic court. The Maggid, as he is known, introduced into Hasidism a much more radical antipathy to the material world than had obtained in the teachings of the Baal Shem Tov. In his reworking of earlier Jewish mysticism, the only true reality is found in the Platonic forms of the *sefirot,* and the material world is an evil realm that must be eradicated by the appropriate spiritual activities. The process of uplifting sparks annihilates the material shells (*kelippot*) and returns the sparks to their divine source, which is the mystical realm of "nothingness."[49]

Scholem's interpretation of Hasidism would seem to be particularly accurate for the Maggid's teachings about sexuality. According to the Maggid, "during the act of intercourse a man must become nothing,"[50] meaning that one should transcend one's materiality and unite with the divine realm of nothingness. Elsewhere, he gives a kabbalistic interpretation to the talmudic dictum "a man has a small organ: if he leaves it hungry, it is satisfied, and if he satisfies it, it remains hungry." He concludes that "even during intercourse," one should ignore the physical in favor of the spiritual.[51] These teachings were not universally accepted by all Hasidic sects, but, because the Maggid developed a circle of disciples who themselves founded sects, his radical ideas formed the basis for a whole school that dominated early Hasidism.

An elaboration of the Maggid's doctrine can be found in the writings of his disciple Elimelech of Lyzhansk (1717–1787). Commenting on the verse from Genesis 4:1, "And Adam knew his wife Eve and she became pregnant and gave birth to Cain," Elimelech offers a radical reading of the word "knew."[52] If the Bible had merely wanted to indicate intercourse, it would have used the phrase "to come into," but the "carnal knowledge" implied by the word "knew," says Elimelech, is profoundly negative. While the appropriate method for engaging in sex is for a man to think only of the upper world and "not to know that he is even with his wife," Adam "knew" that he was with Eve and therefore the product of his intercourse was Cain, the "nest of evil."[53] Adam's sin was not sexuality per se but experiencing desire and pleasure during the act. The consequence of this sin was a cosmic catastrophe that can only be corrected by the proper sexual practice of the righteous, by which Elimelech meant the Hasidic zaddikim.

Mendel of Kotzk echoed this interpretation. Mendel understood the biblical prohibition on adultery to include relations with one's own wife, if they involved sexual desire![54] Mendel's views resemble those of the ascetic extremists who preceded the Baal Shem Tov: sexual desire has no positive function and must be ruthlessly suppressed. Mendel also understood the Hasidic custom of wearing a ceremonial belt (*gartel*) to be a physical sign separating the sexual lower body from the spiritual upper body. Before Adam made himself a belt (Genesis 3:7), his sexual impulses ruled him, and he ate from the fruit of the tree.[55] Like Elimelech, Mendel held that Adam's fall was due to lack of control of his sexuality, a defect that could now be corrected by proper Hasidic asceticism.

Nahman of Bratslav (1772–1810), the great-grandson of the Baal Shem Tov, developed an even more radical position on the sexuality of the zaddik. The "true zaddik" (by which Nahman meant himself) experiences pain rather than pleasure in the act of intercourse:

> Copulation is difficult for the true zaddik. Not only does he have no desire for it at all, but he experiences real suffering in the act, suffering which is like that which the infant undergoes when he is circumcised. The very same suffering, to an even greater degree, is felt by the zaddik during intercourse.[56]

Once again, circumcision stands for the excision of sexual pleasure, but even more, it represents genital pain, perhaps, if one may speculate, castration fear. Nahman's teaching dates from the period shortly after his marriage at age thirteen. Is it possible that his claim represents the deliberate conquest of desire or, rather, the transformation of his own sexual anxiety into a doctrine? In either case, the hagiographical text in which this statement appears claims that Nahman intentionally sought out temptation in order to overcome it:

> When he was still very young, at the time when a person's blood boils, he suffered countless trials in this regard. It was within his power to satisfy his desires and he was in very great danger. But he was a great hero and he succeeded in overcoming his passions several times. Nevertheless, he would not seek to avoid being tested further.... On the contrary, he longed to be tested and would pray to God that He try him once again. He did this because he strongly believed that he certainly would not rebel against God.[57]

Although Nahman does not spell out just how he sought out trials, it would seem that he may have known something of the *musar* doctrine of deliberately seeking out temptation in order to overcome one's desire. According to his biographer, Nahman succeeded so well in suppressing sexual passion that he said "'for me, male and female are exactly the same,' which is to say that he had no special thought when he saw a woman."[58] Living several decades after the Maggid and his disciples, Nahman seems to have been keen on asserting that he, the "true zaddik," had achieved the supreme indifference to sexuality that the earlier masters had only preached.

Nahman believed that the sexual transgressions—and especially nocturnal emissions—encompass all the other transgressions of the law. By performing acts of redemption (*tikkun*) for these transgressions, it is possible to redeem the whole person. For Nahman, this doctrine of a "general *tikkun*" (*ha-tikkun ha-klali*) had messianic meaning: it could lead to the national redemption of Israel and, beyond that, to the redemption of the cosmos.[59]

Nahman seems to have taken his concept either directly or indirectly from Sabbatian or Frankist sources.[60] He believed himself able to redeem the sexual transgressions of the Sabbatians by imitating and transforming their very own practices. Since he judged these transgressions to be part of Sabbatian messianic doctrine, he thought that he could fulfill their messianic mission by inverting their teachings. Nahman's extreme asceticism was therefore prompted on the theoretical level by the sexual excesses of the Sabbatians, but it also had its roots in his own biography as the scion of a great Hasidic family.

Such hostility to pleasure during the act of sexual intercourse certainly had a long history in medieval Judaism, as we have seen, from the earlier philosophers and mystics to the "humble man" who lamented to Baruch of Kosov about the physical pleasure connected with sexuality. Even so, Elimelech's reading of the Garden story appears to be one of the most extreme in the whole tradition, one that resembles the teachings of some of the more ascetic church fathers. Similarly, Nahman of Bratslav's doctrine of sexual suffering goes beyond anything we have previously encountered. Because of the commandments to marry and procreate, Hasidic ascetics like Elimelech and Nahman could not easily prescribe celibacy. Instead, they opted for a much more difficult and radical procedure: fulfilling the commandment to engage in intercourse, but without desire and physical pleasure. The zaddik was to restore the sexual act to its primordial spirituality.

Such a negative attitude toward sexuality was often bound up with frank expressions of misogyny.[61] Hasidism adopted many of the earlier demonic images of women that are scattered through kabbalistic and other Jewish folklore. Because sexual pleasure was so problematic, women had to be turned into nonarousing objects. Like Menachem Nachum, the Maggid compared sexual relations to putting on phylacteries (*tefillin*), chosen by both of them, perhaps, because they involve the physical attachment of an object that does not arouse any erotic or pleasurable feelings.

> One should love one's wife the way in which one loves one's *tefillin*, for one loves them [as an instrument] for fulfilling the commandments of God. One should not think about her [physically]. This is analogous to one who travels to market day and he needs a horse to make the journey. Should he therefore love the horse?... Similarly, in this world, a man needs a wife in order to perform the work of the Creator for the sake of the world to come and if he should leave aside this work in order to think about her, he is committing a great foolishness.[62]

The instrumental view of women expressed in this text is among the most extreme to be found in the Jewish tradition.

Because sexuality was so threatening, women were held guilty by association, serving as metaphors for sexual contamination. Consider this text from Elimelech of Lyzhansk: "[A man] must repair ... the sin of his youth [that is, the sin of masturbation], which is called by the name of the feminine [*nekevut*] and afterward he will arrive at supernal holiness, which is called by the name of the masculine [Aramaic *dukhra*]."[63] Thus, the polluting sin of masturbation is associated with the feminine, while purity and holiness are associated with the masculine. By extension, sexuality as a whole might be seen as feminine, since the feminine is connected to the material, while the masculine represents transcendence of the material—that is, celibacy. While some Jewish Hellenists as well as early Christians sometimes advanced such an equivalence between men and renunciation of sexuality, one searches in vain for such an extreme position in any rabbinic or medieval Jewish text.

This association between spirituality and male celibacy is supported by the extraordinary case of Hannah Rokhel, the "Maid of Ludmir" (1815–95), who functioned for a period as a female zaddik.[64] Rather than proving that Hasidism provided a spiritual place for women, as certain sentimental admirers of Hasidism have claimed, her case suggests exactly the opposite. Hannah Rokhel evidently underwent a psychological breakdown as a result of the death of her mother. She broke off her engagement to the boy she had loved since childhood and began to act like a man, praying and following commandments that pertain only to men. She attracted a group of followers, but, like her contemporary Mendel of Kotzk, she secluded herself and only spoke to them through a closed door. When she was finally persuaded to marry at age forty—that is, to behave like a woman—she lost her following, even though she refused to consummate the marriage and was soon divorced. Hannah Rokhel's attraction for her Hasidim and the danger she posed to the male zaddikim who forced her to marry lay in the perceived paradox of the soul of a male saint residing in the body of a woman. Celibacy was a necessary feature of this paradox. As in some strains of early Christianity, she could achieve authority only by denying her gender. Once it became clear that she really was a woman, she could not be perceived as holy.

## Celibate Marriages

It was one thing to teach that sexual relations within marriage must be carried on without pleasure and quite another actually to achieve it. The unbearable tensions generated by this doctrine pushed some toward a different practice, reminiscent of early Christianity: vows of abstinence within marriage after fulfillment of the commandment to procreate. The legal precedent for taking such vows was, of course, very ancient: it was already discussed in the Mishnah. We have seen how many Babylonian rabbis would absent themselves for long periods from their wives, despite earlier legal prohibitions from doing so. This practice reflected the severe conflict between the duty to study and marital obligations. The talmudic rabbis took vows of abstinence primarily in order to pursue study, rather than to avoid erotic pleasure altogether. Certain earlier mystics, particularly from the Safed school, were also occasionally attracted to abstinence for reasons closer to those of the Hasidim. But in Hasidism, stories of marital celibacy took on a value and a resonance that cannot be found in any earlier Jewish movement.

Many of the tales of marital abstinence appear in the Hasidic hagiographical literature and are therefore primarily of didactic rather than historical value. One story of the Baal Shem Tov that appeared in the first edition of the early-nineteenth-century hagiography *In Praise of the Baal Shem Tov* relates that the founder of Hasidism abstained from sex with his wife for the last fourteen years of her life: "I heard that when the Baal Shem Tov's wife died, his followers and those of his generation suggested that he remarry, but he replied to them in wonder: 'Why do I need a wife? For the last fourteen years I refrained from sleeping with my wife and my son Hersheleh was born by the word.'"[65] Evidently scandalized by even the suggestion of the Christian notion of immaculate conception, the editors of the text omitted this story from later editions.

An elaborated story of such marital abstinence is told of Abraham the Angel, the son of the Maggid of Mezeritch.[66] His angelic quality evidently refers to his renunciation of sexual relations with his wife. Married at thirteen, he "raised his voice in a great cry that it was impossible for him to humiliate himself with an act of physical intercourse, and from this crying, his bride fainted and was ill for a long time." According to some sources, he abstained from sex with her for most if not all of their twelve years of marriage. A similar story is related of the early nineteenth-century zaddik, Israel of Ruzhin (1796–1850).[67] Also married at thirteen, he left his wife because he desired to live like the talmudic celibate Ben Azzai. His mother went to Abraham Joshua Heschel of Apt, another Hasidic master, to complain, and the rabbi promised that her son would yet have children. At another time, the rabbi of Apt wondered whether he had done the correct thing: "Who knows if I will not be punished for having brought down a holy soul like this one into the realm of this world?" Yet another extreme exemplar of a Jewish version of Christian monasticism was Mendel of Kotzk. According to his Hasidim, Mendel stopped living with his wife after his wedding, and after the birth of his son, he separated from her entirely for the next twenty-five years.[68]

These stories of abstinence within marriage seem to valorize the practice, but a careful reading of some of them reveals the great tension that lay just beneath the surface of Hasidic culture. For example, despite the singular importance of marital celibacy in Kotzker Hasidism, the story of Mendel's separation from his wife contains a twist: when his first wife became ill and died in 1837, the doctors blamed it on his ascetic behavior. Since the story stems from a hagiography of Mendel, it clearly preserves a hint of the ambivalence about extreme sexual renunciation in even so strict a sect as this one.[69]

Two stories in the hagiographical *In Praise of the Baal Shem Tov* are similarly ambivalent. The text's version of the story of Abraham the Angel relates a dream by Abraham's wife after his death. She sees him in a great hall sitting with venerable old men, perhaps representing the older generation of zaddikim. Abraham says to these authorities: "Here is my wife, may her days be long. She has a grievance against me because I maintained excessive abstinence. Her complaint is just. I ask her forgiveness before you." She replies: "I forgive you with all my heart." He then vows to provide all her needs if she does not remarry, and her anger against him is dispelled.[70] This story preserves traces of male guilt about the practice of celibacy within marriage. The story is attributed to Abraham's wife, and it glorifies her as a clairvoyant who can avert catastrophes through her visions. Lest we think, though, that a woman could have the same status as a male zaddik, the end of the story intimates that Abraham's wife enjoys her powers because of the celibate relationship between them. This is not a normal marriage: she retains her spiritual gifts even after his death, *and* acquires material wealth by remaining celibate. The story therefore voices resistance to marital celibacy, but it subverts that position by affirming both the supernatural and material advantages to be gained by sexual renunciation.

Another tale in the same collection expresses similar anxieties about vows of abstinence.[71] The Baal Shem Tov claims to have clairvoyantly intuited that an "impression" of adultery hangs over his brother-in-law, Rabbi Gershon. Gershon hotly denies the accusation and strikes his brother-in-law, but the Baal Shem Tov then has another vision, which confirms his initial intuition:

That night, the Baal Shem Tov, in his *yihudim*,[72] saw what Rabbi Gershon had done. The following day, he said to him: "You took upon yourself a vow of abstinence from your wife, and I heard in heaven that Moses Maimonides interpreted it and said: 'It is as if he said of his wife that she is as his mother.'[73] Although it is not a binding vow, the impression of accidental seminal emission [*keri*] which you attempted to absolve by fasting from Sabbath to Sabbath was raised against you. Moreover, because you did not keep your vow of abstinence, the impression against you became more severe so that I perceived it as adultery."

Rabbi Gershon confessed the truth. He did not keep his vow of abstinence because he wanted to go to the Holy Land and his wife would not agree since he would be away from her. Therefore, he did not keep abstinent. Both of them worked to redeem this act until they succeeded. From that union was born the maggid of the holy community of Ladyzhin, about whom the preacher of the holy community of Polonnoye [that is, Jacob Joseph] said that he never experienced an involuntary emission.

The spurious quotation from Maimonides suggests that a marriage without sex, in a sense, turns the husband into a child in relation to his wife. Could this reflect some kind of wishful fantasy of return to the pre-sexual innocence of childhood? Or does it merely turn the wife into a forbidden relation? In either case, Gershon could not attain this state. By remaining with his wife at her behest instead of going to the Holy Land, he fails to remain celibate. The wife here represents an ever-present sexual temptation that makes such vows extraordinarily difficult to maintain. Once he took his vow, Gershon essentially relegated his wife to the status of a forbidden woman, either his mother or, to infer from the accusation of adultery, another man's wife. Forbidden fruit is more passionately desired than what is permitted! Unable to maintain his vow, Gershon fails in two ways: he has an involuntary emission *and* he has intercourse with his wife. But in classic Hasidic fashion, these sins can be turned into the basis for holiness. Gershon and the Baal Shem Tov perform a procedure of redemption (*tikkun*), and the child that is born of the "forbidden" intercourse between Gershon and his wife becomes a holy man who never has an emission. The sins of the father are expressly *not* visited on the son!

Like the story of Abraham the Angel and his wife, this text is both a criticism and an affirmation of the practice of celibacy within marriage. Vows of abstinence cannot be easily kept and wives cannot be relied on to acquiesce in them. Those who take such vows place themselves in danger of transgressions that are, like adultery or incest, sins much worse than the violation of a mere vow. But if the transgressions can be properly repaired, the result is even greater sexual purity. We cannot be sure whether the struggle reflected in narratives like these last two hints at actual conflicts experienced by the Hasidim—conflicts between impossible erotic ideals and the demands of flesh and family.

Despite the appeal of such vows of abstinence, most Hasidic masters were careful to warn against the practice. Perhaps this is the covert motivation of the following commentary by Jacob Isaac, the Seer of Lublin, on God's command to Abraham to leave his home and go to the land of Canaan:

> "Go from your country," [Genesis 11:21] this means that you are to go away in your thoughts from your corporeality... "And from your kindred"—that you should not wish to occupy yourself with procreation and cohabitation ... "and from your father's house" —that you should not think at all of relationship and kinship" ... "to the land that I will show you"—this means, even though it was your wish to go and refrain from corporeality, for on the contrary, you should understand that it is His will that you should occupy yourself with corporeality also.[74]

Just as Abraham is told to leave the land of his family and come to the land God will show him, so the Hasid must leave the material world and then return to it on a new plane.

How did these stories function within the Hasidic communities? It is unlikely that many, if any, of the disciples of the zaddikim followed such practices, and it is not known for sure whether the zaddikim themselves did. Similarly, we have no way of knowing whether the average Hasid tried to eliminate pleasure from his sexual relations. Perhaps these were not doctrines to be emulated at all but were, rather, ideals projected onto the zaddikim. In Hasidism, as often with charismatic movements in general, the cultural or religious hero became the locus for the followers' conflicting values and desires—values and desires that were, in turn, conveyed by the teachings of the leaders themselves.

## The Erotic Theology of Hasidism

The very idea of celibate marriage was highly problematic in Judaism, for it stretched not only the letter but also the spirit of the law. In Western Christianity the practice had been a well-established alternative to total renunciation of marriage until the twelfth-century reforms that dissolved all clerical marriages. For these Catholics, the doctrine of celibacy solved what was to become a thorny problem for some Protestants. German Pietism, the Protestant mystical movement that emerged shortly before Hasidism (and whose doctrines bear some resemblance to those of Hasidism)[75] was plagued by the tension between marriage and mysticism. When Gottfried Arnold, one of the leading theologians of Pietism, decided to marry, another pietist theologian considered his marriage an adulterous betrayal of the divine Sophia.[76]

In this respect, Hasidism did indeed resemble German Pietism, for the

drive toward sexual asceticism within marriage was very much the product of a mystical theology that emphasized the erotic union between the
Hasid and God. Following earlier kabbalistic sources, this unification
(*devekut*) was described in Hasidic literature in highly erotic language—
in stark contrast to the hostility of many Hasidic authorities toward
human sexuality.[77] Instead of human sexuality serving as the hand-
maiden of the *hieros gamos*, one senses a kind of competition in Hasidism between the sexual demands of the divine and the sexual demands of one's wife. To marry and engage in a full sexual life seemed to
the Hasidim, as to some German Pietists, nothing short of adultery
against God, just as the Baal Shem Tov is said to have perceived Rabbi
Gershon's violation of his vow of abstinence as a kind of adultery.

The mystical theology of Hasidism therefore created a demand for
sexual displacement from the human to the divine. Consider, for instance, a comment by Jacob Joseph of Polonnye, one of the less ascetic of
the early Hasidim, on the mishnaic law that "a women is betrothed in
three ways: through money, written deed, and intercourse" (m. Kiddushin 1:1).[78] One must start with the material ("money," which stands
for desire for women), rise to the study of Torah ("written deed"), and
conclude with spiritual unification with God ("intercourse"). Intercourse
here means *spiritual* intercourse with God, the exact opposite of a carnal
act of intercourse. Indeed, the sole purpose of the exercise is to transform the desire for sexual intercourse into intercourse with the realm of
the spirit. In this way, sexual asceticism becomes the necessary companion for an erotic theology.

A parable of erotic desire attributed to the Baal Shem Tov captures
this uneasy relationship between physical and spiritual sexuality:

> A king had a son whom he wanted to teach various wisdoms that are neces-
> sary [for a prince]. He hired a number of scholars to study with him, but
> the prince did not learn anything. Finally, the scholars despaired of ever
> teaching him and only one of them remained with him. One day, the prince
> saw a young maiden and desired her beauty. The scholar complained to the
> king about this, but the king said: "Since he has experienced desire, even in
> this way, through his physical desire, he will attain all wisdom." The king
> summoned the girl to court and instructed her not to allow herself to be se-
> duced by him until he had acquired one teaching. And so she did. After-
> ward, she demanded that he learn yet another teaching until, in this way,
> he had finally acquired all of them. Once he became wise, he came to de-
> spise the girl, for he intended to marry a princess of his own station. The
> meaning of the parable is clear.[79]

If the prince is supposed to be a Hasidic holy man, the class difference
between him and the girl suggests immediately that earthly love is not

appropriate to his spiritual station. He must marry a princess of his own rank: the Shekhinah. His powerful physical desire for the girl nevertheless serves a positive function in the tale. It is used to trick him into learning wisdom until he finally learns enough to overcome his physical needs. (This is the opposite of what happens in the talmudic story of a man whose passion for a certain woman threatens to kill him. There, we recall, the rabbis forbid him even to see her across a wall, since sexual desire has been "taken from those who practice it lawfully and given to sinners.")[80] Consonant with the doctrine of "annihilating the material," the Hasidic parable teaches that the only legitimate function of the physical is as a vehicle for its own elimination. The process of achieving transcendence does not, however, require first satisfying or indulging one's desires; on the contrary, the girl repeatedly withholds herself as a way of enticing the prince to achieve more and more wisdom until he no longer desires her.[81]

To understand the parable fully, it is not sufficient to translate it into a set of abstract mystical symbols; it must also be understood in its concrete human context, which can best be recaptured by reading it from the woman's point of view. The girl has only an instrumental function, just as the Maggid and Elimelech, among others, reduced the wife of the zaddik to the functional equivalent of the *tefillin*. *Her* desire for the prince receives no mention, and she is cast off when he achieves transcendence. To be sure, she is not the same as the Hasidic wife, since she is the agent who actively promotes the prince's spiritual progress. But the subtext of the parable is clear: only by renouncing women and erotic pleasure in this world can the male adepts achieve their spiritual analogues in the world above.

The displacement of eroticism onto theology was not new with Hasidism. We have already seen the remarkable role that erotic theology played in the Kabbalah, in which human sexuality parallels and influences sexual relations between the male and female aspects of God. What is new here is the singular emphasis on sexual relations between the mystic and God in opposition to human intercourse. Conjugal relations might be the starting point for this theological unification, but they had to be emptied of all earthly content.

In addition, Hasidism often spoke of erotic relations between the Hasid and God quite apart from the marital bed. For example, in the court of Baruch of Medzibozh, the grandson of the Baal Shem Tov, the reading of the Song of Songs became an erotic experience of unification with God:

And when [Baruch] read the [Song of Songs] with great passion and desire, the Hasid said to Rabbi Zvi [of Ziditshov, with whom he had come to the court of Baruch] that his mind had become confused from the fire that burned inside him and when he came to the verse "his banner of love was over me ... because I am sick with love," it seemed to him as if a fire actually burned around him and he fled, for he could not withstand the great and awful fire.[82]

One usually thinks of the allegorization of the Song of Songs as a process by which it lost its erotic force in favor of more "lofty" virtues, but here the allegory aroused a sexual response no less powerful than that aroused by a literal reading of the text. The love song between God and Israel had now become a poem of sexual relations between the Hasid and the divine.

The teachings of the Baal Shem Tov himself appear to be the source of this explicit erotic theology of prayer:[83]

> Prayer is a form of intercourse with the Shekhinah and just as in the beginning of intercourse one moves one's body, so it is necessary to move one's body at first in prayer, but afterward one can stand still without any movement when one unites with the Shekhinah. The power of his movement causes a great arousal, for it causes him to think: "Why am I moving myself?" [And he answers himself:] "Because perhaps the Shekhinah is actually standing in front of me." And from this great power, he comes to a great passion.[84]

We have here striking corroboration of the anti-Hasidic accusation cited at the beginning of this chapter that the Hasidim act in prayer as if they are having intercourse with the female emanation of God. There is, to be sure, no talk here of erections or ejaculations, as in the more radical versions of Leib Melamed or David of Makov. But the language is so explicitly erotic that it is easy to see how an author hostile to Hasidism might construe the teaching literally.

In particular, unification with the Skekhinah seems virtually equivalent to orgasm—orgasm associated with death, however: "It is only out of grace from God that man remains alive after prayer, since, from a physical point of view, he should die, for he loses all his life force in prayer."[85] If sexuality on the human plane was perceived as threatening, how much more so was intercourse with God Herself! What a challenge to a virile, young Hasid to conquer the Shekhinah and survive. Might this not be the spiritual version of the male fantasy of seducing an insatiable, seemingly unattainable erotic woman, in this case, literally a goddess?

The association between sexual asceticism and erotic theology is well known from the history of religions, and particularly from Christian asceticism. It is not surprising that celibate monks and nuns might develop powerful erotic feelings for the Virgin Mary or Jesus. It is more surprising to find such ideas in a movement in which virtually all men were married. While neither asceticism nor a theology of eroticism was without precedent in earlier Judaism, Hasidism took them to a radical extreme and gave them a social setting for the first time.

## The Hasidic Court and Anti-Hasidic Polemics

Hasidism made God the object of desire for the purpose of constructing a community of ecstatic worshipers. This male fellowship of the temporarily celibate became the social setting for a powerful erotic theology. The displacement of sexuality from the human to the divine realm must surely have spoken directly to the hearts of those in search of personal and theological answers to the issues raised by early marriage. The zaddik served in loco parentis in a society that banished boys from their parents' house to spend their adolescent years in the families of their in-laws. In search of figures of authority, they turned to the leaders of the new movement, leaders who also provided an ascetic alternative to the sexual anxieties of Jewish adolescence. Because the court was often a considerable distance from their homes, the Hasidim came to experience two very different realities: the family, on the one hand and the intense, celibate male companionship of the court, on the other. I do not mean to suggest that this was necessarily the predominant or conscious reason for the appeal of Hasidism or that all Hasidim had problematic marriages. But in a society in which older forms of authority were waning, more and more teenagers must have failed to find adequate traditional answers to their developmental problems. As an ideological or theological movement that addressed the specific problems of Jewish adolescence, Hasidism, like the other new movements of its time, played a major role in creating the definition of such an age category, which had not existed in quite so clear a way earlier.

We have already noted that some Hasidic masters advocated pilgrimages to the Hasidic court immediately after marriage. Mendel of Kotzk urged his followers to spend at least a year at a time, if not more, in his court. For most of the other sects, absence from home was usually shorter, but it still involved at least several pilgrimages a year, usually on holidays or the Sabbath. With travel, such visits might take up considerable periods of time. The court system thus created a new form of Jewish geography in which the spiritual and emotional center of gravity might lie at some considerable distance from home.

In the courts of its zaddikim, Hasidism constructed an alternative world to the world of family and community in traditional Ashkenazic society. The displacement of sexuality from the human to the divine be-

came, in effect, the theological analogue for the physical displacement of
the Hasid from his family to the court of the zaddik. Nevertheless, in a
culture that still paid legal homage to marriage and procreation, the
court system necessarily created problems for family life. Nahman of
Bratslav, despite his personal ascetic tendencies, was evidently troubled
by the consequences of these new social arrangements:

> It is common for the relations between [our young men] and their wives to
> deteriorate. They separate for a while and sometimes this results in the
> complete breakup of the marriage, Heaven forbid. [Nahman] said that this
> was due to the activities of Satan who is particularly concerned to spoil the
> domestic harmony of young men, so that they fall into his trap by means of
> this.[86]

Nahman assumed that the extended absences from their wives created
sexual temptations for the young men, and he evidently did not believe
that the ascetic practices he prescribed for himself would work for his
Hasidim. But surely the teachings of sexual renunciation must have had
a profound impact on the Hasidim to the point where many of them, too,
wished to strive for the celibate spiritual heights attained by their *rebbe*!

Nahman of Bratslav was not the only one to perceive the threats to the
stability of the family. The opponents of Hasidism were quick to note the
social consequences of Hasidic teachings, and their polemical literature
is filled with accusations that the Hasidic court system was destroying
the Jewish family: "The Hasidim cause girls to cease procreating since
they ensnare the souls of the husbands from their wives and [the wives]
sit as grass widows, while their sons grow up like sheep without a shep-
herd."[87] Viewed from the perspective of the wife and children of the
Hasid, the picture was grim:

> When the visits of the husband to the zaddik became known to his wife and
> sons, they began to cry out bitterly. She bewailed the husband of her youth
> who had left her like a widow, and her sons cried that they had been left as
> orphans, for their husband and father had gone a long distance away and
> had taken a bundle of money in his hands, leaving them bereaved and
> alone, swollen with hunger.[88]

While these descriptions are typically hyperbolic, they no doubt contain
a considerable kernel of truth. Lacking direct sources, we can only imagine that many wives of Hasidim must have had such feelings, although
there are also accounts that claim that women attended the courts frequently in search of miraculous assistance for themselves.

For the opponents of Hasidism, the abandonment of wife and children
by the Hasidim did not serve any holy purpose; they believed, to the con-

trary, that the extreme asceticism was a cover for erotic abandon, just as the mystical doctrine of intercourse with the Shekhinah was nothing but a mask for licentious behavior in the court of the zaddik. The author of the anti-Hasidic *Shever Poshim* claims that when the Hasidim gathered at Amdur on the fast of the ninth of Av, they would sleep together in the attic, use filthy language, and sing love songs all night.[89] This homosexual innuendo was connected to the intense male fellowship of the Hasidic court.

Other polemics ignore the male character of the court and insist that all kinds of promiscuous behavior go on during visits to the zaddik. Men and women are said to sit together and become lustful after drinking wine: "They contaminate the wives of their fellows and pair off with them.... They say that it is permitted to fondle nubile girls on their breasts in order to determine whether they are fertile and after caressing and fondling, they clap their hands."[90] Thus, the *mitnagdim* brought the erotic theology of Hasidism back to earth in their claims that ejaculations and erections during prayer reflected the general collapse of sexual morality in the new sect. As with the opponents of Sabbatianism and Frankism, the *mitnagdim* used sexual innuendo to tarnish the image of those intent on religious innovation.

Why did the *mitnagdim* focus on the sexual mores of the Hasidim? Perhaps they saw in Hasidism something uncomfortably close to home. Despite—or, perhaps, *because* of—their polemics, the *mitnagdim* themselves practiced sexual renunciation and absence from home no less than the Hasidim. Coming from the same general background as their opponents, they must have experienced the same erotic tensions arising from early marriage. But where the Hasidim addressed these problems by directing Eros toward God, the *mitnagdim* invested their energies in the study of Torah. The Lithuanian tradition of single-minded devotion to talmudic study may well have developed in reaction to Hasidism's perceived denigration of study in favor of prayer. The *mitnagdim* were particularly obsessed with what they called *bittul Torah* (failure to study Torah), and they urged that every waking moment be devoted to study. This doctrine fulfilled exactly the same function for them that the ideal of constant *devekut* (unification) did for the Hasidim. The Gaon of Vilna, who had virtually the same holy status among the *mitnagdim* as a zaddik had among his Hasidim, was the model for this extreme negation of worldly concerns. In the words of his son, he represented the superiority of those who "leave the paths of this world in order to labor in Torah and commandments."[91]

The yeshiva movement that began in Volozhin in Lithuania attracted students from great distances, much like the courts of the zaddikim. One description of the yeshiva at Eisiskes focuses on the *perushim* (abstinents), typically young men in their early years of marriage:

They reject all the pleasures of life before they have had a chance to enjoy them. Their young, beloved wives stay at their parents' homes and take pride in their husbands, who exist on dry morsels of bread, sleeping on hard wooden benches at their place of study. They make no distinction between Sabbath and festivals and ordinary weekdays. So they live at the yeshiva for several years without a break, without breathing the fresh air of the world. Many of them do not even find time to remember their families by as much as a letter.[92]

Just as Hasidism represented one of the most extreme and most widespread movements of asceticism in Jewish history, so its opponents in the yeshiva world gravitated toward similar asceticism. The same social and cultural forces generated in both movements. Whatever else separated them, they had this in common.

The anti-Hasidic polemics of the *mitnagdim* fed directly into the polemics of the Haskalah, the new movement of Jewish Enlightenment.[93] The maskilim (disciples of the Haskalah) were also typically adolescents when they joined their new movement. When they attacked the obscurantism of the medieval Jewish tradition, these young literati frequently had in mind primarily Hasidism, or at least Hasidism as they imagined it. Like the *mitnagdim*, they, too, attacked Hasidism for destroying the family by focusing all attention on God and the zaddick and for destroying the sexual morals of the Jews. For instance, Joseph Perl, an Austrian Enlightener who wrote satirical parodies of Hasidic texts, deliberately caricatured the erotic language of Hasidic theology in order to make it sound lascivious.[94] In his novel *Megalleh Temirin*, two of the many interwoven plots involve promiscuous behavior on the part of Hasidim,[95] suggesting that Hasidism has trespassed the bounds of sexual propriety on two counts: its theology is obscenely erotic and the behavior of its followers is promiscuous. The first, he implies, leads to the second. Both religiously and socially, all morality has collapsed and the family is on the road to destruction.

For these maskilim, the system of arranged marriage led to the vices of Hasidism, since the young married men could seek emotional satisfaction only outside the family. Only a new ideology of free choice and romantic love could remove sexuality from the heavens and return it to earth. And only by breaking the authoritarian hold of Hasidism might the husbands be taken out of the zaddik's court and returned to the family.

# CHAPTER 7

# Eros and Enlightenment

I N the winter of 1810, only a few months after his fourteenth birthday, Mordecai Aaron Guenzburg departed from his parents' house in the Lithuanian town of Salant and began his wedding journey to Shavel, to the house of his new in-laws. Engaged two years earlier, at the age of twelve, Guenzburg was following in the footsteps of generations of young Jewish boys from Eastern Europe. But unlike his silent forebears, Guenzburg rebelled publicly against his early marriage, penning an autobiographical confession that was a devastating condemnation of Jewish marital practices. With Guenzburg, the nascent Jewish Enlightenment, or Haskalah, of Eastern Europe turned its sights on the Jewish family as part and parcel of its attack on the medieval practices of the Jews.

The Eastern European Haskalah followed the Jewish Enlightenment movement in Germany, which preceded it by about half a century. In Germany, the emancipation of the Jews, which had begun in the first decade of the nineteenth century, produced a growing mass movement of modernization, as the teachings of the German maskilim (disciples of the Haskalah) were taken up by the new German Jewish middle class. In Eastern Europe, where the much larger Jewish population was not emancipated until the Russian Revolution of 1917, the Jewish Enlightenment remained for a much longer time a small, embattled movement of alienated intellectuals. By the last third of the nineteenth century, however, revolutionary changes began to transform the Eastern European Jews into a more modern society, albeit under far less favorable conditions than in the West. Gradually, the maskilim found a wider and wider audience for their writings, which appeared primarily in Hebrew and Yiddish (and later in Russian). Their voices became increasingly influential as the Jews struggled with anti-Semitism, industrialization, urbanization, and the mass emigration from Russia that began in 1881.

The Haskalah was a movement intent on reordering power within Jewish society. The maskilim attacked the rabbis and the traditional communal leaders and advocated a new kind of community in which power would be shared between the enlightened state and enlightened, acculturated intellectuals like themselves.[1] This reordering of power went hand in hand with a new form of knowledge: secular learning would take the place of rabbinic learning, just as modern leaders would take the place of the rabbis. A new educational system emphasizing European languages and sciences, changes in Jewish dress, moderate religious reform, and a wholesale critique of the unproductive Jewish economy were all the stock-in-trade of the maskilim.[2]

The Haskalah's attack on the traditional Jewish family was part of this new discourse. Power within the family needed to be taken away from parents and placed in the hands of the children; the emotions would now play the role previously played by pragmatic interests. At the same time, sexuality would no longer be an uncontrollable experience inflicted on inexperienced children, but would instead come under the control of the children themselves when they matured. The maskilim were therefore operating in the familiar language of medieval Ashkenazic culture by asking the question that was the central issue of Chapter 3: who would control and define desire? Their revolt against communal and parental authority functioned as a literary version of the alternative discourses of medieval popular culture.

This chapter tells the story of these intellectuals, tracing the interaction between their new marital ideology and their own lives, as it was reflected in their memoirs, letters, fiction, and poetry.[3] The maskilim borrowed most of their ideas from European literature, but their ideology stemmed as well from their personal lives and experiences, especially from the struggles for identity that marked their adolescent years. For it was typically during those years that they, like their counterparts in the Hasidic and yeshiva movements, became converts to the cause. We have already seen how the new religious movements in Eastern Europe were products of such adolescent struggles, catalyzed by the crisis of Polish Jewry in the second half of the eighteenth century. But the followers of these movements saw themselves as the genuine heirs of the long Jewish tradition, even if they actually created new norms and ideals. Their rebellion was not entirely self-conscious, as it was for the maskilim. With the Haskalah, rejection of traditional Jewish life became an explicit ideology centered in a critique of traditional adolescence and an attempt to define new forms of family life.

The maskilim believed first that traditional Jewish adolescence, and particularly premature marriage, created sexual dysfunction and second that only a restructuring of Jewish marriage and family life could produce a normal or healthy sexuality. The "bourgeois" family that they advocated was based on notions of sexual modesty and restraint that, curiously enough, they thought were lacking in traditional society. The body of ascetic thought—from the Talmud through medieval philosophy, mysticism, and *musar* that culminated in Hasidism—seemed to them to be a smokescreen for social practices that distorted sexuality. If anything, the traditional discourse on sexuality appeared to reflect an unhealthy obsession that needed to be tamed by the new bourgeois sobriety. For all their renewed emphasis on modesty, however, the maskilim were no less anxious about sexuality than were the Hasidim. But their solution was different: it did not lie in the displacement of Eros by theology, but instead in the *neutralization* of sexuality within a new family framework.

These ideas resonated with broader developments in Eastern European Jewish society as well. The way the maskilim represented the nature of sexuality and marriage in traditional society gradually came to be accepted as the position of the tradition as a whole. They confused their own sexual complexes with the experience of all Jewish men: in this way, a direct line can be drawn between the literature of the nineteenth century and Roth's *Portnoy*. The importance of this admittedly small movement of writers lies, therefore, in its success in defining the tradition and in creating a set of images that dominate the discourse of Jewish sexuality to this day.

## Eros and Autobiography

In order to effect a power shift within Jewish society, the maskilim felt it necessary to develop a new form of knowledge about the life of the individual in Jewish society, a critical discipline that might be called "self-knowledge." A new sense of the self or the individual was central to this enterprise, and it was therefore essential to construct a personal history of that self. The nature of the literature discussed in this chapter is thus completely different from that of earlier periods, whether the Bible, the Talmud, or the various texts from the Middle Ages. For the first time, Eros was not a cultic, theological, or moral issue, as in earlier periods; instead it became a matter of individual self-definition.

This sense of a self with its own unique history had no real precedent in earlier Ashkenazic Jewish culture, a culture in which neither biography nor autobiography played important roles.[4] One interesting precursor to the autobiographies of the Haskalah is Jacob Emden's *Megillat Sefer*.[5] Emden lived in Germany from 1698 to 1776 and was one of the foremost rabbis of his time. Although a fanatical defender of Orthodoxy in his battles against the eighteenth-century vestiges of the Sabbatian heresy, Emden was a part of a nascent Orthodox Haskalah that prepared the ground for the more secular German Jewish Enlightenment movement of Moses Mendelssohn.[6] In Emden's autobiography, we find for the first time in the Ashkenazic world traditional formulas mingled with hints of genuine introspection and a conscious sense of an erotic self. Emden relates a variety of intimate details of his life, including his sexual problems with his first wife, with whom he could barely get along, and the powerful erotic attraction he felt for his cousin, who apparently tried to seduce him. In the latter incident, he boasts in traditional fashion of his ability to overcome his powerful "evil impulse," but he also speaks of his own sexuality in less externalized terms: "I was very hungry for a woman.... I was a man with all of my powers and impulses."[7] Perhaps Emden's openness to his own sexuality explains the very positive position he took on conjugal relations. Quoting the *Iggeret ha-Kodesh* at length, he goes into great detail about erotic foreplay and concludes, against the philosophers: "To us the sexual act is worthy, good and beneficial even to the soul. No other human activity compares with it."[8]

The need for a new knowledge of the self prompted the profusion of autobiographies that constituted one of the main literary genres of the Haskalah. Virtually every maskil felt compelled to record his personal *Bildungsroman*, a reconstruction of his own life, typically recounting the hero's progress from a traditional childhood to the awakening of enlightenment. The first of these was the famous autobiography of Solomon Maimon, published in Germany in 1792–93 and modeled explicitly on the *Confessions* of Rousseau. Several decades later, similar memoirs began to appear in Eastern Europe, typically in Hebrew, the preferred language of the Eastern European Haskalah, but occasionally in Yiddish. These memoirs follow certain conventions, in part influenced by European literary traditions, and they must be treated more as works of literature than as objective accounts.[9] The maskilim also composed their memoirs long after the events described and under the influence of an already crystallized ideology, thus fulfilling Erik Erikson's dictum that autobiography is an attempt at "recreating oneself in the image of one's own method in order to make that image convincing."[10]

In their autobiographies, the maskilim typically present childhood as a period of innocence and of unproblematic relationship to one's biological parents. Some speak of it metaphorically as being like the Garden of Eden or as the "springtime of life." In most of the memoirs, the writers portray their parents in thoroughly positive and unambivalent terms. They describe their fathers as maskilim, although this is really a play on the traditional meaning of the word, namely, "learned in Torah," since most of the fathers were not maskilim in the sons' sense of the word. This rosy picture of the family was contrasted with the family of the in-laws, since there is a persistent "splitting" in these works between the "good parents" and the cruel outsiders.[11]

With their marriages, the maskilim felt themselves torn out of the arms of their parents and sent into a heartless world. These marriages typically took place during early adolescence. I have examined the biographies of several dozen writers, and the overwhelming majority were married by age sixteen or seventeen, most by age thirteen or fourteen.[12] Abraham Ber Gottlober, whose memoir includes a kind of anthropology of Jewish marriage, asserts that everyone he knew was engaged by the age of eleven.[13] This is probably not reliable evidence for the Jewish community as a whole, since the maskilim typically came from the elite class of merchants and scholars. But, as we have already seen in the last chapter, there is evidence to suggest that even the lower classes were marrying early: if not at thirteen and fourteen, then perhaps at fifteen and sixteen. This traditional pattern persisted in Russia during the first half of the nineteenth century. For instance, a law passed in Russia in 1835, but never enforced, sought to compel the Jews to marry in late adolescence, from which one infers that many Jews were marrying earlier.[14]

The vast majority of Jewish marriages were arranged. For the maskilim, arranged marriage and the particular role of the *shadkhan* (marriage broker) constituted the most offensive symbols of the mindless tyranny and seamy commercialism of traditional Jewish society. They used their fiction and their memoirs to attack this system with bitter sarcasm.[15] In addition to literary denunciations, some rebelled personally against arranged marriages. Reuven Braudes, who was to become an important Hebrew novelist in the second half of the nineteenth century, ran away from home when his mother arranged a match for him in 1868; he did eventually marry—at age forty-six.[16] In the eighteenth century Moses Mendelssohn, the founder of the Berlin Haskalah, wrote to his fiancée, Fromet Guggenheim:

> Your amorousness requires me in these letters to transcend all conventional ceremonies. For, just as we needed no marriage brokers for our [engagement], so we need no ceremonies for our correspondence.... The heart will answer these instead.[17]

Mendelssohn not only broke with the convention of using a marriage broker, but he also dispensed with the custom of writing formulaic letters based on literary models known as *egronim*. Just as writing autobiographies was a way of establishing a unique sense of one's individuality, so writing genuine love letters seemed to be a way of breaking out of the uniformity imposed by tradition. Paradoxically, some of the maskilim were to compose their own letter formularies as ways of educating young Jews to greater romantic spontaneity.

If some maskilim rebelled at the time their engagements were arranged, many of the younger boys who would later become maskilim responded quite differently to their engagements. Some reported experiencing feelings similar to romantic love toward their prospective brides, usually before they actually met them. For instance, Isaac Ber Levinsohn (1788–1860), one of the first Russian maskilim, wrote a love poem to his fiancée; as it turned out, soon after they married some three years later, their relationship turned sour and ended in divorce.[18] Similarly, Abraham Ber Gottlober relates in his autobiography that he began to develop feelings of love for his bride-to-be during their exchange of formulaic letters and before they had even met.[19] Pauline Wengeroff, one of the few women to write an autobiography, recounts the fantasies and dreams she had about her husband during their engagement.[20] These examples reinforce what we have already suggested regarding the status of love in Ashkenazic Jewish society of earlier times. Clearly, some like Levinsohn and Gottlober came to reject the system of arranged marriage only later, either when they became maskilim or when their marriages faltered.

The maskilim also fiercely attacked the practice of not allowing the bride and groom to meet until the day of the wedding. The only contact allowed was usually in the form of formulaic letters. This poses a historical dilemma: in the late Middle Ages, meetings between a couple during the engagement period were not uncommon and might even lead to sexual relations, a Jewish form of "bundling." Yet the memoirs of the maskilim are quite emphatic about the lack of contact until the wedding.[21] It may well be that the custom of keeping bride and groom apart was particularly strong among the elite, the social group from which most of the maskilim themselves came, and that matters were looser among the lower classes. Or this may be a case where a particular social practice was not universal, but those who rebelled against it, either because of their own experience or for ideological reasons, chose to make it appear as such.

Whether the engagement appeared to be a kind of puerile romance from a safe distance or the tyranny of a heartless society, the marriage itself seemed to many of our memoirists like the death of childhood. Adam Hacohen Lebensohn, one of the outstanding poets of the first generation of the Russian Haskalah, was born in 1794 and married in 1807 at age thirteen. He wrote: "I had not yet had a chance to become a young man when they already made me a husband and father while I was still a child."[22] Gottlober speaks of the child snatched out of the paradise of childhood and forced to eat prematurely of the apple of love, which he calls "honey mixed with poison."[23] In this version of Adam's fall, early marriage was the kiss of death. Indeed, the maskilim often portrayed their adolescence as premature old age. Moses Leib Lilienblum, writing at age twenty-nine, characterizes himself as an old man, a tragedy he attributes to his premature marriage. This feeling that one has already failed at the outset of life was characteristic of eighteenth-century German intellectuals as well,[24] but for the maskilim it was a direct product of early marriage.

Some of the maskilim associated premature marriage with sexual trauma, and, as the graphic case of the eighteenth-century minors showed in the last chapter, they did not invent the problem. Guenzburg was the most explicit on this subject. He tells us that he married before he was sexually mature, when he still had no interest in members of the opposite sex. To make matters worse, he describes his wife, who was older than he, as a "masculine female," whereas he was a "feminine male." The wedding night, needless to say, was a sexual catastrophe, and the second night no better. What followed tells us a great deal about sexuality in traditional Jewish culture. Although public displays of sexuality were thoroughly forbidden, a sexual dysfunction such as Guenzburg's impotence became the subject of intense scrutiny by his in-laws. It was obviously discussed by one and all, and the boy's mother-in-law concocted some home-brew medicine that almost did him in. In the end, Guenzburg was sent to a doctor who temporarily cured him with techniques that resemble today's behavior modification; the doctor, a maskil, also prescribed treatment for his intellectual dysfunction in the form of Haskalah ideas. This dual treatment suggests that for Guenzburg, as perhaps for others, the cure for problems of Eros could only come through enlightenment, just as the failure of sexuality could be laid at the doorstep of traditional Jewish life as a whole.

While no other memoir quite matches Guenzburg's for sexual explicitness, a number of the others allude in more circumspect language to sexual problems. These problems also played a role in fiction.[25] For these writers, the trauma of premature sexuality seems to have made a mature relationship with the new wife extraordinarily difficult and, in some cases, contributed to a later divorce. When the maskilim came to adopt European ideals of romantic love, their own premature encounter with Eros created a bitter tension between ideology and reality.

These memoirists were plagued by other problems as well: separation from parents and adaptation to new in-laws. Virtually all wedding contracts stipulated that the in-laws would support the young husband as a student for a number of years, while he and his wife lived in their house. The length of the period of *kest* varied according to the wealth of the parties, but it typically covered a substantial portion of adolescence. Thus, during this critical stage of life the boy lived with his in-laws and not with his biological parents. From the literature on the English public school, we know what it meant to spend one's teenage years away from home, or—closer to our subject—we know of the experiences of apprentices and house servants separated from parents at an early age. While young Jewish boys experienced many of the same problems, their situation as sons-in-law was at once better and worse. They could be pampered as prize possessions, or, as Solomon Maimon, Guenzburg, and Lilienblum attest, their in-laws could become persecutors.

Solomon Maimon's autobiography, written in Germany after he had fled Poland, provides one of the most striking accounts of relations with in-laws—in his case, as in many others, with the mother-in-law. Maimon describes the brutal beatings she inflicted on him, for which he amply repaid her with a variety of cruel practical jokes.[26] Lilienblum states: "It was my mother-in-law who in a real sense was the creator of this autobiography, that is, of the tragic part of it."[27] These youths experienced a distinct tension between their new status as married men and the infantilizing and sometimes violent treatment visited on them by their in-laws.

As the memoirs we have been discussing were all written by men, we might wonder about the experience of the young wives caught between their parents and their new husbands. In an earlier chapter, we tried to glean some evidence of women's experience of marriage from the few texts available to us, but we are at an equal disadvantage when it comes to the wives of the maskilim or of other "modernizing" husbands. Most of the evidence comes through the filter of these male autobiographies. The natural difficulties of marriage in early adolescence must have been exacerbated when the young husband began to espouse the strange ideas of the Haskalah. Many of the maskilim recount the conflicts that their wives experienced between affection for their husbands and loyalty to their parents in whose houses they remained.

The autobiography of Pauline Wengeroff is our only direct evidence from a woman. Wengeroff's husband, although not an intellectual, or maskil, became a highly Russified merchant, and her children all converted to Russian Orthodoxy. Her autobiography is a lament, entitled "The Memoirs of a Grandmother," intended to preserve the memory of an utterly alien world for her grandchildren. She perceives herself in the memoir as the upholder of tradition against the modernizing drive of her husband and children; in this, Wengeroff followed the nineteenth-century German Jewish preachers who extolled women as the defenders of tradition.[28] Wengeroff lived in the house of her in-laws, with all its attendant difficulties, for four years, a reversal of the usual pattern; her situation was therefore comparable to that of most of our male memoirists.

Whether these experiences were also characteristic of those of women in traditional Jewish society as a whole is harder to determine, since the Wengeroff family was so wealthy and so far along the road to assimilation. A fascinating case from the mid-nineteenth century offers us some insight into the experience of a young town girl who goes to live with her husband's family in the countryside—again, the reverse of the usual arrangement. Not only is she disconsolate at leaving her family and lonely in the unfamiliar rural setting, but she is seduced by her father-in-law while her young husband is off at school. The way the scandal developed tells us a great deal about the complex family dynamics in these marital arrangements:

> Her mother-in-law spoke to her husband [that is, the girl's father-in-law] and urged him to befriend her so that she would forget her concerns. He began to befriend her and walked with her a number of times in the forest there. The young wife related this to her husband and said that his father had fondled her and kissed her. Her husband told her not to go walking with him, but she did not listen to him and continued to walk with her father-in-law as before.[29]

Whether this was a case of sexual molestation or of consent cannot be determined, but it is clear that the extraordinary pressures of spending one's adolescence in the house of in-laws could have as dislocating an effect on girls as on boys.

For most males in traditional Jewish society, and some of the females, the battles of adolescence were not waged with their biological parents but with their in-laws. When the maskilim turned this situation into an ideological struggle, they bifurcated the family into the "good" biological family of childhood and the "bad" family of their marriages. Their entrance into the family of the in-laws spelled the end of paradise and the beginning of hopelessness, despair, and senescence. And it was during this period that they typically discovered the ideas of the Haskalah, a discovery that brought them into severe conflict with their in-laws. Gottlober, for instance, was forced to divorce his wife, whom he loved deeply, when his father-in-law learned that he had fallen into the heretical clutches of the Enlightenment. As late as the 1880s the Hebrew writer Micha Yosef Berdichevsky (1865–1921) was forced to divorce his first wife for the same reasons.

Even when not coerced by in-laws, divorce was frequently the result of the trauma of adolescent marriage mixed with Haskalah ideology.[30] The breakup of their marriages rarely led to more successful second marriages. Lilienblum could not imagine turning his extramarital intellectual relationship with an enlightened young woman named Feyge Novakhovitch into a sexual one: he could feel safe only at an epistolary distance, in a relationship based on the word rather than on the flesh.[31] Many of these intellectuals, for whom mature eroticism seemed unattainable, blamed the tradition for their failure.

Since the maskilim often could not realize their ideal family, some despaired of the institution altogether. Abraham Mapu wrote to his brother: "Only one in a thousand will derive joy from family life, and even that will only be a facade."[32] Eliezer Zweifel expressed similar sentiments in a poem entitled "The Woman." Married off at age twelve or thirteen, he fled his wife, who refused for many years to accept a writ of divorce from him. In his poem, which is patterned on the Book of Lamentations, he resolves that rather than marry, it would be better to follow the example of Ben Azzai, the second-century rabbi who preferred marriage to the Torah over marriage to a wife.[33] The Torah here is, of course Haskalah, rather than the rabbinic tradition. Striking indeed is how some maskilim adopted the model of celibacy, which had been rejected by the talmudic rabbis, as a theme in their revolt against the rabbinic tradition. In this, they came unintentionally close to their Hasidic opponents.

Small wonder that the maskilim should turn to male friendships for comfort in their shattered personal lives. Mapu writes to his brother: "Yes, the love of women is strong, but as its price, it takes the souls of the husbands.... Not so is brotherhood whose candle will never be extinguished."[34] Time and again, Mapu, like other Haskalah writers, uses frankly erotic language to describe male friendships. To his brother, for instance, he wrote: "My right hand embraces you and my lips kiss your lips."[35] Would it be too bold to suggest that the erotic energies that some of the maskilim failed to direct toward women found their targets in men? While we must not impute too much to these conventions of epistolary style, it is significant that such language seemed appropriate between men but not between men and women, leading to an almost sectarian comradeship and ideology of friendship in the Haskalah. Whatever the affective valences of these friendships, they provided emotional outlets inconceivable within marriage.

In its cult of male friendship, the Haskalah unwittingly reproduced the feelings of male camaraderie that characterized its hated foe, Hasidism. While the maskilim did not congregate around charismatic leaders as did the Hasidim, they, too, sought solace in relationships with other men. Beyond Hasidism, such male fellowships had an even longer legacy in the mystical brotherhoods in Safed and in the rabbinic academies, both those contemporary with the Haskalah and those throughout Jewish history going back to talmudic times. Unable to create a truly egalitarian community between the sexes, the maskilim ironically returned to the male-oriented pattern of the tradition.

The maskilim also replicated in the Jewish setting a general tendency in Europe since the Enlightenment to create a community of male friendship (*Männerbund*), which often found its highest expression in the experience of warfare.[36] While the Haskalah did not share in this aggressive form of male camaraderie, it did make a similar connection between friendship and the creation of an incipient form of modern nationalism.

## Eros, Marriage, and the Discourse of Capitalism

For the maskilim, the Enlightenment provided an avenue of escape from the pressure cooker of the adoptive family. It allowed them to attack the very social system that had torn them out of their parents' arms, only to bury them in the graveyard of an early marriage. If Hasidism and the yeshivot also offered means of escape from the life of the traditional family, they did not provide the weapons of direct criticism. Those young men who discovered the Haskalah found or, better, invented an ideology that matched their experience. What had been denied to the flesh might be liberated by the word.

As a result of this interplay of ideology and identity in their adolescent years, the maskilim combined their attack on the system of arranged early marriage with their critique of traditional society and their program for reform. This critique was closely tied to an economic vision based on a capitalist ethic. In the 1840s, for example, Adam Hacohen Lebensohn wrote an important memorandum to Moses Montefiore, the English Jewish philanthropist who undertook a mission to investigate the condition of the Russian Jews.[37] Lebensohn listed four reasons for the impoverished and degenerate state of the Jews, the second of which was early marriage. Lebensohn blamed early marriage for the failure of fathers to find productive professions and also for the birth of Jewish children with physical weaknesses, an argument borrowed from eighteenth-century medicine.[38]

As Lebensohn's memorandum to Montefiore demonstrates, the maskilim believed that early marriage contributed to the unproductive nature of the traditional Jewish economy. Instead of learning a worthwhile profession, the young married man was expected to study, a parasite supported first by his in-laws and later by his wife. In Peretz Smolenskin's novel *Ha-Toeh be-Darkhei ha-Hayyim* (Wanderer in the Paths of Life), for instance, a young Hasid tells a maskil who wants to know how he supports himself: "Is my mother-in-law paralyzed that I should have to earn a living? Until the day the worms take up residence in her corpse, she will go on working and supply our needs."[39] The maskilim advocated destroying this system and urged that adolescence be devoted to learning a productive occupation. Marriage should come later, when the boy himself could support a wife. Adolescence should be a period of some autonomy, and the burdens of family life should be delayed.

There was yet a further dimension to the connection between productivization and marriage in Haskalah ideology. For the maskilim, traditional marriage was a commercial transaction unsuited to the modern world. Instead of money being earned by productive labor or capitalist initiative, Jewish financial transactions were epitomized by the *shiddukh,* or engagement. In fact, this portrait of marriage as a financial transaction was largely correct, as we can learn from the autobiographies of Glückel of Hameln and Jacob Emden.[40] For many Jews, these transactions must have been economically among the most significant of their lives. The maskilim were particularly hostile to the institution of the *shadkhan,* or matchmaker, because they considered him an unproductive parasite, living off marriage commissions, and they suspected him of playing a major role in keeping the age of marriage inordinately young.

Israel Aksenfeld's Yiddish novel *Dos Shterntikhl* (The Headband),[41] written in the 1840s, makes this point in an allegory about the conflict between the old commercial values, represented by the marital headband with its valuable stones, and the new ethos of capitalism.[42] The former is based on fixed wealth, and the latter on liquid. Women represent medieval values and are portrayed with an utter lack of sympathy. The novel's hero, Mikhl, symbolically defeats the old world by marrying the heroine but presenting her with a *shterntikhl* made of false pearls. Once the *shterntikhl* and the values it represents are shown up as bogus, the new capitalist spirit that Mikhl has acquired in Germany can prevail.

Influenced by the nascent Russian feminist movement, later Jewish writers such as Y. L. Gordon and Lilienblum sought to liberate the Jewish woman from the yoke of traditional marriage, a modern version of the medieval Spanish and Italian literature "in defense of women." Gordon's poem "Al Kotzo shel Yod" (The Dot on the I) probably remains the most eloquent literary denunciation of the oppression of women by Jewish law and is certainly the first attempt by a man to write from a woman's point of view.[43] Lilienblum, too, wrote several manifestos against the traditional view of women, denouncing in particular what he rather crudely labeled the wife as "chamber pot" (*avit shel shofkhin*).[44] Lilienblum argued that the tasks assigned to the wife by traditional Judaism could as well be discharged by a servant, and he advocated a companionate marriage to replace traditional marriage.

Because of the commercial nature of traditional marriage, women were subject to dangerous sexual temptation. The maskilim believed that women in the marketplace—a role quite common for Jewish women in Eastern Europe—were in moral peril. This was the ostensible reason that the maskilim preached taking women out of commerce, just as they advocated removing marriage from the marketplace. In one of his didactic letter formularies, Guenzburg praises the customs of countries where men work and women stay at home; in his own country, he complains, the women engage in business and their morals have deteriorated.[45] Ayzik Meyer Dik, the best-selling author of Yiddish pulp novels, also considered the marketplace a disaster for feminine morality. With his characteristic lack of subtlety, he writes in one of his novels: "The women of

Israel and their daughters sit selling all kinds of silk and linen and everyone who comes to buy wants to try out the taste of a virgin."[46] For the
maskilim, both marriage and women had to be decommercialized since
both were morally degenerate: their goal was a kind of bourgeois respectability that might be attained only by restricting women to hearth
and home.

The maskilim envisioned a family in which the position of women was
at once better and worse than in the traditional family or, at least, in
their image of the traditional family. While they experienced their moth-
ers-in-law and, to a lesser extent, their wives as powerful and domineering, they imagined an ideal family in which power implicitly lay in the
hands of the husband. Their revolt against the traditional family was a
revolt against a perceived matriarchal family. If the wife was to be liberated from the yoke of traditional marriage, she must also be divorced
from the power that women were thought to wield in the old system.
While the maskilim directed their polemics against a specifically Jewish
system of marriage and family, their goal was the same as that of other
nineteenth-century advocates of domesticity—upholding such values as
privacy and chastity.[47] Their solution to what they saw as the promiscuity
and sexual dysfunction of traditional Jewish society was the imposition
of bourgeois constraints upon desire.

Not all Haskalah writers preached erotic conservatism, however. One
extraordinary exception—perhaps unique—was Judah Leib Ben-Ze'ev
(1764–1811). Ben-Ze'ev was born in Cracow but spent most of his adult
life in Berlin, where he was active in the Berlin Haskalah. There he wrote
a number of scholarly works on Hebrew linguistics. In addition, however, he penned a pornographic poem in Haskalah Hebrew that, although not published until this century, circulated in manuscript in
Eastern Europe and was reputed to be an underground favorite among
young Hasidim.[48] Cleverly adapting phrases from the Song of Songs, the
poet describes in great detail an act of sexual intercourse between his
male narrator and a woman whom he "picks up" at a ball. A typical author of pornography, Ben-Ze'ev was interested only in the physical interaction and ignored any emotional or other transcendent dimension. He
therefore strips the language of the Song of Songs of centuries of theological allegorization and replaces it with pornographic allegory. For example, he turns the biblical phrase "my beloved" (dodi) into a euphemism for the penis. The verse "So my beloved has gone down into his
garden" (6:2) becomes a metaphor for the actual act of intercourse.
When the Shulamit says of her lover, "I held him fast, I would not let him
go / Till I brought him to my mother's house" (3:4), Ben-Ze'ev gives the
verse what we would anachronistically call a "Freudian" interpretation:
the "mother's house" becomes the vagina. Ben-Ze'ev's rendering of the

Song of Songs is surely among the most physically erotic to which the biblical poem has ever been subjected, far exceeding even its original meaning.

Ben-Ze'ev does not limit himself to describing the man's pleasure; he gives full attention to the woman's as well, an extraordinary shift in point of view, given when the poem was written:

> She closed her hand around me and squeezed
> So that my beloved could not spring free
> She thrust her thighs, down and up,
> Racing, racing the horse of her war
> For her heart was stormy with the flame of her love.

Ben-Ze'ev obviously had no doubts that women have orgasms: the poem ends with both partners reaching a graphically described climax.

Ben-Ze'ev's erotic poem was a unique exception in Haskalah literature, occasioned, no doubt, by the desire to explore the full capacities of the Hebrew language. It was certainly not emblematic of the Haskalah's general approach to sexuality, an approach characterized more by frustration and failure. Perhaps as a result of their own traumatic histories, they had difficulty envisioning true erotic liberation. They desired marriages based on companionship in which bourgeois respectability would substitute for traditional chastity and in which women would be placed firmly within the confines of the home. Intent on freeing both men and women from the erotic repression of traditional marriage, the disciples of the Enlightenment constructed modern versions of the ills they believed to be endemic to medieval Judaism.

## New Marital Customs in the Traditional World

The maskilim saw themselves as an isolated and embattled group of rebels in a world still mired in traditional practices, a world in which romantic love and free choice in marriage were alien ideals. But was this an accurate portrait of the Jewish culture of Eastern Europe? We have already seen that the range of possibilities in Jewish society was much broader than rabbinic norms might suggest: not all marriages were arranged in disregard of the emotions, and not all Jews followed the strict sexual ethic proclaimed by the legal codes. During the nineteenth century a variety of modern ideas infiltrated into this world and added new dimensions to the complexities of traditional culture. Moreover, important social changes undermined the stability of traditional norms.

The Jewish population in the Russian empire increased dramatically during the nineteenth century. Under Nicholas I, communal institutions were weakened by a governmental policy of Russification of the Jews. Later in the century, especially following the pogroms of 1881, large portions of the Jewish population were uprooted, some moving into the cities of Russia and others emigrating to the West. All these changes weakened traditional patterns of life. The rise of Jewish prostitution in Russian cities and of a white slave trade abroad were both examples of the breakdown of sexual controls. In the Russian census of 1897, for example, there were forty-four Jewish prostitutes for every hundred thousand women, the highest proportion of any ethnic group.[49]

Even before industrialization and emigration began to have a major effect on the Jewish family at the end of the nineteenth century, a quiet transformation was taking place within the traditional world. Despite the Haskalah portrait of continuing adolescent marriages, the age of marriage began to rise rapidly in the last third of the nineteenth century.[50] Whereas in 1867, some 43 percent of bridegrooms and 61 percent of brides were under the age of twenty, by 1897, the figures were only 5.8 percent and 27.7 percent. The responsa literature of the nineteenth century records a sharp decline in cases of child marriage, a problem that had preoccupied eighteenth-century authorities. Those few cases of boys marrying before the age of thirteen were generally in the Hasidic communities, which tended to preserve old traditions longer than other factions of the Orthodox world; and most of these cases appear to date from the first half of the century.[51]

Independent of Haskalah polemics, Orthodox Jews were also beginning to change their attitudes toward the age of marriage and, perhaps as an unwitting consequence, toward the very nature of marriage itself. Moses Feivish (1817–1887), for instance, authored a popular treatise on the laws of marriage published in 1858. He opposed the marriage of boys at age thirteen and recommended that they marry at eighteen, since "the main period of study is in these years and therefore it is permitted to wait until this age."[52] The maskilim also wanted to reserve the years of adolescence for study, but Feivish's source was the old Palestinian tradition from talmudic times that had not been followed by most Ashkenazic Jews. Feivish also quoted the eighteenth-century Sephardic authority Hayyim Yosef Azulai, who argued against marriage at age thirteen because "the generations have grown weak." This physiological argument against early marriage was to be used repeatedly by rabbis later in the nineteenth century. Feivish, like his Haskalah contemporaries, may have arrived at his position out of his own experience. Married at age fourteen, he ran away with his wife to a yeshiva in Vilna when his in-laws refused to let him study.[53]

The yeshiva world as a whole came to accept the notion of study be-

fore marriage. Naphtali Zvi Berlin (1817–1893), the head of the great
Volozhin yeshiva, stated in 1879 that early marriage was medically un-
sound, even though young people in earlier generations may have been
able to cope with it. In his commentary on Exodus 1:7, which recounts
the population explosion of the Israelites in Egypt, Berlin wrote: "Girls
who begin to give birth when they are young become weak and sickly.
And the same is true of males who use their sexual organs for procreation in the days of their youth. They become weak in health."[54] This
medical argument had already been advanced in the eighteenth century
by Jacob Emden in a responsum against child marriage; it reflected a
widespread opinion of the European Enlightenment that was used in
support of raising the legal age of marriage.

Berlin, as the head of the Volozhin yeshiva, gave this view an institu-
tional dimension. The Lithuanian yeshivot did not accept married men,
and it was only in 1879 that the *kolel* was established as a parallel institution for married students. The age of marriage among the yeshiva students rose dramatically in the second half of the nineteenth century,
until it stood at around twenty-five.[55] By putting study before marriage,
the yeshiva movement may have been a factor in the rising marriage age.
With the claim that young boys were not sexually ready for marriage,
these Orthodox authorities unconsciously placed themselves in the same
camp as their archenemies, the maskilim.

One of the major summaries of Jewish law from the early twentieth
century, the *Arukh ha-Shulhan* of Yehiel Michael Epstein (1829–1908),
confirms this shift in priorities. Epstein echoes Feivish that "the instincts
have weakened in these generations," making marriage to avoid masturbation and temptation less necessary. One should first study and then
wed at age eighteen. Rejecting the earlier Ashkenazic tradition of child
marriage, Epstein concludes: "And there is no reason to discuss this matter at length since it is virtually nonexistent in our time."[56]

As the age of marriage rose, children of traditional families were able
to exercise greater choice in mates, even if parents continued to arrange
the match. Thus, Solomon Schwadron (d. 1911) reported the following
case from Galicia:

> The groom objects in front of a number of people and he also says to his
> mother that he has not yet seen the face of the bride. [But] since it is the fa-
> ther's custom to intimidate the household, they were afraid to tell him [of
> the son's objections], and they wrote the contract of engagement. And now,
> the groom has seen the bride and he does not like her, since she is very
> short and not pretty and is a bit repulsive.[57]

According to this responsum, a meeting between bride and groom before
the engagement would have been possible had the father not been so for-

bidding. Schwadron rules that the engagement may be broken without penalty since the son's wishes should have been taken into account.[58] The rabbi sympathizes with the boy's reasons for rejecting the girl, and he quotes from the Song of Songs to the effect that height is a desirable trait in a bride. The plaintiff makes special mention of the father's domineering behavior—might this mean that the typical Jewish household was less patriarchal than this one?

Schwadron's ruling in favor of the son had precedents in the Middle Ages, especially in the *Sefer Hasidim*, but it appears as well to reflect the growing influence of ideas of romantic love. Pauline Wengeroff reports that her older sister did not meet her fiancé until the day of the wedding, but a few years later, in 1849, she and her husband-to-be met unchaperoned and exchanged love letters.[59] In another case from 1879, two young people tried to arrange their own marriage based on the new notions of romantic love:

> The boy Chaim said that for a long time, perhaps four or five years, the soul of the virgin [Nehama] had adhered to him in love ... and, once, the two of them found themselves by chance together in the community of Likewe [?] and they talked together day and night. She said to him that it seemed to her that their love was eternal. During this whole time, she wrote him many letters containing statements of love and affection. In one of the letters she wrote that he should find a way of avoiding an engagement with another since she would certainly find some trick to become his wife, even though she was already engaged to someone else.[60]

Although there was nothing particularly new about clandestine love, this account does contain some singularly modern elements. The boy and girl meet in a community to which each has traveled independently, suggesting a certain autonomy that may have been a result of a more advanced age. In fact, there are a number of indications of new possibilities for boys and girls to meet unchaperoned. In particular, walks in the fields or forests, beyond the boundaries of the shtetl, became increasingly popular and provided an unsupervised opportunity for intercourse (of all kinds) between the sexes. As the Hebrew writer M. Y. Berdichevsky noted in a story from the end of the nineteenth century: "A generation went and a generation came and a new generation rose in Israel, a generation that began to walk on the Sabbaths at the borders of the city."[61] A new interest in nature can be found in this custom, an interest that went hand in hand with romantic values.

Like Moses Mendelssohn's letters to his fiancée, the letters mentioned in this responsum were not copied from the traditional letter formularies. They were instead spontaneous expressions of affection that would never have been put into writing earlier. But what of the use of the word

"love" in this responsum and in the letters that it quotes? Was this a continuation of the subterranean career of love in the traditional Jewish
world, or was it the result of modern influence? Although there may be
no definitive way of answering this question, the world of nineteenth-
century Eastern European Jews was filled with popular literature and
folk songs that inculcated romantic ideas in the general population.
Much of this literature expanded the medieval folk traditions we have already examined in new directions.

Yiddish chapbooks were one source for romantic ideas, especially for
female readers.[62] Many of these anonymous texts turned traditional practices into vehicles for romance. For example, a girl and boy might fall in
love, only to discover at the end of the story that they were destined for
each other by a vow (tekiyas kaf) sworn between their parents at their
birth. One remarkable anonymous tale tells of the daughter of a rabbi
from Constantinople who is engaged to a rabbi's son from Brisk in
Lithuania, a geographical flight of fancy typical of such literature.[63] She
is the best student in her father's yeshiva in Constantinople, also an improbable detail, since girls were not allowed to study in yeshivot.[64] The
engagement with the boy in Brisk takes place when she is twelve and she
and the groom accept it with enthusiasm, exchanging the traditional formulaic letters with each other. But her curiosity gets the better of her, so,
disguised as a boy, she travels with another yeshiva student to Brisk,
where she enters the yeshiva of her intended. There, she makes a great
impression and encounters the boy, but they do not "know" each other,
implying that the audience would have wondered about such a possibility. At one point, he becomes ill and she cures him by exposing her
breasts!

This story of a transvestite talmudic prodigy, with its erotic innuendo,
resembles Isaac Bashevis Singer's famous "Yentl the Yeshivah Boy."
What is so striking here is the mix of traditional elements, such as the details of the engagement, with the subversive, such as the girl's talmudic
knowledge, her bold initiatives, and, finally, the sexual suggestions. In
this fashion, the story may have appealed to a traditional audience, but it
allowed that audience, particularly if it was female, a fictional reversal of
gender relations.

Signs of the infiltration of modern ideas of romantic love into Jewish
popular culture can also be found in nineteenth-century Jewish folklore
and folk songs.[65] One folk song relates how a girl who falls in love with a
boy commits suicide as a result of opposition from her parents, while another recounts the suicide of a boy for the same reasons. Yet another
song, which may have been based on an actual incident that occurred in
Moldavia in the early 1870s, is the story of a groom who, enraged by the
opposition of his girlfriend's parents, kills her and then attempts, unsuccessfully, to kill himself.[66] Some versions of the song do not mention the

attempted suicide and treat him as a murderer rather than a romantic figure. The parents regret their opposition and call on other parents not to interfere in their children's romantic affairs. This explicit message is, indeed, the implicit message of all these folk songs. In the conflict between parents and children over marital choices, nineteenth-century popular culture increasingly sided with the children.

A number of Yiddish writers who were influenced by the Haskalah exploited this taste for romantic popular literature in order to propagandize explicitly for modern values. Such figures included Shomer and A. M. Dik, both of whom fed their readers an endless diet of the Jewish equivalent of Harlequin romances.[67] While the chapbooks tended to build their romances around the traditional predestined matches, these writers, following the Haskalah, put the young couple more fully in control of their fate, as in the title of one of Dik's romances, "The Match without Matchmakers."[68] Romantic love was now tied to the new bourgeois values. Dik, in particular, emphasized the distinction between his Enlightenment point of view and the older Yiddish romances that, in his opinion, inculcated immorality. He reflected, in 1860, on his phenomenal literary success:

> I wrote ... for the benefit of our women whose eyes look only into a *Taytsh-khumesh* [a Yiddish Bible; Dik is referring to the *Tsene-rene*] written in a language of stammerers which includes unseemly passages that should never be read by pious women and maidens. Not so my own stories written as they are in a fine style, full of ethical teaching, free of any words of eroticism and blemish and they instruct the women to walk in the paths of righteousness and to turn away from all evil.[69]

As we have seen, the maskilim regarded traditional Jewish culture as hypocritical: it preached upright behavior but, in fact, practiced promiscuity. Dik offered his romances as a new form of ethical exempla in which the traditional virtue of modesty might be wedded to bourgeois respectability. But these romances, for all their putative Haskalah values, pandered to the same thirst for romance that informed the chapbook literature he criticized. The line between old and new was often not as clear as the Haskalah writers themselves believed, especially in the works of those who, like Dik and Shomer, wrote in Yiddish for the masses.

The popular culture of nineteenth-century Jews marked a transition from "traditional" to "modern" values, but that transition was not straightforward. Since notions of love, though not necessarily defined in purely modern terms, circulated in Jewish culture throughout the Middle Ages, they formed a kind of foundation for new romantic and erotic attitudes during the nineteenth century. Although the maskilim painted a bleak portrait of traditional society as devoid of any romance, that society was already undergoing changes under the surface that made it increasingly receptive to Haskalah values.

## The Literary Revolution of the Turn of the Century

By the end of the nineteenth century, a new Jewish nationalism had spread through Eastern Europe, transforming the Haskalah in the process. This nationalism was itself the product of broad developments in the Russian empire, including the pogroms and political persecutions of the 1880s and early 1900s and economic impoverishment, especially in the 1890s. The Jewish communities of Eastern Europe spawned a variety of political movements in response to these worsening conditions, from Zionism to the socialist workers' Bund. This new politics was accompanied by a Hebrew and Yiddish literary revival that featured a new stylistic realism.

Influenced by political developments, the writers of this period rejected the Haskalah's optimistic belief that a rational program of reform might change Jewish society. They nevertheless remained indebted to the Haskalah's critique of tradition. They concurred with the Haskalah belief that love and erotic fulfillment were, by definition, foreign to traditional Jewish culture.[70] In the words of a character from an early novel by Berdichevsky: "I am not to blame that I cannot find the love that I seek, but rather my ancestors with all their way of thinking and their books ... which suppressed our spirit and crippled our stature."[71]

One of the sharpest critiques along these lines is the story "The Tale of the Scribe" by the great twentieth-century Hebrew writer S. Y. Agnon (1888–1970). Agnon satirically portrays a Torah scribe who is so consumed with exaggerated sanctity that he lives a virtually celibate life with his wife; her barrenness, Agnon intimates, is really the result of his abstinence. Given the perceived lack of romance in Jewish society, these writers could not envision a Jewish novel in the conventional European sense of the word: the Yiddish writer Shalom Aleichem subtitled one of his early novels, *Sender Blank* (1887), as a *roman on a roman* (a novel without romance).[72]

Some writers did, however, believe that if love and sexuality were foreign to the establishment, they might be found among the lower classes of Jewish society. Shalom Aleichem's early novel *Stempenyu* (1888) describes the licentiousness of Jewish musicians (*klezmorim*). One such musician, Stempenyu, tries to seduce an honorable Jewish girl, Rochelle, into having an extramarital affair with him. After meeting him on *Monastery Road* (sexual license is thus figured as gentile!), she manages to overcome temptation and return to her husband. Although *Stempenyu* appears on the surface to be a celebration of such "good Jewish daughters," Shalom Aleichem, in his typical fashion, satirizes the fate of these Jewish women: they have no hope of real love and any attempt to find it must end in tragedy. The Jewish middle class is doubly cursed by the repressive Jewish tradition and by nascent bourgeois respectability.

Some writers of the period turned to folklore in hopes of recovering there the ostensible erotic traditions of the lower class. Berdichevsky collected vast anthologies of folktales for the purpose of demonstrating that the repressive and passive rabbinic tradition was not monolithic.[73] Under the influence of Nietzsche, Berdichevsky found vitality and eroticism in these popular countertraditions and believed that they might form the basis for a "new Hebrew man." Zionism would resurrect these same ideas in its revolt against the alleged passivity of the Diaspora.

In his fiction, Berdichevsky harnessed elements of traditional folklore to his ideological wagon. The story "In Their Mothers' Wombs,"[74] for example, relates how two Hasidic fathers make an oath to marry their as yet unborn children, a typical theme in popular tales. One father becomes wealthy and the other poor, and the wealthy one wants to renege on his oath. He gets his chance when the boy and the girl are caught walking secretly in the woods: the engagement contract is ripped up and the boy and girl, who had been "joined since they were in their mothers' wombs," are separated. Modern romantic love, symbolized by the walk in the woods, is linked to the traditional *tekiyas kaf*, but the two are destroyed by materialistic parents. The folk has the right instincts, but the oppressive culture of the establishment thwarts it.

Another folklorist motivated by the same ideology was S. An-ski (1863–1920). In 1912, An-ski led an ethnographic expedition to collect Jewish folklore from the vanishing world of the Russian Jewish shtetl. Although An-ski's still-popular play "The Dybbuk," first produced in 1920, is usually considered to be a straightforward retelling of a folktale, it is, in fact, another example of how a writer of this period shaped folklore to advance his own agenda. "The Dybbuk" takes the typical Haskalah form of a conflict between romantic love and the traditional *shiddukh*, but An-ski creates an alliance between popular Jewish culture and modern values against a repressive establishment. At the very outset, he suggests, through the voice of one of the "idlers" who act as a kind of Greek chorus, that in earlier, "purer" times, people made matches based on the virtues of the couple themselves, while, more recently, admiration of wealth and paternity have corrupted Jewish marriage.[75] Following the standard theme from popular culture, Chanon, the brilliant young Kabbalist, is promised to Leah in an oath sworn by their parents before their birth. This *tekiyas kaf* signifies predestination: the love that ultimately develops between them is sanctioned by heaven. But following Chanon's sudden death, Leah is betrothed to another based on purely pragmatic considerations by the parents.

In revenge, Chanon posseses her in the form of a *dybbuk* (the spirit of a deceased person) and refuses to let her marry the boy her father has chosen for her. Like the Maid of Ludmir, Leah becomes both male and female when the *dybbuk* enters her, and this gender confusion subverts the arranged marriage. Possession by the *dybbuk*, with its sexual overtones, symbolizes a kind of erotic revolt against the reactionary establishment of rabbis and parents, but because of the prior pledge between the parents, it is a revolt that has divine backing.

Chanon is a Kabbalist, but his Kabbalah is really a camouflaged form of erotic modernism. Like the talmudic apostate Aher to whom he is compared, he says of himself: "I am one of those who searches for new ways."[76] He propounds a doctrine of the "holiness of sin" and asserts that the greatest sin, lust for a woman, can be purified into the greatest holiness, the Song of Songs. Like Ben-Ze'ev's reworking of the Song of Songs, Chanon therefore restores the erotic biblical poem to its original, nonallegorical meaning: his "Kabbalah" is at once traditional and radically modern.

Yet the tragic end of the story, in which Leah, too, dies and is united with Chanon in the other world, suggests that romantic love cannot yet find a home in this world. While romantic tragedy of this sort could be found in such Yiddish romances of the late Middle Ages as the *Maase Beriah ve-Zimrah*, An-ski's play was a pessimistic reminder that the power of the establishment was still stronger than either the counterculture of the folk or the revolutionary doctrines of modernity. The original title of the play, "Between Two Worlds," may suggest not only the obvious "world of the living" and "world of the dead" but also the dilemma of Jews caught between the vanishing world of popular culture and the still-unborn world of modern values.

Although the power of conservative forces was in fact collapsing throughout the Eastern European Jewish world by the time An-ski wrote his play, his pessimism and that of many other Hebrew and Yiddish writers became the hallmark of the literary renaissance of the age. For the writers of the turn of the century, the Haskalah had failed to provide an alternative to the repressive establishment: on the political plane, its promise of integration was thwarted by the rise of a new anti-Semitism; and on the social plane, it could not deliver healthier institutions of Jewish life. Its rational version of the bourgeois family turned out to be a failure, both for the maskilim themselves and for society at large. Love and sexuality, it now transpired, were beyond rational solutions. Enlightenment now became the enemy of Eros: under the influence of fin de siècle *Lebensphilosophie*, intellectuals came to believe that the study of books, whether modern or traditional, stood in the way of erotic fulfillment. This new literature testified to the failure of Haskalah and therefore, self-referentially, to the failure of literature itself.

While the earlier maskilim had believed in the power of the word to transform the tradition and to liberate the writer, Hebrew writers such as Berdichevsky, Y. H. Brenner, M. Z. Feierberg, and U. N. Gneissin, to name only a few, were far less sanguine. They created new literary genres by turning the themes of the Haskalah autobiographies into fiction and poetry.[77] In this fictional mode of autobiography writers stood at a critical distance from both their fictional narrators and their protagonists. These writers turned their criticism against themselves, portraying their struggles (which the Haskalah memoirists took with the utmost seriousness) as the stuff of contempt and satire. While their antiheroes wallowed in self-pity, trapped in a hopeless internal monologue, they, their creators, stood off at a sardonic distance.

These antiheroes were paralyzed in all aspects of life, emotional and intellectual. But the core symbol of their paralysis was the problem of Eros, which all the writers of the period addressed much more explicitly and insistently than their Haskalah predecessors had done. The new emphasis on sexuality, which characterized European literature of the turn of the century, could only highlight the inadequacies these Jewish writers felt. In turning to *Lebensphilosophie* as an alternative to rationalism, they found themselves in a cruel dilemma: how difficult it must have been for these erotically frustrated intellectuals to try to imagine the liberation of the senses promised by the new irrationalist philosophy! Their predecessors had at least adopted a bourgeois version of modesty.

Love was the goal, but it could never be achieved and the male antiheroes of this literature were trapped in a kind of perpetual adolescence.[78] Presented with the possibility of an actual sexual relationship, the protagonists flee back to their books or, in some other way, abort the erotic encounter. In the words of Berdichevsky's anti-hero Elimelech, in "The Raven Flies":

> There were times I simply wanted her. When we used to sit reading together, our souls enmeshed, I knew that all I had to do would be to take her in my arms and kiss her and then perhaps everything would be different.... But my hands would not perform the commission of my heart, so I would sit there reading, reading and wanting, wanting and reading.[79]

Such passivity and fruitless erotic entanglements became the hallmark of virtually all the male protagonists of the literary renaissance of the turn of the century, as well as in later literature. One extreme expression of this theme was the portrayal of sadomasochistic relationships, in which an aristocratic gentile woman often dominates an ineffectual Jewish man. These bizarre relationships are found at the turn of the century in stories by Berdichevsky and later in works by S. Y. Agnon and David Vogel.[80] In our last chapter, we will see how the comic figure of the male Jew as sexual shlemiel in American Jewish culture recapitulated aspects of these passive antiheroes.

How is one to understand these passive, masochistic literary creations? One need not take such a prevalent theme in a body of literature as a reflection of the actual psychology of its writers; rather, one can see it as a representation of how those writers understood themselves and their contemporaries. The literary renaissance, it should be remembered, took place in the wake of the Russian pogroms of the 1880s and early 1900s and in tandem with the emergence of Jewish nationalism. Passivity became so important a theme in the writing of this period because it represented on a psychological and sexual plane the perceived passivity of the Jewish people that so preoccupied these writers. Berdichevsky, for example, proclaimed a Nietzschean revolt against rabbinical ethics, which had sapped the Jews of their vitality; he called for a nationalist return to nature and to elemental strength in place of bookish learning. In this context, the contrast between erotic desire and reading in "A Raven Flies" actually stands for the opposing values of power and intellection, the latter represented by both Jewish tradition and the Haskalah. To free oneself erotically becomes the individual mode of liberating the Jews as a nation from the passivity of exile. Conversely, the fictional sadomasochistic enslavement of a Jewish man by an aristocratic gentile woman serves as a symbol for the degradation of the Jewish people as a whole in Christian Europe.[81]

The literature of the Jewish national renaissance was caught between erotic passivity and the drive for political power. At a time when Jews were taking up arms and organizing politically in their own defense, the predominant fiction that they produced—a fiction intimately associated with this movement of national awakening—expressed impotence and pessimism. Thus, side by side with the ideology of national liberation, the persistence of passivity in this fiction illustrates that instead of freeing both Jewish sexuality and the Jewish people, this generation's self-image remained constrained by erotic passivity. Each writer need not have himself been passive in his relationships with women: it is enough that writers and readers believed that these difficulties characterized their generation and that they provided the psychological key to the powerlessness of the Jews.

Most of the literature of this renaissance was written by men, using the symbolism of male passivity and erotic confusion. Rebels in their own day against the rabbinic tradition, they later came to be canonized by Zionist culture as the spokesmen of a new national movement. As always, however, there were other discourses that accompanied and challenged the canon as well. By the beginning of the twentieth century, women began to express themselves as writers and poets.[82] The vision of some of these women both corroborated and challenged that of the male writers.

One of the earliest writers of Hebrew fiction from that period was Dvorah Baron (1888–1956), who composed most of her stories about Eastern Europe after emigrating to Palestine in 1911.[83] Baron wrote with outrage at the ill-treatment of women in Jewish family life,[84] but she also explored the theme of female sexuality. In one especially striking story,[85] she describes an Eastern European shtetl consisting only of women; the men have all left for America. As the gentile postman, Fedka, brings the women letters from their husbands, his relationship to them grows increasingly erotic. As opposed to the distant and therefore ineffectual Jewish men, Fedka is strong and attractive; when a fire sweeps through the town, he comes to protect the women. The women seek to seduce him; one of them transparently asks him to pull out a cork stuck in a bottle. Only when some of the husbands return to visit is Fedka shunted aside. Although she does not say so explicitly, Baron implies that the eroticism of Jewish women can only become "uncorked" in the absence of Jewish men and, perhaps, when the object of their desire is a Gentile.

Baron explored a similar dilemma in a bizarre fable about a female "Jewish" dog named Liska.[86] Dogs have a particularly negative valence in Ashkenazic Jewish folklore, generally in association with the gentile world; Liska is a symbol for the vexed relations between Jews and Gentiles in the Eastern European setting. She bears puppies sired by a dog belonging to a local nobleman, but her offspring are stolen from her. At another point, she is kidnapped by Gentiles and gang raped by their dogs. But Liska is driven by her sexual impulses: she falls in love with a "gentile" dog and betrays the Jews she had once belonged to; once she has crossed over to the other side of town, she becomes as vicious as the Gentiles. The Jews take vengeance on her by strangling her to death. Erotic Jewish women, Baron intimates, are doubly cursed, as Jews and as women. Those who challenge erotic norms become victims caught between two worlds, the Jewish and the Gentile.

The problem of erotic relations between Jews and Gentiles also plagued the male authors of the dominant literature of "national renaissance," against whom Baron rebelled, just as it preoccupied Jewish writers in Central Europe and, as we will see, those in twentieth-century America.[87] Hayyim Nachman Bialik (1873–1934), whose name is associated above all others with the generation of national renaissance, devoted a whole story to the issue.[88] "Behind the Fence" tells of the love between a Christian girl, Marinka, and a Jewish boy, Noah; their love stands in opposition to the brutality and xenophobia of his parents and of her witchlike stepmother. At the end of the story, he is forced to marry a Jewish girl, having left Marinka pregnant. The story is an indictment of both traditional Jewish society and of the "fence" between Jews and Gentiles. In what must have been shocking to those of his readers imbued with Jewish nationalism, Bialik seemed to celebrate true love between Jew and Gentile as a protest against convention.

The tension between nationalism and erotic relations with non-Jews was but one of the many personal ambivalences in Bialik's work, ambivalences that were taken as emblematic by a whole generation of writers and readers.[89] With Bialik, all of the themes examined in this chapter found their most eloquent expression: themes of loss of youth, the frustrations of love, and anger at Jewish passivity.[90] A product of the yeshiva world, like so many of his contemporaries and predecessors, Bialik vacillated between the traditional God of his childhood and the secular nationalist revolt of his adolescence, as well as between sexual renunciation and erotic desire.

In his prose poem "Scroll of Fire,"[91] Bialik gave mythic expression to this tension between erotic fulfillment and theological-national redemption. The poem tells the story of two hundred young men and two hundred young women who were exiled from Jerusalem after the destruction of the Second Temple. The hero of the poem rescues the divine torch that was carried from Jerusalem, but he must then choose between ascending with it to heaven or descending to save the one surviving girl—his intended—from the abyss. He falls into her outstretched arms, the torch is extinguished, and he is spewed forth into the distant exile. He wanders through the world, carrying the torch of "unconsummated love and the groan of the world from the night of the destruction."

Trapped between the "fire of love" and the "fire of God," Bialik's narrator captured the dilemmas of the generation. How could the desire for erotic fulfillment be reconciled with the demands of the religious tradition and national goals? If, as appears to be the case, the love of which the poet speaks is pagan and the beloved woman a non-Jew,[92] how can Eros be reconciled with Jewish allegiance? The end of the poem makes it clear that unconsummated love cannot be separated from the experience of exile: both represented dilemmas of powerlessness.

In his love poetry, Bialik was similarly torn between the rebellious desire for Eros and the sense that his desire is polluted and illegitimate. In "It Was a Summer Evening,"[93] he evokes the Lilith myth we recall from the *Alphabet of Ben Sira*:

> And the pure daughters of Lilith are twining-spinning
> shiny silver threads by moonlight,
> weaving one and the same garment for high priests and
> for swineherds.

The "daughters of Lilith" represent erotic women, but their weaving is at once sacred and profane; the very weaving of garments conjures up the biblical account of women in the Temple weaving garments for Asherah, the Canaanite goddess (2 Kings 23:7). The poem oscillates between chastity and lust: "O you chaste stars, come out quickly above, and you, harlots, below." The term for "harlots" is *kedashot,* the prophetic name for the putative cultic prostitutes of Canaanite religion. The erotic tension in the poem thus evokes the old biblical struggle between sexual norms and subversions and between Jewish tradition and pagan liberation.

In "The Hungry Eyes," Bialik blames a lover for having seduced him with the temptations of the flesh away from the "law":[94]

*For a small happy moment I was without a law, and I blessed*
*The hand that grants me the pain of sweet pleasure*
*And at the small moment of pleasure, of happiness and joy,*
*A whole world was destroyed for me—how great is the price that I paid*
*to your flesh.*

Women are the force of antinomian pleasure; they compete with the purity of the law for the heart of the Jewish male.

Given this profound ambivalence toward women and sexuality, Bialik is drawn back to love of the mother as a substitute for problematic Eros. In one of his most popular poems, written in 1905, Bialik mourns the loss of youth and the impossibility of love.[95] The poem is addressed ambiguously to a woman in terms reminiscent of the Jewish mystic's prayer to the Shekhinah, the female aspect of God. Bialik appeals to this woman/goddess to care for him as a substitute for an erotic relationship:

*Take me in under your wing*
*And be a mother and sister to me.*
*Let your lap be a shelter for my head,*
*A nest for my rejected prayers.*

If the legacy of the tradition had frustrated the search for love, it remained the sole, if ambivalent, source of comfort for its wayward sons. With poems such as these, Bialik's generation and its successors found an expression of their own dilemmas, dilemmas that were as much created by literature as they were by reality.

The reordering of power promised by the Haskalah had substantially failed in the minds of its children, and the exploration of the self in the autobiographies and novels had come to a solipsistic and pessimistic dead end. Love and erotic fulfillment seemed doomed. With Bialik, many turned their hopes to the new movement of Jewish nationalism. But could Zionism, which adopted Bialik as its poet laureate, redeem the Jews not only from their historic wanderings but also from their erotic exile?

# CHAPTER 8

# Zionism as an Erotic Revolution

IN February 1932 Magnus Hirsch-
feld, the German Jewish "sexologist" and campaigner for homosexual
rights, visited Palestine and reported admiringly on the young
socialist Zionist pioneers:

> In their simple dress—hatless, bare-necked and with bare legs—in the in-
> genuousness of their manner ... [they] seem so full of joy, strength and af-
> firmation of life that they seem to have overcome all the repressions and
> unconscious feelings of erotic inferiority frequently found at this age.[1]

Hirschfeld believed that in their new attitude toward the body, these
young people had overcome centuries of traditional sexual repression as
well as bourgeois reticence. During his visit, Hirschfeld investigated with
great curiosity the prevalent rumors that in the Zionist communal settlements, marriage partners were freely exchanged and promiscuity and
polygamy were common, a kind of Jewish version of the nineteenth-
century Oneida experiment in sexual utopia. Although he rejected these
rumors as pure fiction, Hirschfeld's report is revealing evidence of the
myth of Zionism as a utopian movement of erotic liberation.

One of the central claims of Zionism was that the Jews lived a disembodied existence in exile and that only a healthy national life could restore a necessary measure of physicality or materiality. This political ideology was not only based on the body as metaphor; it sought, in addition,
to transform the Jewish body itself, and especially the sexual body. Zionism meant both the physical rooting of the "people of the air" (*Luftmen-
schen*) in the soil of Palestine and the reclamation of the body. In the
spirit of the literature of national renaissance, Zionism promised an
erotic revolution for the Jews: the creation of a virile New Hebrew Man

but also the rejection of the inequality of women found in traditional Judaism in favor of full equality between the sexes in all spheres of life.

The reality of Zionism as an erotic revolution is by no means so straightforward. The new nationalism was accompanied, on the one hand, by a strong sense of respectability, inherited from European bourgeois culture, and driven, on the other hand, by the powerful asceticism of a national movement dedicated to goals that transcended the happiness of the individual. Doctrines of "free love" and "puritanism" coexisted in a peculiar dialectic, similar in many ways to the status of sexuality in the Soviet Union after the Bolshevik Revolution.[2] In the Zionist case, the tension between sexual liberation and asceticism channeled erotic energies into the tasks of nation building, a secular form of the sublimation and displacement already encountered in aspects of talmudic and medieval Jewish culture.[3] Out of its own inner dynamic, Zionism, which had sought a radical break with the Jewish past, often ended up returning unwittingly to traditional patterns. The conflicts within the erotic ideology of Zionism can serve as a set of signs for the tensions within Zionism as a whole between revolution and continuity.

This chapter will follow those sons and daughters of Europe who came to Palestine in the years before and after World War I and tried to put their utopian ideologies into practice. Between the years 1903 and 1914, and 1918 and 1924, two waves of immigration to Palestine, primarily from Eastern Europe, known as the Second and Third Aliyot, established the elite culture of the Zionist movement. These agricultural pioneers, or *haluztim*, were a very small minority among the population in the Yishuv, the Zionist community in Palestine before the establishment of the State of Israel in 1948. The overwhelming majority of the immigrants to prestate Israel lived in cities and towns, and their values were often not much different from those of the European Jewish bourgeoisie. Despite that, the *haluztim* were able to transform their utopian ideals and their own experience or, better, the way they *imagined* their experience, into the cultural ethos of Israeli society as a whole. As such, their importance far outweighs their actual numbers. The ideological writings, memoirs, and other literary efforts of this elite created a collective memory that serves to this day as the ambiguous myth of the origins of modern Israel.

## Central European Zionism and the Problem of Degeneration

The Zionist ethos was not rooted only in the Eastern European culture from which many of the pioneers came. Central European Jewish intellectuals in the first decades of the twentieth century contributed just as much to the Zionist argument for reconstituting the Jewish body. As products of a much more acculturated milieu than their cousins in the East, those writers and thinkers in Germany and Austria who became Zionists in the first part of the century reflected the larger drama of sexual liberation of the same period. As I have argued in the introduction to this book, Sigmund Freud, whose name is perhaps most identified with the modern "discovery" of sexuality, personified the ambiguities of this drama in both his life and his theories. The persistent conflict between liberation and sublimation of sexuality that one finds in Freud characterized fin de siècle European culture as a whole and especially the culture of the Central European Jews to which Freud himself belonged. The Viennese Jewish playwright Arthur Schnitzler, for example, explored both Jewish neuroses and erotic compulsions in his plays, leading Freud to hail him as a "colleague" in the investigation of "the underestimated and much-maligned erotic."[4] Franz Kafka, to take another example, was even more conscious of the problematic relationship between Eros and the Jews. In his famous "Letter to His Father," Kafka, like Portnoy, suggests that his sexual paralysis and inability to marry are somehow connected to the failure of his father to transmit Judaism as anything but a hollow shell, a collection of incomprehensible and meaningless rituals.[5]

The sexual paralysis and neurosis that these Central European writers described in their Jewish culture was to become the fertile ground for the Zionist critique of the Diaspora Jews. Like other nationalists of the end of the nineteenth century, the Zionists were preoccupied by the physical and emotional degeneration of the nation and by the threat of demographic decline.[6] Prominent in this general fin de siècle diagnosis was a conception of the physical body as a mirror of emotional disease. The cure for the disturbed soul, therefore, required exercise and physical labor: a healthy body would make for a harmonious psyche, not only for the individual but for the nation as a whole. In this nationalist thought, the individual body became a microcosm for the national body politic. To create a new image of the Jewish body became a symbol for creating a new Jewish nation.

The name most commonly associated with this doctrine was Max Nordau, whose cultural critique *Degeneration* had created a sensation in the 1890s. Within a few years, Nordau became Theodor Herzl's main Western European collaborator, and his Zionist writings exhibit direct links to his general theory of degeneration. For Nordau, degeneration is both a physiological and psychological condition, to be precise, a disease of the nervous system, corresponding to the fashionable diagnosis of "neurasthenia."[7]

Nordau's Zionism reflected this diatribe against degeneration. In 1900, in an important article in the journal of the German Zionist sports association, he popularized the already burgeoning nationalist idea of a

"Judaism with muscles."[8] As he suggested in *Degeneration*, one could adapt the organs to stress through exercise, and the Jews, thought by many physicians to be the quintessential neurasthenics, could overcome their hereditary nervousness by developing their bodies. Jews, according to Nordau, must become men of muscle instead of remaining slaves to their nerves.[9]

The journals of the Zionist sports societies repeated Nordau's arguments in issue after issue, often with learned medical "proof."[10] Return to nature and return to the body were part of the same revolutionary continuum. The iconography of the postcards published by the early Zionist congresses typically featured virile young farmers in Palestine contrasted with old, frail Orthodox Jews in the Diaspora.[11] Physical strength, youth, nature, and secularism were the constellation of Zionist symbols set against the degeneracy, old age, and urban and religious signs of the exile.

To build a Judaism with muscles meant to create a sexually healthy Judaism; indeed, the two went together because, in Nordau's account, their opposites, physical and erotic degeneracy, were linked. Nordau, in his essay from 1900, glorified the modern Jewish sportsmen who proudly proclaimed their connection to their people, and he contrasted them with those Jews in ancient times who would only engage in sports after surgically hiding their circumcisions. By implication, not only are the Zionist Jews of the sports associations—his readers—proud of their bodies, but they also have a healthy attitude toward their sexuality: they no longer need to hide the physical sign of Jewish sexual difference. For Nordau, and for those Zionists who wrote more explicitly than he did on the subject, such sexual health did not demand libertinism. On the contrary, excessive sexual desire, no less than excessive abstinence, was a sign of degeneration. Stable and sober marriage was evidently the cure.[12]

The belief that the Jews were especially "degenerate" was a favorite theme of modern anti-Semitism and was frequently linked to the accusation of Jewish hypersexuality, which posed a purported threat to the purity of the "Aryan" race. By adopting the language of degeneration, the Zionists were unconsciously treading on similar ground, but they tried to use such arguments to show why a national solution outside of Europe was necessary. In 1918 and 1919 Rafael Becker, a Swiss Jewish doctor who was a committed Zionist, wrote two essays about the nervous diseases of the Jews.[13] Becker, like other Zionist writers of the time, offers a purportedly "scientific" analysis of the Jewish condition, based in part on the findings of the new movement of "sexology." He accepts the anti-Semitic argument that the Jews more than others suffer from a variety of psychological abnormalities, but he argues that this is not a result of some racial disposition. Rather, it is a consequence of their political status as a minority and their skewed occupational structure. As a result, they tend to marry late, much later than in traditional Jewish society and also later than their gentile neighbors. Late marriage then becomes the cause of degeneration since the period when sexual desire is greatest is spent in frustration. And as a consequence of degeneration, Jewish fertility has drastically diminished.

In sounding this attack on late marriage, Becker was echoing a very widespread theme in Zionist thinking. What is most striking is that this concern with late marriage, a practice which had become prevalent among Central European Jews as early as the eighteenth century, reversed the preoccupation with *early* marriage among the nineteenth-century maskilim. For Becker and others, sexual dysfunction is considered a result of delayed gratification, while for their Eastern European predecessors, it had been a result of premature sexuality: thus was medical science harnessed to the wagon of ideology.

At the end of one of his essays, Becker offers some homespun medical advice for the treatment of Jewish sexual frustration. He prescribes the elimination of the strong spices "so beloved in Jewish kitchens," as well as of coffee, tea, and alcohol, since they "promote" sexual lust, especially in the young. But he hastens to add that such remedies are mere palliatives. The cure for the sexual neurosis of the Jews must be radical: "the creation of our own home and land. Only this will brings us a healthy body and a free and untroubled spirit."[14] Becker thus seemingly accepted the charge that the Jews are hypersexual and he prescribed a cure that would bring about both sexual restraint *and* increased Jewish fertility.

Becker's recognition of a problem of diminished Jewish fertility was common in discussions of the Jewish community from this period.[15] In part, these discussions reflected the general concern in Germany, France, and elsewhere with the low birth rate resulting from modern urban life and, after World War I, with the population loss caused by the war. But in the minds of many Jews, low Jewish fertility was exacerbated by intermarriage.[16] Zionists were perhaps among the most vocal, though not the only ones, to comment on these issues. Even an opponent of Zionism like the philosopher Franz Rosenzweig appears to have been distressed by the demographic decline of the German Jewish community. His great work of theology, the *Star of the Redemption,* is, in fact, an argument for defining the Jews as a "blood" community of procreation, as opposed to Christianity, which is a faith community of proselytism. In emphasizing blood and procreation as the essence of Judaism, Rosenzweig was engaged in a desperate polemic against the mounting assimilation and intermarriage of the Weimar Jews.[17]

Among the Zionist writings from Central Europe, perhaps the most comprehensive discussion of the connection between Zionism, Jewish fertility, and sexuality is a monograph by an Orthodox Jew, Hans Goslar (1889–1945), entitled *The Sexual Ethic of Jewish Rebirth: A Word to Our*

*Youth.*[18] Like Becker, Goslar decries late marriage among the Jews and urges a return to early marriage as had existed in traditional Jewish society. The late marriages in modern Europe result in a double standard: women are required to remain chaste, while men are encouraged to engage in premarital sex for physical and psychological reasons. Following Nordau, he holds that urbanization has increased sexual drives and created all kinds of social ills, especially prostitution. Jewish youth has succumbed to all these vices, particularly since Jews mature sexually earlier than Germans. Here, Goslar—unlike Becker—resorts to something like a racial argument not so distant from that of some of the anti-Semites: since the Jews come originally from the warm Mediterranean climate, their sexual urges develop at an early age. At this point, Goslar comes perilously close to the myth of Jewish hypersexuality.

He argues that by marrying earlier Jews can control these urges. Since a shift in the age of marriage is impossible in Germany, Zionism is the only possible cure. Adopting the romantic, Zionist attitude toward agriculture, Goslar believes that the creation of a rural, peasant society will cool the overheated erotic drives caused by urban life. More practically, Zionist land and taxation policy will make it economically feasible to marry young and thereby restore a high fertility rate. Thus, like Becker, Goslar sees Zionism as the only solution to the endemic sexual and demographic diseases of Jewish life in modern Europe.

Goslar harked back to the shtetl and denounced modern life as the cause of Jewish sexual problems, but not all Zionists took this nostalgic position. One anonymous author, writing in the short-lived Zionist periodical *Jerubbaal* in 1918, took the Haskalah view and attacked traditional Jewish marriages as being based on commerical arrangements. Few people, even among the bourgeois German Jews, marry for love. He warns against transporting this unhealthy arrangement to Zion:

> It is obvious that marital relations as they are commonly found in Galut [Exile], must not be transferred to Palestine. In the interest of the health of the Volk [*Volksgesundheit*], a new form of relationship between man and woman must be found.[19]

But even this more radical author returns to earlier models in Jewish history, in this case to the biblical custom of the fifteenth of the Hebrew month of Av, when young men and women would dance in the vineyards and create bonds of love totally divorced from material concerns; since the women were not allowed to wear jewelry, he claims, the poor had as good a chance of finding a mate as the wealthy. Here is a case not of "scientific" Zionist sexology, in the style of Becker or Goslar, but rather of a romantic appeal to the Bible as the basis for an erotic revolution. The return to the land of the Bible would resurrect an "antimaterialist" style of life in which family life would be based totally on pure feeling.

This antimaterialism that infected much of early Zionist thought also figured prominently in the critical image of women in some of this writing. Goslar denounced what he called the "cult of women" (*Frauenkult unseres Zeitalters*), which turns them into sexual objects and materialistic "luxury animals" (*Luxustierchen*), rather than treating them as comrades, wives, and mothers.[20] Martin Buber took a similar position in an essay entitled "The Zion of the Jewish Woman."[21] He, too, idealized women in traditional society, in contrast to their degenerate state in the contemporary world (Buber uses Nordau's *Entartung*). In past times the family had been the cornerstone of the Jewish world, the substitute for the lost Jewish state, and women were its main guardians. Given the central role of women, the decline of the Jewish family in modern times is largely their fault, as they have become slaves to their Christian servants. The "regal beauty" of Jewish women in earlier times has given way to ostentation, an early version of the later myth of the Jewish American Princess. Zionism calls upon Jewish women to return to the virtues of motherhood, which would help them overcome the nervous disorders of their lives.

These male voices were not the only ones to be heard. In 1918 Marie Popper, also a Zionist, blamed the structure of the bourgeois Jewish family for the distorted development of its daughters.[22] Although she, too, describes the superficial and materialistic characteristics of adolescent Jewish girls in Germany, she holds the social milieu rather than the girls themselves responsible for these ills. Her solution is not as specific as those of some of the other Zionist writers, but it is clear from her conclusion that the problem of Jewish women can only be solved in a Jewish nationalist context. The curious combination of female liberation and the return of women to their traditional roles as wives and mothers was to characterize much of Zionist thought, including the more radical sexual ideologies of the socialist pioneers.

## Sexual Utopianism in the Second and Third Aliyot

The young pioneers who came to Palestine in the years before and after the First World War were imbued with both the legacy of the Eastern European nationalist revival and the Zionist polemic against Jewish degeneration. Inspired by a mix of socialist Zionism, anarchism, and Tolstoyan populism, they set up a variety of utopian communities in an effort to reconstitute the Jewish people by first revolutionizing their own lives. In the words of a popular song of the era: "We came to the land to build it and to be built by it." To "be built by it" meant to change one's values and practices and, above all, to change one's very body and psyche by agricultural work. In the 1920s the poet Abraham Shlonsky (1900–1973) celebrated physical labor and the body of the worker in a poem entitled "Labor" (*Amal*).[23] Shlonsky adopts phrases from the Song of Songs and from elsewhere in the Bible to glorify the sweating body of the new Jewish worker, concluding with a reference to Joseph's striped shirt as the worker erotically unites with his work:

> *Dress me, pure mother, in a splendid striped shirt*
> *And at dawn deliver me*
> *To Labor.*

This invocation of the mother, like the image of the lost mother in the nineteenth-century literature, was to return again and again in the writings of these pioneers.[24]

The eroticization of labor was closely bound up with images of the land of Israel as a lover, a kind of materialistic transformation of the old allegory of love between God and Israel. Shlonsky invokes the biblical "blessing of breasts," originally associated with the divine name El Shaddai, to refer to the fertility of the land.[25] The poet Uri Zvi Greenberg (1896–1980) uses similar erotic imagery to refer to the connection between the Zionist and the land: "Here is the motherland until the final day; here a canopy of love will be erected."[26]

For the early Zionists, Oriental Palestine promised the liberation of the senses from the suffocation of Europe, a suffocation at once traditional and bourgeois. The image of the Arab as a sensual savage played a key role in this mythology; later, when the national struggle between Zionism and the Palestinians became sharper, the Arab was frequently seen as effeminate in opposition to the virile modernism of Jewish nationalism. The image of the impotent Diaspora Jew was now projected onto the Palestinian, who, like the exilic Jew, refused to free himself from medieval traditions.

Among the ideologists of the Second Aliyah, no one brought together these themes of labor, nature, and return to the body as clearly as Aharon David Gordon (1856–1922). Having joined the young pioneers at the settlement of Kinneret when he was forty-eight, Gordon was a kind of father figure of the Second Aliyah. Under the influence of Tolstoy, Gordon created a veritable religion of agricultural labor, a mystical union of the physical body of the worker with the cosmos. In 1918 Gordon wrote an essay on the problem of marriage among the pioneers.[27] Echoing themes prevalent in the Zionist writings from Central Europe, Gordon argued that the late age of marriage in the Diaspora, which was adopted from non-Jewish society, had had catastrophic physical and psychological effects, from excessive nervousness to poor eyesight, bad teeth, and early balding! The cure for these ills of the exile was a new

form of marriage in which gender relations must be based on pure "natu-
ralness." Consistent with his overall theology of work and nature, Gordon envisioned these new utopian relationships as melding human beings with the forces of nature, which would, in turn, become the basis for
a renewed Jewish nation.

Out of intense disillusionment with marriage and family life in the Diaspora, many of the members of the Second and Third Aliyot agreed with
Gordon that a new form of male-female relations was a necessary, integral part of Zionism. Indeed, this revolution in sexuality was seen as part
of the larger economic and social revolution needed to produce a truly
egalitarian society. One of the most interesting of these ideologues from
the Second Aliyah was the poet and novelist Zvi Shatz (1890–1921), who
developed the idea of an intimate commune, or *kevutzah*.[28] For Shatz, the
commune had to resurrect the family on the basis of love linked to a religion of nature:

> The family is collapsing and religion is dying, but eternal life values are still
> valid; they will only change their forms because the need for family is deep
> and organic and the religious relation to life and nature will yet become
> strong within us and be resurrected in our return to the land and to nature.
> For these are our true Messiah. Thus, a new family on the basis of a new re-
> ligion will establish the laboring nation on its soil. The family will be resur-
> rected not on the basis of blood relations, but on the basis of spiritual inti-
> macy.

Here was a veritable religion of the family, which Shatz, like Gordon,
saw as a manifestation of a new, secular messianic religion of nature.
The return to the soil would revolutionize erotic relations. This appropriation and transformation of traditional language was to recur repeatedly
in the attempts of these Zionist visionaries to construct a new sexual
ethos.

The attempts by Gordon and Shatz to put in writing a theory of erotic
liberation were relatively unusual for the members of the Second Aliyah,
who tended to be quite reticent about sexual matters. Although influenced by Russian feminism and committed to new forms of family life,
they typically unwilling to articulate their ideas fully. Indeed, most
of their memoirs touch only briefly, if at all, on the subject. A kind of
self-censorship suggests the degree to which they remained ambivalent
about their own inchoate ideology.

The Third Aliyah was different. The period immediately following
World War I was an era of sexual experimentation and frankness, especially in Weimar Germany and Soviet Russia. Sexually explicit writers
like D. H. Lawrence threw off bourgeois convention, while Freud's psychology of sexuality became a cultural commonplace. This new culture

of sexuality infected young Jews as well as other Europeans. They read Freud with great interest, as well as, to a lesser extent, the works of "sexologists" like Magnus Hirschfeld and Iwan Bloch. Some of the young Zionists of the Third Aliyah therefore produced much fuller reflections on the connection between Eros and Zion.

Many in the Third Aliyah came to Zionism through the new Jewish nationalist youth movements such as the Blau-Weiss in Germany and the Hashomer ha-Tzair, or Young Guard, that began in Galicia, the Austro-Hungarian portion of Poland, in 1913. In the 1930s this latter movement was to become avowedly Marxist, but in the decade after World War I, it was imbued with a romantic ideology of nature and a cult of youth.[29] The Galician Hashomer ha-Tzair was particularly important since it functioned as a bridge between Central and Eastern European Zionism.

The Zionist youth movements were deeply influenced by the ideas of the German *Wandervogel* (the neo-Romantic youth movement), although the *Wandervogel* itself was frequently anti-Semitic. One of the theoreticians of the *Wandervogel* was Han Blüher. His book, *Die deutsche Wandervogelbewegung als eroticisches Phänomen*, had an important impact on the Jewish youth movements. Blüher's almost mystical celebration of the youth culture of the *Wandervogel* emphasized the strong homoerotic bonds between the male members, and it is not surprising that Magnus Hirschfeld, the leading campaigner in Germany for homosexual rights, wrote the introduction to the book. This aspect of Blüher's book evidently held little appeal for the young Zionists, but his contrast between the revolutionary erotic spirit in the youth movements and the conventions of bourgeois society had very strong resonance.[30]

One of the most important ideological leaders of the early Hashomer ha-Tzair was Meir Yaari (1897–1987), who joined the movement in his native Galicia and immigrated to Palestine after World War I. Already in his early twenties and a veteran of the war, Yaari quickly became the spiritual mentor of the younger Hashomer pioneers. In August 1920 he led a small group to the settlement of Bitania Elite overlooking the Jordan Valley. Although the settlement disbanded half a year later, the group's experience became a kind of mythic crucible of the Third Aliyah, an attempt to create Zvi Shatz's intimate commune. Writing to his comrades in Europe from Bitania, Yaari laid out the erotic ideology of the commune: "The commune is not based only on economic cooperation, but also on the erotic. Bourgeois domestic eroticism is the enemy of the commune. The commune cannot exist without a deeper connection between its members."[31] In terms redolent of Nietzsche, but also of Jewish mysticism, he declared in a 1921 article:

We felt that the person who is suffocating in the private stifling framework ... of mechanical civilization must destroy first and foremost the husks [*ke-*

*lipot*] that weigh on his natural personality.... What will be gained by this destruction is the wild and free communalism of a nation that rules its elemental forces, that answers to them but is not enslaved by them.[32]

The elemental force that needs to be freed is the sexual and the result will be a virile New Man, as opposed to the neurotic Jews of the exile:

[Hashomer ha-Tzair] puts an end to sexual hypocrisy and removes that instinctual impotence ... that distinguishes the conventional type of Jew from the developmental path of the youth.... We love the naked youth who remains a child when he matures, who sanctifies his instinct and the pleasure of his instinct and does not pollute it. I see before me the man who demolishes the walls that generations have put up between spirit and flesh and between reason and instinct. In this way, in an instinctual way, we will create a man who is at once the most primitive and the most cultured, who will unite with his wife and his comrades.[33]

The New Man is a naked child, which raises questions about whether he is sexually mature: Yaari makes no real distinction between sexual union with one's wife and with one's comrades. This, then, is primarily the eroticism of a youth culture rather than a doctrine of free love between men and women. Yaari assaults the Jewish tradition by using its own language: he seizes the rabbinic concept of "sanctification" of the sexual act and presses it into the service of a Dionysian religion of nature.

Yaari's erotic Zionism was based on a cascade of masculine images contrasted to the "feminine" weakness of the Diaspora. For example, in a letter written to a convention of Hashomer leaders in 1918, he asserts, again with Nietzschean bombast:

We want to educate this generation to be tough and strong and not soft and wallowing in their imaginations. Only the [strong] arms of heroes will accomplish this work and not poets.... I view with great trepidation the groups of Hashomer that are dominated not by men but by angels of beauty and love.[34]

In his letter from Bitania, he castigates the women in the group who were not ready to undertake the new erotic life of the commune: "Eroticism for them is only inflated words and, in addition, something that is private for each person. In the final analysis, [the women] say, you cannot change your nature and your instincts."[35]

This ill-concealed misogyny was not uncommon in the overheated writings of this circle. Another veteran of Bitania, Benjamin Dror used very similar terms to describe the relations between men and women in the commune.[36] Dror suggests that a truly healthy human society must give equality to women, that the kind of homoerotic relations celebrated by the Greeks and by the eighteenth-century Hasidim were laudatory but incomplete. In Bitania, he says, two of the four women were erotic magnets for the twenty-four men, and even though only two actually developed relationships with them, "private erotic life [became] the spiritual property of the whole group." The abolition of private property in the commune included the abolition of private erotic relations! But despite his call for the equality of women, Dror observes, the women of Bitania remained appendages of the spiritual life of the men: "The women did not, to be sure, live their spiritual lives with the same intensity and intellectual richness as that of the men, but inasmuch as they served as the center of erotic attraction for the men, they [that is, the women] were educated by them." Clearly, the severe numerical imbalance between men and women at Bitania, as in many of the other settlements of the Second and Third Aliyot, aggravated the sexual frustrations of the men and may have contributed to the patriarchal erotic ideology that some of them espoused.

The struggle for the equality of women in the workplace that accompanied the Second and Third Aliyot reflected the struggle between revolutionary ideology and more conventional attitudes. Yet even within the ideology itself, which was articulated overwhelmingly by men, there was a contradiction between the principle of equality and the homoerotic imagery of the youth movement. As long as Zionism was seen as the creation of a virile New Man against the allegedly feminine impotence of exile, women would have difficulty finding a truly equal place.

Not all women were eager to accept this secondary role. One woman from the Second Aliyah complained bitterly in her diary that the men expected the women to exhibit conventional standards of beauty and their only interest in their female comrades was sexual.[37] Another woman from that period rejected all advances and demanded that every man regard her as a "sister."[38] Advocacy for women found its place in the public realm as well. Dvorah Baron, most of whose protofeminist stories about Eastern Europe were written in Palestine, was a vigorous advocate of women's rights. She put forth these ideas as a writer of fiction and as an editor of the labor movement newspaper, *Ha-Poel ha-Tzair*.[39] In 1921 Ada Fishman, another of the leaders of the movement for equality for women workers, argued that women in Palestine are too much identified with the private realm and they must take equal part in work in order to break out of the private sphere.[40] Her essay explicitly attacked patriarchy and the way that the quest for equality is undermined when the pioneering women become mothers.

But the women of the Second and Third Aliyot should not be seen anachronistically through the eyes of contemporary feminism. For instance, none of the testimonies of women from the Bitania group reflects at all on gender relations. Arriving at an understanding of the independent role of women did not come easily. Rachel Katznelson-Shazar, whose husband Zalman was to become the third president of the State of Israel, wrote in her diary that "woman, too, arouses and creates the man, but first the man must awaken her. They [men] awaken by themselves. Full liberation requires men."[41] As her diary reveals, she only gradually and painstakingly came to the realization that she need not be entirely dependent. Thus, although there was a movement for equality in the workplace, few women systematically resisted the private maternal role assigned to them by Zionist ideology.

The problematic status of women and the role of sexuality in general are quite apparent in the extraordinary collection of documents from the Hashomer group entitled *Kehilyateinu* (Our Community).[42] Two documents are of particular interest, one by the editor, Nathan Bistritsky, and the other by Eliahu Rapoport. Bistritsky evidently believed that the new family in Zion would move beyond patriarchy, but he regarded the present state of sexuality as chaotic: "We have not sufficiently matured to raise the erotic power within us to a sexual power, one that can create a new relationship to woman." What did he envision as this new relationship? Here, Bistritsky reveals the profoundly conservative nature of his erotic philosophy: mature sexuality must have procreation as its primary end. But since Zionist eroticism is still immature, "we are not yet able to see in woman a sister and mother." Despite the desire for sexual liberation that permeates his writing, Bistritsky saw women less as sexual partners than as potential mothers.

This attitude found even more extreme expression in Bistritsky's novel, *Days and Nights*, first published in 1926. The novel is clearly based on *Kehilyateinu*, filled as it is with interminable speeches by members of a fictitious Zionist commune. In one speech that captures particularly well not only his position, but also that of the Hashomer circle, the character Alexander Tsuri denounces bourgeois romantic love and calls for a community in which women are equals. But once again, the need for these women stems from the need to procreate. Women preserve the essence of humanity, whereas men are the force for change. In a mythological moment reminiscent of the blood symbolism of the biblical priestly code, he predicts that at the end of history—in messianic times—matriarchy will return. Abraham will alternate with his son Isaac in suckling from the breasts of Sarah his wife.

> She—the mother—stands outside of our circle, the circle of history, and a strip of blood stands red behind her like a holy, terrifying shadow. She wallows in the blood, her holy blood, the blood of virginity, the blood of her first sacrifice, the blood of childbirth. Humanity washes in the blood of its heroes, but the dove of the holy spirit descends only on the fountain of

blood that flows from the woman. I want to see the face of a young girl, to see in her the mother of my children, to see in her my mother. Mother! What am I and who am I, a man, without my mother ...?[43]

This confusion between woman as one's mother or as the mother of one's children or as one's sister but never, it would seem, as a full equal was not unique to Bistritsky. Rather, it reflected a deep confusion among many of the men of the Second and Third Aliyot. Might it be that the premature abandonment of their own mothers had left these teenage boys still uncertain about just what they expected from women? Or perhaps even earlier separation issues were at stake, traumatic separations that we know of from the nineteenth-century Haskalah critique of traditional Jewish childhood.

The language of blood is also striking. Zionism often used the German *völkisch* language of "blood and soil" before that language became irretrievably corrupted by the Nazis.[44] Bistritsky specifically attributes procreative blood to women, and his allusions to the famous passage in Ezekiel 16 suggest that this blood has a nationalist dimension: in that chapter, Ezekiel describes how God weds Israel, metaphorically portrayed as a girl "wallowing" in the blood of childbirth. So for Bistritsky, female blood will be the force for national renewal.

Eliahu Rapoport's copious contributions to *Kehilyateinu* reflect a similar confusion about women and the role of sexuality. Unlike the younger members of the group, Rapoport (1889–1952) had married in 1910 and had studied philosophy and mathematics at the University of Göttingen. He was a disciple of Martin Buber, and his writings suggest something of Buber's influence. Like Bistritsky, Rapoport considered procreation to be the ultimate value of sexuality. Conventional morality, he claims, considers the sexual instinct something remote from God because there is physical pleasure in it; by severing the generative function of sexuality from its physical aspect, it has polluted the sex act and robbed it of its divinity. For Rapoport, however, "every sexual act returns one to divine purity,"[45] but only when sexuality is intended to produce a child does it become holy; only then does it "unite the body with the soul and become stamped with *hagshamah*"[46] (the peculiar Zionist term that means something like "self-realization" through the material world). He concludes his elegy to eroticism with a feverish appeal to biblical women who broke with conventional morality in order to procreate:

This is what today's generation demands of me: liberate me from the burden of morality; redeem me from the curse of barrenness; redeem me toward the distant image of a blood community.... Tamar, Tamar, you before whom generations from Israel kneel in fear and respect, where are you? ... And you, the heroines, the daughters of Lot, who dared and thus gave life to

nations of the world, where are you? And you, the divine poet who wrote
the Song of Songs, were you writing about love or morality when you asked
anxiously: "We have a little sister and she has no breasts..."? I swear to you,
community of Israel in the name of the sacrifice of your love and your oath:
We have grown sisters and their breasts are like towers and walls built
upon them and they are barren and their breasts are hidden and sealed between the thighs of fanatical priests. Redeem me from the curse of barrenness—such is the cry to me of today's generation.[47]

In this extraordinary passage, the Bible becomes a Nietzschean mani-
festo against conventional morality and religion. The biblical Tamar,
who seduced her father-in-law in order to give birth to the ancestor of
King David,[48] and the daughters of Lot, who committed incest with their
father to create the nations of Moab and Amon,[49] are role models for revolutionary women prepared to shatter bourgeois respectability. The Song
of Songs becomes a broadside for sexual liberation against the priests of
traditional religion. Only the liberation of eroticism, suggests Rapoport,
will restore fertility to the impotent Jews; only an eroticized Zionism will
return them to the glory of the Bible and re-create a mystical, *völkisch*
"blood community."

For many of this period, sexual rebellion came to symbolize the Zionist revolution as a whole. As Abraham Shlonsky wrote in his attack on
the clichéd language of his literary predecessors:

> We rebelled [by proclaiming]: "Free love! Civil marriage!" But our prose is
> like a pure, modest Jewish daughter following the tradition.... [We de-
> mand:] Civil marriage and free love between words, without stylistic en-
> gagements, without genealogies, without a dowry of associations and the
> main point: without *huppah* and *kiddushin* [the required elements in a tra-
> ditional Jewish marriage]. There is too much "family purity" in our lan-
> guage. Every combination of words is an act of promiscuity, a one-night
> stand.[50]

Just as Eros must be freed from the constraints of the tradition in favor
of free love, so the Hebrew language must be liberated from the weight of
the past and allowed to serve the Zionist revolution.

Not only the secular, socialist wing of the Zionist movement called for
the reclamation of the body. Abraham Isaac Kook (1865–1935), who was
the chief Ashkenazic rabbi of Palestine from 1921 until his death, echoed
the secular Zionists on this point, although he avoided any reference to
the erotic:

> The claim of our flesh is great. We require a healthy body. We have greatly
> occupied ourselves with the soul and have forsaken the holiness of the

body. We have neglected health and physical prowess, forgetting that our flesh is as sacred as our spirit.... Our return [to Zion] will only succeed if it will be marked, along with its spiritual glory, by a physical return which will create healthy flesh and blood, strong and well-formed bodies, and a fiery spirit encased in powerful muscles.[51]

Perhaps never before in Jewish tradition had an Orthodox authority placed so much spiritual value on the physical body.

Right-wing Zionism, drawing from modern nationalist rhetoric, also glorified the body. Vladimir Jabotinsky (1880–1940), the leader of the right-wing Revisionist movement, celebrated virility, expressed in military metaphors, as the answer to Jewish impotence.[52] Like Rapoport, Jabotinsky saw the Bible as a model for the sexual liberation of the Jews, which he, too, considered part and parcel of national liberation. In his fascinating novel, *Samson*, first written in Russian and published in 1927, Jabotinsky portrays the Philistines as models of both national pride and sexual health. One passage describes a Philistine ceremony in which the Philistine women are provocatively bare-breasted, their nudity a sign of their vigor. Samson, who is revealed at the end to be the son of an Israelite mother and a Philistine father, serves as the bridge between the still-stunted Israelites and the virile Philistines. His intermarriage with Philistine women represents Israel breaking the chains of sexual bondage in favor of a new, liberated national life.

Jabotinsky's disciple Arthur Koestler reflected similar themes in his later novel *Thieves in the Night*.[53] Koestler spent a period of time in 1926 at Kibbutz Hephzibah, which was one of the two settlements created by the *Kehilyateinu* group. In his novel, which takes place in 1938 on a similar kibbutz, his protagonist, a half Jew named Joseph, adopts Zionism after a gentile lover is repulsed at the sight of his circumcision, a sign, it would seem for Koestler, of Jewish sexual disability. For Koestler, as for Jabotinsky, the Jews are sexually incompetent and require radical Zionism to liberate them and make them more like the erotic Gentiles. But socialist Zionism is a problematic answer, for Koestler portrays the Jewish women of the kibbutz as chaste and asexual and the communal ideology as thwarting the sexual liberation of the individual. *Thieves in the Night* is a political tract disguised as literature, but in his portrait of the romantic relationships in his fictional kibbutz, Koestler managed to capture both the erotic ideology of early pioneering Zionism and also something of its internal contradictions.

The inflated sexual rhetoric of the Hashomer group was not without its internal critics as well. Within the movement itself, there were dissenters, notably David Horowitz, who broke with Yaari at Bitania and was later to become one of the leading figures in creating Israel's modern economy. Horowitz charged that what Yaari thought was erotic was really "neurotic," a sublimation of natural instincts.[54] Yaari himself fell out with his former comrades, in part, it seems, as a result of his marriage to one of the women from Bitania. He refused to allow his contribution to *Kehilyateinu* to appear in the collection and, instead, published a scathing denunciation of *Kehilyateinu* under the title "Alienated Symbols,"[55] an essay that might be considered a self-criticism as well. Among his objections to the bombastic philosophizing of his former comrades, he decried the failure of women's liberation in the movement; women had been turned into "holy mothers" but in reality were no more than servants.[56]

Objections such as these to the erotic ideology of the romantic youth movements were ultimately to predominate, and a more sober, even puritanical view would prevail. Many proclaimed revolutionary ideals, but in establishing their own families, they frequently reverted to either the traditional or the bourgeois marital patterns they knew from childhood. Nevertheless, even if the reality of the communes rarely corresponded to the wild imaginings of these ideologues, the myth of the Second and Third Aliyot as movements of sexual liberation was to persist and to shape the later image of the founders of Israel.

## Asceticism in the Service of the Nation

The ideology of erotic liberation was always a means to realize the broader nationalist goals of Zionism; hence, in part, the repeated insistence on the need for procreation. Sexual liberation was a necessary part of the revolt against the bourgeois, assimilationist culture of the Diaspora; it was not a means of individual fulfillment. Instead, the notion prevailed that one must sacrifice family life and erotic relations for the fulfillment of national goals, which led A. D. Gordon to protest against what he called the artificial division between "life" and "work."[57] Hiyuta Busel, one of the female founders of Degania, the first kibbutz, described this prevalent view:

> Could anyone point to special relationships? Not at all—we would not even admit it to ourselves. We believed with great naïveté that it wasn't proper to think about love between men and women. True love needs to encompass all of humanity and not to be limited to love that is "dependent." We developed an original formulation for this principle: "We are not in love with this or that boy or girl but with the concept of youth united by one human, national idea."[58]

In a similar vein, a young woman, whom we have already mentioned, denied the sexual overtones of her relationships with the men in her commune and insisted on referring to all of them as "brothers." One of them fell so passionately in love with her that he threatened to kill himself if she would not marry him. This left her perplexed:

> She didn't understand how it was possible to concern oneself with matters
> of love at a time when the land needed workers, Hebrew labor.... She said
> to him: "You are my brother, so how can you love me as a woman?" She fi-
> nally persuaded him that he should regard her as only a sister.[59]

Thus, the sublimation of sexual desire in the service of the nation was a common theme in the ideologies of the Second and Third Aliyot and it was often expressed in the notion that the *halutzim* were creating a new family in which all were brothers and sisters. To have an erotic relationship with a comrade in such circumstances was both akin to incest and a betrayal of the national ideal. It may well be that the strong sense of having left families in faraway Russia created the profound need among these adolescents to recapture what they had lost. Indeed, the memoirs of the pioneers are filled with homesickness and longing for parents in the old country.[60] Unable to see themselves in the role of parents, they could only envision themselves as children in need of siblings.

Even among the proponents of an erotic Zionism in Hashomer ha-Tzair, there was a strong tendency toward abstinence and restraint. In his 1921 polemic for liberating the "instincts," Meir Yaari nevertheless expressed concern about those who were enslaved to their sexual drives in terms reminiscent of the talmudic tradition: "They cannot be victorious by conquering their instincts and overcome chaos with the strength of a dominant will."[61] Eliahu Rapoport also celebrated sexual restraint.[62] He confesses that when he was still a youth, his sexual urge had caused him repeatedly to fall in love with women who, because of their devotion to ideals, rejected his advances. Thanks to these virtuous women, he was once again able to experience shame, and now in Palestine work on the land had brought him back to a state of purity. For Rapoport, women are not only mothers but they are also buffers against the dangerous sexuality of men, both notions that he might well have borrowed from tradition.

This puritanical streak among the pioneers found expression in their social arrangements. Courtship rituals followed very definite patterns, which had already characterized gender relations among the educated Jews in Eastern Europe. In memoir after memoir, relationships were established by the couple reading out loud to each other and sharing ideological dreams. Zalman Shazar and Rachel Katznelson read the Hasidic tales of Nahman of Bratslav during their courtship in St. Petersburg,[63] while Rivka Mahnimit, another diarist from the Second Aliyah, relates how she and her fiancé read the Yiddish writer Y. L. Peretz.[64] Typically, the young couple would go to a secluded place to read and talk; according to the mythology, the favored retreat was the *goren*, the wheat threshing floor reminiscent of the seduction scene in the biblical Book of Ruth. If the memoirs are to be trusted, though, little in the way of sexual experimentation took place during these encounters. Zvi Shatz captured these rituals in his novella *Batya*, in particular in a scene in which the two young people, Batya and Dan, slip from an intense ideological discussion into the beginnings of an erotic encounter, only to pull back in adolescent confusion. She is quite explicit about the relationship: "What's the matter with you, Dan. Aren't you ashamed of yourself, you're such a child!"[65]

Once a couple made it through the courtship ritual and declared itself publicly, there was typically no wedding ceremony (at Bet Alfa it was not until about 1948, some twenty-six years after the kibbutz was founded, that an actual wedding party occurred). Those who needed to marry before a rabbi in order to obtain a passport or to register a child would travel to a neighboring village. (On some occasions if the wife or husband was too busy to make this journey, someone else would be sent as a substitute bride or groom!)[66]

In the settlement itself, "marriage" essentially consisted of a request to the secretariat to obtain a joint room.[67] Even here the arrangements often stifled sexual expression. It was not uncommon for a third person to share the room with the couple; often this was a guest, but occasionally it was a regular resident. This "third" in the room (also called "primus" after the primitive cooking stove with which each room was equipped) became a kind of institution that continued for many years. Although all the evidence suggests that it was a product of insufficient housing and not of ideology, it certainly reflected the prevalent insensitivity to private life. An extraordinarily frank diary written by a woman in 1934 reveals the intense sexual frustration that came with the presence of a "third" in the room.[68] She relates that all intimate relations with her husband had ceased and, further, that due to the lack of privacy, she was barely able even to discuss her desperate unhappiness with him.

Arthur Koestler described the lack of private life at Kibbutz Hephzibah in 1926 in his memoir, *Arrow in the Blue*, a text that served as the basis for his novel *Thieves in the Night*. According to Koestler, people no longer shared their sexual feelings and frustrations in the communal meetings, as they had evidently done at Bitania only six years earlier: "Promiscuous tendencies were considered signs of individual selfishness and social maladjustment. Sexual conflicts and tragedies did, of course, occur, but they were exceptional—mainly, one may suppose, because the sexual appetites were blunted by fatigue and by the neutralizing effect of familiarity."[69] If the beginnings of the *kevutza* had been erotically charged, the grueling labor and harsh conditions of life there had in short order extinguished the sexual sparks. One wonders, in fact, to what extent the stories of free love were not mythological from the outset, spawned by the ideology of sexual liberation rather than by reality.[70]

Sexuality was therefore banished to an almost nonexistent private realm, where it would not interfere with communal goals. Relations between men and women were supposed to be concealed, and it was considered improper to make any public display of them. Couples frequently entered the communal dining room separately and ate at separate tables to avoid giving the impression that their private relationship impinged on their solidarity with the commune. In the jargon of the settlements, a woman would refer to her spouse as "my man," rather than "my husband," since in Hebrew, especially, the latter term (*baali*) connoted possession.

In their educational doctrines as well, the utopian youth movements were often fanatically puritanical. The Tenth Commandment of Hashomer ha-Tzair's secular decalogue read: "The Shomer is pure in his thoughts, words, and deeds. He does not smoke or drink alcohol and he guards his sexual purity." In one illustrated version of the Ten Commandments of Hashomer, the words "sexual purity" are highlighted and are framed by a chaste boy and equally chaste girl shaking hands while he holds the flag of the movement.[71] The iconography scarcely differs from the socialist realism of Soviet Russia.

This attitude was also reflected in the child-rearing philosophy of the kibbutz movement in the 1930s and 1940s, especially, but not exclusively, in the settlements of Hashomer ha-Tzair.[72] One of the chief theorists of this philosophy was Shmuel Golan, an early disciple of Meir Yaari at Bitania.[73] In Golan's writings and those of other educational theorists, one senses the almost irreconcilable tensions between utopianism and puritanism, although these contradictions are papered over with "scientific" jargon, frequently adapted from Freud and his disciples.[74] They understood psychoanalysis as teaching the necessity of freeing the child from sexual neurosis. Influenced by such disciples of Freud as Wilhelm Reich and Erich Fromm, they held that patriarchal, capitalist society represses the sexual instinct since the child is an extension of the father's private property. The kibbutz would create an erotic utopia by freeing sexuality from the constraints of property. For Golan, however, erotic utopia did not mean anarchism; sex for the purpose of transient physical pleasure was no less pathological than bourgeois repression. A utopian educational system must be based not on the instincts but on scientific rationality. Borrowing from the behaviorist interpretation of

Freud, Golan insisted that parents exhibit little physical affection, including hugging and kissing, toward their children.

To liberate the child from guilt over sex, it was considered necessary to neutralize sexual attraction during all periods of childhood. Children must sleep apart from their parents to avoid being traumatized by any exposure to adult sexuality. But the main instrument for neutralizing sexual obsession was overexposure, the exact opposite of traditional Jewish or, for that matter, bourgeois repression. Nudity was thought to lessen sexual stimulation rather than encourage it. Communal, coeducational showers, which in some settlements continued through high school, were based on the theory that constant exposure to the naked bodies of the opposite sex would create a more natural attitude toward sexuality. The underlying assumption of this theory was that children should not regard the genitals as differing in meaning from any other organ of the body, a view that corresponded to the medieval depiction of Adam and Eve before the Fall. By affirming nakedness as the way to restrain sexual desire, this utopian theory unconsciously resurrected the belief that sex in the Garden was devoid of unseemly lust.

The child-rearing philosophy of the kibbutz movement therefore tried to demystify eroticism utterly; the consequence was often to suppress sexuality altogether. Adolescents were expected to refrain from any sexual experimentation since their education made it ostensibly unnecessary. Under the guise of eliminating guilt and repression, the new philosophy found its way to a different form of renunciation, in which openness became the instrument for suppression of sexuality. In its educational philosophy, then, the kibbutz movement captured the larger contradiction in the utopian Zionist attitude toward eroticism: the more explicit the discussions around sexuality, the greater the repression. The proclamation of an erotic ideology of Zionism undermined itself by turning Eros into a neutralizing discourse.[75]

This ascetic streak in Zionism was overtly the product of a nationalist ideal of self-sacrifice, part and parcel of a pioneering philosophy that called for renunciation of the pleasures of the present in favor of a utopian future. Viewed in the light of the persistent struggle with the attractions and temptations of asceticism in the Talmud, medieval philosophy and mysticism, and eighteenth-century Hasidism, it is possible that the sexual renunciation practiced by the *halutzim* served unconsciously as a secular version of an old Jewish tradition. These Zionist revolutionaries could no more escape their roots than could the maskilim or, for that matter, rebels against other traditions. But where an ascetic movement like Hasidism displaced its erotic energies into theology, the Zionist pioneers created a more difficult challenge for themselves: to maintain, at one and the same time, contradictory ideologies of erotic liberation and renunciation.

## Romances without Solution

The internal contradictions in the erotic ideology of Zionism had profound consequences for the actual experiences of the pioneers of the Second and Third Aliyot. In his 1918 essay on the need for new erotic relationships, Gordon decried the failure of the *halutzim* to marry. Perhaps reflecting a sense of his own approaching death, Gordon lamented the loss of youth among his young comrades: having failed to find sexual release, the young people with whom he lived and worked had become prematurely old.

The lack of family life that Gordan decried was not only the result of economic and demographic conditions. In a deeper sense, it reflected ideological confusion about the proper place of sexuality in an idealistic movement of national renewal. The persistence of behavioral patterns imported from Europe caused irreconcilable tensions and frustrations in a generation imbued with utopian expectations. One veteran woman of the Second Aliyah reflected on the

> celibacy, distortion of life, waste of energy and hastening of the end, the end of life. The men continued, in effect, the life of yeshiva students from the Diaspora, without any thought to their private lives, as if it was a sin to think of one's own life. In this way, there emerged the phenomenon of "romances without solution" that lasted for decades, which characterized the Second Aliyah. This was the cause of families without children, of the many cases of infertility and failure to marry.[76]

Similarly, a woman from the Third Aliyah wrote: "In relations between men and women, there were many inhibitions. In effect, the mentality of the shtetl continued."[77] It is interesting that women, who were largely excluded from formulating Zionist ideology, were the ones who perceived this problem. If the men thought they had broken thoroughly from the past, their female companions saw the underlying continuities.

Rachel Katznelson-Shazar was a particularly acute observer of the dilemmas of the Second Aliyah in which she took part. She noted in a diary entry from 1918 that it was the very nature of a revolution to render marriage and family life problematic:

> No, we shall not have children. It happens that in the transformation of generations, there comes a generation that takes all the sources of life which eternity has prepared for eternity, for itself, without leaving anything for the generation that follows it.[78]

The purple polemics we have already encountered in Third Aliyah writers like Rapoport and Bistritsky decrying childlessness and urging that sexuality be linked to procreation must have been grounded in this deep despair about ever having children.

The sexual revolution itself created more problems than it solved. Dismayed at the high number of suicides among the *halutzim* over failed romances, the writer A. Z. Rabinowitz reflected on the devastation wrought by the prevalent erotic ideology:

> There are those who commit suicide as a result of sexual disturbances. When the sexual impulse becomes the center of life, it becomes the cause of great suffering, even to the point of suicide. This is an especially difficult problem now, at a time when we stand on the verge of the liberation of women and the relations between the sexes have become freer than what they were in previous generations and the regulator that might preserve some kind of balance has not been found.[79]

Suicide was, in fact, a shockingly prevalent "way out" of the "romances without solution" and out of the other profound frustrations suffered by the pioneers of the Second and Third Aliyot. Zvi Shatz captured this morbid atmosphere in his short story "Without a Voice," in which one of the characters in an impossible romantic triangle commits suicide; his body is discovered by the other two lovers.[80]

The epilogue to Shatz's own biography shows that life sometimes imitated art. After Shatz was killed by Arabs in 1921, both his wife Rivka and his lover Nechama moved to Kibbutz Ein Harod. Nechama married and had a child but then became romantically involved with another man, Aharon Rosen. She ended the affair by shooting Rosen and herself; in a poignant conclusion, Rivka Shatz then raised Nechama's child.[81] Shatz's lover and her second paramour were buried side by side in the old graveyard of Ein Harod, where, like the cemetary at Kinneret, an astonishing number of gravestones bear the phrase "he took his own life," words that would never have appeared in a traditional Jewish graveyard. Suicide had become almost a cult, the most desperate statement of one's commitment to unattainable ideals.

Romantic tragedy thus became a central feature of the collective self-image of the founders. Perhaps not all or even most of the *halutzim* of the Second and Third Aliyot experienced "romances without solution," but those exemplary figures who did become symbols for the others. Berl Katznelson (1887–1944), one of the leading ideologists of the the Second Aliyah, was just such a figure. Berl's affections were torn between two young women, Leah Miron and Sara Schmuckler from his hometown of Bobruisk.[82] He developed a romantic attachment to Leah, but the relationship, in the words of his biographer, "plodded on for years in a tranquil and routine fashion." Suddenly, in 1917, he fell in love with Sara,

Leah's best friend. The three, now in their thirties, tried to juggle this impossible triangle, caught up, as they saw it, in a kind of romantic Russian novel:

> Berl and Sara spent hours "explaining" to Leah that their love was "decreed" from above and that they were unable to control it. Leah, for her part, showed "understanding" and gave them her blessing, like a mature human being, who knew such situations from literature.[83]

In the midst of this torrid, if adolescent, affair, Berl appears to have fallen in love with Rachel Katznelson, also from his hometown. She had already been involved for a good number of years with Zalman Rubashov (Shazar), whom she would later marry.[84]

Despite their tempestuous relations, Berl and Sara decided to marry. Then in the spring of 1919, Sara fell ill with yellow fever and died at age thirty. Berl never recovered from her death and remained deeply attached to her memory, even as he returned to his previous relationship with Leah Miron. He now courted Leah, exploiting her friend Sara's death in order to win her sympathy. Although they never married, the two lived as man and wife in a cheerless and increasingly embittered relationship until Berl's premature death in 1944.[85]

Sara Schmuckler's tragic death clearly fed the fires of Berl's adolescent romanticism. An even better known case of a life cut off without romantic consummation was that of Rachel Blubstein (1890–1931), a poet of the Second Aliyah. Rachel was a pioneer at Kinneret before World War I, but left for France in 1912 to study agronomy. She returned to Russia during the war and only made her way back to Palestine in 1918. Having contracted tuberculosis, she was turned down for membership in Kibbutz Degania and wandered, ill, from place to place until her untimely death in 1931. With her death, she became a romantic figure in the pantheon of the Second Aliyah, a woman who had captured the hearts of half the men of her generation but who died alone.[86] Zalman Shazar, A. D. Gordon, and Uri Zvi Greenberg are among those mentioned as her flames. A minor literary cottage industry in Israel has sought to identify other lovers, and a recent researcher seems to have found the love letters to Rachel from a Michael Bernstein, long believed to have been a fictitious figure.[87] Whether or not Rachel had had all these lovers, the question itself continues to imbue the myth of the Second and Third Aliyot. It is as if for these generations themselves and for subsequent memory, true romance is necessarily doomed.

The Hebrew novelist Yosef Hayyim Brenner, who was killed in 1921 together with Zvi Shatz, blamed the Diaspora for the psychological damage that caused the sexual failures of the Second Aliyah: "You knew that there was no way out for you, for you are eaten with a sense of sin for which you are not guilty, yet you must bear it, and wild, natural, Greek love—that is not to be for you."[88] In Brenner's novel of the Second Aliyah, *Breakdown and Bereavement* (completed in 1914, but first published in 1920) sexual impotence is a metaphor for failure. The antihero, Hefetz (which means, significantly, "desire"), comes to Palestine after a Rabelaisian medical student steals his wife. But his attempt to become one of the pioneers fails when he suffers a hernia and must go to stay with Orthodox relatives in Jerusalem while he undergoes medical treatment. The hernia is cured, but the underlying sexual dysfunction it symbolizes continues to plague Hefetz, as he remains unable to realize a mature erotic relationship. Hefetz sinks irrevocably back into the pathological degeneration of the old Yishuv, the parasitic Orthodox community of Palestine that remains an outpost of the Diaspora. For Brenner, as for many of his contemporaries in the Second Aliyah, cruel reality seemed to drag them down from the high ideals of utopian Zionism to the repression characteristic of traditional life.

Hefetz as a fictional character is a direct descendant of the antiheroes of the fin de siècle literature, in which Brenner himself was a prominent participant. *Breakdown and Bereavement* is but one example of the continuation in Palestine of the prevalent patterns in Eastern European Hebrew literature. S. Y. Agnon portrayed similarly ineffectual male characters and aborted romances in many of his novels and stories set in the Zionist Yishuv.[89] Never has a national revolution been accompanied by such a culture of pessimism in which a mythological ideal of virile national revival coexisted improbably with a poetics of impotence. Moreover, far from being marginal, these works of the imagination formed part of the very canon of Zionist culture! Indeed, this sense of failure and torment was one of the central characteristics of early Zionism and particularly of the Second Aliyah, contrasting sharply with the mythical image of these Zionist pioneers as larger than life. But perhaps the personal and the mythical really went hand in hand, for romantic tragedy became a necessary component in the myth itself.

## Erotic Liberation and the Culture of Modern Israel

The twin myths of erotic liberation and romantic failure lived on in the culture of the state of Israel. The generation that fought in the 1948 War of Liberation perpetuated myths about itself not unlike those of the Second and Third Aliyot. But now sexual liberation was tied to the tragedy of war in the images of men and women fighting side by side in the Pal-mach, the elite unit of Israel's young army. Where the earlier erotic asso-ciations were with agriculture and work, Eros was now mobilized into the service of national self-defense. This romantic view of war and of the equality of the sexes under arms was, of course, a myth with as little basis in reality as the myth of erotic liberation among the *halutzim.*[90]

In more recent years, a cult of nostalgia for the generation of the founders has developed in Israel, but it is nostalgia tinged with ambiva-lence. The later memories reinforce the myths but also censor historical reality. Thus, interviews conducted as part of an oral history of the Sec-ond Aliyah revealed that members of other kibbutzim generally believed that Bet Alfa and other settlements of Ha-shomer ha-Tzair were scenes of wild sexual experimentation. These same people all vehemently denied that such practices occurred in their own communities, and even those interviewed at Bet Alfa rejected the stories of free love as pure myth.[91] These veterans of the heroic days seemed to need to affirm that Zionism had indeed been an erotic revolution but that they themselves never per-sonally participated in something so unrespectable. Such is the unavoid-able tension in a society whose values are essentially bourgeois, yet whose epic past is revolutionary.

This ambivalence signals a loss of self-confidence on the part of the contemporary Labor Zionist culture, a sense of pessimism that it shares with the historical culture of the founders themselves. In the 1970s the playwright Yehoshua Sobel wrote *Twentieth Night,* a play based on the Bitania commune, in which the erotic component of the Bitania experi-ence becomes central. The play itself and its reception suggest that con-temporary Israelis are obsessed with the myth of the founders, like dwarfs on the backs of giants, as if a romantic myth of sexual liberation might serve to liberate a culture whose own dreams have turned sour. In a brilliant satire of this cult of nostalgia, Meir Shalev begins his novel about one of the original agricultural communes with a voice in the night crudely proclaiming: "I'm screwing the granddaughter of Lieberson."[92] This, then, is what remains of the romantic visions and erotic struggles of the founders in the generation of their grandchildren!

The sense that erotic fulfillment can no longer be easily found through Zionist ideals reflects the larger cultural malaise of a revolution now past middle age. In *My Michael,* a classic novel from the 1960s, Amos Oz por-trayed an Israeli woman whose marriage has become passionless; the Is-raeli man has lost his erotic attraction. Her fantasies revolve around Arab twin brothers who are at once sexually alluring and deeply threatening. As with the complex image of the erotic Gentile in European and Ameri-can Jewish culture, the Arab here becomes the ambiguous sexual Other. In the Israeli context, however, the eroticization of the Arab is much more problematic, since the Arab threatens not only the ethnic but also the national boundaries of the state, perhaps analogous to the Canaanites in biblical Israel.

By adopting the voice of a woman in this and other novels, Oz implicitly raised questions about whether the predominantly male orientation of the founding generations of Zionism could still viably represent the contemporary Israeli. If it is women who can best serve as the vehicles for exploring the inner contradictions in Israeli culture, perhaps a revision of the history of the sexes and their relations in the Second and Third Aliyot is necessary in order to understand the current state of gender relations in Israel. Recent historical studies and works of literary criticism have begun this revision of Zionist history, but what effect it will have on contemporary Israeli culture and society remains to be seen.

The feminist challenge to the myth of Zionism as an erotic revolution raises the larger question of which Israelis can identify with the *halutzim*. The Zionist pioneers were, after all, a tiny group, a secular sect that turned its own experience into the collective mythology of the Jewish state. Like all the elites we have studied in this book, these *halutzim* no more represented the experience and attitudes of the wider classes of society than did the rabbis of talmudic times or the Kabbalists and philosophers of the Middle Ages. The Zionist ideology of sexual liberation and its ascetic counterpole could scarcely speak to the many nonideological refugees who came to Palestine and later to Israel. Those whose origins were in Europe and who perpetuated bourgeois patterns must have sensed a profound tension between the myth of Zionist origins and their own experience and values.

An even deeper chasm separates the Ashkenazic founders of Zionism and the Jews who came to Israel from the countries of the Middle East. These "Oriental" Jews were wrenched out of their traditional cultures and forced to adopt the totalizing ideology of the Labor Zionist state, an ideology they were able to repudiate publicly only decades later. What were the attitudes to sexuality of the rabbinic elites and the popular culture of these Middle Eastern Jews? On the one hand, they regarded the putative doctrines and practices of "free love" on the kibbutzim as deeply alienating and threatening to their own traditions.[93] It mattered less whether such free love actually existed; it was enough that such dissolute behavior was imagined to take place among those who governed the state. On the other hand, it would appear on first impression that the traditional culture of these Jews was less bound up with the kind of asceticism that characterized Orthodox Eastern European Jews from the eighteenth century on. Partly in response to Muslim culture, which had fewer anxieties about sexuality than did Christian culture, the Jews of Arab lands do not seem to have developed ascetic mass movements like Hasidism. The early Zionist dialectic of erotic liberation and asceticism had little resonance for a culture less preoccupied, it would seem, with the threat of sexuality.

Nevertheless, I offer this analysis very tentatively and with a caveat: this study focuses on the Ashkenazic culture of the founders of Zionism, and it therefore engages in the same skewing of history against which the Oriental Jews in Israel have rightly rebelled. A complete history of Eros and the Jews still requires a thorough study of the elite and popular cultures of sexuality among the Jews of the Middle East.

For the European founders of Israel themselves, however, Zionism both succeeded and failed as an erotic revolution. Having escaped from the ambivalent embrace of their parents' homes, the young people of the Second and Third Aliyot remained adrift between the desire for autonomy and a longing for parental affections, and between erotic liberation and a return to traditional sexual values. So, too, the national movement they created was torn between two contradictory self-definitions: Zionism as a total break with the past versus Zionism as the culmination and fulfillment of Jewish history. In the final analysis, the ambiguities of Zionism as an erotic revolution prefigured the larger political question, which remains to this day, of how to constitute a Jewish national body in the modern world.

# CHAPTER 9

# Sexual Stereotypes in American Jewish Culture

Alexander        Portnoy, impotent in the Jewish state, is the fictional embodiment of the mythic tension between Israel as the site of Jewish erotic health and the Diaspora as the spawning ground of neurosis. In Portnoy's pursuit of a female Israeli soldier, Philip Roth combined two elements in this myth of modern Israel: the erotic and the military. If Zionism was in reality a highly complex and ambivalent sexual revolution, the myth of an erotic Israel still retains an enormous hold on the American Jewish imagination, as a kind of projection of what American Jews might desire but believe themselves incapable of achieving. The Israeli heroes and heroines of a host of popular American novels are portrayed as highly erotic "tough Jews" who have overcome the impotence of the Diaspora and are now able to wreak vengeance on ex-Nazis and Arabs alike.[1]

The archetype of this fiction was Leon Uris's best-selling novel *Exodus*, first published in 1958. Uris's hero is named Ari Ben Canaan, a name quite deliberately non-Jewish, indeed, a name that conjures up the ancient Canaanites as opposed to the Jews.[2] Ben Canaan fits the Zionist stereotypes: he is ascetic and fanatical but, as a prototypical sabra (native-born Israeli), has his hidden romantic side, which is revealed in his affair with Kitty, a gentile American nurse. Zionism, it seems, has not only liberated the Jew from sexual neurosis, but it has turned him into a quasi *goy*. Where the characters of much American Jewish fiction cannot realize healthy erotic relationships with the Christian women they pursue, the Israeli has no such difficulty. Only in Israel can the desired relationships be realized, either with non-Jewish women or with Israeli women turned into powerful "non-Jewish Jews" like their male counterparts: women with guns.

This popular literature is a product of the struggle with sexuality that characterizes contemporary American Jewish culture, a struggle that brings us back to *Portnoy's Complaint,* the beginning of our long journey through Jewish history. Indeed, this inquiry takes its inspiration precisely from the late-twentieth-century American Jewish preoccupation with sexuality. We now return to the contemporary context and try to understand how the larger, historical picture connects, if at all, to the present.

As with most of the rest of this book, here, too, we shall deal not with social reality but with cultural constructions, with how Jews have imagined and construed their sexuality.[3] Even if these cultural artifacts do not reflect the experience of American Jews as a community in some mimetic way, they can shape the way Jews imagine their experience as well as the Jewish tradition as a whole; that is, even if one's own experience diverges from a stereotype, the stereotype nevertheless defines the standard against which one measures experience. When certain images are eroticized and others are deeroticized in literature, movies, or even theological writing, romantic expectations are unconsiously channeled: discourse creates desire.

Like all historical Jewish cultures, the world of contemporary American Jews is filled with tensions, contradictions, and conflicts. Hollywood and other organs of mass culture put forth stereotypes of Jewish sexuality that are very different from the writings of Jewish theologians. And these in turn differ from the works of fiction and poetry. Nevertheless, for all their differences and contradictions, these strands of American Jewish culture are all dedicated to a common struggle: to harmonize the Jewish experience with American culture and thus to negotiate the integration of Jews in American society. They tackle the age-old problem that has turned up in so many guises: can Jews find sexual satisfaction with other Jews and biologically reproduce the Jewish people in America? How, in brief, can pleasure and procreation, those two contentious poles of the historical dialectic, be reconciled?

## The Jew as Sexual Shlemiel

The image of the sexually and militarily potent Israeli is a projection based on its opposite: the myth of the impotent American Jew. The Jew as sexual shlemiel has its roots in the Yiddish theater of the Lower East Side of New York, in the comedy of the borsht belt in the Catskill Mountains, and in the anti-heroes of fin de siècle Hebrew and Yiddish literature. Indeed, Roth's *Portnoy* is kin to the outrageous, self-deprecating stand-up Jewish comedy routine. By the time Roth composed his fiction, this myth was well established and immediately recognizable: Roth's self-conscious exploration of the myth of Jewish erotic neurosis only works because Roth's readers already know the codes.

Besides Roth, no one has mined this stereotype more than the film-maker and writer Woody Allen. He gets a lot of the credit for disseminating many of the popular stereotypes of the Jewish male, his sexual self-doubt and obsession with gentile women. From *What's New Pussycat?*, the first movie he wrote and acted in, he portrayed what was to become a stock figure, the little man with the big libido and the even bigger sexual neurosis, a character comically unable to consummate his desire. In *Pussycat* we encounter Allen helping Parisian strippers dress, fumbling ridiculously with their costumes as they parade around half naked; later, the girl he tries to bed falls asleep on him.

The sexual insecurities of the characters Allen plays are quintessentially Jewish. Even the sperm in the funniest scene of *Everything You Wanted to Know about Sex* turns out to be Jewish, worrying compulsively before the grand moment whether he will be hurt going in and whether he will be stymied by birth control pills. While his more virile companions yell "Geronimo" as they leap into the unknown, the little-man sperm consoles itself: "At least she's Jewish." As opposed to the theological prescription of sex without guilt, which we shall encounter shortly, Allen suggests that Jews have perfected guilt without sex, a peculiarly secular version of religious asceticism.

At times, this image of the impotent Jewish man takes a vicious turn and the comedy fails. *Everything You Wanted to Know about Sex* offers up an Orthodox rabbi whose sexual fetish is to be whipped by a leather-clad model while his wife eats pork chops at his feet.[4] Traditional Judaism, it would seem, is at the root of the masochism of the Jewish male: violation of the law becomes the source of perverse pleasure. We have already observed how this motif of passivity and even masochism figured importantly in the Hebrew literature of the turn of the century as a symbol of the impotence of the Eastern European Jews. In contemporary America, however, where Jews are no longer powerless, Allen's use of this imagery turns what was initially tragedy into awkward farce.

His characters are not, however, merely impotent; they are also highly erotic. Jews have the libidinal energy to win over gentile women from their desiccated WASP culture, but they seem never to consummate their conquests—the hormones are willing, but the psyche is ambivalent. Like Portnoy, Allen's Jew is ostensibly chaste but secretly hypersexual. The Jew as hypersexual was, of course, a stock-in-trade of racial anti-Semitism, which cultivated a paranoia that Jewish rapists threaten the purity of Christian women and, through them, Christian society as a whole. The Jewish comic takes this anti-Semitic motif and neutralizes it: the Jew does not corrupt gentile America by his hypersexuality so much as he deeroticizes it with his comic fumbling. In some of Allen's movies the Jew's sexual ambivalence infects the gentile women and turns them into mirror images of himself: even gentile Americans become "Jewish." The hidden agenda is to identify America with Jewish culture by generalizing Jewish sexuality and creating a safe, unthreatening space for the shlemiel as American antihero.

Many of the representations of this sexual stereotype, like Allen's or Roth's, are to be found in either comic routines or comic fiction. Comedy is, of course, one of the most powerful weapons in the arsenal of a minority trying to carve out a place in a majority culture. Jewish humor certainly played this role in Europe, and, there, too, it reveled in sexual innuendo, serving as a kind of underside to the chaste official culture of the rabbis.[5] In America a deep insecurity about the Jew's position in American culture seems to underlie this instinctive turn to comedy. Perhaps the distancing afforded by comedy can at once relieve anxiety and win over a potentially hostile gentile audience. If Jewish sexual neurosis is as funny as Allen would have it, if America can laugh at the Jew and see its own neuroses in his, then perhaps the Jew will be accepted as an organic part of the cultural landscape. But this anxiety may not in fact be so deep-seated—if Jews felt that insecure about their sexual identities and their place in America, would they display their neuroses so publicly? On the contrary, Jews in contemporary America appear to have little hesitation about playing out their sexual dilemmas in full public view, whether in movies or literature, which suggests that Jewish sexuality, portrayed comically, is assumed to be a legitimate part of American culture.

Not all sexual jokes about Jews contain this overtly assimilatory strategy. If the sexual persona of the American Jewish male appears relatively harmless, the image of the Jewish woman often takes a vicious turn in the form of jokes about the "Jewish American Princess," or JAP, the latter, dehumanizing term suggestive of the anti-Japanese racism from an earlier era.[6] Although the figure of the JAP has become a staple of American anti-Semitism, it appears to have Jewish origins. The JAP stereotype has two major characteristics: she is obsessively materialistic and she is utterly uninterested in sex. The classic erotic tease, she adorns herself seductively but refuses to consummate sexual relations. Thus: "How do you keep a JAP from having sex? Marry her." Only consumption is erotic: "How do you give a JAP an orgasm? Scream, 'Charge it to Daddy.'"

The JAP, like the male shlemiel, is erotically blocked but he at least is comic and perhaps lovable in his ineptitude, whereas she is typically loathsome. His inner conflicts and neuroses are revealed and thus sympathetic, but her sexual pathology remains purely objectified and superficial, like her overdone makeup. Women become the site for projections of all that seems most hateful about Jewish sexuality.

These profoundly negative images of Jewish women, seething with barely repressed aggression, are not simply products of Jewish self-hatred or anti-Semitism. They are found in rabbinic homily as well. Echoing earlier German Zionist critiques of Jewish women, a Conservative Canadian rabbi, David Kirshenbaum, writing in 1958, specifically blamed the materialism of Jewish women for the increasing rate of intermarriage. The future of the Jews is endangered because of their selfish behavior, and it is no wonder, he charges, that Jewish men prefer to marry Gentiles![7] Jewish women push them into it. Having transmuted sex into empty buying, Jewish women are incapable of the main form of production dictated by tradition: reproduction. The "innocent Jewish daughter" of earlier literary stereotypes, praised for preserving Judaism, has now mutated into the JAP, castigated for bringing about the impending demise of the Jewish people.

The Jewish women of these misogynistic stereotypes are ostentatious representatives of the upper middle class; they consume rather than work. In the film *White Palace* (1990), for example, the materialism of the well-manicured Jewish princesses contrasts unfavorably with the sensuality of a much older, non-Jewish waitress. The young hero, Max, abandons the repressed upper-class world of the JAPs for the eroticism of the working-class gentile woman. Perhaps the underlying anxiety that is projected onto these materialistic Jewish women stems from the meteoric rise of most Jews out of the working class and into the professions, away from manual labor and into consumption. The liaison with the working-class Gentile becomes a kind of fantasy escape into the proletarian Jewish past.

*White Palace* proffers the typical Hollywood solution to the sexual dilemmas of the American Jew, almost always male, by pairing him off with a non-Jew.[8] This is true not only of movies but also television serials, such as the recent "Thirtysomething" and Jackie Mason's ill-fated "Chicken Soup." The few exceptions only prove the rule. The motif of mixed relationships has a very long literary history, dating back to the *belle juive* of Renaissance and Enlightenment literature in works such as Gotthold Lessing's *Nathan the Wise* and Walter Scott's *Ivanhoe* and continuing into the modern Jewish literature of Central and Eastern Europe.[9] In the American context, the theme generally involves a relationship between a Jewish man and a gentile woman, quite the reverse of the more typical European tradition and reflecting to some degree, the higher rate of outmarriage among Jewish men. From the earliest years of Hollywood, films dwelled on this motif. Perhaps the most striking example of this dynamic is the *Jazz Singer,* the first talking picture, which was produced by Warner Brothers in 1927. In a self-referential allegory of the biographies of most of Hollywood's Jews, the film portrays a cantor's son who renounces his religion for success in the entertainment world and a gentile woman.[10]

A more recent movie that brings together all of the myths of the Jew as shlemiel, the JAP, and the gentile temptress in highly charged, explicit terms is the *Heartbreak Kid* (1974). After their ostentatiously Jewish wedding, Lenny Cantrow and Leila Kolodny set out for their honeymoon in Miami Beach. Things immediately turn sour as Leila appears increasingly coarse and unerotic. When Leila becomes sunburned after the first few hours on the beach, she retreats to her room and covers herself with unsightly cream. This explicitly rendered JAP is so divorced from nature that not only can she not tolerate a bit of sun, but she doesn't even know how to swim!

Alone on the beach, Lenny is seduced by a spectacular blonde from Minnesota, named Kelly Corcoran. As he puts it: "A girl like you *would* have a name like Kelly Corcoran." Dropping his marriage "like a bomb," Lenny sets off in pursuit of the mythical *shiksa*, following her all the way to Minnesota. He ends up deracinated, uprooted from Jewish New York, and marooned like an alien being among the Gentiles of the American heartland. Lenny's relationship to Kelly has sadomasochistic overtones. Her seduction proceeds by a series of manipulations, as a result of which he becomes more and more abject and self-debasing. The erotic master-slave relationship implicitly symbolizes the condition of the Jew in America. She first accosts him as he lies on the beach and informs him: "That's my spot"; she later repeats the same line in a bar. In Minnesota her father threatens Lenny: "If you show your face around here again, I'll kick your ass over the Canadian border." The Jew is in America on sufferance; if he oversteps his bounds, he will be expelled.

Kelly turns Jewish insecurity into the stuff of erotic domination: by repeatedly making it clear to Lenny that he is "in her spot," she both seduces him and destroys his self-respect. Although he wins her hand in marriage by outsmarting a muscular gentile competitor and by denouncing her father's anti-Semitic prejudices, the film ends with Lenny an empty shell, able only to mouth vapid clichés. Yes, he wins the prize, but he is left emasculated. Billed as a comedy, the *Heartbreak Kid* is an American Jewish tragedy, a cautionary tale about the fate of the Jewish parvenu who succumbs to gentile temptation in order to climb his way out of the Jewish ghetto.

Such films undoubtedly reflect the social reality of intermarriage, which according to some statistics currently approaches 40 percent of all Jewish marriages.[11] Throughout the history of Hollywood, however, Jewish writers, directors, and producers have been less concerned with the condition of American Jews as a whole than with the specific problems of their own class. Despite their largely unhindered access to success in American culture, these Jews still hold the non-Jewish woman to be the ultimate, if ephemeral, prize, perhaps reflecting their insecurity about their own status. Out of deep inner conflict over this most problematic desire, those who produce mass culture return again and again to the theme of Jewish-Christian erotic relations, like the criminal returning to the scene of his crime. And no doubt the struggles of this particular artistic class, with its own identity and place in American culture, has cast a long shadow over how other Jews view their own erotic expectations.

## Jewish Theologies of Erotic Health

The image of the Jew as sexual shlemiel is one pole of contemporary American Jewish culture. Its polar opposite is represented by Jewish theologians from the Reform, Conservative, and Orthodox movements. Their theologies constitute the contemporary versions of today's "official" or "normative" Jewish literature, but since rabbis are no longer authoritative voices in American Jewish culture, this literature must compete with other cultural forms, just as the writings of the maskilim challenged rabbinic norms in the nineteenth century. Although contemporary Jewish theologies of sexuality are rhetorically far removed from the mythologizing and stereotyping of the material just discussed, they must be understood as responses to the idea of the Jew as erotically inept. If Jewish sexuality in the representations of a Woody Allen or a Philip Roth is neurotic, these thinkers argue that the essence of Judaism is a healthy celebration of Eros within the confines of marriage. Nonetheless, for all that they stand opposed to the stereotypes of Jewish sexuality, these theologies are part of the same discourse and also serve to shape American culture in a way that will make a place for the Jews.

In constructing their counterargument for Jewish sexual health, the Jewish theologians are participating in a characteristically American strategy for confronting sexuality. In the nineteenth and early twentieth centuries certain Christian theologians developed a sexual doctrine of "innocent ecstasy," which dialectically prepared the ground for the new secular sexual morality of the 1960s.[12] According to this theology, proper Christian sex is free of guilt, since it transcends the association with original sin. Margaret Sanger, the founder of the movement for birth control in the 1920s, was herself a devout Christian who believed that sexual pleasure, symbolized by simultaneous orgasm, was a sacrament. Birth control was necessary to allow couples to develop their sexual technique so that at the moment of orgasm, they might attain "the spiritual mystery of this communion of two natures."[13] For Sanger and other like-minded Christians, there is no contradiction between sexual pleasure and Christian faith.

Adapting this peculiarly American Christian tradition to the sexual revolution, some contemporary Christian preachers argue that in a good Christian marriage intercourse becomes a spiritual act that should begin and end with prayer. In the words of one such preacher, a modern Christian must avoid premarital intercourse and abortion but must at the same time "put Jesus Christ right in the center of your sex life."[14] A good Christian marriage is inconceivable without sexual harmony. Orgasm is a form of religious ecstasy to be cultivated in the words of Marabel Morgan, the author of the *Total Woman*, "as clean and pure as eating cottage cheese."[15] Outside the Christian framework, sex is still burdened by guilt, but within it, it is transformed and purified.

Rabbinic writings adopt the same strategy, simply substituting Judaism for Christianity. They are moreover motivated by two specifically Jewish concerns. First, as the rate of intermarriage began to climb dramatically in the postwar period, a host of writers and preachers warned, often stridently, of the "peril that intermarriage poses to the Jewish future." Intermarriage became more than just a statistical fact, although often a contested one. It also became a problem and, for some, *the* problem.[16] To demonstrate that Judaism offers a sexual ethic compatible with modern desire was a strategy against intermarriage or, for those already intermarried, for conversion of the non-Jewish partner.

Second, and related to intermarriage, it was in the 1960s and 1970s that Jews began to feel so fully at home in America that not only did they seek to Americanize their religion and culture, but some also began to proselytize actively for Judaism as a solution to America's presumed moral crisis. Although this argument is rarely advanced explicitly, it appears as a covert subtext in some of the works of the period. For example, Robert Gordis, a Conservative rabbi and the editor of *Judaism*, argued in 1978 that the gravest crisis in modern American life is the lack of a firm sexual identity; all the other social ills of the day might be confronted if the family were not on the road to ruin.[17] Gordis asserts that the new sexual morality is the indirect product of Christianity since both accept a dichotomy between love and sex: the first glorifies sex over love while the second celebrates love over sex. Christian asceticism prepared the ground for the contemporary libertine revolt.

With this indictment of Christianity, Gordis turns to Judaism, which, in his view, integrates love and sex in a healthy way that offers the better model for American culture: "Being a Jew is the least difficult way of being truly human."[18] Sexual pleasure is legitimate, quite apart from procreation, but the only appropriate site for sexuality is within marriage.[19] While Gordis acknowledges that there are some ascetic moments in the history of the Jewish tradition, he attributes them largely to the influence of medieval Christianity. When liberal Christians today try to modify Christian asceticism to fit the modern world, they are really unwittingly recovering the teachings of the Bible and Talmud. Put hyperbolically, for Gordis, American culture can only become healthy by becoming Jewish!

In order to advance their argument, Gordis and the other rabbinical writers had to downplay the persistent strand of asceticism that threads through Jewish history from the talmudic period to the early Zionist collectives. Read through their eyes, historical Judaism appears essentially straightforward and unproblematic; such conflicts and tensions as there are result from outside contamination. In light of the historical record, however, these contemporary theologians are not so much describing an essential Judaism as constructing an *interpretation* that serves their own cultural agenda.

A polemic against modern concepts of love similar to Gordis's can be found in a little pamphlet written in 1966 by Norman Lamm, the president of the Orthodox Yeshiva University.[20] It was the height of the sexual revolution. Lamm denounces the sexual revolution as a modern form of the sacred prostitution of the Canaanites and the debauchery of the ancient Romans, two myths he swallows uncritically. Ancient "hedonism" gave birth to ascetic Christianity, which becomes a kind of inverted paganism. The contemporary "renaissance of paganism" represents the greatest threat to morality and to the family, a threat that he compares to that of nuclear war. The pagan renaissance treats sex as nothing but a biological urge that must be stripped of its shroud of mystery. With no secrets its cardinal theology, this hedonistic religion has *"Playboy* as its Bible [and] its various imitators and mutants—a new Apocrypha and Pseudepigrapha."[21] Sexologists like Freud and Kinsey contribute to this new religion by making a fetish of open sexual discourse; they provide the ostensible "scientific" proof of its veracity.

Against this new paganism, Lamm holds out Judaism as the only plausible bulwark; the contemporary debate over sexuality thus becomes nothing less than the modern version of the age-old struggle between monotheistic Judaism and idolatry. As opposed to the modern religion of openness, Judaism advocates restoring the mystery to sex. At the same time, Judaism rejects any association of sex with guilt, as long as sex takes place within the framework of marriage. Men and women must enter marriage with a positive attitude toward sex: "Any attitude brought to the marital chamber that ... regards sex as evil and identifies desire with lust, can only disturb the harmonious integration of the two forces within man: the moral and the sexual."[22] Although this argument can certainly be found in the historical tradition, by rendering marital sex so unproblematic, Lamm implicitly echoes a peculiarly American discourse. By co-opting one dimension of the sexual revolution into the ostensible Jewish view of marriage, he asserts that the Jews believed in sex without guilt long before the 1960s.

Lamm holds that the laws of family purity, a code phrase for the menstrual laws, inculcate this positive, yet modest attitude toward sexuality. He considers this aspect of Jewish sexual customs at great length and offers nothing short of a contemporary justification for the old laws of cultic purity. He rejects the "superstitious" notion that the laws of *niddah* are a product of repugnance toward menstrual blood or that they have any hygienic meaning. Indeed, Lamm avoids the physical condition altogether since he says nothing about why menstrual blood should prevent sexual contact. Instead, he builds a case based on the psychological, and therefore thoroughly modern, logic of periodic abstinence. Although the Talmud (b. Niddah 31b) does argue for separation in order to increase sexual desire and prevent the boredom of overfamiliarity, Lamm makes this passing comment the centerpiece of his rationale for *niddah*.

Abstinence during marriage, he argues, is eroticizing, just as lack of sexual relations during the engagement period heightens the erotic intensity of the honeymoon. The laws of *niddah* create monthly repetitions of this engagement-honeymoon experience by promoting the replenishment of male "libidinal reserves," a modern formulation of an old medical belief. Without such a regulated sexual rhythm, sex would become mechanical, a kind of "I-It" relationship. The sexual revolution attempts to promote sexual pleasure by liberating Eros from its traditional bonds, but it actually produces the very opposite effect: erotic boredom and exploitation. The laws of family purity, by contrast, enhance eroticism and create a genuine "I-Thou" relationship between the partners.[23] Because of these laws, Orthodox Jewish marriages enjoy a high degree of sexual intensity, that seemingly most contemporary and secular of erotic values. Jewish law is the key to the door of erotic fulfillment, paradoxically slammed shut by the sexual revolution.

In using Martin Buber's concept of I-Thou, Lamm resorts to a modern, even antihalakhic, philosopher to buttress the Halakhah. Another example of exploiting modern arguments is his theory for the symbolic meaning of purifying the menstrual blood by immersion in water. Menstrual blood and other genital discharges are symbols of death, an observation that we also made in the chapter on biblical culture. Lamm quotes an article in *Scientific American* to prove that water is the symbol of life since the percentage of water in living organisms is highest in the embryo and declines as the organism ages. Since loss of water symbolizes death, immersion in the ritual bath is "life affirming"—the essential message of Judaism, Lamm asserts. Not only do the laws of family purity counter the deterioration of marital relations in contemporary America, but they can also inculcate a new set of life-affirming values in a world threatened by atomic weapons. The laws of *niddah* are nothing less than an answer to the threat of nuclear war![24]

Lamm's defense of Orthodox Jewish practice in thoroughly modern terms reflects the influence of modern values on the Orthodox. For example, polls suggest that a high percentage of Orthodox Jews see R- or X-rated movies. There is also a division of opinion among the Orthodox about such aspects of the sexual revolution as premarital relations, homosexuality, and abortion, which the law itself generally condemns.[25] Although this openness to more permissive sexual practices probably has deep historical roots, Orthodox Jews in America clearly participate in the broader culture around them to a greater degree than one might have suspected.

One legal authority who recognized this reality was Moshe Feinstein, perhaps the preeminent halakhist in the American Orthodox community in this century. Feinstein held in an important responsum that the sexual needs of contemporary Jewish women are greater than those of their predecessors and therefore the *onah* of scholars prescribed by early law should be increased:

> As to the innovation of recent authorities in our day, that students of the law should perform the duty of *onah* twice a week, I too support his view....
> Because of the promiscuity of this generation and jealousy for another woman's lot, a woman feels desire and erotic passion more often than once a week. Therefore, her husband is obligated in this respect.[26]

Feinstein implicitly blames women for absorbing the sexual values of the modern world, but the consequence of his ruling is to permit Orthodox men to behave with greater license.[27] Since neither law nor custom legitimates male sexuality to this degree, women become the ambiguous vehicles for male practice.

Within the world of Jewish theological discourse, these affirmations of Jewish sexual ethics have not gone without dissent, especially from feminists.[28] In a recent work of feminist Jewish theology, Judith Plaskow asserts that the Jewish tradition is much more ambivalent toward sexuality than the male writers we have surveyed are prepared to admit.[29] She argues that all too often the tradition identifies sexuality with repugnance toward women's bodies and sees women as sexual temptresses. Male sexuality is identified with the *yetzer ha-ra*, a powerful, alien force triggered by women. With the exception of the kabbalistic tradition, mainstream biblical and rabbinic Judaism associated an asexual God with sexual control for human beings; male-formulated monotheism produced an "energy/control" paradigm of human sexuality. Plaskow therefore calls for reconnecting sexuality with the sacred, first, by attacking the patriarchal inequality of male-female relationships and, then, by reconceptualizing sexuality as the most positive form of human energy that unites the spiritual and the physical:

> Feminist images name female sexuality as powerful and legitimate and name sexuality as part of the image of God. They tell us that sexuality is not primarily a moral danger ... but a source of energy and power that, schooled in the values of respect and mutuality, can lead us to the related, and therefore sexual, God.[30]

While Plaskow clearly breaks with much of the male-oriented sexual theology, she nevertheless remains very close to their conclusions. All share the view that properly constituted Jewish sexuality should affirm erotic pleasure within an egalitarian relationship, although Plaskow argues that this was not the unambiguous ideal of historical Judaism. Like her male counterparts, she castigates American culture for its obsession with sexuality and blames the traditional repressive view for the contemporary culture of sexual "acting out." In her case, however, Judaism is just as much to blame as Christianity for both the repressive tradition and for its irresponsible negation. Despite their differences, however, all of these theologians hold that the dialectic of erotic repression and permissiveness can be overcome by spiritualizing sexuality. Only when Jewish theology subsumes the erotic will both become healthy.

Plaskow's critique is not representative of all Jewish feminist thinking. A group of Orthodox feminists argue that traditional Jewish laws actually enhance and protect women's experience.[31] They hold, with Lamm, that the laws of *niddah*, in particular, serve to eroticize marital relations and give women a set time to regain full control of their own bodies. Here is a fascinating attempt to reformulate Orthodoxy to fit an entirely contemporary agenda and, like the position of a number of the male theologians, to argue for the superiority of traditional Judaism over other sexual ethics.

All of these theological writers believe that it is possible to construct an erotic doctrine in which spirit and body, God and human beings, historical Judaism and modern desire are finally reconciled. Perhaps at no other point in the history of the Jewish tradition, at least since Hellenistic times, has the impulse been so strong to render sexuality unproblematic. For Plaskow, this means returning to the Song of Songs, while for an Orthodox Jew like Lamm or a Conservative Jew like Gordis, talmudic law is an equally viable source. But for all of these thinkers, the goal is profoundly American: to reconcile Judaism with contemporary currents in American culture by achieving the "innocent ecstasy" of sex without guilt.


## Subversions of the Discourse: The Male Jew as Erotic

If a historian five hundred years from today had access only to the works of theology we have just examined, she or he might well conclude that the American Jews had achieved a kind of sexual nirvana, having finally overcome the dilemmas of desire with which the earlier tradition had struggled for several millennia. Even the feminist critique holds out the promise of an erotic utopia. But taken together with the stereotypes of the sexually impotent Jew, there emerges a much more complex picture of conflict and struggle over sexuality. As in earlier periods, the story of Jewish attitudes toward sexuality only becomes complete by describing the full range of culture, from the elite to the popular, and by understanding the inevitable tensions between them.

The dominant discourse of Jewish sexuality in America involves the language of health and disease, an inheritance from the general culture. Yet between the poles of mythic pathology, on the one hand, and theological health, on the other, lies a territory populated by other possibilities. In this territory, one finds a kind of dialectical synthesis in which Jews are portrayed as erotic rather than impotent, but in which their sexuality is either still problematic or can only be healthy when situated somewhere other than in contemporary America.

Let us begin with Lenny Bruce, who perhaps more than any other comedian, broke with the tradition of the Jew as sexual shlemiel in order to outrage conventional American morality with Jewish eroticism. Like Freud's contention that being a marginal Jew allowed him to challenge conventional sexual morality, Bruce saw his role as liberating American culture from the sexual repression of its Puritan heritage. Bruce's comedy was specifically aimed at the intersection between sexual and political hypocrisy in American culture. To "talk dirty" was to outrage convention, but it was also to do publicly what everyone was already doing privately: Bruce's contribution to the sexual revolution was to take sexual discourse out of the closet and put it into the public arena. In no sense, however, was his act erotic; on the contrary, as his numerous trials for obscenity demonstrated, the purpose of his comedy was not to "arouse prurient interest" but to demystify sex by flooding it with sexually explicit language. To be sexually liberated for Bruce meant to be able to *talk* about sex, a verbal characteristic that he shared with Woody Allen, Philip Roth, and many other Jewish writers.

Bruce's act was deliberately Jewish: "My conversation, spoken and written, is usually flavored with the jargon of the hipster, the argot of the underworld, and Yiddish."[32] To talk about sex meant to talk a Jewish language. Bruce idiosyncratically defined "Jewish" as a kind of urban, ethnic, secular irreverence:

> To me, if you live in New York or any other big city, you are Jewish. It doesn't matter even if you're Catholic; if you live in New York you're Jewish. If you live in Butte, Montana, you're going to be goyish even if you're Jewish.... Negroes are all Jews. Italians are all Jews. Irishmen who have rejected their religion are Jews. Mouths are very Jewish. And bosoms.[33]

To be Jewish means to be outside the American mainstream both verbally (mouths) and erotically (bosoms). It means to identify with what was sexually liberated on the margins of American culture.

Jews, Bruce declares, have no concept of obscene words or pornography because they put no value on celibacy:

> There are no words in Jewish that describe any sexual act—*emmis*—or parts or lusts.... Are Jews pornographers? Or is it that the Jew has no concept? To a Jew f-u-c-k and s-h-i-t have the same value on the dirty-word graph.... And the reason for that is that—well, see, rabbis and priests both s-h-i-t, but only one f-u-c-ks. You see, in the Jewish culture, there's no merit badge for not doing that.... And since the leaders of my tribe, rabbis, are *schtuppers*, perhaps that's why words come freer to me.[34]

The theological "leaders of the tribe" we have read here would certainly agree with Bruce that Jewish culture gives no merit badges for celibacy, but one suspects they would balk at his equation between "talking dirty" and the Jewish affirmation of sexuality. Indeed, as an erotic and political rebel, Bruce held no brief for any religious establishment, Christian or Jewish: "Goddamn the priests and the rabbis. Goddamn the Popes and all their hypocrisy. Goddamn Israel and its bond drives."[35] "Hip" Jewish culture was in as much conflict with Jewish convention as with Christian convention and for Bruce, the former was no more sexually liberated than the latter. To be erotic meant to subvert "establishment" Judaism as much as establishment Christianity.

Bruce's hip Jewish eroticism was implicitly male. Although Jewish women come off a bit less repressed than do Gentiles in Bruce's comedy, his basic message is that conventional Jewish culture, associated with women, is antierotic, while a kind of underground, male Jewish identity is liberated.[36] This implied gender division between erotic Jewish men and deeroticized women harks back to the stereotype of the JAP, but if Bruce failed as a feminist, he at least was able to imagine a male Jewish counterculture that was subversively erotic.

The Canadian Jewish writer Mordecai Richler has constructed a similar image of the male Jew. Richler works with a Jewish stereotype very different from the shlemiel: the *pusherke*, or "pushy Jew."[37] His most famous character, Duddy Kravitz, is a classic representative of this type, which goes back to the Eastern Europe shtetl.[38] Duddy is aggressive, crude, ruthlessly self-serving, and materialistic. His story is that of a reverse Horatio Alger: bad boy makes good in America. Duddy's eroticism is part and parcel of his aggressiveness, and he uses sex as a tool in his relentless attempt to make it. Duddy may be erotic, but his main interest lies elsewhere, as his contempt and exploitation of women reveals. For this reason, his seduction of the French Canadian, Yevette, is curiously distracted because Yevette is less a sexual conquest than a vehicle for helping him achieve his material ends: as he makes love to her next to the lake he intends to buy, he cannot help but think about his future possession. For all his ambiguity, though, Duddy Kravitz along with Richler characters in later novels,[39] represents a vital Jewish sexuality strikingly different from the stereotype of erotic incompetence, but equally remote from the healthy optimism of the theologians.

## Eros and Immigration

Richler's *pusherke* Jew has his roots in the great picaresque novel of the immigrant experience, Abraham Cahan's *Rise of David Levinsky*, first published in 1917.[40] Like Duddy Kravitz, David Levinsky is a Jew on the make who succumbs repeatedly to the temptations of "Satan" by seducing his landladies and other available women. His strong sexuality matches his drive for success. By the end of the novel, Levinsky has achieved the great wealth he sought in coming to America, but he fails to find love. All of his sexual escapades have produced nothing but abiding loneliness. Cahan uses Levinsky to depict the dangerous moral depths to which the Jewish immigrant might sink in his desire to make it in America. Having broken the chains of tradition and escaped to the New World, the erotic energy of the Jew has been released, but often to self-destructive ends. Like Duddy, David Levinsky is a negative figure, yet somehow endearing: if only his substantial libido was better directed, he might avoid the temptations of America. But whatever his faults, Levinsky cannot be accused of sexual passivity or impotence.

Abe Cahan was the editor of the *Jewish Daily Forward*, the Yiddish socialist newspaper that played such an important role in acculturating the immigrant Jews during the first decades of the twentieth century. The *Forward* featured a column, known as the *Bintel Brief* (bundle of letters), that contained many a tale of sexual woe and intrigue.[41] Adultery, abandonment, and the difficulties of finding love in a community lacking familiar social practices and networks were common themes. Replacing the traditional rabbi, a role that newspaper editors had already begun to play in Eastern Europe, Cahan became spiritual adviser to his readers, dispensing homey nostrums that mixed vaguely traditional virtues with fervent Americanism. His advice might be considered an attempt to create a new normative system appropriate to the American setting. To a young man with questions about whether a certain woman might be physically and spiritually incompatible, he answered:

> Love conquers all ... it is better for the man to be taller and the woman shorter, not the opposite. People are accustomed to seeing the man more

developed than the woman. People stare? Let them stare! Also, the fact that
the girl is religious and the man is not can be overcome if he has enough influence on her.[42]

These letters to the *Forward* remind us of the earlier responsa literature. Indeed, the sexual intrigues they chronicle, although undoubtedly
exacerbated by the immigrant experience, often resemble the many
"scandalous" practices found in the medieval and nineteenth-century responsa. One writer, for instance, relates how his wife began an affair
with his brother, who was living with them as a boarder, and rumors
began to circulate in the neighborhood. When finally confronted, the
brother committed suicide, but the unrepentant wife went on later to
begin yet another affair. The writer is grateful for a place to "pour out my
suffering on paper," and he hopes that his wife will read his letter and
"blush with shame."[43] While the elements of this case had their earlier
analogues, the novelty here was that the petitioner looks to the newspaper instead of to a rabbi for advice. Publicity, rather than legal coercion,
now became the recourse for those erotically wronged. It was out of material such as this that Cahan drew his inspiration for David Levinsky, a
character who exemplified not only the sexual infractions of real life but
also the tremendous libidinal energy of the immigrant community.

The way in which American Jewish culture preserved the memory of
the immigrant experience played a crucial role in later constructions of
sexuality. The pushy, erotic Jew of Lenny Bruce's comedy or Mordecai
Richler's fiction captured the bawdy tumult of Lower East Side culture,
from the ribald Yiddish theater to the lurid tales in the *Bintel Brief*.[44] Not
all memory emphasized this side, however. The stereotype of the Jew as
chaste found its way into literature as well. In *Call It Sleep*, Henry Roth's
powerful novel of an immigrant family, first published in 1934, the
young boy David discovers that the world outside the Oepidal purity of
his mother's kitchen, the America of the immigrants, is coarse, physical,
and frighteningly sexual. It is in the dark cellar of his building that David
witnesses a gentile boy "playing bad" with a Jewish girl, a sexual and religious transgression that leads inexorably to the novel's nearly fatal de-
nouement. In Roth's dark portrait, the tortuous road to assimilation in
America is marked by sexual shame and confusion.[45] This image of
America as sexual jungle recurs later in Saul Bellow's *Mr. Sammler's
Planet* (1969), in which an enormous black pickpocket exposes his genitals to the elderly Sammler, a European-born Jew living in New York.
Working with the conflicting mythologies of black sexuality and Jewish
chastity, Bellow suggests that the alleged sexuality of the African American is utterly foreign to the cultured European Jew.

Bernard Malamud touched on similar themes in what is perhaps
his most renowned novel, *The Assistant* (1957). Malamud portrays the

conflict-ridden relationship between Frank, a non-Jewish shop assistant, with Morris Bober, his immigrant Jewish employer. Frank falls in love with the shop owner's daughter, Helen, a culturally ambiguous name for a Jewish girl. After he has sex with her against her will, Helen cries: "Dog—uncircumcised dog."[46] Strangely drawn to Jewish suffering, but also feeling guilty over what he has done to both Helen and her father, Frank responds to Helen's rejection by addressing her accusation directly: .

> One day in April Frank went to the hospital and had himself circumcised. For a couple of days he dragged himself around with a pain between his legs. The pain enraged and inspired him. After Passover he became a Jew.[47]

Circumcision thus becomes the symbol of both Jewish suffering and sexual purity, a theme in earlier sources. Malamud contrasts the coarse sexuality of non-Jewish America with Jewish sexual restraint. In his allegory, the bleak life of the Jewish immigrants becomes surprisingly redemptive, serving to uplift Frank, the fallen Gentile, to a higher state of purity. Here, in fictional form, is a version, if much more ambiguous, of the theological claim that Jewish sexual ethics can redeem America.

More recent depictions of working-class, immigrant Jewish culture blend this redemptive dimension with an affirmation of eroticism. One such work is E. L. Doctorow's *Book of Daniel* (1971), a fictional reconstruction of the Rosenberg spy case told from the point of view of their son. The Jewish communists represent the second generation of immigrant Jews, Americanized, but still working class. From their immigrant parents comes a kind of madness that leads to their own suicidal behavior and ultimate destruction. (Doctorow gives the Rosenbergs of the novel the name Isaacson as if to emphasize their descent from the sacrificial biblical Isaac.) But together with this self-destructive madness comes eroticism: "They used to make the house rock. They really went at it, they balled all the time."[48] Their political madness *is* erotic and stands in opposition to the deeroticized immoral culture of capitalist America. Like Lenny Bruce, Doctorow's Rosenbergs are Jewish refutations of America's erotic and political hypocrisy.

The wedding of Jewish political radicalism to sexual liberation is not simply the creation of nostalgic fiction. Emma Goldman (1869–1940), one of the foremost leaders of American anarchism at the beginning of the century, personified the combination.[49] Born in Eastern Europe and an immigrant to America in 1889, she achieved notoriety for advocating free love as an integral part of her anarchistic philosophy. Although she did not spell out her ideas as an explicit reaction against the Jewish tradition, Goldman represents a secular Jewish politics; her utopian philosophy demonstrates that American Jews have a tradition of erotic revolution no less venerable than that of Zionism.

Against the typical Hollywood valorization of intermarriage, several movies of the 1970s and 1980s dissented from the dominant discourse by eroticizing the Jewish working class. *The Way We Were* (1973) was an attack on the intermarriage stereotype, though with a rather ambiguous conclusion. Barbra Streisand, who like Woody Allen, personifies an unabashed Jewish type, plays a Jewish communist from a working-class background in the late 1930s and 1940s who falls in love with a conservative, upper-crust Gentile played by Robert Redford. Their improbable relationship eventually disintegrates under the impact of McCarthyism, and they divorce. At the end of the movie, they meet momentarily some years later, each one now married to his and her appropriate ethnic mate. Returned to her own identity, the Streisand character seems to stand for the political and erotic affirmation of Jewish identity, a refutation of the possibility of finding marital satisfaction with the gentile Other. This conclusion is, in fact, the way the movie was understood when it came out.

The overt message is subtly undermined, however, by the overwhelming nostalgia with which the doomed romance between Jew and Gentile is presented. The "way we were" is not the "way we should be," but "true love" remains the sole property of the failed intermarriage. *The Way We Were* turns a radical Jewish woman of the working class into an erotic symbol, but it romanticizes an intermarriage that can only conflict with its own antiassimilationist message.

Two other movies represent incremental advances over *The Way We Were* in refuting the erotic attraction of the Gentile and affirming that of the Jew. And both, like *The Way We Were*, refer to the Jewish working-class past in doing so. In *Norma Rae*, a New York Jewish union organizer comes to the South to unionize textile workers. Although Reuben Warshawsky is not a worker himself, he proudly proclaims that his forebears were. Reuben is earthy, effusive, and unabashedly proud of being Jewish; he is the closest Hollywood has come to portraying a thoroughly attractive Jew, although his breed of Jewish union organizer is probably on the way to the museum. As erotically compelling as Reuben is, however, he is not allowed to play a sexual role in the movie. He and his native protégée, Norma Rae, acknowledge their attraction to each other but deliberately avoid any entanglement; Reuben has a woman, presumably Jewish, safely offscreen in New York.

Thus, *Norma Rae* indirectly affirms a set of social boundaries: Jews may play a positive political role in the American heartland, but they should return to where they are at home to find erotic satisfaction. Reuben Warshawsky no more belongs with Norma Rae than Lenny Cantrow of *The Heartbreak Kid* belonged with Kelly Corcoran. Although it does not explicitly depict a fully healthy relationship between two contemporary Jews, *Norma Rae* takes a step toward making it more plausible.

*Crossing Delancey* (1988) takes that step. Isabelle, a high-powered professional Jewish woman is frustrated in her attempt to find a suitable man and finds herself repeatedly in problematic relationships with non-Jews. Her Lower East Side grandmother arranges for a matchmaker to fix her up with a traditional pickle vendor and, after the predictable cultural malapropisms, love blossoms. As opposed to the whole stereotyped tradition in which Jews can find satisfaction only with non-Jews, *Crossing Delancey* depicts that rare occurrence: true love between two Jews. Even here, though, a certain note of ambiguity is heard. As in *White Palace*, the upper-middle-class Jew can only find passion in the working class, though in the more self-affirming *Crossing Delancey*, the worker is Jewish. Moreover, the pickle vendor is out of another era, the period of the immigrant, caught in a time warp in the late twentieth century. Thus for the American Jew to find sexual salvation, she must not only cross religious, class, and geographic boundaries, but she must take a leap backward in time to a vanished age.

These three movies, spanning a decade and a half, represent a clear development in the willingness of filmmakers to portray erotic attraction between Jews. In making that statement, all these films dissent from the dominant discourse that continues to be drawn to eroticizing the Other rather than the Self. And all locate the erotic imagination in the nostalgic, politically radical, working-class past rather than the Americanized, middle-class present. For this alternative culture, the past constitutes at once a great strength and a singular weakness.

## I. B. Singer and the Legacy of Eastern Europe

These uses of immigrant, working-class, and left-wing Jews as positive erotic symbols subvert both the male and female stereotypes of much of mass culture and, in their more secular representations, also the doctrines of the theologians. They embody the struggle over how to interpret the Jewish past in America in order to recover models of sexual normalcy. As opposed to the theologians, these works suggest that one can discover erotic truths not in "high culture," in the teachings of the rabbinic tradition, but in the lives of the ordinary working class, the simple Jews.

A similar struggle can be seen over the image of Eastern Europe, the homeland from which most of the immigrants came. We have seen a tendency in some of the assimilatory and apologetic strategies of the more conservative theologies to efface the historical struggles over sexuality and leave an impression of Jewish purity and health. Historical works such as the popular anthropology *Life Is with People*[50] sometimes take the same approach by conjuring up a nostalgic image of the shtetl as a world in which marital and familial harmony reigned. In this mythology, the traditional world of Eastern Europe was a world without internal conflicts and tensions. The struggles that we have noted in Ashkenazic Jewish culture seemed too threatening to the assimilating American Jews in search of a stable past.

Not all Jewish writers have subscribed to this desire for a whitewashed, deeroticized past. The Yiddish writer Isaac Bashevis Singer, himself a transplant from Eastern Europe, gave his American audience a very different image of that world. As opposed to the belief in Jewish purity, Singer depicts sexual perversity and obsession as persistent and important undercurrents in Jewish life in Eastern Europe. In Singer's shtetl eroticism plays a leading role: sexuality is a force for rebellion against a puritanical rabbinic world.

Singer exploits traditional Jewish folklore, with its beliefs in sexual demons, to create an image of an erotic Jewish "underworld" in opposition to rabbinical authority. In the "Destruction of Kreshev,"[51] for example, Satan, the narrator, describes a marriage contracted in classic fashion between Lise, the daughter of a wealthy scholar, and a poor orphan, who is also a talmudic prodigy. But the boy, Shloimele, turns out to be a follower of the seventeenth-century messianic pretender, Sabbatai Zevi, and he and his young wife immerse themselves in sexual perversions based on kabbalistic texts. The story comes to its catastrophic climax when Shloimele convinces Lise to commit adultery with the atheist coachman Mendel, described as "a Jewish Gentile." Although the town punishes them for their crime (Lise ultimately commits suicide), expiation only comes with the destruction of Kreshev by fire and plague. Here Singer goes beyond a mere tale of adultery to construct a fictional Jewish universe in which demonology and sexual libertinism feed on each other. By connecting Shloimele to the antinomian Sabbatian movement, he creates a kind of counter-Judaism in which sexuality, mysticism, and magic stand against the sober legalism of the official religion of the rabbis.

Singer's sexual subversions frequently rest on reversals of traditional roles, much like the biblical stories and folktales we have encountered. In the "Destruction of Kreshev," we are told that Lise studies rabbinic texts, in addition to Yiddish women's literature. Her father "would say sorrowfully: 'It's a shame that she's not a boy. What a man she would have made.'"[52] In "Gimpel the Fool," Gimpel's wife dominates the household and carries on one affair after another.[53] The dangers, as well as the liberating possibilities of such reversals, are the central themes in one of Singer's most famous stories, "Yentl the Yeshiva Boy,"[54] reminiscent of the famous Maid of Ludmir, the female Hasidic charismatic who was thought to have the "soul of a man." Yentl disguises herself as a yeshiva student and falls in love with her study partner, Avigdor. Only in her male disguise can Yentl discover her own sexuality as a woman; only as a result of the reversal of sex roles can love and sexuality be liberated from the constraints of traditional marriage matches.

Far from the comic farce in which such reversals are usually found in other literatures, however, the outcome of Singer's story is tragic. Avigdor marries his original love, Hadass, but their marriage is without joy and Yentl herself disappears. The traditional Jewish world, Singer intimates, could not accommodate either the liberation of women or modern romantic love without tragic consequences. Sexuality in a traditional Jewish context can only be imagined in the form of demonic possession or of radical gender reversals, both of which inevitably wind up in catastrophe. In his great novel of interwar Poland, *The Family Moskat*,[55] Singer's protagonist, Asa Heschel, is unable to fulfill his romantic desires; the deterioration of his personal relations stands for the slide of the Polish Jews into the Holocaust. Asa Heschel is an erotically blocked antihero in the style of the literature of the turn of the century. Singer, the heir to this pessimistic Eastern European tradition, played out many of the problematic themes of Jewish eroticism for his American audience.

His works set in America are similarly full of eroticism, but if the sexual underside of Jewish life in Eastern Europe has continued in America today, it remains just as fraught with problems here as there. In *Enemies, A Love Story*,[56] he depicts the sexual escapades of a Holocaust survivor who becomes a bigamist. As opposed to the frequent beatification of survivors in current literature, Singer realizes characters who are all too human. Although deeply scarred by the Holocaust, they have not lost their prewar sexual drives. Indeed, their sexuality functions as a way of affirming their survival. But Singer is deeply ambivalent about this sexual energy, as he is about the sexuality of the Eastern European Jews. This is eroticism that can easily slide into nihilism, a two-edged sword at once vital and destructive.

## Female Subversions

Like the historical tradition as a whole, most of the images of both male and female Jewish sexuality in America that we have discussed so far were produced by men.[57] Nevertheless, the last two decades have witnessed female voices increasingly challenging and enriching the male domination of American Jewish culture, as seen in feminist theology and films made by women directors, such as *Crossing Delancey*. For the first time in Jewish history, the construction of sexual experience is no longer a male monopoly.

In the essays of the lesbian poets Adrienne Rich and Irena Klepfisz, one finds a synthesis between feminist and Jewish identities: "Like Black and other dark-skinned people, Jews and women have haunted white Western thought as Other, as fantasy, as projected obsession."[58] This sense of double otherness infuses both sides of their identities since both are bound up with mythologies that need to be demolished. Klepfisz points to the specifically sexual dimension of this sense of marginality and alienation: "When you ask me to say something about being a Jewish lesbian, what can I say? You know of course that there are no Jewish lesbians because to begin with Jews are not supposed to be sexual. Especially Jewish women."[59] For a Jewish woman to adopt a sexual identity, and even more to adopt a lesbian identity, is to challenge the myths of the asexual Jewish woman and of an asexual Judaism.

One female writer who deserves special mention in this context is Erica Jong, not only because she has constructed an explicitly Jewish erotic fiction but also because she has set out to challenge the male mythologies of a Woody Allen or a Philip Roth with a countermythology of her own. In her madcap first novel, *Fear of Flying*, her protagonist seeks out the mythical, purely physical "zipless fuck" and along the way encounters an Englishman who seduces her with the line "It's just that Jewish girls are so bloody good in bed."[60] So much for the myth of the asexual JAP! Indeed, Jong's characters seem dedicated to reversing the stereotypes: Jewish women are promiscuous and lusty, while Jewish men are scarcely to be found in their beds.

In *Any Woman's Blues*, Jong's protagonist is Leila Sand, a middle-aged "sexoholic" Jewish artist who, in a gender reversal of *Portnoy*, pursues one gentile man after the other. She says of her greatest obsession, "Dart": "I must admit that my Dyckman Street Jewish childhood had left me with a lifelong fascination for old WASP ways. I was not just fucking a man when I fucked Dart. I was fucking American history, the *Mayflower* myth, the colonial past."[61] Rarely has sex been described so explicitly as a strategy for assimilation (although, alternatively, it might also be strategy for revenge)! Yet Sand is no unadulterated assimilationist. The one man with whom she has children (twin girls) is a Jew: "I realized that they had to be fathered by a hirsute Jew of my blood and bone.... I could no more have brought WASP babies into the world than I could have stopped drawing and painting." She recounts seeing a documentary on Auschwitz while pregnant and "weeping with joy and pain to be replenishing the Jewish race.... [W]here having babies is concerned, all our conservatism seems to burgeon."[62] Procreation, as distinct from pure sex, must somehow remain Jewish.

Jong's strategy is deliberately outrageous, a kind of female Lenny Bruce, in which the outrageousness is specifically Jewish. Yet, for all their seeming erotic liberation and outrageous language, Jong's characters remain mired in sexual confusion and frustration. Leila Sand has no more resolved her sexoholism by the end of the novel than does Portnoy at the end of his complaint or than do Allen's characters after nearly two decades of films. Jong's answer to the male stereotypes is a female version of the same syndrome.

As problematic as Erica Jong's work may be, it nevertheless represents an explicit attempt by a woman to shatter some prevalent myths and create an erotic Jewish woman, stereotyped, perhaps, but still refreshing. Equally challenging, if also problematic, is the recent novel of Marge Piercy, *He, She and It*.[63] Piercy creates a Jewish science fiction set in the middle of the twenty-first century, but it also harks back to the legend of the Golem of Prague. Shira, divorced by her inadequate Jewish husband, returns from the deeroticized world of the multinational corporations to the free Jewish town of Tikva (Hope), where she was born. There, she undertakes to educate a human-like cyborg and eventually falls in love with it/him. Jewish women, Piercy seems to suggest, need to break free of neurotic Jewish men and create their own, autonomous sexuality, much as Shira creates her own sexual partner in the robot Yod. As opposed to the myths of Jewish sexual pathology, Piercy's world is one in which only Jews, and especially Jewish women, are erotically healthy. The erotic utopianism of Zionism is transferred to a future Jewish community. Nevertheless, as a vision of American Jewish sexuality in the future, this novel remains caught in the conflicts of the culture in which it was written: since the cyborg cannot procreate and ultimately self-destructs, Piercy's novel ends without a solution to how healthy and procreative erotic relations between Jewish men and women might become possible. Like other attempts to imagine healthy Jewish sexuality, Piercy's novel projects images of Jewish Eros onto the past and, in her case, also onto the future.

The search for a usable past is not, however a futile or necessarily misleading endeavor. All attempts at a reconstruction of the present must start with history. By contesting male definitions of Jewish women and by rereading classical texts like the Bible from a feminist point of view, Jewish feminists may succeed in identifying models of a healthy eroticism that some believe (rightly or wrongly remains yet to be seen) characterized Jewish women more than men in the past. Adrienne Rich, for example, has suggested that Yiddish women poets represent a tradition "more sexually frank that [that of] the men."[64] Certainly, a figure like Emma Goldman represents a rich antireligious source for those in search of a female erotic past.

The construction of a history of Jewish sexuality from the point of view of women will undoubtedly shed further new light on many of the texts and movements we have examined in this book. How would the thirteenth-century Kabbalah look if we could discover the autobiography of the wife of Moses de Leon, the author of the *Zohar*? How will the talmudic treatment of women and sexuality appear after subjected to a feminist rereading? The past can serve as a kind of escape, a fulfillment elsewhere of what is lacking today, but it can also provide a rich source for the present by illuminating our contemporary reality and by providing models for new identities. Indeed, with feminism, we come back full circle to the Bible, for if the role of feminism today is to serve as a kind of subversion of the traditional canon, this role recapitulates the sexual subversions of biblical culture.

The dialectic of American Jewish culture demonstrates that the struggle around the question of sexuality continues unabated. The powerful forces of assimilation have awakened equally strong forces of cultural resistance. As much as feminism and other subversions of the discourse of American Jewish sexuality have created new possibilities, the stereotypes that have been the subject of this chapter are still powerful and persistent: erotic liberation remains the unfinished business of contemporary Jewish culture.

# Creating Desire

As Alexander Portnoy flies into Israel near the end of *Portnoy's Complaint,* he is suddenly overwhelmed by memories of his father and his friends as they played baseball on Sunday mornings. For just a moment, his self-hatred and sexual obsessions vanish. Here, in the image of his father, is a male model worth emulating: "How I am going to love growing up to be a Jewish man!" It is this reconciliation with memory—and not the projection of fantasies, whether onto the State of Israel or elsewhere—that suggest the hope of psychic repair. Philip Roth has now offered a powerful vision of such a reconciliation with the father in *Patrimony* (1991), his memoir of the death of his father. Here we meet an American Jewish man who has come to terms with the strengths, weaknesses, and ultimately the *reality* of his father. In shifting from fiction to nonfiction, Roth moves his readers from fantasy to the real world.

At stake here is not some psychological development in Philip Roth as a person but the meaning this shift symbolizes for the cultural question of sexual identity. One need not be a Freudian to claim that resolving one's relationship to one's parents is essential to achieving a successful relationship to sexuality. In the larger sense, the parents here stand for the Jewish tradition as a whole. Both the American Jewish community and Israel, the two major centers of Jewish culture in the late twentieth century, established their identities by an effort to reject history and to break with their real and symbolic parents. This effort was necessary to survive in a secular, posttraditional world. But such a rejection of the past could not succeed by itself; it needed to be balanced by a reconciliation with one's origins, the appropriation of a past that was neither stultifying nor paralyzing and that could create new forms of desire.

I believe that the very future of the Jews may depend on whether they can create erotic self-images that are as compelling as their images of either the non-Jew or the Jews of another time or place. The various American Jewish discourses of sexuality demonstrate that who is eroticized and who is not are determined almost unconsciously. To expose the assumptions behind these decisions is perhaps the first step to changing them. This new affirmation of Jewish eroticism will only come when the very integration that Jews have achieved in American society can serve not as the source of sexual anxiety but as a source of self-confidence. Similarly, the ability of contemporary Israeli culture to resolve its own sexual identity involves a reconciliation with its own ambiguous past.

Both of these largely secular societies confront their present problems of Eros out of a common heritage, the historical tradition that has been the subject of this book. That the many voices of this tradition often seem to speak faintly and in foreign tongues does not mean that they are irrelevant or to be ignored; these ghostly voices are the necessary source for whatever modern or postmodern definition of Jewish culture may emerge. Creating Jewish desire today requires a confrontation with all the ambiguities and ambivalences that make up the tradition, since contemporary dilemmas of desire have their analogues and roots in the past.

I have argued throughout this book that the history of Jewish sexuality cannot be reduced to a monolithic message, either liberatory or repressive. Rabbinic norms competed repeatedly with the values of popular culture. From biblical Israel to contemporary America, we have found persistent conflicts between the contrary attractions of asceticism and gratification, procreation and pleasure, collective imperatives and individual needs. The struggles over fertility and sexual fulfillment that characterize contemporary culture repeat in modern form the same themes that preoccupied those who created the Bible, the Talmud, medieval Jewish literature, Hasidism, the Haskalah, and Zionism. And although the modern problem of intermarriage has its own unique dimensions, I believe that the Jews have always had to struggle with the attractions of the erotic Other, never fully succumbing to the temptation but neither ever able fully to ignore it.

The very contradictions and pluralism of these approaches to sexuality in Jewish history demonstrate that there is no one "solution" to the problem of desire. Indeed, the challenge today, it seems to me, is to move beyond the binary opposition of erotic health versus pathology, liberation and repression, and to allow the exploration of a multiplicity of desires: what has been marginalized now needs to be incorporated. In particular, the polarities of male and female sexuality should no longer confine our imagination. Erotic desire operates in a constant tension between attraction to what is familiar and to what is different, even forbidden. True erotic fulfillment, I would argue, is only possible on the personal level when we recognize and accept elements of the other gender in ourselves, whether in a heterosexual or homosexual framework, even as we affirm who we are. To balance the male definitions of Jewish sexuality that have so dominated throughout the tradition with female definitions constitutes the historical and collective dimension of this process, a process essential for both women and men. Since Alexander Portnoy's neurosis involved to such a great degree the objectification and silencing of women, perhaps the best therapy for his famous "complaint" is the reclaiming of female erotic voices.

The issue of intermarriage is based on a related polarity. If the dialectic between Self and Other is a necessary characteristic of the erotic on the gender level, the same is true of relations between Jews and non-Jews. The future of the Jews as a people clearly depends on the ability of Jewish culture to imagine other Jews as erotic, yet the attraction of the Gentile will always be part of this struggle, a struggle that cannot be resolved by the mere rejection of the Other. The challenge in a posttraditional world is to divest the binary opposition between Jew and Gentile of its theological baggage and, thereby, to temper its elements of fantasy and projection. Only when erotic relations between Jews and non-Jews appear less momentous and threatening will they lose part of their fascination.

Erotic relations between Jews and non-Jews both reflect and symbolize the interaction between Jewish culture and the cultures of those among whom Jews have lived. Jewish culture never evolved in a vacuum, but was always the product of the fruitful interaction between Jewish and non-Jewish cultures; Jews have always lived and participated in a multicultural world. In this respect, the search for an authentic definition of Jewish sexuality in contemporary culture recapitulates historical struggles, whether between the biblical Israelites and the Canaanites, between the talmudic rabbis and the Hellenists, or between the medieval Jews and their Christian and Muslim neighbors. The result in all these cases was a distinctive understanding of sexuality in which the textual tradition was both preserved and transformed as the Jews participated in the wider cultures of their times.

It is my hope that this book, as a study growing out of our contemporary fascination with the history of sexuality, may play a similar role, by bringing to bear on the Jewish textual tradition a new set of cultural questions and perhaps by changing the way we see the tradition in the process. Since, as we have seen, texts throughout Jewish history have shaped the erotic, perhaps this book may take its place as one more text seeking to understand, define, and, perhaps, even contribute to creating Jewish desire. Like all works of historical reconstruction, the aim of this study has been to see the present through the past and the past through the present: to discover an erotic tradition that a modern Jew can appropriate, a tradition not dogmatic, but instead the record of real people struggling with questions that have challenged every human culture throughout history.

# N O T E S

## INTRODUCTION:
## Dilemmas of Desire

1. See Chapter 9 for a discussion of this particular interpretation in contemporary American Jewish theology.

2. For accounts of European views of Jewish sexuality, see George Mosse, *Nationalism and Sexuality* (New York, 1985), pp. 133–52; and Sander L. Gilman, *Difference and Pathology: Stereotypes of Sexuality, Race and Madness* (Ithaca, N.Y., 1985), especially pp. 150–62.

3. See the letter by Marie Syrkin to *Commentary* (March 1973). Surprisingly, this was also the argument against *Portnoy* made by the Israeli historian Gershom Scholem, whose own studies of Jewish mysticism shocked those who saw Judaism as a rational, philosophical tradition. See Scholem, *Haaretz* (6 June 1969 and 4 July 1969). Reprinted in Scholem, *Devarim Be-Go* (Tel Aviv, 1976), pp. 534–37. On Scholem, see David Biale, *Gershom Scholem: Kabbalah and Counter-History* (Cambridge, Mass., 1979).

4. Philip Roth, "Imagining Jews," in Roth, *Reading Myself and Others* (New York, 1985), p. 278.

5. See the parody entitled "Peabody's Complaint," which appeared in the *New York Times Book Review*, 23 March 1969, p. 2, shortly after the publication of *Portnoy*. An unintentionally hilarious letter appeared on April 20 in which the writer inquired quite seriously where he might obtain a copy of "Peabody's Complaint."

6. See John Cuddihy, *The Ordeal of Civility* (New York, 1974), in which this stereotype is explored.

7. Philip Roth, *Portnoy's Complaint* (New York, 1969), pp. 37, 84.

8. Roth, *Reading Myself and Others*, p. 199.

9. Roth, *Portnoy's Complaint*, p. 172.

10. Portnoy's equation of women and Gentiles is a curious reversal of the equation between women and Jews in Otto Weininger's notoriously misogynistic turn-of-the-century work, *Sex and Character* (London, 1906). Weininger was driven by self-hate to identify Jews with the feminine. The cases of Portnoy and Weininger suggest that Jewish self-hatred, like anti-Semitism, is frequently bound up with sexual stereotypes.

11. Roth, *Portnoy's Complaint*, p. 52.

12. See Michel Foucault, *The History of Sexuality*, vol. 1, *An Introduction*, trans. Robert Hurley (New York, 1978), pt. 2, for a cogent critique of the concept of repression. Foucault's work has inspired a whole historiography of sexuality that frequently demonstrates how other categories informed the sexual in earlier ages.

13. See, among many other works, Marthe Robert, *From Oedipus to Moses: Freud's Jewish Identity*, trans. Ralph Mannheim (Garden City, N.Y., 1976); Peter Gay, *A Godless Jew: Freud, Atheism and the Making of Psychoanalysis* (New Haven, 1987); Yosef Hayyim Yerushalmi, *Freud's Moses: Judaism Terminable and Interminable* (New Haven, 1991); and Sander L. Gilman, *Freud, Race and Gender* (Princeton, N.J., forthcoming).

14. See David Bakan, *Sigmund Freud and the Jewish Mystical Tradition* (New York, 1958), pp. 271–99; and Moshe Idel, "Sexual Metaphors and Praxis in the Kabbalah," in David Kraemer, ed., *The Jewish Family: Myth and Metaphor* (New York, 1988), p. 213. Idel believes that the Kabbalah's "unequivocal view of sexuality had an important repercussion in modern psychoanalysis through Freud's appreciation of the libido." While Jungian psychology inherited the "reticent and sometimes ambiguous" attitude toward sexuality found in Christianity and Gnosticism, Freud took from Judaism—and from the Kabbalah in particular—the value of an "unrepressed libido." Not only are these assertions highly problematic with respect to the Kabbalah, but they also represent an astonishing misreading of Freud. On the Kabbalah and my different interpretation, see Chapter 5.

15. Sigmund Freud, "Resistance to Psychoanalysis," in Freud, *Collected Papers*, trans. Joan Riviere (New York, 1959), 5:170. For Freud's inner conflict over sexuality, see Peter Gay, *Freud: A Life for Our Time* (New York, 1988), pp. 142–49.

16. Otto Rank, "The Essence of Judaism" (1905), trans. in Dennis Klein, *Jewish Origins of the Psychoanalytic Movement* (New York, 1981), p. 171.

17. See Gay, *Freud: A Life*, pp. 162–64.

18. Sigmund Freud, *Moses and Monotheism*, trans. Katherine Jones (New York, 1939), pp. 147, 152.

19. Howard Eilberg-Schwartz is currently preparing a book on this subject.

20. *New York Times*, 31 March 1969, p. 42. For a similar view of *Portnoy*, see Peter Shaw, "Portnoy and His Creator," *Commentary* 47 (1977): 77–79.

21. Roth, "Imagining Jews," in *Reading Myself and Others*, p. 301.

22. The idea that the physical act of intercourse, or sex, is not the same as various cultural constructs called sexuality can be found perhaps first in Foucault, *History of Sexuality*, vol. 1. See also Arnold Davidson, "Sex and the Emergence of Sexuality," *Critical Inquiry* 14 (1987): 17–48; and David Halperin, "Is There a History of Sexuality?" *History and Theory* 28, no. 3 (1989): 257–74.

23. These ideas are derived primarily from Foucault, *History of Sexuality*, vol. 1.

24. See Chava Weissler, "The Traditional Piety of Ashkenazic Women," in Arthur Green, ed., *Jewish Spirituality* (New York, 1987), 2:245–75; and, on the connection between women and unlearned men, idem, "'For Women and for Men Who Are Like Women': The Construction of Gender in Yiddish Devotional Literature," *Journal of Feminist Studies in Religion* 5, no. 2 (Fall 1989): 7–24.

25. For a discussion of this notion in early Christianity, see Wayne Meeks, "The Image of the Androgyne: Some Uses of a Symbol in Earliest Christianity," *History of Religions* 13 (1974): 165–208; and Peter Brown, *The Body and Society: Men, Women and Sexual Renunciation in Early Christianity* (New York, 1988).

26. That it has also only recently become the subject of scholarly research is attested by the recent book, Howard Eilberg-Schwartz, ed., *People of the Body: Jews and Judaism from an Embodied Perspective* (Albany, NY, 1992). See especially Eilberg-Schwartz's introduction.

27. Roth, "Writing about Jews," in *Reading Myself and Others*, p. 210; emphasis in original.


CHAPTER 1:

Sexual Subversions in the Bible

Abbreviations: m. = Mishnah; b. = Babylonian Talmud


1. A recent example of this kind of argument can be found in Gerda Lerner, *The Creation of Patriarchy* (New York, 1986). Against this view, see Tikva Frymer-Kensky, *In the Wake of the Goddesses: Women, Culture and the Biblical Transformation of Pagan Myth* (New York, 1992). At times, Christian feminist interpretation of the Hebrew Bible unwittingly verges on anti-Semitism. See Susannah Heschel, "Anti-Judaism in Christian Feminist Theology," *Tikkun* (May–June 1990): 25–28, 95–97; Katharina von Kellenbach, "Antisemitismus in biblischer Matriarchatsforschung?" *Berliner Theologische Zeitschrift* 3, no. 1 (1986): 144–47; and idem, "Anti-Judaism in Christian-Rooted Feminist Writings: An Analysis of Major U.S. American and West

German Feminist Theologians" (Ph.D. diss. Temple University, 1990).

2. This discussion parallels and owes much to Regina Schwartz. See Schwartz, "Adultery in the House of David: The Metanarrative of Biblical Scholarship and the Narratives of the Bible," *Semeia* (forthcoming) and her forthcoming book on identity and violence in the Hebrew Bible.

3. For the connection between the theology of fertility and the social life of the ancient Israelites, see Carol Meyers, *Discovering Eve: Ancient Israelite Women in Context* (New York, 1988).

4. Without attempting to solve the still hotly debated question of when it was written, it is clear that Ruth stands at a self-reflective distance from some of the more ancient biblical traditions. It is my contention that the author wrote substantially later than the time of the composition of the Genesis stories. He or she obviously lived *after* the period of the judges (ca. 1200–1050 B.C.E.) but sought to re-create the ambiance of that evidently distant age. For a bibliography of some of the recent scholarship on dating Ruth, see Susan Niditch, "Legends of Wise Heroes and Heroines," in Douglas A. Knight and Gene M. Tucker, eds., *The Hebrew Bible and Its Modern Interpreters* (Philadelphia, 1985), p. 451; and Edward F. Campbell, Jr., *The Anchor Bible Ruth* (Garden City, N.Y., 1975), pp. 23–28. Dates range from the early monarchy (ca. 950) to the late monarchy (ca. 600) to the postexilic period (500–400 B.C.E.). I assume a date during the latter part of the monarchy, probably the time of Deuteronomy (seventh century B.C.E.). It may be that the genealogy at the end of chapter 4 was appended later, but there is no reason to assign even it to a postexilic date.

5. For some acute observations on eroticism and agriculture in Ruth, see Calum Carmichael, "'Treading' in the Book of Ruth," *Zeitschrift für alttestamentliche Wissenschaft* 92 (1980): 248–66. For discussion of the connections between agricultural and human fertility in the Bible, see Howard Eilberg-Schwartz, *The Savage in Judaism: Excursions in an Anthropology of Israelite Religion and Ancient Judaism* (Bloomington, Ind., 1990), Chaps. 5, 6.

6. See Ilana Pardes, *Countertraditions in the Bible: A Feminist Approach* (Cambridge, Mass., 1992), p. 113.

7. The threshing floor may well have been a Canaanite cultic site, and the prophet Hosea claims that it was used for acts of ritual intercourse (Hosea 9: 1–2). On "threshing" or "treading" as a euphemism for sexual intercourse, see Carmichael, "'Treading,'" p. 249 n. 4. For the argument that the story of Ruth was originally a Canaanite cultic myth, see W. E. Staples, "The Book of Ruth," *American Journal of Semitic Literature* 53 (1936–37): 145–47; H. B. May, "Ruth's Visit to the High Place," *Journal of the Royal Asiatic Society* (1939): 75–78; S. L. Shearman and J. Biggs, "Divine-Human Conflicts in the Old Testament," *Journal of Near Eastern Studies* 28 (1969): 235ff; and G. R. H. Wright, "The Mother-Maid at Bethlehem," *Zeitschrift für alttestamentliche Wissenschaft* 98 (1986): 56–72.

8. See Carmichael, "'Treading'"; and idem, *Women, Law and the Genesis*

*Traditions* (Edinburgh, 1979), pp. 74–93. Campbell supports this interpretation, *Anchor Bible Ruth*, p. 121 n. 4 and 131–32, as does, in a different vein, Mieke Bal, *Lethal Love: Feminist Literary Readings of Biblical Love Stories* (Bloomington, Ind., 1987), chap. 3. Against Carmichael, see Anthony Phillips, "The Book of Ruth: Deception and Shame," *Journal of Jewish Studies* 36 (1986): 11–13.

9. Judges 3:24, 1 Samuel 24:3, 2 Kings 18:27, Isaiah 7:20, Ezekiel 16:25.

10. See, for example, Leviticus 18:6–18.

11. See Deuteronomy 23:1, 27:20, and Ezekiel 16:8.

12. For analyses of the book along these lines, see Phyllis Trible, *God and the Rhetoric of Sexuality* (Philadelphia, 1978), pp. 166–99; Bal, *Lethal Love*, chap. 3; and Pardes, *Countertraditions in the Bible*, chap. 6.

13. It is remarkable that Boaz, rather than Elimelech and Ruth's first husband, Mahlon, is the ancestor of David, for the point of the levirate is to perpetuate the name of the childless deceased. In a sense, the death of Elimelech and his sons at the beginning of the book is final; instead of perpetuating their names, Boaz's redemption of Ruth creates a new family with Boaz as the patriarch and Naomi as the matriarch.

14. Bal has suggested the notion of "lethal love" to explain the role of women in many biblical stories. While this point is very persuasive, it seems to me that she makes the biblical view of women's sexuality too one-sidedly negative.

15. See also 1 Kings 11:1–2 and Nehemiah 13:23–28. For an argument that the prohibition on Moabites and Ammonites was an attack on the Davidic lineage, see Jacob Milgrom, "Religious Conversion and the Revolt Model for the Formation of Israel," *Journal of Biblical Literature* 101 (1982): 169–76. The rabbis tried to harmonize the law with Ruth by arguing that the law applied only to male Moabites and Ammonites (m. Yevamot 8.3), but since the two passages above refer specifically to women, the rabbinic exegesis is not plausible. Some have argued that by celebrating King David's Moabite origins, the Book of Ruth served as a polemic against either the laws of Deuteronomy that forbade intermarriage or Ezra's dissolution of marriages between Jews and foreigners after the return from Babylonia (ca. 440 B.C.E.). If David's own great-grandmother was a Moabite, then perhaps lesser Israelites might be equally justified in taking foreign spouses. Nevertheless, Ruth does not have the flavor of a polemic, and a more likely explanation for the contradiction is that it was written before the laws of Deuteronomy were in force.

16. For a structuralist analysis of Ruth in the context of this and other stories of sexual subversion (Genesis 38), see Harold Fisch, "Ruth and the Structure of Covenant History," *Vetus Testamentum* 32 (1982): 425–37.

17. See Pardes, *Countertraditions in the Bible*, chap. 6.

18. The Israelites were a young nation, not an old people like the Egyptians and the Sumerians. They evolved a theology of election that explained

why, contrary to nature, God had chosen this weakest and youngest of nations to inherit the land. This is also the explanation for the narratives in which younger sons supplant elder sons in violation of the law of primogeniture in Deuteronomy 21:15–17. In story after story, the younger son is preferred over the older: Abel over Cain, Isaac over Ishmael, Jacob over Esau, Joseph and Benjamin over their older brothers, Perez over Zerah, Ephraim over Manasseh, David over his older brothers. Primogeniture was common practice throughout the ancient Near East. See, for example, the Middle Assyrian law that is quite close to the biblical: James B. Pritchard, ed., *Ancient Near Eastern Texts* (Princeton, N.J., 1958), 1:185. See further I. Mendelsohn, "On the Preferential Status of the Elder Son," *Bulletin of the American Schools of Oriental Study* 156 (1959): 38–40. But there are also accounts of the younger son eclipsing the older in ancient Near Eastern literature. See Pritchard, pp. 289, 557, 603–4 (pars. 23–24).

19. For some recent analyses of the Tamar and Judah story, including its connections to Ruth, see Susan Niditch, "The Wronged Woman Righted: An Analysis of Genesis 38," *Harvard Theological Review* 72 (1979): 143–49; J. A. Emerton, "Judah and Tamar," *Vetus Testamentum* 29 (1979): 403–15 and bibliography; Carmichael, *Women, Law and the Genesis Traditions,* pp. 57–73; and Fisch, "Ruth and the Structure of Covenant History."

20. Robert Alter has shown how the editor of Genesis artfully tied Genesis 38 to the Joseph cycle. See Alter, *The Art of Biblical Narrative* (New York, 1981), pp. 3–12. For a very different analysis that also places the story in its context, see Bal, *Lethal Love,* chap. 4.

21. For a recent summary of the bibliography on levirate in Ruth compared with the levirate law of Deuteronomy 25:5ff., and Genesis 38, see Niditch, "Legends of Wise Heroes and Heroines," pp. 452–53. See, in particular, D. R. G. Beattie, "The Book of Ruth as Evidence for Israelite Legal Practice," *Vetus Testamentum* 24 (1974): 251–67; Calum Carmichael, "A Ceremonial Crux: Removing a Man's Sandal as a Female Gesture of Contempt," *Journal of Biblical Literature* 96 (1977): 321–36; Robert Gordis, "Love, Marriage and Business in the Book of Ruth: A Chapter in Hebrew Customary Law," in Howard Bream et al., eds., *A Light unto My Path: Old Testament Studies in Honor of Jacob M. Myers* (Philadelphia, 1974), pp. 241–64; Baruch Levine, "In Praise of the Israelite *Mispaha:* Legal Themes in the Book of Ruth," in H. B. Huffmon et al., eds., *The Quest for the Kingdom of God: Studies in Honor of George E. Mendenhall* (Winona Lake, Ind., 1983), pp. 95–108; and H. H. Rowley, "The Marriage of Ruth," in Rowley, *The Servant of the Lord and Other Essays on the Old Testament* (Oxford, 1965), pp. 171–94.

22. The striking tension between sexual prohibitions and the levirate can also be deduced from a very interesting law in Deuteronomy:

If two men get into a fight with each other, a man and his brother, and the wife of one comes up to save her husband from his antagonist and puts out her hand

and seizes him by the genitals, you shall cut off her hand; show no pity. (25:11–12)

The wife is mentioned, rather than any other intervener, presumably because she is forbidden to have sexual contact with any other man. If she touches the other's genitals, even to defend her husband, she crosses a sexual boundary and causes him the shame of illegitimate exposure (the rare term *mevoshav* used for genitals is derived from "shame" [*bosh*]). The text also states, seemingly superfluously, that it is not just any two men who are fighting, but two *brothers*. This law follows immediately after the law of levirate marriage (Deuteronomy 25:5–10). As in the Levitical law prohibiting incest with a brother's wife, the legislator here is giving a warning: a woman is only allowed to touch the genitals of her brother-in-law in the exceptional circumstance when her husband dies childless; in all other cases, including a fight between the brothers, she is forbidden any sexual contact with him.

23. For a very useful collection of such myths, see Otto Rank, *The Myth of the Birth of the Hero*, ed. Philip Freund (New York, 1959), pp. 14–64. For some interesting reflections on the Bible, with less persuasive psychoanalytic observations, see Avshalom Elitzur, *Into the Holy of Holies: Psychoanalytic Insights into the Bible and Judaism* (in Hebrew) (Tel Aviv, 1988), pp. 173–211.

24. See Judah Goldin, "The Youngest Son or Where Does Genesis 38 Belong," *Journal of Biblical Literature* 96 (1977): 27–44. Goldin argues that this theme in the Genesis stories is a folkloristic way of turning the world upside down, a built-in correction to the abuse of the law: "The folk love such stories because they are a weapon against the powerful." This is an attractive theory and probably partly true, but it ignores the ideological function the stories fulfilled for Israelite identity.

25. See the interpretations of the Bathsheba story in Schwartz, "Adultery in the House of David"; Meir Sternberg, *The Poetics of Biblical Narrative: Ideological Literature and the Drama of Reading* (Bloomington, Ind., 1985), pp. 190–222; Alter, *The Art of Biblical Narrative*, pp. 75–76; and Bal, *Lethal Love*, chap. 1. None of these commentators points out the connections to the Abigail story.

26. On the theme of drunkenness in the Bible, see Hirsch H. Cohen, *The Drunkenness of Noah* (University, Ala., 1974).

27. A concubine probably had the same status as a wife with respect to the incest prohibitions. Three other instances of the same kind of behavior can be found from the period of the early monarchy (2 Samuel 3:7, 16:20–22, 1 Kings 2:28). It would appear from these passages that either marrying or having intercourse with the father's concubine may have been a symbolic way of claiming rights of inheritance or succession in the case of the monarchy. See the analysis of these incidents by Raphael Patai, *Sex and Family in the Bible and the Middle East* (Garden City, N.Y., 1959), pp. 98–103.

28. Regina Schwartz will treat incest and exogamy in her forthcoming book on identity and violence in the Hebrew Bible.

29. See the parallel law in Exodus 34:15 and in Joshua 23:12. On intermarriage in the Bible and beyond, see Leopold Loew, *Gesammelte Schriften* (Szegedin, 1893), 3:108–200; Louis Epstein, *Marriage Laws in the Bible and Talmud* (Cambridge, Mass., 1942), pp. 145–219; Lou H. Silberman, "Reprobation, Prohibition, Invalidity: An Examination of the Halakhic Development Concerning Intermarriage," in Daniel Jeremy Silver, ed., *Judaism and Ethics* (New York, 1970), pp. 177–98; and Shaye J. D. Cohen, "From the Bible to the Talmud: The Prohibition on Intermarriage," *Hebrew Annual Review* 7 (1983): 23–39.

30. See Elaine J. Adler, "The Background for the Metaphor of Covenant as Marriage in the Hebrew Bible" (Ph.D. diss. University of California, Berkeley, 1989).

31. Ezra 9 and 10.

32. Genesis 26:34, 27:46–28:2 (these are probably priestly texts), and Judges 14:3.

33. See, for example, Malachi 2:11 and Jubilees 30:7. Jubilees interprets the prohibition against giving one's seed to Molech to refer to intermarriage.

34. b. Avodah Zara 36b. See further Cohen, "From the Bible to the Talmud." We cannot know to what extent this norm was actually accepted, and there is evidence that intermarriage continued even in rabbinic times.

35. See Bal, *Lethal Love*, chap. 2; and idem, *Death and Dissymmetry* (Chicago, 1988).

36. See the very detailed reading of this story in Sternberg, *The Poetics of Biblical Narrative*, pp. 445–74.

37. See A. van Selms, *Marriage and Family Life in Ugaritic Literature* (London, 1954), pp. 81–82. Van Selms admits that he cannot find sacred prostitution in the Ugaritic texts. See also G. E. Mendenhall, *The Tenth Generation: The Origins of the Biblical Tradition* (Baltimore, 1974), pp. 105–21; Eugene J. Fisher, "Cultic Prostitution in the Ancient Near East? A Reassessment," *Biblical Theology Bulletin* 6 (1976): 225–36; Robert A. Oden, Jr., *The Bible without Theology: The Theological Tradition and Alternatives to It* (San Francisco, 1987), chap. 5; and Adler, "The Background for the Metaphor of Covenant." While some ritual intercourse may well have been part of certain religions (particularly the hierogamy, or sacred marriage, in Babylonia), it is not at all clear if it even existed among the Canaanites. On the Sumerian rites, see S. N. Kramer, *Sacred Marriage Rite: Aspects of Faith, Myth and Ritual in Ancient Sumer* (Bloomington, Ind., 1969).

38. The son of the surrogate was considered the child of the principal wife. See Genesis 16:2, 30:3, 9–13. This custom evidently had Assyrian parallels. See A. K. Grayson and J. Van Seters, "The Childless Wife in Assyria and the Stories of Genesis," *Orientalia* 44 (1975): 485–86. See further Savina Teubal, *Sarah the Priestess: The First Matriarch of Genesis* (Athens, Ohio, 1984).

39. The Midrash proposes a variant on this dichotomy between the loved and the fecund wife. It says in its story of Lamech (Genesis Rabbah 23.3) that before the flood men had one wife for procreation and another for purposes of sexual intercourse. The latter would drink a sterilizing potion so as not to get pregnant.

40. The birth of Perseus is a good example from Greek mythology. See Rank, *The Myth of the Birth of the Hero*, pp. 25–26.

41. See the very suggestive analysis by Jane Schaberg, *The Illegitimacy of Jesus: A Feminist Theological Interpretation of the Infancy Narratives* (San Francisco, 1987). Matthew's genealogy of Jesus mentions four women, Tamar, Rahab, Ruth, and Bathsheba (referred to only as "Uriah's wife"), all of whom are accused of transgressing sexual conventions. Might he be hinting at something illegitimate in Jesus' origins? But perhaps, as in the case of biblical heroes, this very illegitimacy is the proof of divine election.

42. For an excellent summary of various arguments concerning the priestly documents, especially in connection with fertility issues, see Jeremy Cohen, *"Be Fertile and Increase, Fill the Earth and Master It": The Ancient and Medieval Career of a Biblical Text* (Ithaca, N.Y., 1989), pp. 46–56. See also the excellent treatment of fertility in priestly culture in Eilberg-Schwartz, *The Savage in Judaism*, chap. 5.

43. See Frank Moore Cross, *Canaanite Myth and Hebrew Epic* (Cambridge, Mass., 1973), pp. 301–5. Cross is one of those who holds that P is postexilic and uses archaizing language. See pp. 322–25.

44. Genesis 1:28, 9:1, 17:2ff., 28:3–4, 35:11–12, 48:3–4. See the excellent discussion of the career of these blessings in Cohen, *"Be Fertile and Increase,"* chap. 1. The Hebrew word for "blessing" (*berakhah*) may originally have meant "to make fertile." See van Selms, *Marriage and Family Life in Ugaritic Literature*, p. 40.

45. For a bibliography and my own interpretation, see David Biale, "The God with Breasts: El Shaddai in the Bible," *History of Religions* 21, no. 3 (1982): 240–56.

46. For an extensive discussion of why the P blessings and Genesis 49 should be connected and what their provenance and date were, see ibid., pp. 249–51.

47. I am indebted to Howard Eilberg-Schwartz for these insights, which are the basis of his forthcoming work.

48. See Trible, *God and the Rhetoric of Sexuality*, pp. 31–71; and Raphael Patai, *The Hebrew Goddess* (New York, 1967).

49. Cyrus Gordon, *Ugaritic Literature* (Rome, 1949), p. 75. (text 128, pars:25–28).

50. Ibid., text 52, par. 28. The translation is debatable. Gordon translates "fields," but B. Vawter translates "breasts." See Vawter, "The Canaanite Background to Gen. 49," *Catholic Biblical Quarterly* 17 (1955): 1–18. Genesis 49 betrays knowledge of the epithet of El's consort Rahmay as well as of

other Canaanite mythological characters such as *Tehom* (Deep).

51. See William Reed, *The Asherah in the Old Testament* (Fort Worth, Tex., 1949); John Day, "Asherah in the Hebrew Bible and Northwest Semitic Literature," *Journal of Biblical Literature* 105 (1986): 385–408; Walter A. Maier II, *'Aserah: Extrabiblical Evidence* (Atlanta, 1986); and Saul Olyan, *Asherah and the Cult of Yahweh in Israel* (Atlanta, 1988).

52. W. F. Albright, *The Archaeology of Palestine and the Bible* (New York, 1932), p. 110.

53. See Day, "Asherah in the Hebrew Bible," pp. 391–94; William Dever, "Asherah, Consort of Yahwe? New Evidence from Kuntillet 'Arjud," *Bulletin of the American Schools of Oriental Research* 255 (Summer 1984): 21–37; and Ziony Zevit, "The Khirbet el Qom Inscription Mentioning a Goddess," *Bulletin of the American Schools of Oriental Research* 255 (Summer 1984): 39–47.

54. God changes his name to Yahweh (YHWH) in Exodus 6:3, which is the last priestly text that uses El Shaddai. Historians have pointed out that this was a device for assimilating different gods into one divinity.

55. See Exodus 33:20.

56. See Gordon J. Wenham, *The Book of Leviticus* (Grand Rapids, 1979), pp. 222–24, for bibliography; and Jacob Milgrom, *Anchor Bible Leviticus* (Garden City, N.Y., 1991), pp. 1766–67.

57. See also Exodus 19:12–13, Leviticus 16:2.

58. See Mary Douglas, *Purity and Danger* (London, 1966). My interpretation focuses less on bodily fluids that are out of their proper place, as Douglas does, than on why specifically semen and menstrual blood are polluting. Douglas makes the mistake of considering all bodily fluids to be equally polluting in the Bible and therefore misses the importance of procreative fluids. I agree with Milgrom that it is the association with death rather than dirt that is at stake. A rabbinic example of the paradoxical defiling capacity of a sacred object is the peculiar statement in the Mishnah that "all sacred writings defile the hands" (m. Yadayim 3.5). As Milgrom notes (*Anchor Bible Leviticus*), there may well be a connection between the biblical concept of purity and this later rabbinic saying (p. 1004).

59. Genesis 9:4–5 and Leviticus 17:11, 14. See further *Interpreter's Dictionary of the Bible*, Supplementary Volume, S.V. "blood."

60. For recent interpretations of why semen defiles along these lines see G. J. Wenham, "Why Does Sexual Intercourse Defile (Lev. 15:18)?" *Zeitschrift für alttestamentliche Wissenschaft* 95 (1983): 432–34; Eilberg-Schwartz, *The Savage in Judaism*, pp. 182–86; and Milgrom, *Anchor Bible Leviticus*, pp. 927–28, 933–34.

61. For a comparison of the Levitical laws on menstruation with those of other cultures, see Milgrom, *Anchor Bible Leviticus*, pp. 948–53. One might even argue that a man had greater impurity after ejaculation than a woman had after menstruation, since a man must wait until nightfall, whereas a woman could purify herself immediately after her flow stopped.

62. The evidence for such a belief is the rather ambiguous statement in 2

Samuel 11:4 that Bathsheba was "sanctifying herself from her impurity" when she slept with David. According to the next verse, she immediately conceived. There is difficulty in deciding from the language whether she had already completed her menstrual period. The term "sanctifying" (*mitkadeshet*) does not, however, appear in the priestly texts. On this verse and its possible implications, see Martin Krause, "II Sam 11:4 und das Konzeptionsoptimum," *Zeitschrift für alttestamentliche Wissenschaft* 95 (1983): 434–37.

63. See Eilberg-Schwartz, *The Savage in Judaism*, pp. 183–84. Another interesting example is the bizarre law of Numbers 5:11–31, the *sotah* ordeal, in which a woman accused by her husband of adultery is made to drink a magical potion called "the waters of bitterness." If she is guilty, "her belly shall distend and her thigh shall sag," but if she is innocent, "she shall be unharmed and shall conceive." The waters evidently cause her to miscarry if she is pregnant, or perhaps to become sterile; if she is pure, however, the waters have the opposite effect of inducing fertility.

64. See Baruch Levine, *JPS Torah Commentary: Leviticus* (Philadelphia, 1989), pp. 241–42.

65. My translation based on New JPS.

66. Proverbs 5:18 refers to a wife as a "fountain" or "source" (*mekor*).

67. Ezra 9:11–12.

68. Eilberg-Schwartz is now developing an entire analysis of this biblical trope.

69. Most of the references to the divine in Ruth are essentially formulaic: "the Lord has dealt harshly with me," "the Lord let her conceive," etc. See Campbell, *Anchor Bible Ruth*, pp. 28–29. The Midrash implicitly recognized this theological weakness in Ruth by claiming that Ruth bore her son as a result of a miracle. See Ruth Rabbah 7.14.

70. Marvin Pope has argued that the Song reflects rituals in which eroticism and funeral rites were bound up together. See Pope, *Anchor Bible Song of Songs* (Garden City, N.Y., 1977), pp. 210–29. For other cultic interpretations, see Pope, 145–53.

71. See Ariel and Chana Bloch, *The Song of Songs: A Translation and Commentary* (New York, forthcoming).

72. I am indebted in this analysis and in my reading of the Song of Songs as a whole to Pardes, *Countertraditions in the Bible,* chap. 7.

73. See Frymer-Kensky, *In the Wake of the Goddesses,* pp. 97–99.


CHAPTER 2:
## Law and Desire in the Talmud
Abbreviations: m. = Mishnah; b. = Babylonian Talmud; y. = Palestinian Talmud


1. Sifre Numbers 99–100; Avot de-Rabbi Nathan, ver. A, chaps. 2 and 9, ver. B, chap. 2; b. Shabbat 87a; Yalkut Shimoni, Numbers, 4:738, pp. 222–23. See also Louis Ginzberg, *Legends of the Jews* (Philadelphia, 1911), 3:255–56.

That this midrash was based on a very old tradition going back at least to the first century C.E. is attested by Philo, who reports that Moses had disdained sexual intercourse "almost from the time when, possessed by the spirit, he entered on his work as prophet." See Philo, *Life of Moses* 2.68–69, in F. H. Colson, *Philo* (Cambridge, Mass., 1935), 6:483.

2. Sifre Numbers 99–100.

3. My reading of this text shares much with that of Daniel Boyarin, *Carnal Israel: Reading Sex in Talmudic Judaism* (Berkeley and Los Angeles, forthcoming), chap. 4. The present chapter has evolved in dialogue with Boyarin over several years, and I shall note where my readings have been influenced by his. As I shall also make clear in the notes, my interpretation of the rabbinic materials differs from his in placing greater weight on the ascetic pole of talmudic culture. An early draft of this chapter is to appear under the title "From Intercourse to Discourse: Rabbinic Control of Sexuality" (Center for Hermeneutical Studies Colloquy, Berkeley, forthcoming). Readers will note that my position has shifted somewhat in the interim.

4. Genesis Rabbah 35.1.

5. b. Yevamot 63b. For a superb history of the rabbinic attitude toward procreation, see Jeremy Cohen, *"Be Fertile and Increase, Fill the Earth and Master It": The Ancient and Medieval Career of a Biblical Text* (Ithaca, N.Y., 1989). See also David Feldman, *Marital Relations, Birth Control and Abortion in Jewish Law* (New York, 1968), pp. 46–59; and Rachel Biale, *Women and Jewish Law* (New York, 1984), pp. 198–218.

6. For some useful cautions and two different approaches to this vast literature, see Jacob Neusner, "The Formation of Rabbinic Judaism: Yavneh (Jamnia) from A.D. 70 to 100," in H. Temporini and W. Haase, eds., *Aufsteig und Niedergang der romischen Welt* (Berlin, 1977), sec. 2, vol. 19:2, pp. 3–42; and Daniel Boyarin, *Intertextuality and the Reading of Midrash* (Bloomington, Ind., 1990).

7. For Augustus' population policy, see David Daube, *The Duty to Procreate* (Edinburgh, 1977); and R. I. Frank, "Augustus's Legislation on Marriage and Children," in *California Studies in Classical Antiquity* 8 (1975): 44–52. For the influence of Roman policy on the commandment to procreate, see Daube and Robert Gordis, "Be Fruitful and Multiply: Biography of a Mitzvah," *Midstream* 28 (1982): 21–29.

8. Cohen, *"Be Fertile and Increase,"* pp. 158–65.

9. b. Pesahim 49b. On the Palestinian rabbis as a social elite, see Lee I. Levine, *The Rabbinic Class of Roman Palestine in Late Antiquity* (Jerusalem, 1989).

10. b. Pesahim 49b. See Levine, *The Rabbinic Class* and Aharon Oppenheimer, *The 'Am ha-Aretz: A Study in the Social History of the Jewish People in the Hellenistic-Roman Period* (Leiden, 1977), pp. 171–73.

11. b. Pesahim 49b.

12. m. Sotah 3.4. For a close analysis of the differences between the Pales-

tinian and Babylonian positions on this question, see Boyarin, *Carnal Israel*, chap. 5. See also R. Biale, *Women and Jewish Law*, pp. 29–41.

13. All of the following works, many of which are quite valuable in terms of sources, share this view to one degree or another: Louis Epstein, *Sex Laws and Customs in Judaism* (New York, 1948); Robert Gordis, *Sex and the Family in Jewish Tradition* (New York, 1967); Menachem M. Brayer, *The Jewish Woman in Rabbinic Literature*, 2 vols. (Hoboken, N.J., 1986); and Feldman, *Marital Relations*.

14. These ideas about culture came out of intensive conversations with Daniel Boyarin and Howard Eilberg-Schwartz.

15. See Saul Lieberman, *Hellenism in Jewish Palestine* (New York, 1950).

16. See Peter Brown, *The Body and Society: Men, Women and the Renunciation of Sexuality in Early Christianity* (New York, 1988), p. 18; and Paul Veyne, "The Roman Empire," in Veyne and Georges Duby, eds., *A History of Private Life*, trans. A. Goldhammer (Cambridge, Mass., 1987), 1:16–233.

17. Epictetus, *The Discourses*, ed. and trans. W. A. Oldfather (Cambridge, Mass., 1928), 2:154–55. Many of his practical arguments against marriage appear again in Saadia Gaon's *Book of Beliefs and Opinions*. Saadia writes against this philosophical opposition to marriage.

18. Musonius Rufus, *Fragment* 12 in Cora Lutz, ed., "Musonius Rufus: The Roman Socrates," *Yale Classical Studies* 10 (1947): 86. See further Brown, *Body and Society*, p. 21; and John Noonan, *Contraception: A History of Its Treatment by the Catholic Theologians and Canonists* (Cambridge, Mass., 1965), pp. 46–49, 75.

19. I thank David Winston for clarifying this point for me.

20. See Michel Foucault, *History of Sexuality; vol. 3, The Care of the Self*, trans. Robert Hurley (New York, 1986).

21. The "heat" associated with sexuality was the thesis of Galen, *On the Usefulness of the Parts of the Body*, ed. and trans. Margaret May (Ithaca, N.Y., 1968), 1:382, 2:628, 630. See Thomas Laqueur, "Orgasm, Generation and the Politics of Reproductive Biology," *Representations* 14 (Spring 1986): 4–7; and idem, *Making Sex: Body and Gender from the Greeks to Freud* (Cambridge, Mass., 1990), pp. 46–52. See also Veyne, "The Roman Empire," p. 202; and Brown, *Body and Society*, pp. 17–18. For control, see Plutarch, *Advice on Marriage*, in F. C. Babbitt, ed. and trans., *Plutarch's Moralia* (Cambridge, Mass., 1969), 2:331.

22. *Soranus' Gynaecology*, trans. O. Temkin (Baltimore, 1956), p. 27. See Brown, *Body and Society*, pp. 18–19.

23. Epistle of Barnabas 10:1–12, 19:4; Clement of Alexandria, *Stromateis* 3, in J. Oulton and H. Chadwick, eds., *Alexandrian Christianity* (Philadelphia, 1954), p. 61. For recent treatments of early Christian attitudes toward sexuality, see Elaine Pagels, *Adam, Eve and the Serpent* (New York, 1988); and Brown, *Body and Society*.

24. Philo, *The Special Laws* 3.113, trans. F. H. Colson (Cambridge, Mass.,

1937), 7:547. See also idem, *Joseph* 43, 6:165; and idem, *Moses* 1.28, 6:291, in which Philo says that Moses had suppressed all sexual pleasure, except for the "lawful begetting of children." See also *Special Laws* 3.34, p. 497, where he forbids sex with an infertile wife, although he does not require the husband to divorce her. For further references and discussion, see Isaak Heinemann, *Philons griechische und jüdische Bildung* (Hildesheim, 1962), pp. 261–92; and Richard Baer, *Philo's Use of the Categories Male and Female* (Leiden, 1970), pp. 94–95. For a survey of some Hellenistic Jewish attitudes toward sexuality and purity, see L. William Countryman, *Dirt, Greed and Sex: Sexual Ethics in the New Testament and Their Implications for Today* (Philadelphia, 1988), pp. 57–64.

25. Philo, *Special Laws* 3.9, pp. 480–81.

26. Ibid.

27. Philo, *The Contemplative Life*, p. 34.

28. Philo, *Special Laws* 1.8–9, p. 105.

29. Josephus, *Contra Apion* 2.25, in William Whiston, trans., *The Life and Works of Flavius Josephus* (Philadelphia, n.d.) p. 893.

30. Josephus, *The Jewish War*, trans. G. A. Williamson (New York, 1959), 2.165, p. 137.

31. See Ross Kraemer, "Monastic Jewish Women in Greco-Roman Egypt: Philo on the Therapeutrides," *Signs* 14 (1989): 342–70.

32. *Messianic Rule* 1:9–11, trans. in Geza Vermes, *The Dead Sea Scrolls in English* (Middlesex, 1962), p. 119. On the still-disputed question of celibacy at Qumran and among the Essenes, see Abel Isaksson, *Marriage and Ministry in the New Temple* (Lund, 1965); Antoine Guillaumont, "A propos du celibat des Esseniens," in *Hommages à André Dupont-Sommer* (Paris, 1971), pp. 395–404; and Lawrence Schiffman, *Sectarian Law in the Dead Sea Scrolls: Courts, Testimony, and the Penal Code* (Chico, Calif., 1983), pp. 13, 64, 214–15.

33. *War Rule* 7, p. 132. The biblical prohibition on sex during warfare can be found in 1 Samuel 21:6.

34. *Damascus Rule* 12, p. 113, and *Temple Scroll* 45:11–12, Yigael Yadin, ed., (Jerusalem, 1977).

35. P. W. Van Der Horst, *The Sentences of Pseudo-Phocylides* (Leiden, 1978), vv. 175–76, 189–90, 192–94; pp. 100–101 and notes, pp. 225–41.

36. For a discussion of the concepts of "natural" and "unnatural" sexuality in Greek culture, see John Winkler, *The Constraints of Desire: The Anthropology of Sex and Gender in Ancient Greece* (New York and London, 1990).

37. *Wisdom of Solomon* 3:13–14, 4:1, trans. in David Winston, ed. and trans., *Anchor Bible Wisdom of Solomon* (Garden City, N.Y., 1979), p. 130. Winston dates the text to the period 30 B.C.E.–50 C.E., with the strong likelihood that it was composed between 37 and 41 C.E. It might therefore have been influenced by Philo, and, indeed, this passage bears some similarities to

Philo's text on barren women in *Deus* 13–15. Eunuchs were excluded from public worship.

38. m. Yevamot 8.4 and b. Yevamot 79b.

39. Matthew 19:12. See also Acts 8, which reports the conversion of an Ethiopian eunuch by Philip. The Ethiopian, who was on his way to Jerusalem and was reading from the Book of Isaiah, was evidently a Jew or at least close to the Jewish religion.

40. See Steven Fraade, "Ascetical Aspects of Ancient Judaism," in Arthur Green, ed., *Jewish Spirituality* (New York, 1986), 1:253–88.

41. Foucault, *History of Sexuality* 3:41.

42. See Gary Anderson, "Celibacy or Consummation in the Garden? Reflections on Early Jewish and Christian Interpretations of the Garden of Eden," *Harvard Theological Review* 82 (1989): 121–48.

43. b. Ketubot 8a. Anderson ("Celibacy or Consummation in the Garden?") notes the contrast between the joy associated with eating, anointing with oil, bathing, and sex, on the one hand, and mourning, during which sex is forbidden, on the other.

44. Genesis Rabbah 8.1. See Boyarin, *Carnal Israel*, chap. 1.

45. See Alon Goshen-Gottstein, "The Body as Image of God in Rabbinic Literature" (Paper given at the Conference on People of the Book–People of the Body, Stanford University, 1991); and Gershom Scholem, "Tselem: The Concept of the Astral Body," in *On the Mystical Shape of the Godhead*, trans. Joachim Neugroschel (New York, 1991), pp. 251–73.

46. Sura 78:31–34. See also Suras 37:39–48, 44:51–55, 52:18–21, 55:45–76, and 56:10–39.

47. b. Berakhot 17a. For an analysis of these and other statements on asceticism, see Fraade, "Ascetical Aspects of Ancient Judaism."

48. y. Kiddushin 4.12 (66d).

49. Avot de-Rabbi Nathan, ver. A., chap. 28. This text contains a great deal of ascetic material relating to sexuality, and although parallels to many of these passages can be found elsewhere in rabbinic literature, the fact that they are collected in this text suggests an editor with a particularly ascetic point of view.

50. Midrash Psalms 146.4. On this passage, see W. D. Davies, "The Rabbinical Sources," in Leo Landmann, ed., *Messianism in the Talmudic Era* (New York, 1979), pp. 163–64 and additional bibliography.

51. b. Berakhot 57b.

52. For a discussion of this saying, see Cohen, *"Be Fertile and Increase,"* p. 77.

53. Genesis Rabbah 8.11, Pirke de-Rabbi Eliezer, chap. 11, 9:101–2.

54. b. Yevamot 63b and b. Niddah 13b. See further Cohen, *"Be Fertile and Increase,"* pp. 114–20.

55. b. Avodah Zara 5a.

56. Genesis Rabbah 51.10.

57. y. Yevamot 11:1 (11d) and b. Sanhedrin 58b. The midrash is a word-play on the verse in Leviticus 20:17 in which incest is termed a "disgrace" using the word *hesed*, which normally means the opposite, "grace." See further David Novak, "Some Aspects of the Relationship of Sex, Society and God in Judaism," in Frederick Greenspahn, ed., *Contemporary Ethical Issues in the Jewish and Christian Traditions* (Hoboken, N.J., 1986), pp. 145–46.

58. Genesis Rabbah 9.9. I follow Daniel Boyarin in translating this key term as "evil desire" rather than "evil inclination." The former seems to me to reflect the rabbis' view that it is something like the libido. See also the midrash about how the rabbis capture the *yetzer* responsible for sexual sin but are then unable to find a freshly laid egg for a sick person, since there was no longer any impetus for procreation. They therefore blinded the personified erotic impulse, thereby guaranteeing that procreation would continue, while eliminating the desire to commit incest (b. Yoma 69b). For variants, see Ephraim Elimelech Urbach, *The Sages: Their Concepts and Beliefs*, trans. Israel Abrahams (Cambridge, Mass., 1975), p. 895 n. 24.

59. Leviticus Rabbah 14.5. The midrash is based on the peculiar verse in Psalms 51:7: "Indeed I was born with iniquity; with sin my mother conceived me." This verse looks almost like a biblical doctrine of original sin. On the medieval history of interpretation of the verse that consistently avoided such a "Christianizing" doctrine, see Feldman, *Marital Relations*, p. 87. But when Feldman mentions our midrash elsewhere (see p. 98), he neutralizes its radical connection between sexuality and sin by quoting a *nineteenth-century* interpretation of the midrash. This unhistorical procedure is characteristic of much of the scholarship on sexuality. The medieval and modern understandings of the biblical, talmudic, and midrashic literature may reflect the attitudes of those later periods, but they cannot be used as accurate indicators of the earlier texts they interpret.

60. For treatments of this concept, see Urbach, *The Sages*, pp. 471–83; and Emero Stiegman, "Rabbinic Anthropology," in H. Temporini and W. Haase, eds., *Aufsteig und Niedergang der romischen Welt* (Berlin, 1977), sec. 2, vol. 19:2, pp. 516–27.

61. See, for example, b. Yoma 69b and Avodah Zara 17b, in both of which the *yetzer* is said no longer to incite Jews to idolatry. In both these texts as well as in a good many others, it is exclusively sexual.

62. Avot de-Rabbi Nathan, ver. B, chap. 30, and b. Sanhedrin 91b, where Rabbi Judah the Prince learns this from the Greek philosopher Antoninus.

63. Avot de-Rabbi Nathan, ver. A, chap. 16. And in the same text: "The evil impulse begins to develop in the mother's womb and is born with the person."

64. Genesis Rabbah 8.11 and Avot de-Rabbi Nathan, ver. A, chap. 16.

65. Avot de-Rabbi Nathan, ver. A, chap. 16.

66. Foucault has made the same point for Hellenistic culture. See his *History of Sexuality*, vol. 3. Similarly, Elaine Pagels argues in *Adam, Eve and the Serpent* that most of the pre-Augustinian church fathers believed that the will

could be controlled; the problem was not primarily a soul-body dualism. Augustine divorced desire from the will and therefore made the body essentially incorrigible.

67. m. Avot 3.1.

68. Numbers Rabbah 9.7.

69. Thus, the *yetzer ha-ra* is called "impure" (*tamei*) in b. Sukkah 52a. See also the apocryphal Testament of Benjamin, which associates sexual relations with scatalogical pollution and impurity: "A person with a mind that is pure with love does not look on a woman for the purpose of having sexual relations. He has no pollution in his heart.... For just as the sun is unpolluted though it touches dung and slime, but dries up both and drives off the bad odor, so also the pure mind, though involved with the corruptions of earth, edifies instead and is not itself corrupted." Testament of Benjamin 8:2–3, in James Charlesworth, ed., *Old Testament Pseudepigrapha*, vol. 1 (Garden City N.Y., 1985).

70. b. Avodah Zara 22b, Shabbat 145b–146a, and Yevamot 103b. On the theme of the snake's lust for Eve, see Genesis Rabbah 18.6.

71. b. Shabbat 152a.

72. Eilberg-Schwartz suggested this interpretation in his response, "Damned If You Do, Damned If You Don't," to my early draft of this chapter, "From Intercourse to Discourse."

73. b. Berakhot 24a.

74. b. Moed Katan 9b. I am indebted to Boyarin for this text. See his analysis of the difference between rabbinic and Greek evaluations of women in Boyarin, *Carnal Israel*, chap. 2.

75. See Julius Preuss, *Biblical and Talmudic Medicine*, trans. Fred Rosner (New York, 1978), chaps. 2, 13, 14, 16.

76. b. Gittin 70a.

77. b. Shabbat 152a.

78. b. Nedarim 20a–b, b. Eruvin 100b, b. Gittin 70a.

79. Sifre Deuteronomy, sec. 45, p. 103.

80. b. Kiddushin 30b. See also b. Berakoht 5a and Avot de-Rabbi Nathan, ver. A, chap. 16, in which Rabbi Zadok resisted the seductions of a Roman maidservant by studying Torah.

81. b. Yevamot 64b.

82. b. Sukkah 52a. See Boyarin's analysis of this text in *Carnal Israel*, chap. 6.

83. See the brilliant and poetic analysis of Ari Elon, "Alma Di," *Shdemot* 114 (Summer 1990): 57–104.

84. b. Kiddushin 29b. See Boyarin's very persuasive analysis of these different traditions in *Carnal Israel*, chap. 4.

85. b. Yevamot 62b. See further Cohen, *"Be Fertile and Increase,"* p. 135; and Boyarin, *Carnal Israel*.

86. b. Avodah Zara 22b, Shabbat 146a, and Yevamot 103b. A strong bibli-

cal and rabbinic countertradition obviously held that Israel was not immune from sexual transgression, since many texts blame the exile on just such sins.

87. Intercourse is permitted during the period of purification after childbirth. This period lasts for thirty-three days, starting a week after the birth of a boy, and sixty-six days, starting two weeks after the birth of a girl (Leviticus 12:4). The variant text in Leviticus Rabbah states, "I have forbidden you the blood of a menstruant but have permitted you the blood of virginity." (Sex is allowed with a virgin even though it will result in bleeding.)

88. b. Hulin 109b. See also Leviticus Rabbah 22.10, where the variant text is in the name of Rabbi Levi.

89. Sifra, Kedoshim 20.26.

90. See b. Berakhot 51b and b. Niddah 20b. I am indebted to Rachel Adler for these references and for a brilliant literary analysis of the texts in an unpublished paper, "Skotsk Kumt: En/gendering Judaism" (Conference on Judaism for the Twentieth-first Century, Brandeis-Bardin Institute, 1991).

91. For some very interesting observations connecting circumcision to fertility, see Michael Fox, "The Sign of the Covenant: Circumcision in the Light of the Priestly 'ot Etiologies," *Revue Biblique* 81 (1974):557–96; and Eilberg-Schwartz, *The Savage in Judaism*, chap. 5.

92. Genesis Rabbah 80.10.

93. Avot de-Rabbi Natan, ver. A, chap. 2.

94. Midrash Tadshe 8, p. 152.

95. b. Yevamot 61b.

96. Ibid., 62b.

97. For a discussion of differences between Palestine and Babylonia as well as other facets of rabbinic views of marriage, see Isaiah Gafni, "The Institution of Marriage in Rabbinic Times" in David Kraemer, ed., *The Jewish Family* (New York, 1988), pp. 13–30.

98. W. Wright, *The Homilies of Aphraates, the Persian Sage* (London, 1869), 1:345–55. See further Isaiah Gafni, "Marriage in Rabbinic Times," pp. 20–21; and Jacob Neusner, *Aphrahat and Judaism: The Christian-Jewish Argument in Fourth-Century Iran* (Leiden, 1971), p. 76.

99. Another unmarried rabbi was Rav Hamnuna. See b. Kiddushin 29b.

100. Leviticus Rabbah 20.7, Peskita de-Rav Kahana on Numbers 3:2–4, and Tanhuma on Numbers 3:2–4. See also Ginzberg, *Legends of the Jews* 3:188. I thank my student Kenneth Cohen for bringing this midrash to my attention.

101. b. Yevamot 62b. Early marriage for the purpose of suppressing sexual desire was also the impetus for John Chrysostom. See Brown, *Body and Society*, p. 309.

102. b. Yevamot 62b.

103. b. Kiddushin 29b.

104. b. Nedarim 20b. See Boyarin's incisive analysis of this text and others in *Carnal Israel*, chap. 6. My interpretation places the emphasis more on the

side of control than his does, but I am indebted to him for a number of local readings.

105. See Avot de-Rabbi Natan, ver. A, chap. 2.

106. b. Nedarim 20a. See also b. Pesahim 112b: "If one has intercourse by the light of a lamp, he will have epileptic children."

107. b. Gittin 70a.

108. This law does not, however, allow a man to coerce his wife into having sex against her will, but it does grant him the patriarchal right to choose sexual practices. See b. Eruvin 100b.

109. b. Nedarim 20b.

110. The editor understands the term "to converse" in the Imma Shalom story to mean actual conversation, which is what concerns Johanan ben Dahabai, when, in fact, Imma Shalom is using it in the euphemistic rabbinic sense of sexual intercourse (le-sapper im isha).

111. b. Shabbat 86a and b. Niddah 17a. King David is said to have violated this law by having sexual relations during the day in order to quench his desire and not think about women during the daytime. But this procedure failed, for he succumbed to his desire to have relations with Bathsheba. See b. Sanhedrin 107a.

112. b. Niddah 17a.

113. Ibid. and Rashi's commentary on b. Niddah 17a. See Boyarin's analysis of this text in *Carnal Israel*.

114. Leviticus Rabbah 21.7.

115. b. Ketubot 48a.

116. Veyne, "The Roman Empire," pp. 25, 203.

117. b. Berakhot 8b.

118. Genesis Rabbah 70.12.

119. For the possible influences of the Persians on Jewish practices, see Gafni, *Marriage in Rabbinic Times*, pp. 20–21; and M. Shaki, "Sassanian Matrimonial Relations," *Archiv Orientalni* 39 (1971):340.

120. b. Sukkah 52b.

121. b. Sanhedrin 107a.

122. b. Berakhot 22a. The context here is nocturnal emissions (keri), which the rabbis, unlike the later, medieval Jewish mystics, did not regard as necessarily sinful. Such emissions only caused impurity in the biblical sense. The rabbis did, however, believe that especially holy men, such as the biblical Jacob, never suffered from them. See b. Yevamot 76a. According to another opinion, such emissions are actually a healthy sign for a sick person (b. Berakhot 57a).

123. b. Berakhot 62a.

124. There is, however, a version of the Kahana story that appears in b. Hagiga 5b without the final line that seems to support Rav's practice against Kahana's initial condemnation.

125. m. Ketubot 5.6 and b. Ketubot 62b. For an extensive discussion of

*onah*, see Feldman, *Marital Relations*, pp. 60–80; and R. Biale, *Women and Jewish Law*, pp. 121–46.

126. b. Ketubot 62b, b. Baba Kama 82a, and y. Ketubot 5.6. Contrast this with the prohibition in Jubilees 50:8.

127. b. Ketubot 48a.

128. Laqueur, "Orgasm, Generation, and the Politics of Reproductive Biology," pp. 6–7.

129. Leviticus Rabbah 14.4.

130. 1 Corinthians 7:3–5. Paul may have addressed his remarks equally to men and women, because both made up his audience of disciples; the rabbis, however, were concerned exclusively with a male audience.

131. b. Sanhedrin 7a. See R. Biale, *Women and Jewish Law*, p. 122.

132. b. Baba Metzia 84a.

133. b. Yevamot 62b.

134. b. Eruvin 100b.

135. Boyarin has given the most subtle account of the rabbinic view of women in *Carnal Israel*, especially chap. 3. See also Judith Wegner, *Chattel or Person?: The Status of Women in the Mishnah* (New York, 1988).

136. m. Ketubot 5.6.

137. b. Ketubot 62b–63a. See Boyarin, *Carnal Israel*, chap. 5, for a brilliant analysis of these texts; and Shulamit Weller, "The Collection of Stories in the Passages of Ketubot 62b–63a" (in Hebrew), *Tura* (1989):95–102.

138. The rabbis added a week of "clean" days to the biblically prohibited period of bleeding. For two excellent summaries of the laws of *niddah*, see R. Biale, *Women and Jewish Law*, pp. 147–74; and *Encyclopedia Judaica*, s.v. "niddah." See also Shaye J. D. Cohen, "Menstruants and the Sacred in Judaism and Christianity," in Sarah B. Pomeroy, ed., *Women's History and Ancient History* (Chapel Hill and London, 1991), pp. 273–99.

139. Leviticus 15:25–30. Martin Krause has recently suggested that even Leviticus may have assumed a seven-day clean period after normal menstrual bleeding had ceased. He derives this by a different way of parsing the verses in Leviticus 15 and by an analysis of 2 Samuel 11:4, in which Bathsheba is said to have "sanctified herself from her impurity," after which she immediately becomes pregnant. Krause holds that the Bible believed, as did the rabbis later, that conception occurs immediately after menstruation; in order to hold this belief, they had to assume a two-week period of abstention. See Martin Krause, "II Sam 11:4 und das Konzeptionsoptimum," *Zeitschrift für alttestamentliche Wissenschaft* 95 (1983):434–37. While Krause's argument is intriguing, there is no reason to believe that the author of Samuel had modern medical knowledge.

140. It is important, however, not to exaggerate this effect unduly, since before the modern era, women probably menstruated far less than they do today. They married earlier and were therefore pregnant more often. If they did not use wet nurses and breast-fed their babies for a relatively long time,

the contraceptive effect of pregnancy would be extended significantly past the birth of the last child. A woman might typically menstruate a few times before her marriage, then until she became pregnant, and possibly only infrequently after that.

141. There was a great deal of ancient medical wisdom that assumed incorrectly that the period immediately after the actual menstrual flow is ideal for conception. See Soranus, *Gynaecology* 1.10.36. See further Noonan, *Contraception*, p. 16; and Feldman, *Marital Relations*, p. 247 n. 77. Philo, too, believed that menstrual blood "purges the womb as if it were a cornfield" and therefore makes conception impossible. Philo argued that since the only justification for intercourse was procreation, sex had to be prohibited during menstruation. Philo, *Special Laws* 3.32–33, pp. 495–96. There was also some medical opinion that conception could occur during menstruation, although the child would be born deformed. See Pliny, *Natural History* 7.15.67; and after him Jerome, *Commentary on Ezekiel* 6:18. See Noonan, p. 85.

142. b. Niddah 31b, Sotah 27a, and Leviticus Rabbah 14.5 The latter midrash uses the interesting expression "the woman absorbs or receives" (*koletet*). Although there is a contrary opinion that conception occurs *prior* to menstruation, the opinion of Rabbi Johanan appears to have been more widespread.

143. Leviticus Rabbah 14.9.

144. b. Yevamot 34b. Rabbi Eliezer, however, permitted it during the twenty-four months of nursing, presumably as a form of birth control. For a history of the term, see Feldman, *Marital Relations*, pp. 144–55.

145. b. Yevamot 34b, 59a and b. Sanhedrin 58b. According to Sanhedrin 58b, "unnatural intercourse" is forbidden to the Gentiles but allowed to the Jews! The Talmud is quite puzzled by this ruling and fails to offer a convincing explanation. It is possible, although speculative, that the rabbis may have considered anal intercourse potentially procreative. See Feldman, *Marital Relations*, pp. 155–62, for a history of the interpretation of the term. Feldman does not adequately distinguish between nonvaginal intercourse (anal and oral) and nonconventional vaginal positions. The term "unnatural" means "nonvaginal" in the talmudic literature, even though it may have become a more generic term during the Middle Ages. For corroboration, see Cohen, *"Be Fertile and Increase,"* p. 137.

146. For an excellent collection of material on masturbation, see Feldman, *Marital Relations*, pp. 109–31, 144–68.

147. For the rabbis, onanism, the sin of Onan in Genesis 38, meant coitus interruptus; for the Bible, the crime of Onan was violation of his levirate obligation (see Chapter 1). Although the use of onanism to refer to masturbation became prevalent only in the eighteenth century, it was occasionally used by the church fathers. See John Cassian, *Collationes*, 12:3, cited in Aline Rousselle, *Porneia: On Desire and the Body in Antiquity*, trans. Felicia Pheasant (Oxford, 1988), p. 153.

148. m. Niddah 2.1. It is not only the act of masturbating that is forbidden, but even the thoughts that might lead to wasting semen: "He who excites himself by lustful thoughts will not be allowed to enter the domain of the Holy One, blessed be He" (b. Niddah 13b). The context makes it clear that the excitement is illicit because it leads to masturbation.

149. b. Niddah 13a–b. See also the view attributed to Simeon bar Yohai in Leviticus Rabba 21.7.

150. Johanan refers here to the position of Rabbi Eliezer in b. Yevamot 63b–64a, that failure to procreate is equivalent to murder, but the context is masturbation rather than some nonprocreative intercourse.

151. b. Sanedrin 108b and Rosh ha-Shanah 12a.

152. m. Avot 4.1.

153. See Thomas Laqueur, "The Social Evil, the Solitary Vice and Pouring Tea," in Michel Feher, ed., *Fragments for a History of the Human Body* (New York, 1989), 3:334–43.

154. Genesis Rabbah 23.2.

155. b. Yevamot 64a.

156. See Foucault, *History of Sexuality* 3:41.

157. See R. Biale, *Women and Jewish Law*, p. 158.

158. 1 Corinthians 6:19.

159. b. Sotah 17a, b. Yevamot 64a, and b. Yoma 54a (based on Numbers 7:89). See Moshe Idel, "Sexual Metaphors and Praxis in the Kabbalah," in Kraemer, *The Jewish Family*, pp. 201–2.

160. y. Ketubot 5.6.

161. b. Sanhedrin 75a.

162. m. Yadayim 3.5. I use Rabbi Akiva's statement that the Song of Songs is like the Holy of Holies as a shorthand for the overall midrashic approach to the Song. See Song of Songs Rabbah. For the canonization process in general, see Sid Z. Leiman, *The Canonization of Hebrew Scripture: The Talmudic and Midrashic Evidence* (Hamden, Conn., 1976). On the Song of Songs, see Gerson D. Cohen, "The Song of Songs and the Jewish Religious Mentality," in *The Samuel Friedland Lectures 1960–66* (New York, 1966). Boyarin has argued for the essential difference between the midrashic and Christian allegorical readings of the Song in his *Intertextuality and the Reading of Midrash*, pp. 105–16. While I accept his distinction between midrash and allegory, I would still argue that there is a basic similarity underlying the two with respect to the Song.

CHAPTER 3:
## Rabbinic Authority and Popular Culture in Medieval Europe
Abbreviations: m. = Mishnah; b. = Babylonian Talmud

1. Rashi on b. Sanhedrin 75a.

2. I take issue on this point with Jacob Katz, who argued that those who

transgressed the sexual norms nevertheless accepted these norms, that transgressions represent deviations rather than alternative cultures. See Katz, "Marriage and Marital Relations at the End of the Middle Ages" (in Hebrew), *Zion* 10 (1945–46): 21–54. Katz published a shortened English version of this article with additional material from Eastern Europe. See Katz, "Family, Kinship and Marriage among Ashkenazim in the Sixteenth to Eighteenth Centuries," *Jewish Journal of Sociology* 1 (1959): 4–22; and idem, *Tradition and Crisis* (New York, 1961), pp. 135–48. Azriel Shochat argued against Katz that for seventeenth- and eighteenth-century Germany, sexual deviations were harbingers of a new, modern sexual ethic. See Shochat, *Im Hilufei Tekufot* (Jerusalem, 1960), pp. 162–73. But Shochat has no way of accounting for similar "deviations" in earlier centuries or in Eastern Europe.

3. Isserles gloss to *Shulhan Arukh,* Even ha-Ezer 1. On the relaxation of the laws of procreation, see Jeremy Cohen, *"Be Fertile and Increase, Fill the Earth and Master It": The Ancient and Medieval Career of a Biblical Text* (Ithaca, N.Y., 1989), pp. 169–80.

4. For cases of this sort in the thirteenth century, see Meir of Rothenburg, *Responsa* (Prague, 1608), nos. 226, 595, and 938; and idem, *Responsa* (Cremona, 1557), nos. 32–33, 305, 307. The problem is also dealt with in the thirteenth-century *Sefer Hasidim*. See *Sefer Hasidim,* ed. Reuven Margaliot (Jerusalem, 1957, based on the Bologna manuscript), no. 564, p. 371.

5. *Shulhan Arukh,* Even ha-Ezer 2.2.

6. This system has been exhaustively described by Katz in the articles cited in note 2. It can be contrasted with the practice in medieval Christian Europe of intellectually talented boys entering the celibate clergy and therefore not having children. Where inheritance practices among the Christian upper classes effectively concentrated wealth in the hands of the oldest son and made celibacy the only viable financial option for other male children, the Jewish practice of exchanging wealth through substantial dowries for sons meeting the standard criteria created a very different kind of social matrix.

7. On the theology of the Ashkenazic Hasidim, see Gershom Scholem, *Major Trends in Jewish Mysticism,* 3d ed. (New York, 1961), pp. 80–118; and Joseph Dan, *Torat ha-Sod shel Hasidut Ashkenaz* (Jerusalem, 1968). For their social views, see Ivan G. Marcus, *Piety and Society: The Jewish Pietists of Medieval Germany* (Leiden, 1981). For analyses of the literary and folkloristic aspects of the *Sefer Hasidim,* see Tamar Alexander, "The Formation of Hasidic-Ashkenazic Stories: The Folktale in Its Theological Context" (in Hebrew), *Studies in Aggada and Jewish Folklore* 7 (1983): 197–206; and Eli Yassif, "The Exemplum Story in *Sefer Hasidim*" (in Hebrew), *Tarbits* 57 (1988): 217–55.

8. Judah the Hasid, *Sefer Hasidim,* no. 562, pp. 370–71.

9. See the classic article by Monford Harris, "The Concept of Love in *Sepher Hassidim,*" *Jewish Quarterly Review* 50 (1959): 13–44. See also Haim Hillel Ben Sasson, *A History of the Jewish People* (Cambridge, Mass., 1976), p. 553. See in particular *Sefer Hasidim,* no. 141, p. 148, in which the author

warns against covering a holy book with pages on which are written *romantz*.

10. *Pinkas Medinat Lita,* ed. Simon Dubnow (Berlin, 1925), no. 43. For other such communal legislation, see A. H. Freiman, *Seder Kiddushin ve-Nisuin* (Jerusalem, 1964), pp. 210–16.

11. For a comparison of Jewish and Christian marriage law, see Ze'ev W. Falk, *Jewish Matrimonial Law in the Middle Ages* (Oxford, 1966), pp. 35–112.

12. *Pinkas Vaad Arba Aratzot,* ed. I. Halpern (Jerusalem, 1945), no. 165. In Lithuania, the stipulated age was eighteen. See *Pinkas Medinat Lita,* no. 52.

13. The Council of the Four Lands also enacted different legislation in 1624 and 1644 barring men from giving loans during the first two or three years of marriages, which suggests that they were typically in their teens at the time of marriage and therefore considered still fiscally immature. See *Pinkas Vaad Arba Aratzot,* nos. 123, 125, 167, 189. For two discussions of the definitions of adolescence, see David Kraemer, "Images of Childhood and Adolescence in Talmudic Literature," in Kraemer, ed., *The Jewish Family: Metaphor and Memory* (New York, 1989), pp. 65–80; and Gershon David Hundert, "Jewish Children and Childhood in Early Modern East Central Europe," in Kraemer, pp. 81–94.

14. Jacob Reischer, *Shevut Yaakov* (Halle, 1710; Offenbach, 1719; Metz, 1789), pt. 2, no. 112.

15. See some of the cases collected by Freiman, *Seder Kiddushin,* pp. 213–14.

16. Joseph Hahn, *Yosef Ometz* (Frankfurt, 1928), pp. 186–87.

17. See Katz, "Family, Kinship and Marriage," p. 13.

18. Yair Hayyim Bachrach, *Havat Yair* (Frankfurt, 1699), no. 60.

19. For more on this argument, see David Biale, "Love, Marriage and the Modernization of the Jews," in Marc Raphael, ed., *Approaches to Modern Judaism* (Chico, Calif. 1983), pp. 1–17. I disagree with Katz, who insisted that love played no role in the normative values of the culture; only with the eighteenth-century Enlightenment was romantic love set against the resolutely pragmatic marital criteria of wealth, lineage, and learning. See Katz, "Marriage and Marital Relations"; and idem, *Tradition and Crisis.* For another critique of Katz on this issue, see Haim Hillel Ben Sasson's review of Katz's *Tradition and Crisis* in *Tarbits* 29 (1960): 300–301, and Katz's rejoinder in *Tarbits* 30 (1961): 62–72.

20. Published in its earliest versions by M. Erik (Zalmon Merkin) in *Vegn Alt-Yidishn Roman un Novele* (Warsaw, 1926), pp. 147–72. For analysis, see Yitzhok Schipper, "A Yiddish Love Novel from the Middle Ages" (in Yiddish), *YIVO Bleter* 13 (1938): 232–45; and Israel Zinberg, *A History of Jewish Literature,* trans. Bernard Martin (Cincinnati and New York, 1975), 7:181–84.

21. For the way in which folktales can function as projections of fantasies and also as outlets for anxieties, see Alan Dundes, *Interpreting Folklore* (Bloomington, Ind., 1980), pp. 33–61.

22. See Zinberg, *History of Jewish Literature* 7:177. The story was written down in the early sixteenth century but is most likely of earlier provenance, as is typical of folktales.

23. For some examples of joke marriages in the responsa, see *Teshuvot Baalei ha-Tosafot*, ed. Irving Agus (New York, 1954), no. 85; and Meir of Rothenburg, *Responsa* (Prague, 1608), no. 993, p. 103b. For two parallels to this folktale, see Micha Joseph Bin Gorion, *Mimekor Yisrael*, trans. I. M. Lask (Bloomington and London, 1976), 2:858–60.

24. For a discussion of the theme of marriage between men and female demons in Ashkenazic folklore from the seventeenth to the nineteenth century, see Sarah Tzefetman, *Nisuei Adam ve-Shedah: Gilgulim shel Motif be-Sifrut shel Yehudei Ashkenaz be-Mayot ha-17–19* (Jerusalem, 1988).

25. Some of the legal issues have been discussed by Eliakim Ellenson, *Nisuin she-lo ke-Dat Moshe ve-Yisrael* (Tel Aviv, 1975).

26. *Pinkas Vaad Arba Aratzot*, no. 94.

27. Ezekiel Landau, *Noda be-Yehudah* (Prague, 1811), pt. 2, no. 23.

28. *Sefer ha-Pardes* (Budapest, 1924), no. 149, trans. in Irving Agus, *Urban Civilization in Pre-Crusade Europe* (New York, 1965), 2:728–29. For additional material on legal attempts to segregate the sexes, see Louis Epstein, *Sex Laws and Customs in Judaism* (New York, 1948), chap. 3.

29. The song appears in a collection by Isaac Wallich of Worms. See Felix Rosenberg, "Über eine Sammlung von Volks und Gesellschaftsliedern in hebräischen Lettern," *Zeitschrift für die Geschichte der Juden in Deutschland* 2 (1888): 232–96, and 3 (1889): 14–28. This particular poem appears in translation in Zinberg, *History of Jewish Literature* 7:90.

30. See, in particular, the ribald poem written by one Eizik Kitel, in Rosenberg, "Über eine Sammlung," p. 258.

31. Translated in Zinberg, *History of Jewish Literature* 7:90. See also the *Tsukhtshpigl* of Seligmann Ulma (Hanau, 1610) in Zinberg, pp. 269–70.

32. Elijah ben Solomon Abraham ha-Kohen, *Shevet Musar* (Jerusalem, 1963), p. 189.

33. Joel Sirkis, *Sefer Bayit Hadash ha-Hadashot* (Jerusalem, 1959), no. 56.

34. Katz based his model of marriage on first marriages and failed to take into account the high rate of second or third marriages. See Ben Sasson in *Tarbits* 29 (1960): 301.

35. See David Sabean, *Power in the Blood: Popular Culture and Village Discourse in Early Modern Germany* (New York, 1984).

36. Bachrach, *Havat Yair*, no. 211.

37. The period of engagement in Ashkenazic tradition was usually one to two years. Engagement (*shiddukhin*) was a contract, and the penalty for breaking it off was a fine. Engagement must be distinguished from the two formal stages of the marriage: betrothal (*kiddushin* or *erusin*) and marriage (*nisuin*). In the early Middle Ages (at least up until the thirteenth century),

these last two stages were themselves often separated by a long period of time during which the relationship could only be dissolved, as after marriage, with a writ of divorce. In the later Middle Ages, the two stages of marriage were usually combined in one ceremony, as they are today. See Falk, *Jewish Matrimonial Law*.

38. Meir of Rothenburg, *Responsa* (Lemberg, 1860), no. 141.

39. Isaiah Horowitz, *Shnei Luhot ha-Berit* (Amsterdam, 1649), p. 100a. For corroborating evidence that Horowitz was not inventing the practice, see Moses Isserles, *Responsa* (Jerusalem, 1971), no. 30, a case from Cracow in the sixteenth century in which a girl comes to live in the house of her fiancé.

40. Landau, *Noda be-Yehudah*, pt. 2., no. 27.

41. For France, see J. L. Flandrin, *Les amours paysannes* (Paris, 1975); and idem, "Repression and Change in the Sexual Life of Young People in Medieval and Early Modern Times," *Journal of Family History* 2, no. 3 (1977): 196–210. For England, see Lawrence Stone, *The Family, Sex and Marriage in England, 1500–1800* (New York, 1977), pp. 605–7.

42. Jonah Landsofer, *Meil Tzedakah* (Prague, 1756), no. 19.

43. Jonathan Eibeschutz, *Yaarot Devash* (Warsaw, 1889), 1:2, p. 22a. See further Epstein, *Sex Laws*, pp. 106–8.

44. Judah the Hasid, *Sefer Hasidim*, ed. J. Wistinetzki (Berlin, 1891, based on the Parma manuscript), no. 53, p. 45, also no. 52, p. 44.

45. See Yassif, "The Exemplum Story," p. 224 n. 20.

46. The talmudic basis for this notion is the saying that "even a righteous man cannot stand in the place of penitent." A minority position attributed to Rav Judah holds that if one has sinned with a woman, one should return to the same place and the same woman and, this time, resist the temptation (b. Yoma 86b).

47. Judah the Hasid, *Sefer Hasidim* (Parma ed.), no. 19, p. 23.

48. See the collection of cases in Irving Agus, *Meir of Rothenburg* (Philadelphia, 1947), 2:279–85.

49. Meir of Rothenburg, *Responsa* (Prague ed.), no. 98.

50. Judah the Hasid, *Sefer Hasidim* (Parma ed.), no. 1886, p. 457.

51. See Georges Duby, *The Knight, the Lady and the Priest: The Making of Modern Marriage in Medieval France*, trans. Barbara Bray (New York, 1983), p. 169.

52. See Rachel Biale, *Women and Jewish Law* (New York, 1984), chap. 4.

53. See Irving Agus, *The Heroic Age of Franco-German Jewry* (New York, 1969), pp. 289–302.

54. On the attribution of the bans on polygamy and divorce against a woman's consent to Rabbenu Gershom, see Avraham Grossman, *Hakhmei Ashkenaz ha-Rishonim* (Jerusalem, 1981), pp. 132–49.

55. For these innovations, see Falk, *Jewish Matrimonial Law*, pp. 113–43; and Louis Finkelstein, *Jewish Self-Government in the Middle Ages* (New York, 1964), p. 105. The requirement for consent of the communities was initially

promulgated by the communities of Speyer, Worms, and Mainz and required the consent of all three.

56. Jacob Moeln, *Hilkhot Gitin*, quoted in Falk, *Jewish Matrimonial Law*, p. 131.

57. On the status of women, see Kenneth Stow, "The Jewish Family in the Rhineland in the High Middle Ages: Form and Function," *American Historical Review* 92 (1987): 1085–1110; Ivan G. Marcus, "Mothers, Martyrs and Moneymakers: Some Jewish Women in Medieval Europe," *Conservative Judaism* 38 (1986): 34–45; and Irving Agus, *The Heroic Age*, pp. 294–305. Joseph Shatzmiller is presently preparing a study of this subject.

58. See R. Biale, *Women and Jewish Law*, chap. 1. For the debate about educating women in the later Middle Ages, see Moritz Güdemann, *Geschichte des Erziehungswesens und der Culture der Juden in Deutschland* (Vienna, 1888), pp. 113–15.

59. For an account of this affair, see Israel Yuval, "Legislation against the Increase in Divorces in Fifteenth-Century Germany" (in Hebrew), *Zion* 48 (1983): 177–213. Yuval has assembled statistics that suggest an extraordinarily high rate of divorce. For instance, for a portion of the fifteenth century, close to two out of every three couples in Nuremberg divorced!

60. Eliezer of Worms, *Sefer ha-Rokeah ha-Gadol* (Jerusalem, 1968), Hilkhot Teshuvah, no. 12, p. 27.

61. Judah the Hasid, *Sefer Hasidim* (Parma ed.), no. 69, p. 50.

62. Ibid., no. 19, p. 24.

63. *Mordecai Ha-Gadol*, 358d. Cited in Agus, *Meir of Rothenburg*, p. 279; see also pp. 281–82.

64. See Salo Baron, *Social and Religious History of the Jews* (New York, 1957), 11:77–87; Solomon Grayzel, *The Church and the Jews in the XIIIth Century*, vol. 2, ed. Kenneth R. Stow (New York, 1989); and Guido Kisch, *The Jews in Medieval Germany: A Study of Their Legal and Social Status*, 2d ed. (New York, 1970), pp. 205–7, 315.

65. See Baron, *Social and Religious History* 11:83–84; and Chone Shmeruk, *Sifrut Yidish be-Polin* (Jerusalem, 1981), pp. 206–79.

66. See Livia Bitton-Jackson, *Madonna or Courtesan? The Jewish Woman in Christian Literature* (New York, 1982); and, more generally, Harold Fisch, *The Dual Image: The Figure of the Jew in English and American Literature* (New York, 1971). Michael Nutkiewicz is working on a systematic history of the *belle juive* motif.

67. See Shmeruk, *Sifrut Yidish be-Polin*, pp. 206–79.

68. Isaac ben Eliakum, *Lev Tov* (Frankfurt, 1681), chap. 6, p. 45. Cited in Zinberg, *History of Jewish Literature* 7:164. The *Lev Tov* was a popular Yiddish ethical advice book.

69. See Agus, *The Heroic Age of Franco-German Jewry*, pp. 341–57; and Joseph Shatzmiller, *Shylock Reconsidered: Jews, Moneylending and Medieval Society* (Berkeley and Los Angeles, 1989).

70. Judah the Hasid, *Sefer Hasidim* (Parma ed.), no. 1301, p. 321.

71. See Christopher N. L. Brooke, *The Medieval Idea of Marriage* (Oxford, 1989), chap. 5.

72. For a statement of the asceticism of the Ashkenazic pietists, see Eliezer of Worms, *Sefer ha-Rokeah*, Hilkhot Hasidut, p. 5. On the Christian penitentials, see James Brundage, *Law, Sex and Christian Society in Medieval Europe* (Chicago, 1987), pp. 152–69.

73. Eliezer of Worms, *Sefer ha-Rokeah*, Hilkhot Teshuvah, no. 14, p. 27.

74. See Jacob ben Asher, *Tur*, Oreh Hayyim, no. 240, where the talmudic phrase "scholars should not be found with their wives like roosters" is applied to all men (that is, Jews).

75. Eliezer of Worms, *Sefer ha-Rokeah*, Hilkhot Teshuvah, no. 20, p. 30.

76. Judah the Hasid, *Sefer Hasidim* (Parma ed.), no. 1084, p. 275.

77. Ibid. (Bologna ed.), no. 509, pp. 340–41.

78. Ibid., no. 50, p. 44.

79. See Brundage, *Law, Sex and Christian Society*, pp. 165–66.

80. Judah the Hasid, *Sefer Hasidim* (Parma ed.), no. 71, p. 50.

81. See Maimonides, *Mishne Torah*, Laws of Forbidden Intercourse, 21.9; and Jacob ben Asher, *Tur*, Even ha-Ezer, no. 25. See further David Feldman, *Marital Relations, Birth Control and Abortion in Jewish Law* (New York, 1968), pp. 21–45; and R. Biale, *Women and Jewish Law*, pp. 121–46.

82. See Feldman, *Marital Relations*, pp. 65–71, for a collection of legal sources.

83. Rabbi Isaac in Tosafot to b. Yavamot 34b and Sanhedrin 58a. For a review of the medieval positions on "unnatural intercourse," see Feldman, *Marital Relations*, pp. 155–65. Some authorities understood unnatural intercourse as being vaginal, but in a nonmissionary position.

84. Rashi on b. Shabbat 140b.

85. Elijah ben Solomon, *Shevet Musar*, pp. 188–90.

86. See Chava Weissler, "The Traditional Piety of Ashkenazic Women," in Arthur Green, ed., *Jewish Spirituality* (New York, 1987), 2:245–75; and idem, "'For Women and for Men Who Are Like Women': The Construction of Gender in Yiddish Devotional Literature," *Journal of Feminist Studies in Religion* 5, no. 2 (Fall 1989): 7–24.

87. Cited in Weissler, "Traditional Piety," p. 258.

88. See Moritz Güdemann, *Geschichte des Erziehungswesens und der Culture der Juden in Frankreich und Deutschland* (Vienna, 1880), pp. 264–72; and Simha Asaf, *Mekorot le-Toldot ha-Hinukh be-Yisrael* (Tel Aviv, 1954), 1:6–16.

89. Rashi on b. Niddah 17a.

90. Joseph Bekhor Shor on Genesis 38:7 in his *Perush le-Hamishah Humshei Torah* (Jerusalem, 1978), p. 63. That economic concerns might influence the decision to have children is reflected also in Judah the Hasid, *Sefer Hasidim*, (Parma ed.), nos. 1913–1914, p. 463.

91. Eliezer of Worms, *Sefer ha-Rokeah*, Hilkhot Teshuvah, no. 14, p. 27. On observance of menstrual laws in the polemical literature, see David

Berger, *The Jewish-Christian Debate in the High Middle Ages: A Critical Edition of the Nizzahon Vetus* (Philadelphia, 1979), p. 224.

92. Landau, *Noda be-Yehudah*, 2d ed., Even ha-Ezer, no. 91.

93. For the most recent analysis of the book, its variant manuscripts, and bibliography, as well as a critical edition of the texts themselves, see Eli Yassif, *Sippurei Ben Sira be-Yemei ha-Benayim* (Jerusalem, 1985).

94. For a list of Yiddish translations, see Abraham Haberman, *Hadashim gam Yeshanim* (Jerusalem, 1976), pp. 110–12, 224–27. Even early in its career, the *Alphabet* evidently became so popular that Moses Maimonides, in the twelfth century, felt compelled to condemn it as a worthless and frivolous book, while, in France, Peter the Venerable quoted it in order to ridicule the absurdities of the "Talmud." Maimonides, *Commentary on the Mishnah*, Sanhedrin 10; and Peter the Venerable, *Tractatus adversus Judaeorum inveteratam duritiem*, in *Patrologiae Latinae*, vol. 189, cols. 645 and 648. This judgment was seconded by many modern rationalist scholars who were palpably embarrassed by the book's shocking stories. For discussions of some of these scholars, see Eli Yassif, "'The History of Ben-Sira': Ideational Elements in a Literary Work" (in Hebrew), *Eshel Beer-sheva* 2 (1980): 104; and Samuel Lachs, "The Alphabet of Ben Sira: A Study in Folk-literature," *Gratz College Annual of Jewish Studies* 2 (1973): 28.

95. Yassif, *Sippurei Ben Sira*, pp. 197–99, version A (I have used this version since it was the one that circulated in France).

96. A wide variety of interpretations have been offered to explain the original intention of the author. One holds that the text was intended as an anti-Christian polemic. Some see it as evidence of a Jewish-Persian syncretistic sect. Others have argued that the work was intended as a critique of rabbinic law, as part of some intramural Jewish struggle. Finally, some recent folklorists have claimed that it was not directed against Judaism or Christianity specifically but against religion in general, an early attempt by Jews to write secular literature. For a summary of these interpretations, see Yassif, *Sippurei Ben Sira*, pp. 130–34. My interest here is not with the text's original intention but with how it might have resonated in Ashkenazic culture.

97. Ibid., pp. 231–34.

98. Ibid., pp. 246–50. On animal tales in general in Jewish folklore, see Dov Noy, *Sippurei Baalei Hayyim be-Edot Yisrael* (Haifa, 1976); and in relation to the *Alphabet of Ben Sira*, see Eli Yassif, "Medieval Hebrew Tales on the Mutual Hatred of Animals and Their Methodological Implication" (in Hebrew), *Studies in Aggada and Jewish Folklore* 7 (1983): 227–46.

CHAPTER 4:
## Sensuality, Asceticism, and Medieval Jewish Philosophy

1. For a recent treatment of Spanish Jewish poetry with texts, see Raymond P. Scheindlin, ed. and trans., *Wine, Women and Death: Medieval He-*

*brew Poems on the Good Life* (Philadelphia, 1986). See further Dan Pagis, *Hiddush u-Masoret be-Shirat ha-Hol ha-Ivrit: Sefarad ve-Italya* (Jerusalem, 1976).

2. For a detailed summary of cases from Spain, see Yom Tov Assis, "Sexual Behaviour in Mediaeval Hispano-Jewish Society," in Ada Rapoport-Albert and Steven J. Zipperstein, eds., *Jewish History: Essays in Honour of Chimen Abramsky* (London, 1988), pp. 25–60.

3. For Spain, see ibid. For a number of fascinating cases from Provence, see Rodrigue Lavoie, "La délinquance sexuelle à Monosque (1240–1430): Schéma général et singularités juives," *Provence Historique* 37, no. 150 (1987): 571–87. For papal complaints about relations between Jews and Christians, especially nurses and servants, see Solomon Grayzel, *The Church and the Jews in the XIII Century*, Vol. 1 (New York, 1966), Vol. 2 (Detroit, 1989).

4. For evidence on this ban and its lack of effect, see Assis, "Sexual Behaviour," p. 39. The sources are the poems of Todros ben Judah Halevi, *Diwan*, ed. D. Yellin (Jerusalem, 1932–36), poems 540–43, 595; and Solomon ben Adret, *Sheelot u-Teshuvot* (Leghorn, 1825), 5:238–43.

5. Moses of Coucy, *Sefer Mitzvot ha-Gadol* (Venice, 1522), negative commandment 112, n.3.

6. M. Lazar, "Catalan-Provencal Wedding Songs (14th–15th centuries)" (in Hebrew), in *Hayyim Schirmann Jubilee Volume* (Jerusalem, 1970), pp. 159–77. See further Assis, "Sexual Behaviour," pp. 30–36. In general, Assis seems to draw rather far-reaching conclusions about Spain per se from his material. Had he compared his cases with a similar selection from, say, Eastern Europe in the sixteenth through eighteenth centuries, he might have been surprised at the similarities.

7. Solomon ben Adret, *Responsa* (Bologna, 1539), Vol. 1, no. 1209.

8. Cited in Assis, "Sexual Behaviour," pp. 28–29, 41.

9. Moses Nachmanides, "Letter to his Son" (in Hebrew), in C. D. Chavel, *Kitvei ha-Ramban* (Jerusalem, 1964), 1:370.

10. *Zohar* 2:3b.

11. See F. Y. Baer, "The Historical Background of the 'Raaya Meheimna'" (in Hebrew), *Zion*, n.s. 5, no. 1 (1939): 1–44.

12. Ibid., 28; F. Y. Baer, "Todros ben Judah Halevi and His Time" (in Hebrew), *Zion* 2 (1937): 12–55; and idem, *A History of the Jews in Christian Spain* (Philadelphia, 1966), 1:236–42.

13. Scheindlin, *Wine, Women and Death*, pp. 90–91. I have modified Scheindlin's translation based on the original.

14. See Annemarie Schimmel, "Eros—Heavenly and Not So Heavenly—in Sufi Literature and Life," in Afaf al-Sayyid-Marsot, ed., *Society and Sexes in Medieval Islam* (Malibu, Calif.: 1979). For the Koran's views of sex in heaven, see above, Chapter 2.

15. For some varying views, see Scheindlin, *Wine, Women and Death*, p.

82; J. Schirmann, "The Ephebe in Medieval Hebrew Poetry" (in Hebrew), *Sefarad* 15 (1955); Nehemiah Allony, "The Zevi in the Hebrew Poetry of Spain" (in Hebrew), *Sefarad* 23 (1963): 311–21; Norman Roth, "'Deal Gently with the Young Man': Love of Boys in Medieval Hebrew Poetry of Spain," *Speculum* 57 (1982): 33–59; and Jacob Press, "'What in the World Is the Sin If I Thrill to Your Beauty?': The Homosexual Love Poems of the Medieval Rabbis," *Mosaic* (1989): 12–26.

16. See Monford Harris, "Marriage as Metaphysics: A Study of the 'Iggeret ha-Kodesh," *Hebrew Union College Annual* 33 (1962): 197–200; and Israel Davidson, *Parody in Jewish Literature* (New York, 1907), p. 9.

17. See *Tikkunei Zohar*, Tikkun 56, pp. 92b–93b. On this radical idea, see Isaiah Tishby, *Mishnat ha-Zohar* (Jerusalem, 1971), 2: 621–26.

18. See Arthur Green, "The Song of Songs in Early Jewish Mysticism," *Orim: A Jewish Journal at Yale* 2, no. 2 (Spring 1987): 49–63.

19. The best survey of medieval Jewish philosophy remains Julius Guttmann, *Philosophies of Judaism* (New York, 1964).

20. For the medieval philosophical attempts to reconcile the law with philosophy, see Isaac Heinemann, *Taamei ha-Mitzvot be-Sifrut Yisrael* (Jerusalem, 1966). On the question of asceticism in medieval Jewish philosophy, see Georges Vajda, "Continence, mariage et vie mystique selon la doctrine du Judaism," in *Mystique et continence: Travaux scientifiques du VII^e Congrès International d'Avon* (Paris, 1951), pp. 82–93.

21. For the medieval philosophical and mystical theologies of love of God, see Georges Vajda, *L'amour de Dieu dans la théologie juive de moyen âge* (Paris, 1957).

22. For a discussion of how this theory is connected to his exegetical philosophy, see David Biale, "Philosophy and Exegesis in the Writings of Abraham Ibn Ezra," *Comitatus* (UCLA Medieval and Renaissance Center) 5 (1974): 43–62.

23. Perhaps the first to advance this view was Saadia Gaon in the tenth century. See Saadia, *Book of Beliefs and Opinions*, Book 10, chap. 6, in which he gives a lengthy account of the social consequences of excessive sexual desire and concludes that it is proper to have sex only in order to procreate.

24. Maimonides, *Guide of the Perplexed*, trans. Shlomo Pines (Chicago, 1963), intro., p. 13. See further 3:8, p. 431.

25. Ibid. 2:36, p. 371. See also 3:8. Maimonides quotes Aristotle's *Nichomachean Ethics* iii.10.1118b2.

26. Maimonides, *Guide*, 3:8, p. 433.

27. Ibid., 3.49, pp. 602, 606. See also intro., p. 13, and Maimonides, *Commentary on the Mishnah*, Avot 1.5.

28. Maimonides, *Guide*, 3:8, pp. 435–36.

29. Ibid., p. 609. Maimonides was not the only medieval Jewish philosopher to take this position. See also Judah Halevi, *Sefer ha-Kuzari*, ed. Y. Even Shmuel (Tel Aviv, 1972), 1:115.

30. See Thomas Laqueur, *Making Sex: Body and Gender from the Greeks to Freud* (Cambridge, Mass., 1990), chap. 3, on the "discovery" of the clitoris; on the foreskin, see pp. 100–101. The sixteenth-century medical writer Gabriello Fallopio echoed Maimonides: "God ordained circumcision among the Jews so that they might concentrate on His service rather than on the pleasures of the flesh." See Fallopio, *De decoratione*, in *Opuscula* (Padua, 1566), p. 49; cited in Laqueur, *Making Sex*, p. 271 n. 75.

31. Maimonides was not the first to advance this interpretation of circumcision. We saw in Chapter 2 that Philo of Alexandria said something very similar in the first century, but Maimonides could not have read Philo. Perhaps Maimonides took the idea from belief current in the surrounding Muslim culture, which practiced male and female circumcision. The latter practice, which still exists today in places like Egypt, was specifically designed to excise the promiscuous desire of young girls. I have not, however, been able to find a Muslim source about male circumcision excising pleasure.

32. See Saadia, *Book of Beliefs and Opinions*, Book 10, chap. 9.

33. See Vajda, "Continence, mariage et vie mystique," p. 87. For the Islamic mystical stance on asceticism, see Louis Massignon, "Mystique et continence en Islam," in *Mystique et continence*, pp. 93–99.

34. Maimonides, *Guide* 3:12, p. 445.

35. Ibid. 3:8, p. 433.

36. Ibid. 3:12, p. 445.

37. See Maimonides, *Mishne Torah*, Hilkhot Deot 3.2, 5.4, 5.5, Hilkhot Issurei Biah 21.9–14, and *Medical Aphorisms* 7.61, 17.8.

38. See Madelain Farah, *Marriage and Sexuality in Islam: A Translation of al-Ghazali's Book on the Etiquette of Marriage from the Ihya* (Salt Lake City, 1984), pp. 49, 61.

39. Maimonides, *Guide* 2:49, pp. 601–2.

40. For some reflections on Maimonides' political theory, see Shlomo Pines, "Translator's Introduction," in Maimonides, *Guide*, pp. lxxxvi–xcix; and David Hartman, *Maimonides: Torah and Philosophical Quest* (Philadelphia, 1976).

41. Levi ben Gerson, *Perush al ha-Torah* (Venice, 1547), 1:12a. On various doctrines of procreation in medieval Jewish thought, see Jeremy Cohen, *"Be Fertile and Increase, Fill the Earth and Master It": The Ancient and Medieval Career of a Biblical Text* (Ithaca, N.Y., 1989), chap. 4.

42. On Isaac ben Yedaiah, see Marc Saperstein, *Decoding the Rabbis* (Cambridge, Mass., 1980), especially pp. 90–102. The following analysis is based largely on this excellent work. Saperstein has published portions of Isaac's commentary on the Midrash Rabbah in Hebrew in Isadore Twersky, ed., *Studies in Medieval Jewish History and Literature* (Cambridge, Mass., 1979), pp. 283–306.

43. Cited in Saperstein, *Decoding the Rabbis*, p. 93.

44. Ibid., p. 98; original text in Twersky, *Studies*, pp. 294–97.

45. See *Encyclopedia Judaica*, s.v. "Maimonidean Controversy"; and D. J.

Silver, *Maimonidean Criticism and the Maimonidean Controversy* (New York, 1965).

46. On Rabad, see Isadore Twersky, *Rabad of Posquières* (Philadelphia, 1980), pp. 19–29, including bibliography.

47. Rabad on Hilkhot Deot 3.2.

48. Abraham ben David, *Baalei ha-Nefesh* (Jerusalem, 1975), pp. 104–24.

49. Maimonides, perhaps reflecting Muslim belief, holds that excessive drinking of alcohol is even worse than sexual excess, since it affects the intellect. See Maimonides, *Guide* 3:8, p. 434. See also Bachya ibn Pakuda, *Hovot ha-Levavot*, Shaar ha-Perishut, chap. 5.

50. I am in substantial agreement with Dahlia Hoshen that the *Baalei ha-Nefesh* is a more ascetic text than other interpreters have argued. See "Sexual Relations between Husband and Wife: The Rishonim's Approach and the Talmudic Sources," *Jewish Quarterly Review* (forthcoming). Interpretations that emphasize Rabad's permissive views include Twersky, *Rabad*, pp. 92–97; David Feldman, *Marital Relations, Birth Control and Abortion in Jewish Law* (New York, 1968), pp. 69, 94ff; and Rachel Biale, *Women and Jewish Law* (New York, 1984), pp. 132–33.

51. Rabad, *Baalei ha-Nefesh*, p. 13.

52. One wonders if Rabad may have had this latter metaphor indirectly from Muslim sources, since the Koran states that "your wives are your fields; go to your fields whenever you desire" (Sura 4, v. 231). In Rabad's rendering, use of one's fields is regulated by divine commandment.

53. Rabad, *Baalei ha-Nefesh*, pp. 14–16.

54. This is not to say that mortification of the flesh did not play an important role in the mystical tradition. In fact, the sixteenth-century Kabbalists and later *musar* preachers advocated severe physical penances. But here, too, the theory was that punishing the body could influence one's spiritual intention rather than producing a direct effect, as in the *Sefer Hasidim* or the *Sefer ha-Rokeah*.

55. I am indebted in this discussion to Jeremy Cohen. See Cohen, "Rationales for Congual Sex in RaAvaD's *Ba'ale ha-Nefesh*," in *Frank Talmage Memorial Volume*, special issue of *Jewish History* (forthcoming).

56. See Ze'ev W. Falk, *Jewish Matrimonial Law in the Middle Ages* (Oxford, 1966), chap. 2.

57. On Catharism, see A. Borst, *Die Katharer* (Stuttgart, 1953).

58. For the impact on the church, see Eric Fuchs, *Sexual Desire and Love: Origins and History of the Christian Ethic of Sexuality and Marriage*, trans. Marsha Daigle (Cambridge, 1983), p. 126; and James A. Brundage, *Law, Sex and Christian Society in Medieval Europe* (Chicago, 1987), pp. 399, 423.

59. See Brundage, *Law, Sex and Christian Society*, chap. 5.

60. See David Berger, *The Jewish-Christian Debate in the High Middle Ages: A Critical Edition of the Nizzahon Vetus* (Philadelphia, 1979), pp. 69, 205, 223–24.

61. For Augustine's views, see Peter Brown, *The Body and Society: Men,*

*Women, and the Renunciation of Sexuality in Early Christianity* (New York, 1988), chap. 19; and John Noonan, *Contraception: A History of Its Treatment by the Catholic Theologians and Canonists* (Cambridge, Mass., 1965), pp. 46–139.

62. See Cohen, "Rationales for Conjugal Sex"; and Brundage, *Law, Sex and Christian Society*, pp. 278–88, 447–50.

63. See Christopher N. L. Brooke, *The Medieval Idea of Marriage* (Oxford, 1989), chap. 5.

64. Peter Abelard, *Ethica*, ed. D. E. Luscombe (Oxford, 1971), pp. 18–21.

65. He omits reasons of health but includes Rabad's fifth reason, sensual pleasure.

66. See Brundage, *Law, Sex and Christian Society*, pp. 281–82.

67. Thomas Aquinas, *Summa Theologica* (New York and London, 1963), 1a.98.2. Aquinas's position was somewhat different in his *Scriptum Super Libros Sententiarum Magistre Peter Lombardi*, Distinctio XX, where he holds that if the first couple had been able to have sex in the Garden, they would have done it without any desire. See Shlomo Pines, "Nahmanides on Adam in the Garden of Eden in the Context of Other Interpretations of Genesis, Chapters 2 and 3" (in Hebrew), *Galut Ahar Golah* (Haim Beinart Festschrift) (Jerusalem, 1988), p. 163. Pines does not take the position of the *Summa* into account.

68. Aquinas, *Summa* 2a2ae, 153.2.2.

69. Aquinas, Commentary to *Sentences* 4.31.2.3 and *Summa* (Supplement) 3.41.3 and 3.64.2.

70. On Jewish knowledge of Catharist or Albigensian doctrines, see Shulamit Shahar, "Catharism and the Origins of Kabbalah in Languedoc" (in Hebrew), *Tarbits* 40 (1971): 483–508; Frank Talmage, "A Hebrew Polemical Treatise, Anti-Cathar and Anti-Orthodox," *Harvard Theological Review* 60 (1967): 323–48; and Joseph Shatzmiller, "The Albigensian Heresy in the Eyes of Contemporary Jews" (in Hebrew) in Reuven Bonfil, ed., *Tarbut ve-Hevrah be-Toldot Yisrael be-Yemei ha-Benayim*, Memorial Volume for Haim Hillel Ben Sasson (Jerusalem, 1989), pp. 333–52.

CHAPTER 5:
### Sexuality and Spirituality in the Kabbalah
Abbreviation: b. = Babylonian Talmud

1. The *Iggeret ha-Kodesh* was traditionally attributed to Moses Nachmanides, but Gershom Scholem definitively showed that this attribution is false. See his article in *Kiryat Sefer* 25 (1944–45): 179–86. Scholem suggested that it was written by Joseph Gikatilla, another Spanish Kabbalist, but later modified this judgment. Gikatilla's authorship has received recent support from Charles Mopsik in his *Lettre sur la sainteté: Le secret de la relation entre*

*l'homme et la femme dans la cabale* (Lagrasse, 1986), pp. 20–29. See further C. D. Chavel, ed., *Kitvei ha-Ramban* (Jerusalem, 1964), pp. 315–19. Chavel suggests that the author was either Azriel of Gerona or one of his students. Chavel's edition of the text is the most scientific and is the one I have used here.

2. *Iggeret ha-Kodesh* in Chavel, *Kitvei ha-Ramban*, pp. 323–24.

3. Gershom Scholem was probably the first to articulate this point of view about the Kabbalists in *Major Trends in Jewish Mysticism*, 3d ed. (New York, 1961), p. 235. For a similar analysis of the "Philonic, the talmudic-midrashic, and the kabbalistic perceptions of sexuality ... [as] unambiguously positive," see Moshe Idel, "Sexual Metaphors and Praxis in the Kabbalah," in David Kraemer, ed., *The Jewish Family* (New York, 1989), p. 211. See further David Feldman, *Marital Relations, Birth Control and Abortion in Jewish Law* (New York, 1968), pp. 73–74, 99–100 on *Iggeret ha-Kodesh* and the whole work for an interpretation of the medieval textual tradition along these lines.

4. See Scholem, *Major Trends*, pp. 23–25.

5. See James Brundage, *Law, Sex and Christian Society in Medieval Europe* (Chicago, 1987), pp. 451–52, 467; and Helen Rodnite Lemay, "Some Thirteenth and Fourteenth Century Lectures on Female Sexuality," *International Journal of Women's Studies* 1 (1978): 391–400.

6. See Madelain Farah, *Marriage and Sexuality in Islam: A Translation of al-Ghazali's Book on the Etiquette of Marriage from the Ihya* (Salt Lake City, 1984), pp. 106–7. See further G. H. Bousquet, *L'éthique sexuelle de l'Islam* (Paris, 1966), pp. 7–8, 161–84.

7. *Iggeret ha-Kodesh*, p. 336.

8. For a discussion of medieval Jewish treatments of female orgasm, see Feldman, *Marital Relations*, chap. 7. For medieval Christian views, see Brundage, *Law, Sex, and Christian Society*, pp. 450–51.

9. See Laqueur, *Making Sex: Body and Gender from the Greeks to Freud* (Cambridge, Mass., 1990), pp. 46, 49–52, 99–103. Medieval Christian theologians generally accepted this medical opinion. Not all Jewish authors necessarily agreed with the connection between female orgasm and conception. In the fifteenth century Simon ben Zemah Duran of North Africa held that female "semination" is for pleasure alone, designed to make marriage and childbirth more attractive. See his *Magen Avot* (Livorno, 1785), p. 40b. See further Feldman, *Marital Relations*, pp. 138–39.

10. *Sifrei*, par. Ekev, 49.

11. Maimonides *Guide* 1:2, p. 25, and 3:8, p. 434.

12. See Abraham Ibn Ezra, Commentary on Genesis 2:17 and 3:7; and David Kimchi, *Perushei Rabbi David Kimchi al ha-Torah*, ed. M. Kamalher (Jerusalem, 1982), p. 30 (on Genesis 2:17) and p. 33 (on Genesis 2:25): "'And they were not ashamed' comes to inform you that before they ate from the tree of knowledge, they did not have shame regarding their exposed genitals, because they had not yet had sexual intercourse since they did not yet have

the desire for intercourse. Their genitals were exactly like the rest of their limbs and they were not ashamed of them." See also Moses Nachmanides on Genesis 2:9. For an analysis of Jewish and Christian sources on this problem, see Shlomo Pines, "Nahmanides on Adam in the Garden of Eden in the Context of Other Interpretations of Genesis, Chapters 2 and 3" (in Hebrew), *Galut Ahar Golah* (Haim Beinart Festschrift) (Jerusalem, 1988), pp. 159–64.

13. *Iggeret ha-Kodesh*, pp. 323–24.

14. See Jeremy Cohen, *"Be Fertile and Increase, Fill the Earth and Master It": The Ancient and Medieval Career of a Biblical Text* (Ithaca, N.Y., 1989), pp. 245–64; and Margaret Miles, *Carnal Knowing: Female Nakedness and Religious Meaning in the West* (Boston, 1989), p. 94.

15. See Monford Harris, "Marriage as Metaphysics: A Study of the 'Iggeret ha-Kodesh," *Hebrew Union College Annual* 33 (1962): 197–220. I am basically in agreement with Harris's revisionist reading of the *Iggeret*, but he too readily applies the word "gnostic" to the text. Although the *Iggeret* is clearly indebted to the *Sefer ha-Bahir*, which Gershom Scholem labeled a kind of medieval Jewish Gnosticism, it has a much more complex position on this world than did the dualistic Gnostics of late antiquity. Moreover, Harris believes that the *Iggeret* should be read as a sex manual on the exoteric level and as an antimaterialist kabbalistic code on the esoteric level. This division of the book into exoteric and esoteric seems to me overdrawn. On the contrary, the author was striving to reconcile the physical act of intercourse with its kabbalistic meaning.

16. But see Harris, "Marriage as Metaphysics," pp. 219–20; and Mopsik, *Lettre sur la sainteté*, pp. 295–97.

17. See Mopsik, *Lettre sur la sainteté*, p. 295 n. 114.

18. *Iggeret ha-Kodesh*, p. 326.

19. This is the term used by Giles of Rome, whose *De Formatione Corporis Humani in Utero* appeared a few decades after our text. See Mopsik, *Lettre sur la sainteté*, pp. 192–93; and D. Jacquart and C. Thomasset, *Sexuality and Medicine in the Middle Ages*, trans. Matthew Adamson (Princeton, 1988), p. 59. Giles's text reveals a similar notion, taken from Aristotelian medicine, of the sperm as the force that gives shape to the embryo. As Mopsik notes, however, Giles's doctrine does not contain the mystical element of the *Iggeret*. The term *res divina* must be understood metaphorically in Aristotelian terms as "form" that combines with passive female "matter."

20. See especially b. Yoma 29a: "Sinful thoughts are worse than sins."

21. *Iggeret ha-Kodesh*, p. 334.

22. The idea goes back to Plato but was known during the Middle Ages from Hippocrates. See Laqueur, *Making Sex*, p. 35.

23. *Iggeret ha-Kodesh*, pp. 326, 332.

24. Ibid., p. 326. Other kabbalistic texts of the period connect adultery with idolatry. For references, see Elliot Wolfson, "Circumcision, Vision of

God and Textual Interpretation: From Midrashic Trope to Mystical Symbol," *History of Religions* 27 (1987–88): 190 n. 2.

25. b. Nedarim 20a–b. See above, Chapter 2.

26. *Iggeret ha-Kodesh*, p. 326.

27. Emphasis added. Harris, "Marriage as Metaphysics," p. 208, was the first to notice this phrase.

28. See Maimonides, *Guide*, pt. 1.

29. Abraham Abulafia, *Ozar Eden Ganuz* (Oxford ed., 1580) fol. 130b, in Moshe Idel, *The Mystical Experience in Abraham Abulafia*, trans. Jonathan Chipman (Albany, N.Y., 1988), p. 204. See also the almost identical position of Isaac of Acre in *Meirat Eynaim*, quoted in Idel, p. 203.

30. For an excellent summary of kabbalistic doctrines of sexuality, see Mopsik, *Lettre sur la sainteté*, pp. 45–162.

31. On the *Zohar*'s views of sexuality, see I. Tishby, ed., *Mishnat ha-Zohar* (Jerusalem, 1975), 2:607–53.

32. *Zohar* 2:3a–b.

33. Ibid. 1:57a, 1:62a. The name "Er" is the Hebrew word for evil—*ra*—written backward!

34. Ibid. 1:219b.

35. Ibid. 1:54b. For talmudic statements on *keri* (nocturnal emissions), see b. Ketubot 46a: "One should not indulge in evil thoughts by day that might lead one to impurity at night"; and b. Yoma 88a: "He who has a nocturnal emission on Yom Kippur, let him be anxious over this for the entire year. And if he survives the year, he is assured of being destined for the future world." *Keri* is one of six characteristics that are noted as a good sign for one who is sick (b. Berakhot 57b). Finally, Jacob never had a *keri* (Genesis Rabbah 98.4 and b. Yavamot 76a).

36. *Zohar* 1:49b.

37. *Zohar* 2:89a. See, further *Tikkunei Zohar*, Tikkun 56, p. 93b.

38. For a discussion of the kabbalistic meaning of the Sabbath seen through the prism of the sixteenth-century kabbalist Meir ibn Gabbai, see Elliot K. Ginsburg, *The Sabbath in the Classical Kabbalah*, 2 vols. (Albany, N.Y., 1989).

39. *Zohar* 3:90a.

40. Ibid. 3:168a.

41. Isaiah Horowitz, *Shnei Luhot ha-Berit* (Amsterdam, 1649), p. 102b. David Feldman misunderstood this passage as support for nonprocreative intercourse. See Feldman, *Marital Relations*, p. 68.

42. Nachmanides on Leviticus 18:10.

43. Nachmanides on Leviticus 18:19. Nachmanides understood menstrual blood to be nonprocreative and, in fact, destructive (anyone who drinks it will die).

44. See Mopsik, *Lettre sur la sainteté*, p. 196.

45. See Gershom Scholem, "Shekhinah: The Feminine Element in Divinity," in *On the Mystical Shape of the Godhead: Basic Concepts in the Kabbalah*, trans. Joachim Neugroschel (New York, 1991), pp. 140–96.

46. This appears to be Mopsik's view in *Lettre sur la sainteté*, p. 198.

47. *Zohar* 1:50b.

48. See Maria Warner, *Alone of All Her Sex: Myth and the Cult of the Virgin Mary* (New York, 1976).

49. Idem, "Sexual Metaphors and Praxis," p. 199. See above, Introduction, n. 14, for further comments on Idel's views of sexuality in Judaism.

50. See Abraham Abulafia, *Sefer Mafteah ha-Sefirot*, in Idel, *Abulafia*, p. 186.

51. See Arthur Green, "The Song of Songs in Early Jewish Mysticism," *Orim: A Jewish Journal at Yale* 2, no. 2 (Spring 1987): 49–63; and Scholem, "Shekhinah," p. 184.

52. Isaac of Acre, *Sefer Ozar Hayyim*, p. 73b, cited in Moshe Idel, *Studies in Ecstatic Kabbalah* (Albany, N.Y., 1988), p. 153 n. 66.

53. See Solomon Schechter's still excellent essay, "Safed in the Sixteenth Century," in his *Studies in Judaism*, 2d series (Philadelphia, 1908), pp. 202–306, 317–28.

54. The dissemination of the sixteenth-century Lurianic Kabbalah has been documented by Gershom Scholem in his *Sabbatai Sevi: The Mystical Messiah, 1626–1676*, trans. R. J. Zwi Werblowsky (Princeton, 1973), pp. 22–77.

55. See Gershom Scholem, "Tradition and New Creation in the Ritual of the Kabbalists," in his *On the Kabbalah and Its Symbolism* (New York, 1965), pp. 138–42; and Lawrence Fine, "The Contemplative Practice of Yihudim in Lurianic Kabbalah," in Arthur Green, ed., *Jewish Spirituality* (New York, 1987) 2:77.

56. See, for example, Hayyim Vital, *Shaar Ruah ha-Kodesh* (Jerusalem, 1963). The most interesting section pertaining to sexual offenses is Vital's discussion of homosexuality in which he gives an elaborate kabbalistic explanation for the effect of anal intercourse on the *sefirot*. Whether this points to the existence of homosexual acts in Safed cannot be answered. See *Tikkunim* 22–26, pp. 57–62.

57. See, for example, Hayyim Vital, *Sefer ha-Hezyyonot*, a collection of Vital's dreams interpreted kabbalistically.

58. See R. J. Zwi Werblowsky, *Joseph Karo: Lawyer and Mystic* (Philadelphia, 1977).

59. Ibid., chap. 12.

60. Joseph Karo, *Maggid Mesharim* (Amsterdam, 1708), p. 51a, cited in Werblowsky, *Joseph Karo*, pp. 138–39.

61. Hayyim Vital, *Sefer Shaar ha-Mitzvot* (Tel Aviv, 1951), par. Bereshit, p. 8. Vital, who was Luria's student and one of those responsible for transmitting his teachings, claims that he himself never heard this report directly

from his teacher. Indeed, it contradicts Vital's own teaching that sex on a non-Sabbath night is forbidden for the scholar.

62. Karo, *Maggid Mesharim,* pp. 13b–14a and 7a, cited in Werblowsky, *Joseph Karo,* pp. 245–46.

63. Karo, *Maggid Mesharim* (Jerusalem, 1960), p. 64.

64. Karo, *Shulhan Arukh,* Orah Hayyim, no. 240.

65. Vital, *Sefer Shaar ha-Mitzvot,* par. Bereshit, p. 8; emphasis added.

66. Ibid., p. 7. Only procreative intercourse involves the *sefirot* by causing them to unite and produce a holy soul. See also Vital, *Etz Hayyim,* pt. 1, Shaar ha-Zivvugim, chap. 1.

67. Elijah da Vidas, *Reshit Hokhmah,* p. 196b.

68. Horowitz, *Shnei Luhot ha-Berit,* p. 56a.

69. Ibid., pp. 49a–b and 110a.

70. See Eliezer Azkari, *Sefer Haredim* (Jerusalem, 1966), pp. 199–202. See also Horowitz, *Shnei Luhot ha-Berit,* pp. 100a–b.

71. Vital, *Shaarei Kedushah* (Jerusalem, 1967), pt. 2, chap. 6, p. 70. I have not found an earlier source that explicitly addressed the problem of child masturbation.

72. Vital, *Shaar Ruah ha-Kodesh,* Tikkun 27, pp. 62–64.

73. Horowitz, *Shnei Luhot ha-Berit,* pp. 98a–99b.

74. The subtitle of Moses Graf, *Zera Kodesh* (Furth, 1696). See also Joseph Hahn, *Yosef Ometz* (Frankfurt a.M., 1723), pp. 195–96, 286ff; Joseph ben Solomon of Posen, *Yesod Yosef* (Frankfurt a.O., 1679); and Joseph Kanafi, *Ot Brit Kodesh* (The Sign of the Holy Covenant) (Livorno, 1884).

75. Solomon Alkabez, *Ayelet Ahavim* (reprint, Jerusalem, 1973). I thank Arthur Green for this reference.

76. Eliezer Azkari, *Sefer Haredim,* pt. 7, chap. 4, cited in Werblowsky, *Joseph Karo,* p. 136. This kind of erotic relationship with a text can be found as early as the fourteenth century in Israel ibn al-Nakawa's *Menorat ha-Maor,* ed. H. G. Enlow (New York, 1931), 3:275–76, in which a mystic who studied only the talmudic tractate Hagigah dies and a figure "like a woman mourning her husband" comes to weep over his grave. The woman is the tractate Hagigah.

77. Horowitz, *Shnei Luhot ha-Berit,* p. 49b.

78. *Zohar* 3:83b. For a history of this theme, see above, Chapter 2. The early-thirteenth-century Kabbalist Ezra of Gerona speaks of the purely spiritual nature of Adam before he ate the fruit. The Raaya Meheimna section of the *Zohar,* written sometime after Moses de Leon composed the main section, developed a whole spiritual world, with its own Torah, in opposition to the material world.

79. Abraham Azulai, *Hesed le-Avraham* (Vilna, 1877), "Eyn ha-Kore," p. xi, cited in Scholem, *Sabbatai Sevi,* p. 320. See also the statement of da Vidas quoted above.

80. Horowitz, *Shnei Luhot ha-Berit*, p. 21a.

81. Solomon Alkabez, *Berit ha-Levi* (Jerusalem, 1980), p. 42d. The source for this idea is the *Zohar* 1:21b–22a, which speaks of Moses as married to the Shekhinah. The same spiritualized view of Moses can be found in the writings of the sixteenth-century Polish halakhist Moses Isserles: "Moses our teacher, because he had removed from himself all corporeality and there was none of the dark matter from without left in him, saw naught but the brilliant light itself." See Isserles, *Torat ha-Olah* (Prague, 1569), par. 14, fol. 19b–d, cited in Scholem, "Tselem: The Concept of the Astral Body," in *On the Mystical Shape of the Godhead*, trans. Joachim Neugroschel (New York, 1991), pp. 258–59.

82. In a personal communication, however, Arthur Green wrote me that Yehuda Yaari, one of the founders of the kibbutz movement, informed him that Yaari himself proposed the name kibbutz, but he took it from the phrase *ha-kibbutz ha-kadosh*, which referred to the gathering of Bratslav Hasidim at Nahman's grave.

83. For the definitive history of Sabbatianism during Sabbatai Zevi's life, see Scholem, *Sabbatai Sevi*.

84. This history has been recounted by Gershom Scholem in his classic essay "Redemption through Sin," in *The Messianic Idea in Judaism and Other Essays on Jewish Spirituality* (New York, 1971), pp. 78–141.

85. Scholem, *Sabbatai Sevi*, p. 113.

86. Ibid., pp. 159–60.

87. Ibid., pp. 191–97, 387.

88. Ibid., pp. 403–4.

89. Ibid., pp. 61–63.

90. Nathan of Gaza, *Treatise on the Menorah*, published in Gershom Scholem, *Be-Ikvot Mashiah* (Jerusalem, 1944), p. 104.

91. Ibid., p. 102, translated in Scholem, "Redemption through Sin," p. 117.

92. Idel, "Sexual Metaphors and Praxis," p. 212. Idel believes that Sabbatianism merely took the Kabbalah's sensual stance to its logical conclusion once halakhic prohibitions were weakened.

CHAPTER 6:
## The Displacement of Desire in Eighteenth-Century Hasidism
### Abbreviation: b. = Babylonian Talmud

1. David of Makov, *Shever Poshim: Zot Torat ha-Kanaot*, pp. 33a–b, published in Mordecai Wilensky, *Hasidim u-Mitnagdim* (Jerusalem, 1970), 2:108. This accusation appears as a gloss on an alleged statement by the Gaon of Vilna: "The Gaon of Vilna already wrote about them: 'They commit transgressions against holy flesh,' thus hinting that they waste their seed." See also *Shever Poshim*, p. 30a (Wilensky, p. 103): "They say that in their prayers it is

necessary to give birth and therefore they need a 'living organ' to make unifications and to move themselves like a man having intercourse with his wife when they are performing unifications."

2. Among the so-called *haredim*, or ultra-Orthodox, in Israel today, for instance, the Hasidim are generally thought to be the most extreme ascetics with respect to sexuality in a world generally characterized by an ascetic ideal. See Amnon Levi, *Ha-Haredim* (Jerusalem, 1988).

3. See Bernard Weinryb, *The Jews of Poland* (Philadelphia, 1972), pp. 308–20.

4. On Sabbatianism in Poland, see Gershom Scholem, "The Sabbatian Movement in Poland" (in Hebrew), *Bet Yisrael be-Polin* (Jerusalem, 1954), 2:36–76; and a criticism of Scholem's view in Weinryb, *Jews of Poland*, pp. 232–35. On the Frankists, see Weinryb, pp. 236–61; Scholem, "Jacob Frank and the Frankists," in his *Kabbalah* (Jerusalem, 1974), pp. 287–309; and Meir Balaban, *Le-Toldot ha-Tenuah ha-Frankit* (Tel Aviv, 1934). The Satanow proceedings were published in large part by Jacob Emden, *Sefer Shimmush* (Altona, 1762), pp. 5a–7a.

5. See Isaiah Tishby, "The Messianic Idea and Messianic Tendencies in the Rise of Hasidism" (in Hebrew), *Zion* 32 (1967):1–45; and Mendel Piekarz, *Bi-Yemei Zemihat ha-Hasidut* (Jerusalem, 1978). Against the hypothesis of Gershom Scholem, both of these authors see Sabbatianism as a relatively unimportant factor in the early-eighteenth-century religious revival that culminated in Hasidism.

6. See Gershom Scholem, "The Historical Figure of the Baal Shem Tov" (in Hebrew), in Scholem, *Devarim be-Go* (Tel Aviv, 1976), p. 294.

7. Baruch of Kosov, *Amud ha-Avodah*, p. 29b. See Tishby, "Messianic Idea," pp. 27–28 n. 122.

8. Baruch, *Amud ha-Avodah*, p. 88b. See Piekarz, *Bi-Yemei Zemihat ha-Hasidut*, p. 219. See also Baruch's statement in *Amud ha-Avodah*, p. 237c, that "it is permitted to transgress one of the negative commandments in order to fulfill the commandment to repent."

9. Leib's teachings have come down to us through an anti-Hasidic text, and some therefore concluded that he was invented as a way of tarnishing the image of Hasidism by making the new movement appear much more antinomian than it actually was. For a discussion of his historicity, see Wilensky, *Hasidim u-Mitnagdim* 2:109–12. Opinions range from identifying him as a Hasid (S. Dubnow), as a Frankist (D. Kahane and G. Scholem), and as an anti-Hasidic fabrication (A. Rubinstein and M. Wilensky). Piekarz believes that he was a non-Hasidic, but also non-Frankist, radical. See Piekarz, "Religious Radicalism at the Time of the Spread of Hasidism" (in Hebrew), *Molad* nos. 243–44 (1975):435–36, Leib Melamed's purported text is a commentary on the *Tur* law code, which came into the hands of the *mitnagdim* of Shklov in 1787.

10. For the earlier sources for this tradition, see Piekarz, *Bi-Yemei Zemihat*

*ha-Hasidut*, chap. 5. Horowitz's *Shnei Luhot ha-Berit* (Amsterdam, 1649) was a key text for this concept. See pp. 49a–b.

11. *Shever Poshim*, pp. 36a–b, in Wilensky, *Hasidim u-Mitnagdim* 2:117.

12. *Shever Poshim*, pp. 34b–35a, in Wilensky, *Hasidim u-Mitnagdim* 2:115.

13. *Shever Poshim*, pp. 37b–38a, in Wilensky, *Hasidim u-Mitnagdim* 2:119–20.

14. See Piekarz, *Bi-Yemei Zemihat ha-Hasidut*, chaps. 4, 5; and Simon Dubnow, "Heretical Hasidim" (in Hebrew), *Ha-Shiloah* 7 (1901):312–30.

15. Leib Melaned, *Shever Poshim*, pp. 62b–63a, in Wilensky, *Hasidim u-Mitnagdim* 2:157.

16. Ezekiel Landau, *Derushei ha-Zalah* (reprint, Jerusalem, 1966), p. 4a. Landau was familiar with the cultural practices of the areas in which Hasidism later emerged. He studied in Brody between 1735 and 1745 and had contact with Nahman of Kosov. See Ben-Zion Dinur, "The Origins of Hasidism" in Gershon Hundert, ed., *Essential Papers in Hasidism* (New York, 1991), pp. 160–61.

17. I am endebted to Gershon Hundert for this observation. See Hundert, "The Jewish Family in Early Modern Poland-Lithuania," in Steven Cohen and Paula Hyman, eds., *The Jewish Family: Myths and Reality* (New York, 1986), pp. 19–20, 26 n. 2 for demographic bibliography. For my own speculations along these lines, see David Biale, "Childhood, Marriage and the Family in the Eastern European Jewish Enlightenment," in Cohen and Hyman, pp. 46–47. In this discussion and in the next chapter, on the Jewish Enlightenment, I accept Erik Erikson's suggestion that every generation experiences a struggle for a viable adult identity. See Erikson, *Young Man Luther* (New York, 1958), pp. 14, 41–42, for the way in which this developmental struggle finds expression in religious innovation.

18. On the legal history of child marriage, see *Otzar ha-Poskim*, Even ha-Ezer, sec. 1, chap. 3:15.

19. See Jacob Katz, "Marriage and Marital Relations at the End of the Middle Ages," *Zion* 10 (1945–46) p. 35, n. 98.

20. See Israel Halpern, "Panic Marriages in Eastern Europe" (in Hebrew), in Halpern, *Yehudim ve-Yahadut be-Mizrah Europa* (Jerusalem, 1969), pp. 289–309.

21. See Jacob Emden, *She'elat Yavetz* (Altona, 1738–59), no. 14, p. 18; and Ezekiel Landau, *Noda be-Yehudah*, pt. 2 (Prague, 1811), no. 54, p. 63.

22. On the Polish Enlighteners, see Jacob Goldberg, "Jewish Marriages in Old Poland in the Public Opinion of the Enlightenment Period" (in Hebrew), *Galed* 4–5 (1978): 25–33. For a foreign observation about the hypersexuality of the Polish Jews, see F. L. De La Fontaine, *Chirurgish-Medicinische Abhandlungen verschiedenen Inhalts Polen betreffend* (Breslau, 1792). On La Fontaine, see Sander L. Gilman, *Difference and Pathology: Stereotypes of Sexuality, Race and Madness* (Ithaca, N.Y., 1985) p. 110.

23. *Pinkas Medinat Lita*, ed. Simon Dubnow (Berlin, 1925), no. 968, p. 266.

24. See, for example, Hayyim ha-Kohen Rapoport, *She'elot u-Teshuvot* (Lvov, 1861), Even ha-Ezer, no. 1; Ephraim Zalman Margaliot, *Sefer Bet Ephraim* (Warsaw, 1883), Even ha-Ezer, pt. 1, nos. 41 and 42; and Ezekiel Katzenellenbogen, *Knesset Yehezkel* (Altona, 1733), no. 55.

25. Landau, *Noda be-Yehudah*, pt. 2, no. 52. pp. 45–46 (for the description of the case).

26. Responsum by Rabbi Meshulam, the court president of Pressburg, in Moses Teitelbaum, *Heshiv Moshe* (Lemberg, 1866), end of book.

27. *The Memoirs of Glückel of Hameln*, trans. Marvin Lowenthal (New York, 1977), pp. 23ff.

28. Eliezer Zweifel, *Shalom al Yisrael* (Zhitomir, 1870), vol. 2, pt. 3, pp. 30–31. Nahman of Bratslav began to gather his Hasidim shortly after his marriage at age thirteen; many were roughly the same age. See Arthur Green, *Tormented Master: A Life of Rabbi Nahman of Bratslav* (New York, 1981), p. 39. For the adolescent character of Hasidism in general, see also Simon Dubnow, *Toldot ha-Hasidut* (Tel Aviv, 1975), p. 369; Jacob Katz, *Masoret u-Mashber* (Jerusalem, 1963), p. 282 n. 18; and Ada Rapoport-Albert, "On Women in Hasidism," in Ada Rapoport-Albert and Steven J. Zipperstein, eds., *Jewish History: Essays in Honour of Chimen Abramsky* (London, 1988), p. 510 n. 13.

29. Menachem Nachum of Chernobyl, "Meor Eynayim," trans. in Arthur Green, ed., *Upright Practices—The Light of the Eyes: Menahem Nahum of Chernobyl* (New York, 1982), p. 121.

30. Arthur Green pointed out to me in a personal communication that Ger Hasidism, which derived from Kotzk, lacks this ascetic element.

31. Abraham J. Heschel, *Kotzk* (Tel Aviv, 1973), 1:246–47. The Maggid of Kosnitz also advocated becoming a Hasid in the year after marriage.

32. Jacob Joseph of Polonnye, *Toldot Yaakov Yosef* (Korzec, 1780), pp. 88b–c.

33. Ibid., p. 19b. Nahman was less a disciple than a companion of the Baal Shem Tov. See Abraham J. Heschel, *The Circle of the Baal Shem Tov: Studies in Hasidism*, ed. Samuel H. Dresner (Chicago, 1985), pp. 113–51.

34. *Tzavaat ha-Ribash* (New York, 1975), no. 56, p. 10.

35. Jacob Joseph, *Toldot Yaakov Yosef*, p. 151a.

36. Jacob Joseph of Polonnye, *Ben Porat Yosef* (Korzec, 1781), p. 66b. The saying is based on a misinterpretation of Saadia Gaon. See Joseph Weiss, "The Beginnings of Hasidism" (in Hebrew), *Zion* 16 (1951):101.

37. Benjamin of Zalozce, *Ahavat Dodim* (Lemberg, 1795), 35:3.

38. See Heschel, *The Circle of the Baal Shem Tov*, pp. 122–23. Heschel lists the source as "from a MS."

39. See, for example, Jacob Joseph of Polonnye, *Toldot Yaakov Yosef*, p. 50a. See further Weiss, "Beginnings of Hasidism," pp. 92ff.

40. Quoted in Dov Baer of Mezeritch, *Maggid Devarav le-Yaakov*, ed. Rivka Schatz (Jerusalem, 1976), no. 160, pp. 256–57. Dov Baer's own position was much more traditional in its hostility to involuntary emissions. See ibid., no.

207, pp. 331–33. For a discussion of the Baal Shem Tov's teaching, see Heschel, *The Circle of the Baal Shem Tov*, pp. 147–48, 189–91 n. 149.

41. On Hasidic attitudes towards *keri*, see Rivka Schatz, *Ha-Hasidut ke-Mistikah* (Tel Aviv, 1968), p. 48, and below on Nahman of Bratslav.

42. Jacob Joseph of Polonnye, *Ktonet Pasim* (Lvov, 1866), p. 33a. For a commentary on this text, see Weiss, "Beginnings of Hasidism," pp. 92–93. See also Elimelech of Lyzhansk, *Noam Elimelech*, ed. Gidaliah Nigal (Jerusalem, 1978), 1:280: "In general, the sin [for men] of these fantasies and desires comes from a woman who, God forbid, has evil fantasies."

43. Menachem Nachum of Chernobyl, *Meor Eynayim*, Toldot, trans. in Arthur Green, *Upright Practices*, p. 175. See also *Hanhagot Yesharot* in ibid., p. 40. For a parallel text from Jacob Joseph, also attributed to the Baal Shem Tov, see *Toldot*, p. 67b.

44. b. Yevamot 12b.

45. See Rapoport-Albert, "On Women in Hasidism," pp. 495–525. For some additional observations on Hasidic attitudes toward sexuality, see Abraham J. Heschel, *Kotzk* 1:235–41.

46. Menachen Nachum, *Meor Eynayim*, par. Lekh Lekha, trans. in Arthur Green, *Upright Practices*, p. 117; emphasis added.

47. Martin Buber, *The Origin and Meaning of Hasidism*, trans. M. Friedman (New York, 1960).

48. Gershom Scholem, "Martin Buber's Interpretation of Hasidism," in *The Messianic Idea and Other Essays on Jewish Spirituality* (New York, 1971), pp. 221–50. See further Schatz, *Ha-Hasidut ke-Mistikah*.

49. For an account of the meaning of "nothingness" (*ayin*) in Jewish mysticism and Hasidism, see Daniel Matt, "*Ayin*: The Concept of Nothingness in Jewish Mysticism," in Robert M. C. Forman, ed., *The Problem of Pure Consciousness* (New York, 1990), pp. 121–59.

50. *Tzavaat ha-Ribash*, no. 35, p. 101.

51. Dov Baer, *Maggid Devarav le-Yaakov*, no. 54, pp. 76–77. See also no. 15, p. 30: "You are not permitted to desire her for your physical pleasure."

52. Elimelech of Lyzhansk, *Noam Elimelech* 1:10–11.

53. The reference is to the *Zohar* 3:60a.

54. Mendel of Kotzk, *Emet ve-Emunah*, p. 635. See Heschel, *Kotzk* 1:247.

55. Mendel of Kotzk, *Emet ve-Emunah*, p. 840. See Heschel, *Kotzk* 1:245.

56. *Shivhei ha-Ran* (Jerusalem, 1989), sec. 17, p. 20. See further Green, *Tormented Master*, p. 39.

57. *Shivhei ha-Ran*, sec. 16, p. 18.

58. Ibid, sec. 18, p. 20.

59. See Nahman of Bratslav, *Sihot ha-Ran* (Jerusalem, 1989), sec. 141, pp. 139–45.

60. See Yehudah Liebes, "R. Nahman of Bratslav's *Ha-tikkun Ha-klali* and His Attitude towards Sabbatianism" (in Hebrew), *Zion* 45 (1980):201–45.

61. See Rapoport-Albert, "On Women in Hasidism."

62. *Tzavaat ha-Ribash*, no. 35, p. 101.

63. Elimelech of Lyzhansk, *Noam Elimelech* 2:305. On Elimelech, see Rivka Schatz-Uffenheimer, "On the Essence of the Zaddik in Hasidism" (in Hebrew), *Molad* nos. 144–50 (1960):369–70.

64. Rapoport-Albert, "On Women in Hasidism," has given the definitive account and analysis of this story. Her article also includes an extensive bibliography. See especially S. A. Horodetsky, *Ha-Hasidut ve-ha-Hasidim* (Tel Aviv, 1951), 4:70–71; Mordecai Biber, "The Maid of Ludmir" (in Hebrew), *Reshumot* 2 (1946):69–76; and Ephraim Taubenhaus, *Be-Netiv ha-Yahid* (Haifa, 1959), pp. 37–41. I thank Shimon Brisman of the UCLA Library for initially drawing my attention to these last two works. (I undertook this aspect of my research before the appearance of Rapoport-Albert's excellent article. My initial analysis coincided with her conclusions, but she deserves full credit for publishing them first.)

65. Dan Ben-Amos and Jerome R. Mintz, eds. and trans., *In Praise of the Baal Shem Tov* (Bloomington, Ind., 1970), no. 249, p. 258. Based on the 1814 edition of *Shivhei ha-Besht*. See p. 342 n. 1.

66. Ibid., no. 75, 94–99. See also *Seder ha-Dorot he-Hadash* (reprint; Jerusalem, 1965), p. 29; and Horodetsky, *Ha-Hasidut ve-ha-Hasidim* 1:53, quoting from Israel of Ruzhin, *Irin Kadishin*.

67. See Horodetsky, *Ha-Hasidut ve-ha-Hasidim* 2:102, quoting from a manuscript entitled *Keneset Yisrael*, p. 19.

68. See Heschel, *Kotzk*, 1:241.

69. Ibid. The source is *Emet ve-Emunah*, p. 742.

70. *Shivhei ha-Besht* (Jerusalem, 1969), p. 83, translated in Ben-Amos and Mintz, *In Praise of the Baal Shem Tov*, no. 75, p. 98 (trans. slightly altered).

71. *Shivhei ha-Besht*, p. 71; translated in Ben-Amos and Mintz, *In Praise of the Baal Shem Tov*, no. 54, pp. 71–72.

72. The mystical-theurgic practice of uplifting divine sparks by unifying divine names.

73. I have not been able to find such a statement in the *Mishne Torah*. By referring to a heavenly source, the text seems to suggest that the reference is spurious.

74. *Zot Zikaron* (Munkacs, 1942), p. 126, cited in Rachel Elior, "The Doctrine of the Zaddik—The Seer of Lublin," in Rapoport-Albert and Zipperstein, *Jewish History*, p. 435.

75. See Schatz, *Ha-Hasidut ke-Mistikah*.

76. See Erich Seeberg, *Gottfried Arnold* (Meerane, 1923), pp. 6–7, 27–28.

77. On *devekut*, see Gershom Scholem, "*Devekut* or Communion with God," in *The Messianic Idea*, pp. 203–26.

78. Jacob Joseph of Polonnye, *Toldot Yaakov Yosef* (Jerusalem, 1965), vol. 2, par. Hukat, p. 559.

79. Jacob Joseph of Polonnye, *Ben Porat Yosef*, p. 66b; *Keter Shem Tov* (reprint; New York, 1972), pp. 16–17. For a translation and commentary, see

Ada Rapoport-Albert, "God and the Zaddik," in Hundert, *Essential Papers in Hasidism*, pp. 302–3. My translation is based on this one with changes from the original.

80. b. Sanhedrin 75a. See above, Chapter 2.

81. I therefore disagree with Rapoport-Albert's conclusion that "the satisfaction of physical desire is rendered a precondition for the spiritual desire to know God."

82. *Seder ha-Dorot he-Hadash* pp. 23–24. See further Dubnow, *Toldot ha-Hasidut*, p. 209.

83. The relevant texts are in the *Tzavaat ha-Ribash*, the ostensible "will" of the Baal Shem Tov, which was first published in 1794. The texts appear to stem from the school of the Maggid and while these passages cannot with certainty be attributed to the Baal Shem Tov himself, they do not contradict his teachings on *devekut* (union with the divine) found elsewhere.

84. *Tzavaat ha-Ribash*, no. 21, p. 68.

85. Ibid., no. 35, p. 11.

86. *Sihot ha-Ran* (Lemberg, 1901), sec. 261, p. 77a, translated in Rapoport-Albert, "On Women in Hasidism," p. 511 n. 16.

87. *Shever Poshim*, p. 139b, in Wilensky, *Hasidim u-Mitnagdim* 2:47.

88. Wilensky, *Hasidim u-Mitnagdim* 2:46.

89. *Shever Poshim*, p. 74a, in Wilensky, *Hasidim u-Mitnagdim* 2:41.

90. *Shever Poshim*, pp. 137b–138b, in Wilensky, *Hasidim u-Mitnagdim* 2:105.

91. Introduction to Elijah Gaon's commentary to the *Shulhan Arukh*. For the concept of *bittul torah*, see Hayyim of Volozhin, *Nefesh ha-Hayyim* (Vilna, 1824). On the Gaon and the whole Lithuanian tradition, see Immanuel Etkes, "Marriage and Study among the Lithuanian *Lomdim* in the Nineteenth Century," in David Kraemer, ed., *The Jewish Family* (New York, 1989), pp. 153–78.

92. Ephraim Deinard, *Zikhronot Bat Ami* (St. Louis, 1920), pt. 1, pp. 38–39, translated in Rapoport-Albert, "On Women in Hasidism," p. 512 n. 19.

93. See Shmuel Werses, "Hasidism in the Eyes of Haskalah Literature" (in Hebrew), *Molad* 144–45 (1960):379–91.

94. Joseph Perl, *Uiber das Wesen der Sekte Chassidim*, ed. Abraham Rubinstein (Jerusalem, 1977), pp. 41–43, 125, 146.

95. Joseph Perl, *Megalleh Temirin* (Vienna, 1819). In one story, two Hasidim rape and impregnate a gentile woman, while in another, the son of the rebbe sleeps with a Jewish woman.

CHAPTER 7:
Eros and Enlightenment

1. For an extended discussion of this argument, see David Biale, *Power and Powerlessness in Jewish History* (New York, 1986), chap. 4.

2. For Germany, see David Sorkin, *The Transformation of German Jewry, 1780–1840* (New York, 1987). For Eastern Europe, see Mordecai Levin, *Arkhei Hevrah ve-Kalkalah be-Ideologiyah shel Tekufat ha-Haskalah* (Jerusalem, 1975); J. S. Raisin, *The Haskalah Movement in Russia* (Philadelphia, 1913); and Raphael Mahler, *Ha-Hasidut ve-ha-Haskalah* (Merhaviya, 1961).

3. A recent study of the Scottish Enlightenment takes an approach similar to the one taken here to correlate youthful experience and ideology. See Charles Camic, *Experience and Enlightenment* (Chicago, 1984).

4. There were, however, several important precursors for the Haskalah autobiographies. Starting in the sixteenth century, there emerged a new genre of mystical hagiography, which was later adopted by the Hasidim. Because the life of the zaddik was taken to be exemplary, his personal struggles assumed didactic importance, just as the maskilim were to turn their own lives into counter-*exempla*. Another genre of literature that could provide a source for autobiography was that of the "ethical will" (or *tzavaah*). These documents, typically written by a father for his children, might merge details of autobiography with moralistic pronouncements. A particularly interesting example of this kind of literature, which pays particular attention to marital relations, is the memoir of Glückel of Hameln (1646–1724), often considered a unique testimony of a woman's life in traditional Jewish society: *The Memoirs of Glückel of Hameln*, trans. Marvin Lowenthal (New York, 1977). Glückel wrote her memoirs in the second decade of the eighteenth century. Although she proclaims that her memoir will be "no book of morals," it is in fact filled with conventional advice to her children and copious quotations from the moralistic literature available to a woman of her class.

5. Jacob Emden, *Megillat Sefer*, ed. David Kahana (Warsaw, 1897). Emden wrote his autobiography about 1752.

6. For this argument, see Azriel Shochat, *Im Hilufei ha-Tekufot* (Jerusalem, 1960).

7. Emden, *Megillat Sefer*, p. 82.

8. Jacob Emden, *Siddur Beit Yaakov* (Lemberg, 1884), pp. 158b–159b. See also David Feldman, *Marital Relations, Birth Control and Abortion in Jewish Law* (New York, 1968), pp. 101–2.

9. Solomon Maimon, *An Autobiography*, ed. Moses Hadas (New York, 1947). On these memoirs, see Alan Mintz, *"Banished from Their Father's Table": Loss of Faith and Hebrew Autobiography* (Bloomington, Ind., 1989), pp. 1–54; and Samuel Werses, "The Patterns of Autobiography in the Period of the Haskalah" (in Hebrew), *Gilyonot* 17 (1945):175–83. Other important memoirs include Mordecai Aaron Guenzburg, *Aviezer* (Vilna, 1863); Avraham Ber Gottlober, *Zikhronot u-Masaot*, 2 vols., ed. R. Goldberg (Jerusalem, 1976); and M. L. Lilienblum, *Ketavim Autobiografim*, 3 vols., ed. S. Breiman (Jerusalem, 1970). Guenzburg (1795–1846) began his memoir in 1828 but did not complete it. Gottlober (1810–99) published the first part of his autobiography in 1881 and the second in 1886, but the section on his youth seems to

have been written in 1854. Lilienblum (1843–1910) lived a generation later and published his *Hatteot Neurim*, the relevant part of his autobiography, in 1876 (it was written in 1872–73). Thus, Lilienblum was the only one of the three to have written the memoir close to the time described.

10. Erik Erikson, *Life History and the Historical Moment* (New York, 1975), p. 125.

11. The literature of ego psychology argues that such "splitting" results from a very early inability to separate properly from the mother. Those who split the world in this fashion typically idealize certain people while exhibiting aggression toward others. In addition, such personality types often have considerable difficulty in realizing mature love relationships. See Otto Kernberg, "Barriers to Falling and Remaining in Love," *Journal of the American Psychoanalytic Association* 22 (1974):486–511. On the concept of splitting generally, see Gertrude and Rubin Blanck, *Ego Psychology*, vol. 2 (New York, 1979). If this theory is helpful in understanding the maskilim, it must be put into the specific social setting of Eastern Europe in which boys were taken from their homes at a very early age, first to be sent to the heder or school and then to the houses of their in-laws after their marriages in early adolescence.

12. For sources of the biographies of maskilim, see Israel Zinberg, *A History of Jewish Literature*, trans. Bernard Martin (Cleveland, 1972–78), esp. vol. 11; and Joseph Klausner, *Historiya shel ha-Sifrut ha-Ivrit ha-Hadashah* (Jerusalem, 1953).

13. Gottlober, *Zikhronot u-Masaot*, 1:85. The typical goal was to celebrate the bar mitzvah and the marriage at the same party. Since a two-year engagement was frequently considered necessary, the *shiddukh* (engagement) was often concluded when the boy was eleven.

14. See Israel Halpern, "Panic Marriages in Eastern Europe" (in Hebrew), in Halpern, *Yehudim ve-Yahadut be-Mizrah Europa* (Jerusalem, 1969), pp. 289–309.

15. A particularly acute analysis is in Gottlober, *Zikhronot*, 1:85–89, 92. For other evidence, see David Knaani, *Ha-Batim she-Hayu* (Tel Aviv, 1986), pp. 29–33.

16. For Braudes's memoirs, see "Memoirs from The Days of My Youth" (in Hebrew), in *Zekanim im Na'arim* (Vienna, 1886), p. 65. See further Klausner, *Historiya shel ha-Sifrut ha-Ivrit*, 5:402.

17. Moses Mendelssohn, *Gesammelte Schriften Jubiläumsausgabe* (Berlin, 1929–38), vol. 16, May 15, 1761, letter 103, p. 205 (and April 27, 1762, letter 200, p. 324).

18. The poem is quoted in Klausner, *Historiya shel ha-Sifrut ha-Ivrit*, 3:36.

19. Gottlober, *Zikhronot*, 1:90–92, 94–95. See also Guenzburg, *Aviezer*, p. 54.

20. Pauline Wengeroff, *Memoiren einer Grossmutter* (Berlin, 1913), p. 40.

21. Gottlober, *Zikhronot*, 1:89.

22. See Klausner, *Historiya shel ha-Sifrut ha-Ivrit*, 3:175.

23. Gottlober, *Zikhronot*, 1:93.

24. See Henri Brunschwig, *Enlightenment and Romanticism in Eighteenth Century Prussia*, trans. Frank Jellinek (Chicago, 1974), pp. 147–55.

25. See for example, A. M. Dik, *Yankele Goldshlager* (1895); Isaac Linetski, *Dos Polishe Yingel;* and Y. L. Gordon, *Olom ki-Minhago Noheg* (Odessa, 1868).

26. Maimon, *Autobiography*, pp. 31–33.

27. Lilienblum, *Ketavim*, 1:108.

28. Wengeroff, *Memoiren*, pp. 100–102, 138–40. For some examples of this sermonic literature in nineteenth-century Germany, see *Sulamith* 7, no. 2 (1833):390; Gotthold Salomon, *Das Familienleben: Drei Predigten gehalten im neuen Israelitischen Tempel zu Hamburg* (Hamburg, 1821); and J. Maier, J. N. Mannheimer, and G. Salomon, ed., *Israelitische Festpredigten und Casualreden* (Stuttgart, 1840). See further David Sorkin, *Transformation of German Jewry*, p. 89, and Marion Kaplan, *The Making of the Jewish Middle Class: Women, Family and Identity in Imperial Germany* (New York, 1991).

29. Hayyim Halbershtam, *Divrei Hayyim* (Lemberg, 1875), no. 29, pp. 96–97.

30. Guenzburg claims that early marriage produced a very high rate of divorce: of every two women, one had had two husbands. See Guenzburg, *Aviezer*, p. 104. His testimony is suspect because of his own unhappy marriage, but when compared with a survey of the biographies of other maskilim, if not the population as a whole, his observation is not far off the mark.

31. See the excellent analysis of this affair in Mintz, *"Banished from Their Father's Table,"* pp. 44–45.

32. Ben-Zion Dinur, ed., *Mikhtavei Avraham Mapu* (Jerusalem, 1970), October 29, 1860, p. 133.

33. For Zweifel's biography, see Klausner, *Historiya she ha-Sifrut ha-Ivrit*, 6:14. The poem appeared in *Makhbarot le-Sifrut* 1 (September 1941):96–102.

34. Dinur, *Mikhtavei Avraham Mapu*, January 12/26, 1861, p. 138.

35. Ibid., November 7, 1857, p. 23. See further his letters to Shneur Sachs from 1843 (pp. 3–7), which include a "love" poem on friendship.

36. See Brunschwig, *Enlightenment and Romanticism*, pp. 208–213; and George Mosse, "Friendship and Nationhood: About the Promise and Failure of German Nationalism," *Journal of Contemporary History* 17, no. 2 (April 1982):351–67.

37. The memorandum can be found in Adam Hacohen Lebensohn, *Kol Shirei Adam* (Vilna, 1895), 3:68–70.

38. See above, Chapter 6, n. 22.

39. (Warsaw, 1905), pt. 3, pp. 22ff. Translated in David Patterson, "Hasidism in the Nineteenth-Century Novel," *Journal of Semitic Studies* 5 (1960):367–68.

40. See above, this chapter, ns. 4 and 5.

41. Joachim Neugroschel, ed. and trans., *The Shtetl* (New York, 1979), pp.

49–172. The novel was probably written in the 1840s, but pressure from Hasidim prevented its publication. It appeared in Leipzig in 1862. Another novel, this time in Hebrew, that makes a similar point is Mendele Mokher Sforim's *Ha-Avot ve-ha-Banim* ("Fathers and Sons"), published in 1868. See *Kol Kitvei Mendele*, vol. 6 (Tel Aviv, 1935).

42. For this analysis, see Dan Miron, *Ben Hazon le-Emet* (Jerusalem, 1979), pp. 177–216.

43. Y. L. Gordon, *Kol Shirei Yehudah Leib Gordon* (Tel Aviv, 1930), 4:4–34. On this poem and Gordon in general, see Michael Stanislawski, *For Whom Do I Toil? Judah Leib Gordon and the Crisis of Russian Jewry* (New York, 1988), pp. 125–28.

44. Lilienblum, *Ketavim* 2:89–93.

45. M. A. Guenzburg, *Kiryat Sefer* (Vilna, 1847), p. 59.

46. A. M. Dik, *Masekhet Aniyut* (n.p., n.d.), p. 26. For a fuller treatment of this theme in Dik and other Yiddish authors, see David Roskies, "Yiddish Popular Literature and the Female Reader," *Journal of Popular Culture* 10, no. 4 (1977):852–58. Roskies quotes a similar passage from Dik's *Royze Finkl* (1874): "Our Jews only consider it shameful for (a Jewish woman) to flirt with a young Jewish fellow, but not with a Christian, because in the latter case, it is a matter of business."

47. Peter Gay has shown how despite the cultivation of these values in nineteenth-century bourgeois culture, the erotic lives of middle-class Europeans were far more sensual within marriage than the so-called Victorian ideal suggests. See Gay, *The Bourgeois Experience: Victoria to Freud*, 2 vols. (New York, 1984 and 1986).

48. The poem was published in a limited edition by G. Kressel under the title *Shir Agavim* (Love Poem) (Tel Aviv, 1977). In his introduction, Kressel brings references to the poem from Shimon Bernfeld, Ephraim Deinard, and Ahad Ha-Am. For the evidence on the Hasidic readership of the poem, see Deinard, *Zikhronot Bat Ami* (St. Louis, 1920), pt. 2, p. 31.

49. *Zeitschrift für Demographie und Statistik der Juden* 8–9 (1906):141. See further Abraham Shtal, "Prostitution among Jews as a Phenomenon Accompanying the Transition from Culture to Culture" (in Hebrew), *Megamot* 24 (1978):202–25. For a contemporary view of prostitution and the breakdown of morals, particularly in the cities of the Pale such as Vilna, see the anonymous article in *Ha-Dor* 1, no. 24 (June 13, 1901):4–6.

50. For the census data of the late nineteenth century, see *Die sozialen Verhältnisse der Juden in Russland* (Veröffentlichungen des Bureaus für Statistik der Juden, Berlin 1906), vol. 2. See further Andrejs Plakans and Joel M. Halpern, "An Historical Perspective on Eighteenth-Century Jewish Family Households in Eastern Europe," in Paul Ritterband, ed., *Modern Jewish Fertility* (Leiden, 1981), pp. 18–32; and Jacques Silber, "Some Demographic Characteristics of the Jewish Population in Russia at the End of the Nineteenth Century," *Jewish Social Studies* 42 (Summer–Fall 1980):277–78.

51. See, for example, Menachem Mendel Schneersohn (1789–1866), *Sefer Tzemach Tzedek* (1870–74; New York, 1945), Even ha-Ezer, no. 34, pp. 89–91, and no. 114, pp. 106–10. The latter case is from 1828. See also Isaac Judah Shmelkes (1828–1906), *Sheelot u-Teshuvot Beit Yitshak* (Przemysl, 1901), pt. 1, no. 1; and Isaac Meir Alter of Gur (d. 1866), *Sheelot u-Teshuvot ha-Rim* (Biozefotz, 1867), Even ha-Ezer no. 21 and no. 26. The latter case is from Warsaw in 1850.

52. Moses Feivish, *Netivot Shalom* (Königsberg, 1858), sec. 1, par. 1.

53. For Feivish's biography, see Jacob Galis, *Encyclopedia Toldot Hakhmei Eretz Yisrael* (Jerusalem, 1977), 2:317–20.

54. Naphtali Zvi Berlin, *He'amek Davar* (Vilna, 1879–80), commentary on Exodus 1:7.

55. See Shaul Stampfer, *Shelosha Yeshivot Litaiot be-Meah ha-19* (Ph.D. diss., Hebrew University, 1981), appendix.

56. Yehiel Michael Epstein, *Arukh ha-Shulhan*, Even ha-Ezer (1905–6), sec. 1, p. 11:3.

57. Solomon Mordecai Schwadron, *Sheelot u-Teshuvot Marasham* (Warsaw, 1902), pt. 1, no. 195.

58. For a similar opinion from early-twentieth-century Hungary, see Isaac Zvi Leibovitch, *Sefer Shulhan Ezer al Dinei Nisuin* (Bergsas, 1932), secs. 1–2.

59. Wengeroff, *Memoiren*, pp. 100ff.

60. Abraham Landau Bornstein, *Avnei Nezer* (Pieterkov, 1916), pt. 1, no. 119.

61. M. Y. Berdichevsky, "In Their Mothers' Wombs" (in Hebrew), *Kitvei M. Y. Bin-Gurion (Berdichevsky)* (Tel Aviv, 1965), 1:102.

62. See David Roskies, "Ayzik-Meyer Dik and the Rise of Yiddish Popular Literature" (Ph.D. diss., Brandeis University, 1975), pp. 48–101.

63. Anonymous, *Ayn Sheyne Historye fun aynem Ekhtikn Rovs Tokhter fun Konstantinopl un fun ayn Rov Zayn Zun fun Brisk* (n.p, n.d.); see further Roskies, "Ayzik-Meyer Dik," pp. 67–68.

64. A similar anonymous story, also featuring a girl who studies in a yeshiva, is *Mordecai un Ester—Eyn Shayne Vunderlikhe Historiye fun ayn Hosen mit ayn Kala* (Warsaw, 1860).

65. For a collection of this Yiddish material, including quotations and extensive bibliography of sources, see Meir Noy, "The Theme of the Canceled Wedding in Yiddish Folksongs: A Bibliography Survey" (in Hebrew), in *Studies in Marriage Customs* (Jerusalem, 1974), especially pp. 61–65.

66. A song based on an incident like this, entitled "Di Geshterte Liebe" (The Interrupted Love), was published in *Makel Noam* in 1873. Other versions of the folk song can be found in Noy, "The Theme of the Canceled Wedding," pp. 63–64.

67. See Roskies, "Yiddish Popular Literature"; idem, "Azik-Meir Dik"; and Dan Miron, *A Traveler Disguised* (New York, 1973), chaps. 1, 2.

68. A. M. Dik, *Der Shidekh on Shadkhonim* (Vilna, 1871).

69. H. D. S. (Ayzik-Meyer Dik), *Mahaze mul Mahaze* (Warsaw, 1861), p. 4.

Quoted in Roskies, "Yiddish Popular Literature," p. 853. For another Haskalah attack on popular literature and theater for encouraging promiscuity, see the anonymous article in *Ha-Dor* 1, no. 24 (June 13, 1901):4–6.

70. For the examples of such literary sources, see Knaani, *Ha-Batim She-Hayu*, pp. 43, 62–64.

71. "The Raven Flies" (in Hebrew), in Micha Yosef Bin-Gorion (Berdichevsky), *Romanim Ketzarim* (Jerusalem, 1971), p. 87.

72. See also Mendele's letter to Shalom Aleichem, quoted in the introduction to the latter's *Stempenyu* (New York, 1900; English translation, New York, 1913): "I doubt if there is anything that is romantic in the life of our people."

73. Berdichevsky's *Mi-Mekor Yisrael* remains one of the best collections of Jewish folktales, and it served as one of our main sources for medieval popular culture in Chapter 3.

74. *Kitvei M. Y. Bin-Gurion (Berdichevsky)* 1:101–2.

75. S. An-ski, *Der Dybbuk*, in *Di Yidishe Drame fun 20sten Yorhundert* (New York, 1977), p. 14.

76. Ibid., p. 44.

77. See Mintz, "*Banished from Their Fathers' Tables*," pts. 2, 3; and Gershon Shaked, *Ha-Siporet ha-Ivrit: 1880–1970*, vol. 1 (Tel Aviv, 1977).

78. Baruch Kurzweil, *Sifrutenu ha-Hadashah: Hemshekh o-Mahapekhah?* (Tel Aviv, 1971), pp. 234ff.

79. *Romanim Ketzarim*, p. 82. The translation is from Mintz, "*Banished from Their Fathers' Tables*," p. 103.

80. See, for example, Berdichevsky's "Two Camps," Agnon's story "The Lady and the Peddler" (1943), and David Vogel's *Married Life* (Tel Aviv, 1920–30; English translation, New York, 1988). Other such sadomasochistic themes in which the woman is Jewish can be found in Berdichevsky's "The Master of the Story" and Agnon's posthumous novel, *Shira*. It is fascinating that the literary namesake of masochism, Leopold von Sacher-Masoch, was himself a philo-Semite who advocated a Haskalah program for the Jews. See David Biale, "Masochism and Philosemitism: The Strange Case of Leopold von Sacher-Masoch," *Journal of Contemporary History* 17 (Spring 1982): 305–24.

81. See Robert Stoller, *Perversion* (New York, 1975), for one theory of sadomasochism and bibliography.

82. For a recent treatment of female Hebrew poets, see Dan Miron, *Imahot Miyasdot, Ahayot Horgot* (Tel Aviv, 1991); and Michael Gluzman, "The Exclusion of Women from Hebrew Literary History," *Prooftexts* 11 (1991):259–78.

83. For biographical information and analysis of the stories, see Nurit Govrin, *Ha-Mahatzit ha-Rishonah: Dvora Baron—Hayyeiha u-Yetzirotah* (Jerusalem, 1988).

84. See, for example, Dvorah Baron, "A Quarreling Couple" (in Hebrew), in Govrin, *Ha-Mahatzit ha-Rishonah*, pp. 374–76, first published 1905.

85. Dvorah Baron "Fedka" (in Hebrew), in Govrin, *Ha-Mahatzit ha-Rishonah*, pp. 442–49, first published in 1909.

86. Dvorah Baron, "Liska" (in Hebrew), in Govrin, *Ha-Mahatzit ha-Rishonah*, pp. 543–50, first published in 1911. Use of a dog as a symbol of projection can also be found in S. Y. Agnon's *Just Yesterday*.

87. One of the most popular novels among German Jews at the beginning of the twentieth century was Georg Hermann's *Jettchen Gebert* (1906), in which a virtuous Jewish daughter falls in love with a déclassé Christian.

88. Hayyim Nachman Bialik, "Behind the Fence" (in Hebrew), *Kol Kitvei H. N. Bialik*, 6th ed. (Tel Aviv, 1945), pp. 112–29. On Bialik as a prose writer, see Shaked, *Ha-Siporet ha-Ivrit*, pp. 278–86.

89. For a discussion of the concept of "Bialik's generation," see Dan Miron, *Bodedim be-Moadam* (Tel Aviv, 1987), especially pt. 2.

90. Bialik's clearest attack against Jewish passivity is in his bitter poem written in the wake of the Kishinev pogroms, "In the City of Slaughter."

91. Bialik, "Scroll of Fire" (in Hebrew), *Kol Kitvei Bialik* (Tel Aviv, 1945), pp. 88–94. The poem was written in the summer of 1905.

92. Yonatan Ratosh suggested this possibility in his reading of the line that describes the two hundred girls with Christian imagery as "wearing crowns of thorns and on their faces were frozen the sufferings of the Messiah." Moreover, the goddess that protects the girls is Venus (the morning star), suggesting pagan associations in contrast to the Israelite "God of vengeance," who is implicated in the destruction of the Temple. See Ratosh, "Bialik's Poem of Foreign Love" (in Hebrew), in Gershon Shaked, ed., *Bialik* (Jerusalem, 1974), pp. 261–65.

93. Original and translation in T. Carmi, ed., *The Penguin Book of Hebrew Verse* (New York, 1981), pp. 513–14.

94. Bialik, "The Hungry Eyes" (in Hebrew), *Kol Kitvei Bialik*, p. 30.

95. Bialik, "Place Me under Your Wing" (in Hebrew), in *Kol Kitvei Bialik*, p. 41.

CHAPTER 8:
Zionism as an Erotic Revolution

1. Magnus Hirschfeld, *Men and Women: The World Journey of a Sexologist*, trans. (New York, 1935), pp. 275–76. See also Charlotte Wolf, *Magnus Hirschfeld: A Portrait of a Pioneer in Sexology* (London, 1986), p. 358. Rumors of free love in the kibbutzim were confirmed in an August 1990 interview the author did with Eliezer Sklartz, a founder of Kibbutz Bet Alfa, where Hirschfeld lectured on his tour. Sklartz reported that when he visited his family in Berlin in the mid-1920s, he was confronted with questions about free love among the pioneers, stories that he rejected as pure fancy.

2. See Vera S. Dunham, "Sex: From Free Love to Puritanism," in A. Inke-

les and K. Geiger, eds., *Soviet Society* (Boston, 1961), pp. 540–46.

3. See S. Diamond, "Kibbutz and Shtetl," *Social Problems* 5 (1957): 71–99.

4. See Carl Schorske, *Fin-de-Siècle Vienna* (New York, 1981), p. 11.

5. The pathological family relations in many of Kafka's stories may well be fictional refractions of his own self-perception. See Robert Alter, "Literary Refractions of the Jewish Family," in David Kraemer, ed., *The Jewish Family* (New York, 1989), pp. 228–33.

6. See Robert A. Nye, "Degeneration and the Medical Model of Cultural Crisis in the French Belle Epoque" and Anson Rabinbach, "The Body without Fatigue: A Nineteenth-Century Utopia," in Seymour Drescher, David Sabean, and Allan Sharlin, eds., *Political Symbolism in Modern Europe: Essays in Honor of George L. Mosse* (New Brunswick, 1982), pp. 19–62. See also George Mosse, *Nationalism and Sexuality* (New York, 1985), pp. 48–65.

7. On neurasthenia, see Anson Rabinbach, *The Human Motor: Energy, Fatigue and the Origins of Modernity* (New York, 1990), chap. 6.

8. Max Nordau, "Muskeljudentum," in *Jüdische Turnzeitung* (June 1900): 10–11; and idem, "Was bedeutet Turnen für uns Juden?" (July 1902): 109–12.

9. I owe this felicitous phrase to George Mosse, in Nordau, *Degeneration*, introduction, p. xxvii.

10. See, for example, "Jüdische Erziehungsprobleme," *Jüdische Turnzeitung* 2, no. 1 (January 1901): 5–8; and "Diskussionen über die Frage der körperlichen Hebung der Juden," *Jüdische Turnzeitung* 3, no. 1 (January 1902): 1–5.

11. Michael Berkowitz, "'Mind, Muscle and Men': The Imagination of a Zionist National Culture for the Jews of Central and Western Europe, 1897–1914" (Ph.D. diss., University of Wisconsin, 1989), pp. 219–20.

12. See Max Nordau, *Degeneration*, 1895 English translation of 2d ed., introduction by George Mosse (New York, 1968), pp. 167–68. Man marries out of love, but the marriage is held fast out of "unsexual friendship" and "considerations of duty towards children and State." Around the same time that he wrote *Degeneration*, Nordau also penned a play called *The Right to Love*, aimed at the "degenerate" Ibsen. In it he gives dramatic expression to these conventional bourgeois platitudes. Nordau's bourgeois doctrine of marriage was known to the Zionists of the Second Aliyah. See Y. H. Brenner, *Breakdown and Bereavement*, trans. Hillel Halkin (Ithaca, N.Y.: 1971), p. 158.

13. Rafael Becker, *Die jüdische Nervosität: Ihre Art, Enstehung und Bekämpfung* (Zurich, 1918); and idem, *Die Nervosität bei den Juden: Ein Beitrag zur Rassenpsychiatrie für Ärzte und gebildete Laien* (Zurich, 1919). On these essays, see Sander L. Gilman, *Difference and Pathology: Stereotypes of Sexuality, Race and Madness* (Ithaca, N.Y., 1985), pp. 159–61.

14. Becker, *Jüdische Nervosität*, pp. 26–27.

15. See, for example, Max Besser, "Der Einfluss der ökonomischen Stellung der deutschen Juden auf ihre physische Beschaffenheit," in *Körperliche Renaissance der Juden* (Berlin, 1909), pp. 6–13. Besser argues that lack of

physical work by Jews and urban conditions cause a diminution of marital fertility and a decrease in Jewish population. One of the oft-quoted studies was by Felix Theilhaber, *Der Untergang der deutschen Juden* (Munich, 1911).

16. A dissenting opinion to this common condemnation of intermarriage was offered by Max Marcuse, *Über die Fruchtbarkeit der christlich-jüdischen Mischehe* (Bonn, 1920). Marcuse argued that in principle intermarriage could actually contribute to Jewish population growth. Marcuse's statistical analysis concealed a polemical attempt to justify intermarriage.

17. Franz Rosenzweig, *The Star of Redemption,* trans. William Hallo (Boston, 1971), pp. 298, 326, 341–42.

18. Hans Goslar, *Die Sexualethik der jüdischen Wiedergeburt. Ein Wort an unsere Jugend* (Berlin, 1919). I am grateful to Professor Paul Mendes-Flohr for bringing this important work to my attention. Like others writing on this subject, Goslar was influenced by sexologists like Max Marcuse and Iwan Bloch, as well as Sigmund Freud, in his effort to ground the erotic ideology of his Zionism on ostensibly scientific premises.

19. K. B., "Von der Familie," *Jerubbaal* 1 (1918–19): 315–16.

20. Goslar, *Die Sexualethik,* pp. 5, 10.

21. Martin Buber, "Das Zion der jüdischen Frau," *Die jüdische Bewegung* (Berlin, 1920), pp. 28–38.

22. Marie Popper, "Jüdische Mädchen," *Jerubbaal* 1 (1918): 391–96.

23. Abraham Shlonsky, *Shirim* (Tel Aviv, 1961), 1:163–65.

24. See, for example, also from the 1920s, Uri Zvi Greenberg, "The Sixth Millennium" (*Ha-Elef ha-Shishi*), in *Emah Gdolah ve-Yareah* (Tel Aviv, 1925), p. 14.

25. Shlonsky, "Desert Wind" (*Sharav*), in *Shirim,* p. 309. See also "Soil" (*Adamah*), in *Shirim,* p. 176.

26. Uri Zvi Greenberg, "The Blood and the Flesh" (*Ha-Dam ve-ha-Basar*), in *Emah,* p. 16. The term *motherland* (*moledet*) means literally the place that gives birth.

27. A. D. Gordon, *Ha-Umma ve-ha-Avodah* (Tel Aviv, 1962), pp. 475–76. See also his letter to Shlomo Tzemach on the problem of celibacy among the hired workers, in Shmuel Dayan, *Im Avot ha-Hityashvut* (Givatayim, 1967).

28. On Shatz, see Menachen Poznansky, in Zvi Shatz, *Al Gevul ha-Demamah,* ed. Muki Tsur (Tel Aviv, 1990), pp. 13–22; and Muki Tsur, *Aviv Mukdam: Zvi Shatz ve-ha-Kevutzah ha-Intimit* (Tel Aviv, 1984).

29. For a history of Hashomer ha-Tzair, see Elkana Margalit, *Hashomer ha-Tzair: Mi-Edat Neurim le-Marxism Mahapkhani (1913–1936)* (Tel Aviv, 1971).

30. On Blüher's influence on the Zionist youth movements, see Margalit, *Hashomer ha-Tzair,* p. 32; Shlomo Rekhev, *Hashomer ha-Tzair: Mi-Tenuat ha-Noar le-Kibbutz ha-Artzi* (Tel Aviv, 1952–53), pp. 54ff.; and Muki Tsur, "Introduction," *Kehilyateinu* (Jerusalem, 1988), p. 11. Blüher himself was an anti-Semite, but this apparently did not diminish the impact of his ideas.

31. *Kehilyateinu,* p. 276.

32. Meir Yaari, "Within the Ferment" (in Hebrew), in *Kehilyateinu,* p. 267.

33. Ibid., p. 269.

34. Yaari, *Be-Derekh Arukah* (Merhaviyah, 1947), p. 11.

35. *Kehilyateinu,* p. 276.

36. Ibid., pp. 28–31.

37. Quoted in Muki Tsur, Ta'ir Zevulun, and Hanina Porat, eds., *Kan al Penei ha-Adamah* (Tel Aviv, 1981), p. 70.

38. Ibid., p. 71.

39. See Nurit Govrin, *Ha-Mahatzit ha-Rishonah: Dvorah Baron-Hayyeiha u-Yetzirotah* (Jerusalem, 1988).

40. Ada Fishman, "The Question of the Female Worker," *Ha-Poel ha-Tzair* 15, no. 1–2 (November 11, 1921): 12–14. For a study of the question of women and labor in the Zionist movement, although with a particular focus on the cities, see Deborah Bernstein, *The Struggle for Equality: Urban Women Workers in Prestate Israeli Society* (New York, 1987).

41. Rachel Katznelson-Shazar, *Adam Kemo Shehu* (Tel Aviv, 1989), pp. 64–65. The entry is from around 1910, when she was still in St. Petersburg. See further Dan Miron, *Imahot Miyasdot, Ahayot Horgot* (Tel Aviv, 1991), pp. 249–71.

42. On *Kehilyateinu,* see Aviva Opaz, "The Symbolic World of the Collection 'Kehilyateinu' (in Hebrew), *Kathedra* 59 (March 1991): 126–41. I thank Ehud Luz for this reference.

43. *Yamim ve-Leilot* (Jerusalem, 1926), p. 197.

44. See George Mosse, *The Crisis of German Ideology* (New York, 1964) and idem, "The Influence of the Volkish Idea on German Jewry," in Mosse, *Germans and Jews* (New York, 1970), pp. 77–115. Martin Buber also used the language of "blood and soil" (*Blut und Boden*) in his prewar writings. It is striking how even a non-Zionist like Franz Rosenzweig resorted to such language: the term *blood community* is central in his vocabulary of Judaism in *The Star of Redemption.*

45. *Kehilyateinu,* p. 179.

46. Ibid., p. 40.

47. Ibid.

48. Genesis 38. For a discussion of this story, see Chapter 1.

49. Genesis 19: 30–38.

50. "Ha-Melitzah," *Hedim* 2 (1923). I thank Chana Kronfeld for providing me with this text from an anthology put together by Benjamin Hrushovsky, *Yorshei ha-Simbolism ba-Shirah* (Tel Aviv University, 1973), pp. 154–55.

51. Abraham Isaac Kook, *Orot,* 2nd. ed. (Jerusalem, 1950), "Orot ha-Tehiyah," par. 33. Translated in Arthur Hertzberg, ed., *The Zionist Idea* (New York, 1971), p. 431.

52. See Shlomo Avineri, "Jabotinsky: Integralist Nationalism and the Illusion of Power" in Avineri, *The Making of Modern Zionism* (New York, 1981), pp. 159–86.

53. Arthur Koestler, *Thieves in the Night* (London, 1946). On Koestler, see Bernard Avishai, "Koestler and the Zionist Revolution," *Salmagundi* 87 (Summer 1990): 234–59. For Avishai's analysis of the sexual component of *Thieves*, see pp. 252–53.

54. David Horowitz, *Ha-Etmol Sheli* (Jerusalem, 1970), p. 106.

55. "Semalim Telushim," first published in *Hedim* (1923); reprinted in Yaari, *Be-Derekh Arukah*.

56. Yaari, *Be-Derekh Arukah*, pp. 29–30.

57. See Gordon, "An Irrational Solution" in *Ha-Umma ve-ha-Avodah*, p. 99.

58. *Kan al-Penei ha-Adamah*, p. 71.

59. Ibid.

60. See the diary of Rivka Mahnimit, *Haverot be-Kibbutz* (Ein Harod, 1943), 1: 35–48, entries from 1911 to 1917. She speaks much more about her family of origin than about her husband, whom she mentions only in passing. Zvi Shatz captured this homesickness in "Batya," *Al Gevul ha-Demamah*, p. 39.

61. Yaari, *Be-Derekh Arukah*, p. 13.

62. *Kehilyateinu*, pp. 38–39.

63. Katznelson-Shazar, *Adam Kemo Shehu*, p. 61.

64. Rivka Mahnimit, diary entry for March 4, 1912, in *Haverot be-Kibbutz*, p. 40.

65. Shatz, "Batya," *Al Gevul ha-Demamah*, pp. 50–53.

66. I am grateful to the archivists at Kibbutz Bet Alfa for relating some of these stories to me.

67. For an analysis of relations between men and women in Bet Alfa, see Melford Spiro, *Kibbutz: Venture in Utopia*, 2d ed. (Cambridge, Mass., 1970), pp. 110–20.

68. Mahnimit, *Haverot be-Kibbutz*, pp. 360–63.

69. Arthur Koestler, *Arrow in the Blue* (New York, 1952), p. 141.

70. Interview with Eliezer Sklartz, Kibbutz Bet Alfa, August 1990. I also wish to thank Melford Spiro, whose intimate knowledge of Bet Alfa is reflected in his several books on the kibbutz, for discussing this question with me.

71. The illustrations are by Shraga Weill. The booklet is undated but is probably from the late 1930s.

72. See Melford Spiro, *Children of the Kibbutz*, 2d ed. (Cambridge, Mass., 1975); and Yonina Talmon-Garber, *Yahid ve-Hevrah ba-Kibbutz* (Jerusalem, 1970). For an excellent critique of the psychoanalytic assumptions of this philosophy, see Immanuel Berman, "Communal Education in the Kibbutz: The Attraction and Dangers of Psychoanalytic Utopia" (in Hebrew), *Ha-Hinukh ha-Mishutaf* 53 (1990): 64–77.

73. See Horowitz, *Ha-Etmol Sheli*, p. 107.

74. See, for example, the set of principles laid out by a committee headed by Golan, "Principles of Sex Education in the Kibbutz Artzi of Ha-Shomer ha-Tzair" (in Hebrew), *Ha-Hinukh ha-Mishutaf* 1 (1937): 28–32; and idem, "On the Means for Communal Education" (in Hebrew), *Ofakim* 3, no. 4

(1946): 51–52. See also *Ha-Hinukh ha-Shomri* (Warsaw, 1939), pp. 72–75.

75. This analysis owes much to Michel Foucault in his *History of Sexuality*, vol. 1, *An Introduction*, trans. Robert Hurley (New York, 1978).

76. Quoted in Tsur, Zevulun, Porat, *Kan al-Penei ha-Adamah*, p. 70.

77. Ibid., p. 177.

78. Katznelson-Shazar, *Adam Kemo Shehu*, 153. See also p. 161, also written in 1918: "We are people of the commune and not people with families."

79. Quoted in Tsur, *Le-Lo Kutonet Passim*, p. 36.

80. Shatz, "Be-Lo Niv," *Al Gevul ha-Demamah*, p. 34. In his essay on the intimate commune, Shatz refers explicitly to the problem of suicide among his comrades. See ibid., p. 95.

81. Muki Tsur relates the story in *Aviv Mukdam*, p. 87.

82. The story is well told by Anita Shapira, *Berl: The Biography of a Socialist Zionist*, trans. Haya Galai (Cambridge, 1984), pp. 65–67, 91–97.

83. Ibid., p. 66.

84. Katznelson-Shazar, *Adam Kemo Shehu*, pp. 16, 158. Although Katznelson-Shazar is quite reticent in her memoir about what went on between her and Berl, it is clear that the relations between these old friends had become quite romantic by about 1918.

85. Shapira recounts the deterioration of Berl's relationship with Leah and his affair in the last years of his life with a younger woman, Sara Zayit. See Shapira, *Berl*, pp. 305–6.

86. See *Rahel: Shirim, Mikhtavim, Reshimot, Korot Hayyeha*, ed. Uri Milstein (Tel Aviv, 1985), pp. 46–47. See further Miron, *Imahot Miyasdot*, pp. 151–60.

87. The Shazar connection is fairly well attested from the 1920s when he was already married to Rachel Katznelson. It seems less likely that an actual affair took place between Rachel Blubstein and A. D. Gordon, who was already in his fifties when they met. But his letters to her bear the unmistakable mark of a man deeply infatuated. See Gordon, *Mikhtavim* (Jerusalem, 1954), pp. 53–62. The letters are from 1913–14. Hannan Hever reported the liaison with Uri Zvi Greenberg. On Michael Bernstein, see Binyamin Hakhlili, ed., *Le-kha ve-Alekha: Ahavat Rahel ve-Michael* (Tel Aviv, 1987).

88. Quoted in Tsur, *Le-Lo Kutonet Passim*, p. 60.

89. See, for example, Agnon's great novel of the Second Aliyah, *Just Yesterday*, and stories like "In the Heart of the Seas" and "The Hill of Sand."

90. For a debunking of this myth by a female veteran of the Palmach, see Netivah Ben Yehuda, *1948: Ben ha-Sefirot* (Jerusalem, 1981), p. 105.

91. See the interviews with Reuven Levin, Oral History Division, Institute for Contemporary Jewry, Hebrew University 45/9, p. 43; with Yaakov Raz, 45/3, p. 59; with Hadassah Kimelman, 45/5, p. 9; and with Shimon Shnipper, 45/1, p. 47.

92. Meir Shalev, *Roman Russi* (Tel Aviv, 1988), p. 5.

93. This conflict was captured beautifully in *Sallah Shabbati*, a film from

the 1960s that relates the tribulations of a family of Oriental Jewish immi-grants and their relations to the neighboring kibbutz.

## CHAPTER 9:
## Sexual Stereotypes in American Jewish Culture

1. A recent, partial treatment of this theme is Paul Breines, *Tough Jews* (New York, 1990).

2. A group of Israeli writers in the 1950s identified as the Canaanites also sought to replace Jewish identity with a new Israeli identity drawn in part from the historical Canaanites. Whether or not Uris knew of this literary movement, the name Ari Ben Canaan accurately captured a trend in Israeli culture.

3. For the approach to the material of this chapter, I am particularly in-debted to the work of Riv-Ellen Prell on gender stereotypes in American Jew-ish culture. See Prell, "Rage and Representation: Jewish Gender Stereotypes in American Culture," in Faye Ginsburg and Anna Tsing, eds., *Uncertain Terms: Negotiating Gender in American Culture* (Boston, 1990), pp. 248–68; idem, "Why Jewish Princesses Don't Sweat: Desire and Consumption in Post-war American Jewish Culture," in Howard Eilberg-Schwartz, ed., *People of the Body: Jews and Judaism from an Embodied Perspective* (Albany, N.Y., 1992); and idem, *Fighting to Become American: Jewish Women and Men in Conflict in the Twentieth Century* (New York, forthcoming).

4. See also Erica Jong, *Any Woman's Blues: A Novel of Obsession* (New York, 1990), p. 269, in which Jong's protagonist, Leila Sand, visits a domina-trix and observes two yarmulka-clad yeshiva students in the waiting room: traditional Jewish men, we are led to believe, are masochists. The extent to which this extreme stereotype of the Jew as masochist may have penetrated American culture in general is attested by Xaviera Hollander in her memoir as a New York madam in which she claims that Orthodox Jewish men often sought to play out sadomasochistic fantasies. See Hollander, *The Happy Hooker* (New York, 1972).

5. See Sander L. Gilman, *Difference and Pathology: Stereotypes of Sexuality, Race and Madness* (Ithaca, N.Y., 1985), pp. 175–90; Elliot Oring, *The Jokes of Sigmund Freud: A Study in Humor and Jewish Identity* (Philadelphia, 1984); and William Novak and Moshe Waldocks, eds., *The Big Book of Jewish Humor* (New York, 1981).

6. See J. Allen, *500 Great Jewish Jokes* (New York, 1990), pp. 13–21; S. W. Schneider, "In a *Coma!* I Thought She Was *Jewish:* Some Truths and Some Speculations about Jewish Women and Sex," *Lilith* (1977): 5–8; Esther Fuchs, "Humor and Sexism: The Case of the Jewish Joke," *Jewish Humor* (1986), pp. 111–22; and Riv-Ellen Prell, "Why Jewish Princesses Don't Sweat." I am particularly indebted to Prell's analysis.

7. David Kirshenbaum, *Mixed Marriage and the Jewish Future* (New York, 1958), pp. 69–75.

8. See Robert Jancu, "Jackie Mason's World According to Hollywood," *Judaism* 40 (Spring 1991): 134–47; and Patricia Erens, *The Jew in American Cinema* (Bloomington, Ind., 1984). Jewish women are either left out of the picture entirely, presumably to remain unwed, or are depicted in the derogatory JAP images already described.

9. On the *belle juive* tradition in non-Jewish literature, see Livia Bitton-Jackson, *Madonna or Courtesan? The Jewish Woman in Christian Literature* (New York, 1982).

10. See Neal Gabler, *An Empire of Their Own: How the Jews Invented Hollywood* (New York, 1989).

11. See Charles Silberman, *A Certain People: American Jews and Their Lives Today* (New York, 1985).

12. This is Peter Gardella's persuasive thesis in *Innocent Ecstasy: How Christianity Gave America an Ethic of Sexual Pleasure* (New York and Oxford, 1985). I thank Daniel Boyarin for suggesting a comparison between Gardella's Christians and the Jewish theologians.

13. Margaret Sanger, *Happiness in Marriage* (New York, 1939), p. 141, quoted in Gardella, *Innocent Ecstasy*, p. 134.

14. Quoted in Gardella, *Innocent Ecstasy*, p. 4.

15. Marabel Morgan, *The Total Woman* (Old Tappan, N.J., 1975), p. 141.

16. See, for example, Kirshenbaum, *Mixed Marriage and the Jewish Future*. For two works that look more objectively at the consequences of intermarriage, see Egon Mayer, *Love and Tradition: Marriage between Jews and Christians* (New York, 1985); and Silberman, *A Certain People*.

17. Robert Gordis, *Love and Sex: A Modern Jewish Perspective* (New York, 1978), p. 240.

18. Ibid.

19. A much more scholarly work by another Conservative rabbi is David Feldman, *Marital Relations, Birth Control and Abortion in Jewish Law* (New York, 1968). Like Gordis, Feldman has constructed his book as a polemic against Christianity. Feldman was also responding to the debate over birth control and abortion; his book came out between the *Griswold v. Connecticut* decision of 1966, making birth control a constitutional right, and the *Roe v. Wade* decision of 1973, legalizing abortion. The burden of his argument from the Jewish tradition tends to support both birth control and abortion (albeit with many qualifications); it thus implicitly shows that Judaism is more modern and in tune with contemporary American trends than is Christianity.

20. Norman Lamm, *A Hedge of Roses: Jewish Insights into Marriage and Married Life*, 1st ed. (New York, 1966), 5th ed. (New York, 1977). The number of editions, plus translations into Spanish, Portuguese, and Hebrew, suggests the popularity of the treatise, probably particularly among Orthodox Jews. Lamm's little book is the basic source for a larger work by his brother, Maurice Lamm, *The Jewish Way in Love and Marriage* (New York, 1980).

21. Lamm, *Hedge of Roses*, p. 19.

22. Ibid., pp. 31–32.

23. Ibid., pp. 63–65.

24. Ibid., p. 90. Eugene Borowitz, a leading Reform theologian, embraces no less a messianic goal with respect to sexual ethics. As opposed to Lamm, Borowitz does not stake his claim on the commandments of Jewish law but instead constructs an argument based on the Kantian principle of autonomy. He adopts a set of ethical principles that lead him to reject the doctrines of a healthy orgasm, mutual consent, and love in favor of marriage as the most legitimate locus for sexual relations. Borowitz's conclusion is therefore no less conservative than Gordis's or Lamm's, although he arrives at it by a very different route, and he remains tolerant of other approaches. See Borowitz, *Choosing a Sex Ethic: A Jewish Inquiry* (New York, 1969).

25. See Samuel C. Heilman and Steven M. Cohen, *Cosmopolitans and Parochials: Modern Orthodox Jews in America* (Chicago, 1989), pp. 158, 167, 173–78. The division of the self-declared Orthodox Jews into "traditionalists," "centrists," and "nominalists" is explained in terms of ritual practice on pp. 40–56. The group of traditionalists does not include Hasidic Jews or other so-called *haredim* (ultra-Orthodox). Sixty-four percent of the most Orthodox Jews surveyed reported having seen an R- or X-rated movie in the previous year; 72 percent of "centrist" Orthodox and 57 percent of "nominal" Orthodox had as well. While 100 percent of young (ages 18–35) "traditional" Orthodox Jews disapprove of sex between casual acquaintances, only 81 percent of "centrist" and 55 percent of "nominal" Orthodox Jews in the same age bracket would agree.

26. Moshe Feinstein, *Iggrot Moshe,* Even ha-Ezer (New York, 1961), 3:28, translated in Rachel Biale, *Women and Jewish Law* (New York, 1984), p. 134. Feinstein bases himself on Jonah Landsofer, the eighteenth-century authority, who was responding to the changes in sexual mores of his own day.

27. Daniel Boyarin reported to me a case of a legal authority who permitted an Orthodox man plagued by impotence to read *Playboy* as a way of stimulating him to fulfill his sexual obligations to his wife, a striking case of how the importance of sexual performance in Jewish law can even permit resort to otherwise negative forms of secular, popular culture.

28. See especially the writings of Rachel Adler, Lynn Gottleib, and Susannah Heschel, all of which can be found in Heschel, *On Being a Jewish Feminist* (New York, 1983).

29. Judith Plaskow, *Standing Again at Sinai: Judaism from a Feminist Perspective* (San Francisco, 1990), chap. 5.

30. Ibid., p. 210.

31. See Susan Weidman Schneider, *Jewish and Female: Choices and Changes in Our Lives Today* (New York, 1984), esp. chap. 5; and Tamar Frankiel, *The Voice of Sarah: Feminine Spirituality and Traditional Judaism* (San Francisco, 1990).

32. Lenny Bruce, *How to Talk Dirty and Influence People* (Chicago, 1963), p. 5.

33. Ibid.

34. *The Essential Lenny Bruce*, ed. John Cohen (New York, 1967), pp. 32–33.

35. Bruce, *How to Talk Dirty*, p. 71.

36. Ibid., p. 5.

37. See Arnold Davidson, *Mordecai Richler* (New York, 1983), pp. 81–105.

38. Mordecai Richler, *The Apprenticeship of Duddy Kravitz* (Boston, 1959).

39. See particularly *St. Urbain's Horsemen* (New York, 1971) and *Joshua, Then and Now* (New York, 1980).

40. Abraham Cahan, *The Rise of David Levinsky* (New York, 1917).

41. A selection of these letters has been published in English by Isaac Metzker, ed., *A Bintel Brief: Sixty Years of Letters from the Lower East Side to the Jewish Daily Forward* (New York, 1971).

42. Ibid., p. 50 (1906).

43. Ibid., pp. 44–45 (1906).

44. The flavor of this culture has been beautifully captured by Irving Howe, *World of Our Fathers* (New York, 1976).

45. Henry Roth, *Call It Sleep* (New York, 1962). The relevant scene is chapter 14. See also pp. 52–55; and Alfred Kazin, "The Art of 'Call It Sleep,'" *New York Review of Books* (October 10, 1991):15–18.

46. Bernard Malamud, *The Assistant* (New York, 1957), p. 168.

47. Ibid., p. 246.

48. E. L. Doctorow, *The Book of Daniel* (New York, 1971), p. 53.

49. See especially Emma Goldman, "Marriage and Love," in Goldman, *Anarchism and Other Essays* (New York, 1969), pp. 227–40; and her autobiography, *Living My Life* (New York, 1970). On her extraordinary erotic relationship to Ben Reiter, see Alice Wexler, *Emma Goldman: An Intimate Life* (New York, 1984). See also Candace Falk, *Love, Anarchy and Emma Goldman* (New York, 1984).

50. Mark Zborowski and Elizabeth Herzog, *Life Is with People* (New York, 1952), pp. 269–90. Some of the same idealization can be seen in the film *Fiddler on the Roof*, which softened much of the satirical sting of the original Shalom Aleichem "Tevye" stories.

51. Isaac Bashevis Singer, *The Collected Stories* (New York, 1982), pp. 94–131.

52. Ibid., p. 98.

53. Ibid., pp. 3–14

54. Ibid., pp. 149–69.

55. Singer, *The Family Moskat*, trans. A. H. Gross (New York, 1950).

56. Singer, *Enemies, A Love Story* (New York, 1972).

57. JAP jokes are not, however, exclusively the products of men. The Jewish comedian Joan Rivers, on her record *What Becomes a Semi Legend Most?*, offers some of the more offensive examples. See Prell, "Why Jewish Princesses Don't Sweat."

58. Adrienne Rich, "If Not with Others, How?" in Rich, *Blood, Bread and Poetry* (New York, 1986), p. 203. See also idem, "Split at the Root" in Evelyn Torton Beck, ed., *Nice Jewish Girls: A Lesbian Anthology* (New York, 1982), pp. 67–84.

59. Irena Klepfisz, "Resisting and Surviving in America," in Beck, *Nice Jewish Girls*, p. 106.

60. Erica Jong, *Fear of Flying* (New York, 1973), p. 30.

61. Jong, *Any Woman's Blues* (New York, 1990), p. 32.

62. Ibid., p. 59.

63. Marge Piercy, *He, She and It* (New York, 1991).

64. Adrienne Rich, "Stepmother Tongues," *Tikkun* (September–October 1990):36.

# BIBLIOGRAPHY OF SELECTED SECONDARY WORKS

Adler, Elaine J. "The Background for the Metaphor of Covenant as Marriage in the Hebrew Bible." Ph.D. diss., University of California, 1989.

Agus, Irving. *The Heroic Age of Franco-German Jewry.* New York, 1969.

——. *Urban Civilization in Pre-Crusade Europe.* 2 vols. New York, 1965.

Alexander, Tamar. "The Formation of Hasidic-Ashkenazic Stories: The Folktale in Its Theological Context" (in Hebrew). *Studies in Aggada and Jewish Folklore* 7 (1983): 197–206.

Allony, Nehemiah. "The Zevi in the Hebrew Poetry of Spain" (in Hebrew). *Sefarad* 23 (1963): 311–21.

Alter, Robert. *The Art of Biblical Narrative.* New York, 1981.

Anderson, Gary. "Celibacy or Consummation in the Garden? Reflections on Early Jewish and Christian Interpretations of the Garden of Eden." *Harvard Theological Review* 82 (1989): 121–48.

Assis, Yom Tov. "Sexual Behaviour in Mediaeval Hispano-Jewish Society." In Ada Rapoport-Albert and Steven J. Zipperstein, eds., *Jewish History: Essays in Honour of Chimen Abramsky.* London, 1988.

Avishai, Bernard. "Koestler and the Zionist Revolution." *Salmagundi* 87 (Summer 1990): 234–59.

Baer, F. Y. "The Historical Background of the 'Raaya Meheimna'" (Hebrew). *Zion*, n.s. 5, no. 1 (1939): 1–44.

——. *A History of the Jews in Christian Spain.* 2 vols. Philadelphia, 1966.

——. "Todros ben Judah Halevi and His Time" (in Hebrew). *Zion* 2 (1937): 12–55.

Baer, Richard. *Philo's Use of the Categories Male and Female.* Leiden, 1970.

Bakan, David. *Sigmund Freud and the Jewish Mystical Tradition.* New York, 1958.

Bal, Mieke. *Death and Dissymmetry.* Chicago, 1988.

———. *Lethal Love: Feminist Literary Readings of Biblical Love Stories.* Bloomington, Ind., 1987.

Balaban, Meir. *Le-Toldot ha-Tenuah ha-Frankit.* Tel Aviv, 1934.

Beattie, D. R. G. "The Book of Ruth as Evidence for Israelite Legal Practice." *Vetus Testamentum* 24 (1974): 251–67.

Berger, David. *The Jewish-Christian Debate in the High Middle Ages: A Critical Edition of the Nizzahon Vetus.* Philadelphia, 1979.

Berkowitz, Michael. "'Mind, Muscle and Men': The Imagination of a Zionist National Culture for the Jews of Central and Western Europe, 1897–1914." Ph.D. diss., University of Wisconsin, 1989.

Berman, Immanuel. "Communal Education in the Kibbutz: The Attraction and Dangers of Psychoanalystic Utopia" (in Hebrew). *Ha-Hinukh ha-Mishutaf* (1990): 64–77.

Bernstein, Deborah. *The Struggle for Equality: Urban Women Workers in Prestate Israeli Society.* New York, 1987.

Biale, David. "The God with Breasts: El Shaddai in the Bible." *History of Religions* 21:3 (1982): 240–56.

———. "Love, Marriage and the Modernization of the Jews." In Marc Raphael, ed., *Approaches to Modern Judaism.* Chico, Calif., 1983.

———. "Masochism and Philosemitism: The Strange Case of Leopold von Sacher-Masoch." *Journal of Contemporary History* 17 (Spring 1982): 305–24.

Biale, Rachel. *Women and Jewish Law.* New York, 1984.

Biber, Mordecai. "The Maid of Ludmir" (in Hebrew). *Reshumot* 2 (1946): 69–76.

Bitton-Jackson, Livia. *Madonna or Courtesan? The Jewish Woman in Christian Literature.* New York, 1982.

Borst, A. *Die Katharer.* Stuttgart, 1953

Bousquet, G. H. *L'éthique sexuelle de l'Islam.* Paris, 1966.

Boyarin, Daniel. *Carnal Israel: Reading Sex in Talmudic Judaism.* Berkeley and Los Angeles, forthcoming.

———. *Intertextuality and the Reading of Midrash.* Bloomington, Ind., 1990.

Brayer, Menachem M. *The Jewish Woman in Rabbinic Literature.* 2 vols. Hoboken, N.J., 1986.

Breines, Paul. *Tough Jews.* New York, 1990.

Brooke, Christopher N. L. *The Medieval Idea of Marriage.* Oxford, 1989.

Brown, Peter. *The Body and Society: Men, Women and the Renunciation of Sexuality in Early Christianity.* New York, 1988.

Brundage, James A. *Law, Sex and Christian Society in Medieval Europe.* Chicago, 1987.

Brunschwig, Henri. *Enlightenment and Romanticism in Eighteenth Century*

*Prussia.* Translated by Frank Jellinek. Chicago, 1974.

Buckley, Thomas, and Alma Gottlieb, eds. *Blood Magic: The Anthropology of Menstruation.* Berkeley and Los Angeles, 1988.

Camic, Charles. *Experience and Enlightenment.* Chicago, 1984.

Campbell, Edward F., Jr. *The Anchor Bible Ruth.* Garden City, N.Y., 1975.

Carmichael, Calum. "A Ceremonial Crux: Removing a Man's Sandal as a Female Gesture of Contempt." *Journal of Biblical Literature* 96 (1977): 321–36.

———. "'Treading' in the Book of Ruth." *Zeitschrift für Alttestamentliche Wissenschaft* 92 (1980): 248–66.

———. *Women, Law and the Genesis Traditions.* Edinburgh, 1979.

Cohen, Gerson D. "The Song of Songs and the Jewish Religious Mentality." In *The Samuel Friedland Lectures, 1960–66.* New York, 1966.

Cohen, Jeremy. *"Be Fertile and Increase, Fill the Earth and Master It": The Ancient and Medieval Career of a Biblical Text.* Ithaca, N.Y., 1989.

———. "Rationales for Conjugal Sex in RaAvaD's *Ba'ale ha-Nefesh.*" In *Frank Talmage Memorial Volume* (special issue of *Jewish History*). Forthcoming.

Cohen, Shaye J. D. "From the Bible to the Talmud: The Prohibition on Intermarriage." *Hebrew Annual Review* 7 (1983): 23–39.

———. "Menstruants and the Sacred in Judaism and Christianity." In Sarah B. Pomeroy, ed., *Women's History and Ancient History.* Chapel Hill and London, 1991.

Cohen, Steven, and Paula Hyman, eds. *The Jewish Family: Myths and Reality.* New York, 1986.

Countryman, L. William. *Dirt, Greed and Sex: Sexual Ethics in the New Testament and Their Implications for Today.* Philadelphia, 1988.

Cross, Frank Moore. *Canaanite Myth and Hebrew Epic.* Cambrige, Mass., 1973.

Cuddihy, John. *The Ordeal of Civility.* New York, 1974.

D'Emilio, John, and Estelle B. Freedman. *Intimate Matters: A History of Sexuality in America.* New York, 1988.

Daube, David. *The Duty to Procreate.* Edinburgh, 1977.

Davidson, Arnold, "Sex and the Emergence of Sexuality." *Critical Inquiry* 14 (1987): 17–48.

Day, John. "Asherah in the Hebrew Bible and Northwest Semitic Literature." *Journal of Biblical Literature* 105 (1986): 385–408.

Dever, William. "Asherah, Consort of Yahwe? New Evidence from Kuntillet 'Arjud." *Bulletin of the American Schools of Oriental Research* 255 (Summer 1984): 21–37.

Douglas, Mary. *Purity and Danger.* London, 1966.

Dubnow, Simon. "Heretical Hasidim" (in Hebrew). *Ha-Shiloah* 7 (1901): 312–30.

Duby, Georges. *The Knight, the Lady and the Priest: The Making of Modern Marriage in Medieval France.* Translated by Barbara Bray. New York, 1983.

Dundes, Alan. *Interpreting Folklore.* Bloomington, Ind., 1980.

Dunham, Vera S. "Sex: From Free Love to Puritanism." In A. Inkeles and K. Geiger eds., *Soviet Society.* Boston, 1961.

Eilberg-Schwartz, Howard. *The Savage in Judaism: Excursions in an Anthropology of Israelite Religion and Ancient Judaism.* Bloomington, Ind., 1990.

Eilberg-Schwartz, Howard, ed. *People of the Body: Jews and Judaism from an Embodied Perspective.* Albany, N.Y., 1992.

Elitzur, Avshalom. *Into the Holy of Holies: Psychoanalytic Insights into the Bible and Judaism* (in Hebrew). Tel Aviv, 1988.

Ellenson, Eliakim. *Nisuin she-lo ke-Dat Moshe ve-Yisrael.* Tel Aviv, 1975.

Elon, Ari. "Alma Di," *Shdemot* no. 114 (Summer, 1990): 1–173.

Emerton, J. A. "Judah and Tamar." *Vetus Testamentum* 29 (1979): 403–15.

Epstein, Louis. *Marriage Laws in the Bible and Talmud.* Cambridge, Mass., 1942.

———. *Sex Laws and Customs in Judaism.* New York, 1948.

Erens, Patricia. *The Jew in American Cinema.* Bloomington, Ind., 1984.

Erikson, Erik. *Life History and the Historical Moment.* New York, 1975.

———. *Young Man Luther.* New York, 1958.

Falk, Candace. *Love, Anarchy and Emma Goldman.* New York, 1984.

Falk, Ze'ev W. *Jewish Matrimonial Law in the Middle Ages.* Oxford, 1966.

Farah, Madelain. *Marriage and Sexuality in Islam: A Translation of al-Ghazali's Book on the Etiquette of Marriage From the Ihya.* Salt Lake City, 1984.

Feldman, David. *Marital Relations, Birth Control and Abortion in Jewish Law.* New York, 1968.

Fisch, Harold. *The Dual Image: The Figure of the Jew in English and American Literature.* New York, 1971.

———. "Ruth and the Structure of Covenant History." *Vetus Testamentum* 32 (1982): 425–37.

Fisher, Eugene J. "Cultic Prostitution in the Ancient Near East? A Reassessment." *Biblical Theology Bulletin* 6 (1976): 225–36.

Flandrin, J. L. *Les amours paysannes.* Paris, 1975.

———. "Repression and Change in the Sexual Life of Young People in Medieval and Early Modern Times." *Journal of Family History* 2, no. 3 (1977): 196–210.

Foucault, Michel. *History of Sexuality.* Vol. 1, *An Introduction.* Translated by Robert Hurley. New York, 1978.

———. *History of Sexuality.* Vol. 3, *The Care of the Self.* Translated by Robert Hurley. New York, 1986.

Fox, Michael. "The Sign of the Covenant: Circumcision in the Light of the Priestly *'ot* Etiologies." *Revue Biblique* 81 (1974): 557–96.

Fraade, Steven. "Ascetical Aspects of Ancient Judaism." In Arthur Green, ed., *Jewish Spirituality.* Vol. 1. New York, 1986.

Frank, R. I. "Augustus's Legislation on Marriage and Children." In *California Studies in Classical Antiquity* 8 (1975): 44–52.

Freiman, A. H. *Seder Kiddushin ve-Nisuin*. Jerusalem, 1964.

Freud, Sigmund. *Moses and Monotheism*. Translated by Katherine Jones. New York, 1939.

Frymer-Kensky, Tikva. *In the Wake of the Goddesses*: *Women, Culture and the Biblical Transformation of Pagan Myth*. New York, 1992.

Fuchs, Eric. *Sexual Desire and Love: Origins and History of the Christian Ethic of Sexuality and Marriage*. Translated by Marsha Daigle. Cambridge, 1983.

Fuchs, Esther. "Humor and Sexism: The Case of the Jewish Joke." *Jewish Humor* (1986): 111–22.

Gabler, Neal. *An Empire of Their Own: How the Jews Invented Hollywood*. New York, 1989.

Gardella, Peter. *Innocent Ecstasy: How Christianity Gave America an Ethic of Sexual Pleasure*. New York and Oxford, 1985.

Gay, Peter. *The Bourgeois Experience: Victoria to Freud*. Vols. 1 and 2. New York, 1984 and 1986.

———. *Freud: A Life for Our Time*. New York, 1988.

———. *A Godless Jew: Freud, Atheism and the Making of Psychoanalysis*. New Haven, 1987.

Gilman, Sander. *Difference and Pathology: Stereotypes of Sexuality, Race and Madness*. Ithaca, N.Y., 1985.

———. *Jewish Self-Hatred: Anti-Semitism and the Hidden Language of the Jews*. Baltimore, 1986.

Ginsburg, Elliot K. *The Sabbath in the Classical Kabbalah*. 2 vols. Albany, NY, 1989.

Gluzman, Michael. "The Exclusion of Women from Hebrew Literary History." *Prooftexts* 11 (1991): 259–78.

Goldberg, Jacob. "Jewish Marriages in Old Poland in the Public Opinion of the Enlightenment Period" (in Hebrew). *Galed* 4–5 (1978): 25–33.

Goldin, Judah. "The Youngest Son or Where Does Genesis 38 Belong." *Journal of Biblical Literature* 96 (1977): 27–44.

Gordis, Robert. "Be Fruitful and Multiply: Biography of a Mitzvah." *Midstream* 28 (1982): 21–29.

———. "Love, Marriage and Business in the Book of Ruth: A Chapter in Hebrew Customary Law." In Howard Bream et al., eds., *A Light unto My Path: Old Testament Studies in Honor of Jacob M. Myers*. Philadelphia, 1974.

———. *Sex and the Family in Jewish Tradition*. New York, 1967.

Gordon, Cyrus. *Ugaritic Literature*. Rome, 1949.

Govrin, Nurit. *Ha-Mahatzit ha-Rishonah: Dvora Baron—Hayyaiha u-Yitzirotah*. Jerusalem, 1988.

Grayson, A. K., and J. Van Seters. "The Childless Wife in Assyria and the Stories of Genesis." *Orientalia* 44 (1975): 485–86.

Grayzel, Solomon. *The Church and the Jews in the XIIIth Century*. 2 vols.

Edited by Kenneth R. Stow. New York, 1989.

Green, Arthur. "The Song of Songs in Early Jewish Mysticism." *Orim: A Jewish Journal at Yale* 2, no. 2 (Spring 1987): 49–63.

———. *Tormented Master: A Life of Rabbi Nahman of Bratslav.* University, Ala., 1979.

Güdemann, Moritz. *Geschichte des Erziehungswesens und der Culture der Juden in Deutschland.* Vienna, 1888.

———. *Geschichte des Erziehungswesens und der Culture der Juden in Frankreich und Deutschland.* Vienna, 1880.

Guillaumont, Antoine. "A propos du celibat des Esseniens." In *Hommages à Andre Dupont-Sommer.* Paris, 1971.

Hakhlili, Binyamin, ed. *Le-kha ve-Alekha: Ahavat Rahel ve-Michael.* Tel Aviv, 1987.

Halperin, David. "Is There a History of Sexuality?" *History and Theory* 28, no. 3 (1989): 257–74.

Halpern, Israel. "Panic Marriages in Eastern Europe" (in Hebrew). In *Yehudim ve-Yahadut be-Mizrah Europa.* Jerusalem, 1969.

Harris, Monford. "The Concept of Love in *Sepher Hassidim.*" *Jewish Quarterly Review* 50 (1959): 13–44.

———. "Marriage as Metaphysics: A Study of the 'Iggeret ha-Kodesh.'" *Hebrew Union College Annual* 33 (1962): 197–200.

Heilman, Samuel C., and Steven M. Cohen. *Cosmopolitans and Parochials: Modern Orthodox Jews in America.* Chicago, 1989.

Heschel, Abraham J. *The Circle of the Baal Shem Tov: Studies in Hasidism.* Edited by Samuel H. Dresner. Chicago, 1985.

———. *Kotzk.* 2 vols. Tel Aviv, 1973.

Heschel, Susannah. "Anti-Judaism in Christian Feminist Theology." *Tikkun* (May–June 1990): 25–28, 95–97.

Horodetsky, S. A. *Ha-Hasidut ve-ha-Hasidim.* Tel Aviv, 1951.

Hoshen, Dalia. "Sexual Relations between Husband and Wife: The Rishonim's Approach and the Talmudic Sources." *Jewish Quarterly Review.* Forthcoming.

Howe, Irving. *World of Our Fathers.* New York, 1976.

Idel, Moshe. *The Mystical Experience in Abraham Abulafia.* Translated by Jonathan Chipman. Albany, N.Y., 1988.

Isaksson, Abel. *Marriage and Ministry in the New Temple.* Lund, 1965.

Jacquart, D., and C. Thomasset. *Sexuality and Medicine in the Middle Ages.* Translated by Matthew Adamson. Princeton, 1988.

Jancu, Robert. "Jackie Mason's World according to Hollywood." *Judaism* 40 (Spring 1991): 134–47.

Kaplan, Marion. *The Making of the Jewish Middle Class: Women, Family and Identity in Imperial Germany.* New York, 1991.

Katz, Jacob. "Family, Kinship and Marriage among Ashkenazim in the Sixteenth to Eighteenth Centuries." *Jewish Journal of Sociology* 1 (1959): 4–22.

———. "Marriage and Marital Relations at the End of the Middle Ages" (in Hebrew). *Zion* 10 (1945–46): 21–54.

———. *Tradition and Crisis.* New York, 1961.

Kellenbach, Katharina von. "Anti-Judaism in Christian-Rooted Feminist Writings: An Analysis of Major U.S. American and West German Feminist Theologians." Ph.D. diss., Temple University, 1990.

Klausner, Joseph. *Historiya shel ha-Sifrut ha-Ivrit ha-Hadashah.* Jerusalem, 1953.

Klein, Dennis. *Jewish Origins of the Psychoanalytic Movement.* New York, 1981.

Knaani, David. *Ha-Batim she-Hayu.* Tel Aviv, 1986.

Kraemer, David, ed. *The Jewish Family: Metaphor and Memory.* New York, 1989.

Kraemer, Ross. "Monastic Jewish Women in Greco-Roman Egypt: Philo on the Therapeutrides." *Signs* 14 (1989): 342–70.

Kramer, S. N. *Sacred Marriage Rite: Aspects of Faith, Myth and Ritual in Ancient Sumer.* Bloomington, Ind., 1969.

Krause, Martin. "II Sam 11:4 und das Konzeptionsoptimum." *Zeitschrift für alttestamentliche Wissenschaft* 95 (1983).

Kurzweil, Baruch. *Sifrutenu ha-Hadashah: Hemshekh o-Mahapekhah?* Tel Aviv, 1971.

Lachs, Samuel. "The Alphabet of Ben Sira: A Study in Folk-literature." *Gratz College Annual of Jewish Studies* 2 (1973): 9–28.

Laqueur, Thomas. *Making Sex: Body and Gender from the Greeks to Freud.* Cambridge, Mass., 1990.

———. "Orgasm, Generation and the Politics of Reproductive Biology." *Representations* 14 (Spring 1986): 1–41.

———. "The Social Evil, the Solitary Vice and Pouring Tea." In Michel Feher, ed., *Fragments for a History of the Human Body.* Vol. 3. New York, 1989.

Lavoie, Rodrigue. "La délinquance sexuelle à Monosque (1240–1430): Schéma général et singularités juives." *Provence Historique* 37, no. 150 (1987): 571–87.

Lazar, M. "Catalan-Provencal Wedding Songs (14th–15th Centuries)" (in Hebrew). In *Hayyim Schirmann Jubilee Volume.* Jerusalem, 1970.

Lemay, Helen Rodnite. "Some Thirteenth and Fourteenth Century Lectures on Female Sexuality." *International Journal of Women's Studies* 1 (1978): 391–400.

Lerner, Gerda. *The Creation of Patriarchy.* New York, 1986.

Levi, Amnon. *Ha-Haredim.* Jerusalem, 1988.

Levin, Mordecai. *Arkhei Hevrah ve-Kalkalah be-Ideologiyah shel Tekufat ha-Haskalah.* Jerusalem, 1975.

Levine, Baruch. "In Praise of the Israelite *Mispaha*: Legal Themes in the Book of Ruth." In H. B. Huffmon et al., eds., *In The Quest for the Kingdom of God: Studies in Honor of George E. Mendenhall.* Winona Lake, Ind., 1983.

————. *JPS Torah Commentary: Leviticus*. Philadelphia, 1989.

Levine, Lee I. *The Rabbinic Class of Roman Palestine in Late Antiquity*. Jerusalem, 1989.

Liebes, Yehudah. "R. Nahman of Bratslav's *Ha-tikkun Haklali* and His Attitude towards Sabbatianism" (in Hebrew). *Zion* 45 (1980): 201–45.

Loew, Leopold. *Gesammelte Schriften*. Vol. 3. Szegedin, 1893.

Mahler, Raphael. *Ha-Hasidut ve-ha-Haskalah*. Merhaviya, 1961.

Maier, Walter A., II. *'Aserah: Extrabiblical Evidence*. Atlanta, 1986.

Marcus, Ivan G. "Mothers, Martyrs and Moneymakers: Some Jewish Women in Medieval Europe." *Conservative Judaism* 38 (1986): 34–45.

————. *Piety and Society: The Jewish Pietists of Medieval Germany*. Leiden, 1981.

Margalit, Elkana. *Hashomer ha-Tzair: Mi-Edat Neurim le Marxism Mahapkhani (1913–1936)*. Tel Aviv, 1971.

Massignon, Louis. "Mystique et continence en Islam." In *Mystique et continence: Travaux scientifiques du VII$^e$ Congrès International d'Avon*. Paris, 1951.

May, H. G. "The Fertility Cult in Hosea." *American Journal of Semitic Languages and Literatures* 48 (1932): 73–98.

————. "Ruth's Visit to the High Place." *Journal of the Royal Asiatic Society* (1939): 75–78.

Mayer, Egon. *Love and Tradition: Marriage between Jews and Christians*. New York, 1985.

Meyers, Carol. *Discovering Eve: Ancient Israelite Women in Context*. New York, 1988.

Miles, Margaret. *Carnal Knowing: Female Nakedness and Religious Meaning in the West*. Boston, 1989.

Milgrom, Jacob. *Anchor Bible Leviticus*. Vol. 1. Garden City, N.Y., 1991.

Mintz, Alan, *"Banished from Their Father's Table": Loss of Faith and Hebrew Autobiography*. Bloomington, Ind.: 1989.

Miron, Dan. *Ben Hazon le-Emet*. Jerusalem, 1979.

————. *Bodedim be-Moadam*. Tel Aviv, 1987.

————. *Imahot Miyasdot, Ahayot Horgot*. Tel Aviv, 1991.

————. *A Traveler Disguised*. New York, 1973.

Mopsik, Charles. *Lettre sur la sainteté: Le secret de la relation entre l'homme et la femme dans la cabale*. Lagrasse, 1986.

Mosse, George. "Friendship and Nationhood: About the Promise and Failure of German Nationalism." *Journal of Contemporary History* 17:2 (April 1982): 351–67.

————. "Jewish Emancipation: Between *Bildung* and Respectability." In Jehuda Reinharz and Walter Schatzberg, eds., *The Jewish Response to German Culture: From the Enlightenment to the Second World War*. Hanover, N. H., 1985.

————. *Nationalism and Sexuality*. New York, 1985.

Neusner, Jacob. *Aphrahat and Judaism: The Christian-Jewish Argument in Fourth-Century Iran.* Leiden, 1971.

———. "The Formation of Rabbinic Judaism: Yavneh (Jamnia) from A.D. 70 to 100." In H. Temporini and W. Haase, eds., *Aufsteig und Niedergang der romischen Welt.* Berlin, 1977, sec. 2, vol. 19:2, pp. 3–42.

Niditch, Susan. "Legends of Wise Heroes and Heroines." In Douglas A. Knight and Gene M. Tucker, eds., *The Hebrew Bible and Its Modern Interpreters.* Philadelphia, 1985.

———. "The Wronged Woman Righted: An Analysis of Genesis 38." *Harvard Theological Review* 72 (1979): 143–49.

Noonan, John. *Contraception: A History of Its Treatment by the Catholic Theologians and Canonists.* Cambridge, Mass., 1965.

Novak, David. "Some Aspects of the Relationship of Sex, Society and God in Judaism." In Frederick Greenspahn, ed., *Contemporary Ethical Issues in the Jewish and Christian Traditions.* Hoboken, N.J., 1986.

Novak, William, and Moshe Waldocks, eds. *The Big Book of Jewish Humor.* New York, 1981.

Noy, Meir. "The Theme of the Canceled Wedding in Yiddish Folksongs: A Bibliography Survey" (Hebrew). In *Studies in Marriage Customs.* Jerusalem, 1974.

Oden, Robert A., Jr. *The Bible without Theology: The Theological Tradition and Alternatives to It.* San Francisco, 1987.

Olyan, Saul. *Asherah and the Cult of Yahweh in Israel.* Atlanta, 1988.

Opaz, Aviva. "The Symbolic World of the Collection 'Kehilyateinu'" (in Hebrew). *Kathedra* 59 (March 1991): 126–41.

Oppenheimer, Aharon. *The 'Am ha-Aretz: A Study in the Social History of the Jewish People in the Hellenistic-Roman Period.* Leiden, 1977.

Oring, Elliot. *The Jokes of Sigmund Freud: A Study in Humor and Jewish Identity.* Philadelphia, 1984.

Pagels, Elaine. *Adam, Eve and the Serpent.* New York, 1988.

Pardes, Ilana. *Countertraditions in the Bible: A Feminist Approach.* Cambridge, Mass., 1992.

Patterson, David. "Hasidism in the Nineteenth-Century Novel." *Journal of Semitic Studies* 5 (1960): 367–68.

Patai, Raphael. *The Hebrew Goddess.* New York, 1967.

———. *Sex and Family in the Bible and the Middle East.* Garden City, N.Y., 1959.

Phillips, Anthony. "The Book of Ruth: Deception and Shame." *Journal of Jewish Studies* 36 (1986): 11–13.

Piekarz, Mendel. *Bi-Yemei Zemihat ha-Hasidut.* Jerusalem, 1978.

Pines, Shlomo. "Nahmanides on Adam in the Garden of Eden in the Context of Other Interpretations of Genesis, Chapters 2 and 3" (in Hebrew). In Aharon Mirsky, ed., *Galut Ahar Golah* (Haim Beinart Festschrift). Jerusalem, 1988.

Plakans, Andrejs, and Joel M. Halpern. "An Historical Perspective on Eighteenth-Century Jewish Family Households in Eastern Europe." In Paul Ritterband, ed., *Modern Jewish Fertility*. Leiden, 1981.

Pope, Marvin. *Anchor Bible Song of Songs*. Garden City, N.Y., 1977.

Prell, Riv-Ellen. *Fighting to Become American: Jewish Women and Men in Conflict in the Twentieth Century*. New York, forthcoming.

———. "Rage and Representation: Jewish Gender Stereotypes in American Culture." In Faye Ginsburg and Anna Tsing, eds. *Uncertain Terms: Negotiating Gender in American Culture*. Boston, 1990.

———. "Why Jewish Princesses Don't Sweat: Desire and Consumption in Postwar American Jewish Culture." In Howard Eilberg-Schwartz, ed., *People of the Body: Jews and Judaism from an Embodied Perspective*. Albany, N.Y., 1992.

Press, Jacob. "'What in the World Is the Sin If I Thrill to Your Beauty?': The Homosexual Love Poems of the Medieval Rabbis." *Mosaic* (1989): 12–26.

Preuss, Julius. *Biblical and Talmudic Medicine*. Translated by Fred Rosner. New York, 1978.

Rabinbach, Anson. *The Human Motor: Energy, Fatigue and the Origins of Modernity*. New York, 1990.

Rank, Otto. *The Myth of the Birth of the Hero*. Edited by Philip Freund. New York, 1959.

Rapoport-Albert, Ada. "On Women in Hasidism." In Ada Rapoport-Albert and Steven J. Zipperstein, eds., *Jewish History: Essays in Honour of Chimen Abramsky*. London, 1988.

Ratosh, Yonatan. "Bialik's Poem of Foreign Love" (in Hebrew). In Gershon Shaked, ed., *Bialik*. Jerusalem, 1974.

Reed, William. *The Asherah in the Old Testament*. Fort Worth, Tex., 1949.

Robert, Marthe. *From Oedipus to Moses: Freud's Jewish Identity*. Translated by Ralph Mannheim. Garden City, N.Y., 1976.

Rosenberg, Felix. "Über eine Sammlung von Volks-und Gesellschaftsliedern in hebräischen Lettern." *Zeitschrift für die Geschichte der Juden in Deutschland* 2 (1888): 232–96, and 3 (1889): 14–28.

Roskies, David. "Ayzik-Meyer Dik and the Rise of Yiddish Popular Literature." Ph.D. diss., Brandeis University, 1975.

———. "Yiddish Popular Literature and the Female Reader." *Journal of Popular Culture* 10:4 (1977): 852–58.

Roth, Norman. "'Deal Gently with the Young Man': Love of Boys in Medieval Hebrew Poetry of Spain." *Speculum* 57 (1982): 33–59.

Rousselle, Aline. *Porneia: On Desire and the Body in Antiquity*. Translated by Felicia Pheasant. Oxford, 1988.

Rowley, H. H. "The Marriage of Ruth." In Rowley, *The Servant of the Lord and other Essays on the Old Testament*. Oxford, 1965.

Sabean, David. *Power in the Blood: Popular Culture and Village Discourse in Early Modern Germany*. New York, 1984.

Saperstein, Marc. *Decoding the Rabbis*. Cambridge, Mass., 1980.

Schaberg, Jane. *The Illegitimacy of Jesus: A Feminist Theological Interpretation of the Infancy Narratives.* San Francisco, 1987.

Scheindlin, Raymond P., ed. and trans. *Wine, Women and Death: Medieval Hebrew Poems on the Good Life.* Philadelphia, 1986.

Schimmel, Annemarie. "Eros—Heavenly and Not So Heavenly—in Sufi Literature and Life." In Afaf al-Sayyid-Marsot, ed., *Society and Sexes in Medieval Islam.* Malibu, Calif., 1979.

Schipper, Yitzhok. "A Yiddish Love Novel from the Middle Ages" (in Yiddish). *YIVO Bleter* 13 (1938): 232–45.

Schirmann, J. "The Ephebe in Medieval Hebrew Poetry" (in Hebrew). *Sefarad* 15 (1955).

Schneider, S. W. "In a *Coma!* I Thought She Was *Jewish:* Some Truths and Some Speculations about Jewish Women and Sex." *Lilith* (1977): 5–8.

Scholem, Gershom. "*Devekut* or Communion with God." in *The Messianic Idea in Judaism and Other Essays on Jewish Spirituality.* New York, 1971.

———. "Jacob Frank and the Frankists." In *Kabbalah.* Jerusalem, 1974.

———. *Major Trends in Jewish Mysticism.* 3d ed. New York, 1961.

———. "Redemption through Sin." In *The Messianic Idea in Judaism and Other Essays on Jewish Spirituality.* New York, 1971.

———. *Sabbatai Sevi: The Mystical Messiah, 1626–1676.* Translated by R. J. Zwi Werblowsky. Princeton, 1973.

———. "The Sabbatian Movement in Poland" (in Hebrew). *Bet Yisrael be-Polin.* Vol. 2. Jerusalem, 1954.

———. "Shekhinah: The Feminine Element in Divinity." In *On the Mystical Shape of the Godhead: Basic Concepts in the Kabbalah.* Translated by Joachim Neugroschel. New York, 1991.

———. "Tradition and New Creation in the Ritual of the Kabbalists." In *On the Kabbalah and Its Symbolism.* New York, 1965.Schorske, Carl. *Fin-de-Siècle Vienna.* New York, 1981.

———. "Tselem: The Concept of the Astral Body." In *On the Mystical Shape of the Godhead: Basic Concepts in the Kabbalah.* Translated by Joachim Neugroschel. New York, 1991.

Schwartz, Regina. "Adultery in the House of David: The Metanarrative of Biblical Scholarship and the Narratives of the Bible." *Semeia.* Forthcoming.

Seeberg, Erich. *Gottfried Arnold.* Meerane, 1923.

Selms, A. van. *Marriage and Family Life in Ugaritic Literature.* London, 1954.

Shahar, Shulamit. "Catharism and the Origins of Kabbalah in Languedoc" (in Hebrew). *Tarbiz* 40 (1971): 483–508.

Shaked, Gershon. *Ha-Siporet ha-Ivrit, 1880–1970.* Vol. 1. Tel Aviv, 1977.

Shaki, M. "Sassanian Matrimonial Relations." *Archiv Orientalni* 39 (1971): 322–45.

Shapira, Anita. *Berl: The Biography of a Socialist Zionist.* Translated by Haya Galai. Cambridge, England, 1984.

Shatzmiller, Joseph. "The Albigensian Heresy in the Eyes of Contemporary Jews" (in Hebrew). In Reuven Bonfil, ed., *Tarbut ve-Hevrah be-Toldot Yis-*

*rael be-Yemei ha-Benayim* (Memorial Volume for Haim Hillel Ben Sasson). Jerusalem, 1989.

Shaw, Peter. "Portnoy and His Creator." *Commentary* 47 (1977): 77–79.

Shochat, Azriel. *Im Hilufei ha-Tekufot.* Jerusalem, 1960.

Shtal, Abraham. "Prostitution among Jews as a Phenomenon Accompanying the Transition from Culture to Culture" (in Hebrew). *Megamot* 24 (1978): 202–225.

Silber, Jacques. "Some Demographic Characteristics of the Jewish Population in Russia at the End of the Nineteenth Century." *Jewish Social Studies* 42 (Summer–Fall 1980): 277–78.

Silberman, Charles. *A Certain People: American Jews and Their Lives Today.* New York, 1985.

Silberman, Lou H. "Reprobation, Prohibition, Invalidity: An Examination of the Halakhic Development Concerning Intermarriage." In Daniel Jeremy Silver, ed., *Judaism and Ethics.* New York, 1970.

Sorkin, David. *The Transformation of German Jewry, 1780–1840.* New York, 1987.

Spiro, Melford. *Children of the Kibbutz.* 2d ed. Cambridge, Mass., 1975.

———. *Kibbutz: Venture in Utopia.* 2d ed. Cambridge, Mass., 1970.

Stampfer, Shaul. *Shelosha Yeshivot Litaiot be-Meah ha-19.* Ph.D. diss., Hebrew University, 1981.

Staples, W. E. "The Book of Ruth." *American Journal of Semitic Literature.* 53 (1936–37): 145–47.

Sternberg, Meir. *The Poetics of Biblical Narrative: Ideological Literature and the Drama of Reading.* Bloomington, Ind., 1985.

Stiegman, Emero. "Rabbinic Anthropology." In H. Temporini and W. Haase, eds., *Aufsteig und Niedergang der romischen Welt.* Berlin, 1977, sec. 2, vol. 19:2, pp. 516–27.

Stone, Lawrence. *The Family, Sex and Marriage in England, 1500–1800.* New York, 1977.

Stow, Kenneth. "The Jewish Family in the Rhineland in the High Middle Ages: Form and Function." *American Historical Review* 92 (1987): 1085–1110.

Talmage, Frank. "A Hebrew Polemical Treatise, Anti-Cathar and Anti-Orthodox." *Harvard Theological Review* 60 (1967): 323–48.

Talmon-Garber, Yonina. *Yahid ve-Hevrah ba-Kibbutz.* Jerusalem, 1970.

Teubal, Savina. *Sarah the Priestess: The First Matriarch of Genesis.* Athens, Ohio, 1984.

Tishby, Isaiah. "The Messianic Idea and Messianic Tendencies in the Rise of Hasidism" (Hebrew). *Zion* 32 (1967): 1–45.

Tishby, Isaiah, ed. *Mishnat ha-Zohar.* 2 vols. Jerusalem, 1975.

Trible, Phyllis. *God and the Rhetoric of Sexuality.* Philadelphia, 1978.

Tsur, Muki. *Le-Lo Kutonet Passim.* Tel Aviv, 1976.

———. *Aviv Mukdam: Zvi Shatz ve-ha-Kevutzah ha-Intimit.* Tel Aviv, 1984.

Twersky, Isadore. *Rabad of Posquières.* Philadelphia, 1980.

Tzefetman, Sarah. *Nisuei Adam ve-Shedah: Gilgulim shel Motif be-Sifrut shel Yehudei Ashkenaz be-Mayot ha-17-19*. Jerusalem, 1988.

Urbach, Ephraim Elimelech. *The Sages: Their Concepts and Beliefs*. Translated by Israel Abrahams. Cambridge, Mass., 1975.

Vajda, Georges. "Continence, mariage et vie mystique selon la doctrine du Judaism." In *Mystique et continence: Travaux scientifiques du VIII<sup>e</sup> Congrès International d'Avon*. Paris, 1951.

———. *L'amour de Dieu dans la théologie juive de moyen âge*. Paris, 1957.

Vawter, B. "The Canaanite Background to Gen. 49." *Catholic Biblical Quarterly* 17 (1955): 1–18.

Veyne, Paul, and Georges Duby, eds. *A History of Private Life*. Vol. 1. Translated by A. Goldhammer. Cambridge, Mass., 1987.

Warner, Maria. *Alone of All Her Sex: Myth and the Cult of the Virgin Mary*. New York, 1976.

Wegner, Judith. *Chattel or Person?: The Status of Women in the Mishnah*. New York, 1988.

Weiss, Joseph. "The Beginnings of Hasidism" (in Hebrew). *Zion* 16 (1951): 46–105.

Weissler, Chava. "'For Women and for Men Who Are Like Women': The Construction of Gender in Yiddish Devotional Literature." *Journal of Feminist Studies in Religion* 5:2 (Fall 1989): 7–24.

———. "The Traditional Piety of Ashkenazic Women." In Arthur Green, ed., *Jewish Spirituality*. Vol. 2. New York, 1987.

Weller, Shulamit. "The Collection of Stories in the Passages of Ketubot 62b–63a" (in Hebrew). *Tura* (1989): 95–102.

Wenham, G. J. "Why Does Sexual Intercourse Defile (Lev 15:18)?" *Zeitschrift für alttestamentliche Wissenschaft* 95 (1983): 432–34.

Wenham, Gordon J. *The Book of Leviticus*. Grand Rapids, Mich., 1979.

Werblowsky, R. J. Zwi. *Joseph Karo: Lawyer and Mystic*. Philadelphia, 1977.

Werses, Samuel. "Hasidism in the Eyes of Haskalah Literature" (in Hebrew). *Molad* 144–45 (1960): 379–91.

———. "The Patterns of Autobiography in the Period of the Haskalah" (in Hebrew). *Gilyonot* 17 (1945): 175–83.

Wexler, Alice. *Emma Goldman: An Intimate Life*. New York, 1984.

Wilensky, Mordecai. *Hasidim u-Mitnagdim*. Jerusalem, 1970.

Winkler, John. *The Constraints of Desire: The Anthropology of Sex and Gender in Ancient Greece*. New York and London, 1990.

Wolf, Charlotte. *Magnus Hirschfeld: A Portrait of a Pioneer in Sexology*. London, 1986.

Wolfson, Elliot. "Circumcision, Vision of God and Textual Interpretation: From Midrashic Trope to Mystical Symbol." *History of Religions* 27 (1987–88): 189–215.

Wright, G. R. H. "The Mother-Maid at Bethlehem." *Zeitschrift für alttestamentliche Wissenschaft* 98 (1986): 56–72.

Yassif, Eli. "Medieval Hebrew Tales on the Mutual Hatred of Animals and

Their Methodological Implication" (in Hebrew). *Studies in Aggada and Jewish Folklore* 7 (1983): 227–46.

———. *Sippurei Ben Sira be-Yemei ha-Benayim*. Jerusalem, 1985.

———. "The Exemplum Story in *Sefer Hasidim*" (in Hebrew). *Tarbits* 57 (1988): 217–55.

Yuval, Israel. "Legislation against the Increase in Divorces in Fifteenth-Century Germany" (in Hebrew). *Zion* 48 (1983): 177–213.

Zevit, Ziony. "The Khirbet el Qom Inscription Mentioning a Goddess." *Bulletin of the American Schools of Oriental Research* 255 (Summer 1984): 39–47.

Zinberg, Israel. *A History of Jewish Literature*. Translated by Bernard Martin. Cleveland, Ohio, 1972–78.

# INDEX